Advances in Information Security

Volume 62

Series Editor

Sushil Jajodia, Center for Secure Information Systems, George Mason University, Fairfax, VA 22030-4444, USA

For further volumes:
http://www.springer.com/series/5576

Alexander Kott • Cliff Wang • Robert F. Erbacher
Editors

Cyber Defense
and Situational Awareness

 Springer

Editors
Alexander Kott
United States Army Research Laboratory
Adelphi, MD, USA

Cliff Wang
United States Army Research Office
Research Triangle Park, NC, USA

Robert F. Erbacher
United States Army Research Laboratory
Adelphi, MD, USA

ISSN 1568-2633
ISBN 978-3-319-38026-1   ISBN 978-3-319-11391-3 (eBook)
DOI 10.1007/978-3-319-11391-3
Springer Cham Heidelberg New York Dordrecht London

Contents

About the Authors

Keith Abe (of the chapter titled Inference and Ontologies) is a program manager at Referentia Systems. His areas of interest include network performance management and cyber and cloud security. Key sponsors of this research include the Office of Naval Research, Naval Research Laboratory, and other DoD organizations. His prior work included research and development in the telecommunications test, digital video, and satellite systems fields. He received his B.S. in electrical engineering from the University of Hawaii and his M.S. in electrical engineering from Stanford University.

Massimiliano Albanese (of the chapter titled Formation of Awareness) is an assistant professor in the Department of Applied Information Technology at George Mason University. He serves as the associate director of the Center for Secure Information Systems (CSIS) and as a codirector of the Laboratory for IT Entrepreneurship (LITE). Dr. Albanese received his Ph.D. in computer science and engineering in 2005 from the University of Naples Federico II. He joined the University of Maryland in 2006 as a postdoctoral researcher, before joining George Mason University in 2011. His current research interests are in the areas of modeling, recognition and scalable detection of cyber attacks, network hardening, cyber situational awareness, and moving target defense. A common theme that characterizes Dr. Albanese's research is the development of efficient techniques for reducing massive amounts of raw security data to a manageable amount of actionable intelligence. This theme is also reflected in his contribution to this volume, which illustrates the process of cyber situational awareness (CSA) in cyber defense and presents a CSA framework to automate, in a scalable way, many of the tasks that cyber analysts would normally execute in a mostly manual fashion. Dr. Albanese has authored or coauthored 1 book, 12 book chapters, and 50 publications in refereed journals and conference proceedings.

Noam Ben-Asher (of the chapter titled Cognition and Technology) is a postdoctoral fellow in the Dynamic Decision Making Laboratory at Carnegie Mellon University. His primary interests lie at the intersection of cognitive science, decision science, and human factors engineering, with a particular interest in cyber security.

In this field, he combines behavioral studies with computational cognitive modeling to study cyber situation awareness and dynamic decision making in cyber warfare and social conflicts. His research experience also includes work performed in industrial environment, working as usable-security expert in Deutsche Telekom Innovation Laboratories at Ben-Gurion University. Dr. Ben-Asher holds a Ph.D. and an M.S. in human factors engineering and a B.S. in industrial engineering from Ben-Gurion University.

Norbou Buchler (of the chapter titled Kinetic and Cyber) is a cognitive scientist engaged in network science research at the Army Research Laboratory (ARL) in Aberdeen Proving Ground, MD. He is currently serving as Government Lead for the human dynamics (psycho-social) cross-cutting research initiative on the Cyber Security Collaborative Research Alliance. Prior to joining ARL in 2009, Dr. Buchler did two postdoctoral fellowships, first at Carnegie Mellon University examining computational and behavioral approaches to cognition and second at the Center for Cognitive Neuroscience at Duke University applying functional magnetic resonance imaging and diffusion tensor imaging. Dr. Buchler received his B.S. in psychology from the University of North Carolina in Chapel Hill in 1996 and his Ph.D. in experimental psychology from Syracuse University in 2003. Dr. Buchler's basic research interests lie in network science, cognitive modeling, and behavioral experimentation, both at the individual and team level, while his applied research focuses on human system integration and developing decision-support technologies.

Yi Cheng (of the chapters titled Network-Wide Awareness and Metrics of Security) received his B.E. degree in electrical engineering from Tianjin University, Tianjin, China, in 1997, M.S. degree in mathematics, and Ph.D. degree in computer science and engineering, both from the University of Cincinnati, Ohio, the USA, in 2003 and 2008, respectively. He is currently a lead scientist at Intelligent Automation Inc., where he has been working on multiple SBIR/STTR projects related to enterprise security, cyber mission assurance, attack graph, security metrics, and misbehavior detection, funded by ARO, ARL, AFRL, and NIST. Dr. Cheng's primary research interests include computer and network security, cyber situational awareness, security metrics, mission asset mapping and modeling, intrusion/misbehavior/malware detection, network vulnerability assessment, attack risk analysis and impact mitigation, cryptography, and key management.

Erik S. Connors (of the chapter titled Foundation and Challenges) is a senior research associate at SA Technologies, Inc., in Marietta, GA, where he leads research projects on situation awareness for domains such as military command and control, electric power transmission and distribution, and cyber defense. His research interests include user interface design, technology integration, collaborative tools for complex teams, and cognitive modeling. He received a Ph.D. in information science and technology from Penn State University.

Scott A. DeLoach (of the chapter titled Metrics of Security) is a professor in the department of Computing and Information Sciences at Kansas State University. He is retired from the U.S. Air Force, having served in systems acquisition, intelligence, and the Air Force Research Laboratory. He received his Ph.D. from the Air Force Institute of Technology. Dr. DeLoach is best known as the creator of the Multi-agent Systems Engineering methodology and the Organization Model for Adaptive Computational Systems (OMACS). OMACS defines the knowledge needed about a system's structure and capabilities to allow it to reorganize at run-time in the face of a changing environment and its own capabilities. His current research interests focus on applying software engineering methods, techniques, and models to the design and development of intelligent, complex, adaptive, and autonomous multi-agent and distributed systems.

Julia Deng (of the chapter titled Metrics of Security) currently is a principal scientist and director of Network and Security at IAI. Her primary research interests include cyber security, cloud computing, trust computing, information assurance, and distributed systems. At IAI, serves as a PI and leads numerous projects in closely related areas. Some example projects include Secure Cloud Computing Framework, Trusted Computing Framework for Embedded Systems, Secure Content Delivery System for Tactical Networks, Trusted Querying Framework for Wireless Sensor Networks, and Secure Routing in airborne networks. Dr. Deng received her Ph.D. in electrical engineering from University of Cincinnati in 2004, majoring in network and system security. She has published more than 20 papers in leading international journals and conference proceedings.

Haitao Du (of the chapter titled Attack Projection) received his Ph.D. degree in the Computing and Information Sciences at Rochester Institute of Technology in 2014. His research focuses on machine learning, data mining and algorithm design for analyzing sequential data produced by network and host intrusion detection systems, particularly in the presence of obfuscation techniques. He has published six conference papers and two book chapters as the primary author and coauthored another book chapter and a paper in IEEE Communications magazine during his Ph.D. study. He has been working on several research projects with Air Force Research Laboratory, DARPA, and Boeing Phantom Works. He was a graduate research intern with CSX Corporation and Xerox. Currently, he works for Xerox PARC as a postdoc data scientist researcher.

Mica R. Endsley (of the chapter titled Foundation and Challenges) is the chief scientist of the U.S. Air Force. Prior to assuming this position she served as president and CEO of SA Technologies and served on the faculty at Texas Tech University and MIT. Dr. Endsley received her Ph.D. from the University of Southern California in industrial and systems engineering. She is widely recognized for her pioneering work on situation awareness in individuals and teams and creating effective human-automation integration across a wide variety of systems. She has edited or coauthored three books, including *Designing for Situation Awareness*.

Robert F. Erbacher (of the chapters titled Preview, Cognitive Process and Concluding Thoughts) is a computer scientist performing computer security research at the Army Research Laboratory (ARL) in Adelphi, MD. He received his B.S. in computer science from the University of Lowell in 1991, his M.S. and Sc.D.

degrees in computer science from the University of Massachusetts-Lowell in 1993 and 1998, respectively. He is cooperative agreement manager (CAM) for the science for cyber cooperative agreement and technical lead for the detection focal area of the cyber security CRA. Before joining ARL, he was a senior principal scientist with the Northwest Security Institute (NWSI) and was on the faculty of the Computer Science Department at Utah State University. He was a Summer Faculty Fellow at AFRL's Rome Labs from 2004 through 2006. He is an associate editor for the *Journal of Electronic Imaging*, a chair and a member of the steering committee of the SPIE Conference on Visualization and Data Analysis, and the Workshops on Systematic Approaches to Digital Forensics Engineering. His research interests lie in digital forensics, situational awareness, computer security, information assurance, intrusion detection, visualization, cyber-terrorism, and cyber command and control. He has over 80 referred publications in these areas.

Nicholas Evancich (of the chapter titled Network-Wide Awareness) holds bachelor's and master's degrees in electrical engineering from the Purdue University. His area of research is in cyber security focusing on network security. Specifically his research centers on automated exploitation generation. His work at Intelligent Automation Inc. covers a wide variety of cyber topics: process introspection, anonymization, and situational awareness. Prior to joining Intelligent Automation Inc., he worked at JHU/APL where he worked on anti-submarine warfare, chem/bio detection systems, and unattended ground sensors; additionally he worked on DARPA's TIGR program which improved tactical situational awareness. His academic interests include malware detection, mobile security, and compiler design.

Cleotilde Gonzalez (of the chapter titled Cognition and Technology) is a professor of decision sciences and the founding director of the Dynamic Decision Making Laboratory at Carnegie Mellon University. She is affiliated with the Social and Decision Sciences department and has additional affiliations with many other departments and centers in the university. She is a fellow of the Human Factors and Ergonomics Society and associate editor of the *Journal of Cognitive Engineering and Decision Making*. She is also part of the editorial board of the *Journal of Behavioral Decision Making*, the *Human Factors* journal, and the *System Dynamics Review*. She has widely published across many fields deriving from her contributions to Cognitive Science. Her work includes a substantial cognitive modeling component building on Instance-Based Learning Theory (IBLT), from which many computational models have been built, including a run-up winner of a modeling competition focused on the prediction in repeated Market Entry Games. She has been principal or co-investigator on a wide range of multi-million and multi-year collaborative efforts with government and industry.

Lihua Hao (of the chapter titled Visualizations and Analysts) is a Ph.D. student in the Department of Computer Science at North Carolina State University. She received her B.S. from the Computer Science Department at Peking University in Beijing, China. Her research interests include visualization, graphics, and data management.

Richard Harang (of the chapter titled Learning and Semantics) is currently a researcher in the Network Security Branch of the U.S. Army Research Laboratory. He received his Ph.D. in statistics from the University of California, Santa Barbara, and performed additional postdoctoral research in the computational science and engineering research group there. His research focuses on the intersection of machine learning, statistical modeling, and network security, with an emphasis on using those techniques to extract meaningful information from large amounts of unstructured or poorly structured data. His academic interests include exploring the role of randomization in machine learning for such tasks as classification, clustering, and feature extraction.

Christopher G. Healey (of the chapter titled Visualizations and Analysts) is a professor in the Department of Computer Science at North Carolina State University. He received a B.Math. from the University of Waterloo in Waterloo, Canada, and an M.Sc. and a Ph.D. from the University of British Columbia in Vancouver, Canada. He is an associate editor for *ACM Transactions on Applied Perception*. His research interests include visualization, graphics, visual perception, and areas of applied mathematics, databases, artificial intelligence, and aesthetics related to visual analysis and data management.

Jared Holsopple (of the chapters titled Impact Assessment and Attack Projection) is a software engineer at Avarint, a wholly owned subsidiary of CUBRC, Inc, in Buffalo, NY. Primary research interests are in higher levels of information fusion such as threat and impact assessment. More specifically, he has been working with colleagues to develop a software suite for higher-level information fusion called FuSIA: Future Situation and Impact Awareness, which is focused on the processing of actual data to determine the current and future impacts of objects in a given environment. Most of the research has focused on implementing the FuSIA architecture for computer security applications. He has additional research interests in command and control simulations. He obtained his bachelor of science and master of science in computer engineering from Rochester Institute of Technology. He is currently a Ph.D. candidate in industrial and systems engineering at the University at Buffalo.

Steve E. Hutchinson (of the chapter titled Visualizations and Analysts) is a researcher-analyst with ICF International. He received an M.S. in mathematics education from Drexel University, pursued graduate studies in computer science at Rochester Institute of Technology, and received a B.S. in electrical engineering from SUNY at Buffalo. As an engineer in the chemical/pharmaceutical industry, he led projects in manufacturing control, laboratory data acquisition, web-based applications, and knowledge-based systems development. His current research interests concern visual representation of network traffic features to support quality decision making and recognition of the importance of state (history) to allow more effective team-decisions in hybrid human-algorithmic processes.

Sushil Jajodia (of the chapter titled Formation of Awareness) is University Professor, BDM International Professor, and the founding director of Center for Secure Information Systems at George Mason University. He received his Ph.D.

from the University of Oregon, Eugene. His research interests include security, privacy, databases, and distributed systems. He has authored or coauthored 7 books, edited 43 books and conference proceedings, and published more than 425 refereed journal and conference papers. He is also a holder of 13 patents and has supervised 27 doctoral dissertations. He received the 1996 IFIP TC 11 Kristian Beckman award, 2000 Volgenau School Outstanding Research Faculty Award, 2008 ACM SIGSAC Outstanding Contributions Award, and 2011 IFIP WG 11.3 Outstanding Research Contributions Award. He was elected a fellow of IEEE in January, 2013. He was recognized for the most accepted papers at the 30th anniversary of the IEEE Symposium on Security and Privacy. His h-index is 84 and Erdos number is 2.

Gabriel Jakobson (of the chapter titled Mission Resilience) is chief scientist at Altusys Corp., a firm which is developing situation management technologies for cyber security and defense applications. He received his Ph.D. degree in computer science from the Institute of Cybernetics, Estonia. Dr. Jakobson's research interest has been in the area of automata theory, artificial intelligence, expert systems, databases, event correlation, and semantic information processing. His recent research is in cognitive situation theory, situation management, cyber security situation awareness, resilient cyber defense, and adaptive multi-agent systems. He holds the honorary degree of Doctor Honorius Causa from the Tallinn Technical University, Estonia, and is Distinguished IEEE ComSoc Lecturer. He is the general chair of the IEEE Conference on Cognitive Methods of Situation Awareness and Decision Support (CogSIMA 2011–2014) and TPC cochair of the NATO and IEEE Conference on Cyber Conflict (CyCon 2012–2014). Dr. Jakobson is the chair of the IEEE ComSoc Sub-Committee on Situation Management.

Mieczyslaw M. Kokar (of the chapter titled Inference and Ontologies) is a professor in the Department of Electrical and Computer Engineering at Northeastern University in Boston, Massachusetts. He is also president of VIStology, Inc. His research interests include information fusion (situation awareness), cognitive radios (the use of ontologies and formal reasoning for interoperability and policy based control), software engineering (sefl-controlling software), and modeling languages. He has authored and coauthored over 180 journal and conference papers. He is on editorial board of *Journal of Information Fusion* and program committee member of numerous conferences. He is a senior member of IEEE and member of ACM.

Alexander Kott (of the chapters titled Preview, Kinetic and Cyber, and Concluding Thoughts) serves as the chief, Network Science Division, Army Research Laboratory headquartered in Adelphi MD. In this position, he is responsible for fundamental research and applied development in performance and security of tactical mobile and strategic networks. Between 2003 and 2008, Dr. Kott served as a Defense Advanced Research Programs Agency (DARPA) Program Manager responsible for a number of large-scale advanced technology research programs. His earlier positions included technical director with BBN Technologies, Cambridge, MA; director of R&D at Logica Carnegie Group, Pittsburgh, PA; and IT research department manager at AlliedSignal, Inc., Morristown, NJ. Dr. Kott received the Secretary of

Defense Exceptional Public Service Award and accompanying Exceptional Public Service Medal, in October 2008. He earned his Ph.D. from the University of Pittsburgh, Pittsburgh, PA in 1989; published over 70 technical papers; and coauthored and edited six technical books.

Christian Lebiere (of the chapter titled Cognition and Technology) is research faculty in the Psychology Department at Carnegie Mellon University. He received his B.S. in computer science from the University of Liege (Belgium) and his M.S. and Ph.D. from the School of Computer Science at CMU. During his graduate career, he studied connectionist models and was co-developer of the Cascade-Correlation learning algorithm. Since 1991, he has developed the ACT-R cognitive architecture and coauthored with John Anderson for the book *The Atomic Components of Thought*. His research interests include cognitive architectures and their applications to cognitive psychology, artificial intelligence, human-computer interaction, decision making, intelligent agents, cognitive robotics, cybersecurity, and neuromorphic engineering.

Jason Li (of the chapters titled Network-Wide Awareness and Metrics of Security) received his Ph.D. degree from the University of Maryland at College Park. He is currently a vice president and senior director at Intelligent Automation Inc., where he has been working on research and development programs in the area of networks and cyber security. Over the years he has initiated and worked on numerous R&D programs related to protocol design and development for satellite networks, mobile code technology and its applications in security, realistic and repeatable wireless networks test and evaluation, moving target defense, cyber situational awareness, attack impact analysis, airborne networks, complex networks, ad hoc and sensor networks, efficient network management, and software agents. Dr. Li has led the effort of architecting the networks and security programs at IAI, establishing enduring trust relationship with various customers, and working with the IAI team and the collaborators to deliver quality results that meet the customer's needs.

Peng Liu (of the chapter titled Cognitive Process) received his B.S. and M.S. degrees from the University of Science and Technology of China and his Ph.D. degree from George Mason University in 1999. Dr. Liu is a professor of information sciences and technology, founding director of the Center for Cyber-Security, Information Privacy, and Trust, and founding director of the Cyber Security Lab at Penn State University. His research interests are in all areas of computer and network security. He has published a monograph and over 220 refereed technical papers. His research has been sponsored by NSF, ARO, AFOSR, DARPA, DHS, DOE, AFRL, NSA, TTC, CISCO, and HP. He is a recipient of the DOE Early Career Principle Investigator Award. He has coled the effort to make Penn State a NSA-certified National Center of Excellence in Information Assurance Education and Research. He has coled the effort to make Penn State a NSA-certified National Center of Excellence in Information Assurance Education and Research. He has advised or co-advised over 20 Ph.D. dissertations to completion.

Zhuo Lu (of the chapter titled Network-Wide Awareness) is a research scientist at Intelligent Automation Inc, where he has been working on multiple network and security projects from NASA and DoD. He earned his Ph.D. degree at North Carolina State University. His area of research covers a wide range of cyber security topics, including wireless and mobile security, cyber physical system security, data forensics and analytics, attack analysis, and countermeasure design.

Jakub J. Moskal (of the chapter titled Inference and Ontologies) is a research scientist at VIStology, Inc. in Framingham, MA. He is currently leading two efforts in the area of cognitive electronic warfare. Dr. Moskal has been a principal investigator for several projects funded by MDA, DARPA, AFRL, and OSD. He completed his Ph.D. at Northeastern University's Department of Electrical and Computer Engineering.

Alessandro Oltramari (of the chapter titled Cognition and Technology) is a postdoctoral research associate at Carnegie Mellon University, CyLab. He received his Ph.D. from University of Trento (Italy) in cognitive science and education, in co-tutorship with the Institute for Cognitive Science and Technology of the Italian National Research Council (ISTC-CNR). He has held a research position at the Laboratory for Applied Ontology (ISTC-CNR) in Trento from 2000 to 2010. He has been a visiting research associate at Princeton University (Cognitive Science Laboratory) in 2005 and 2006. His primary interests are centered around theoretical and applied research on knowledge representation and agent technologies. In particular, his research activity at Carnegie Mellon University mainly deals with integrating ontologies and cognitive architectures for high-level reasoning in knowledge-intensive tasks.

Xinming Ou (of the chapter titled Metrics of Security) is associate professor of computer science at Kansas State University. He received his Ph.D. from Princeton University in 2005. Before joining Kansas State University in 2006, he was a postdoctoral research associate at Purdue University's Center for Education and Research in Information Assurance and Security (CERIAS) and a research associate at Idaho National Laboratory (INL). Dr. Ou's research is primarily in enterprise network security defense, with a focus on attack graphs, security configuration management, intrusion analysis, and security metrics for enterprise networks. He is a recipient of 2010 NSF Faculty Early Career Development (CAREER) Award and three-time winner of HP Labs Innovation Research Program (IRP) award.

Kristin E. Schaefer (of the chapter titled Kinetic and Cyber) is an ORAU postdoctoral fellow with U.S. Army Research Laboratory, Aberdeen Proving Ground, MD. She earned her M.S. and Ph.D. in the area of modeling and simulation from the University of Central Florida, Orlando, Florida, and a B.A. in psychology from Susquehanna University, Selinsgrove, Pennsylvania. She currently has over 20 journal publications, technical reports, and conference proceedings specific to the topics of trust, situation awareness, human-robot interaction, and modeling and simulation. Dr. Schaefer also currently serves as the vice chair for the IEEE Cognitive

Methods in Situation Awareness and Decision Support (CogSIMA) conference and the Technical Subcommittee on Situation Management, Emerging Technologies.

Anoop Singhal (of the chapter titled Metrics of Security) is currently a senior computer scientist in the Computer Security Division at the National Institute of Standards and Technology (NIST) in Gaithersburg, MD. He received his Ph.D. in computer science from Ohio State University, Columbus, Ohio. His research interests are in network security, cloud computing security, security metrics, and data mining systems. He is a member of ACM and a senior member of the IEEE and has coauthored over 50 technical papers in leading conferences and journals. He has also co-edited a book on Secure Cloud Computing.

John Kei Smith (of the chapter titled Inference and Ontologies) is the chief technology officer of LiveAction, a network analytics company specializing in high performance network flow and IPFIX based performance analysis on complex networks. In the past, Mr. Smith has served as principal investigator in R&D projects to support network and security management and analytics for military networks. Key sponsors of this research include the Office of Naval Research, Naval Research Laboratory, and other DoD organizations. He received his M.S. in computer science from University of Hawaii and his B.S. in electrical engineering from University of Washington.

Moises Sudit (of the chapters titled Impact Assessment and Attack Projection) is the executive director of the Center for Multisource Information Fusion at the University at Buffalo. Primary research interests are in the theory and applications of Discrete Optimization and Information Fusion. More specifically, he has been concerned in the design and analysis of methods to solve problems in the areas of integer programming and combinatorial optimization. One primary goal of this research has been the development of efficient exact and approximate (heuristic) procedures to solve large-scale engineering and management problems. As a research professor in the School of Engineering at the University at Buffalo he has merged the interests of operations research with information fusion. He also has a faculty appointment in the Kate Gleason College of Engineering at the Rochester Institute of Technology. Dr. Sudit is a NRC fellow trough the Information Directorate at the Air Force Research Laboratory and has received a number of scholarly and teaching awards. He also received the prestigious IBM Faculty Scholarship Award. Dr. Sudit has a number of publications in distinguished journals and has been the principal investigator in numerous research projects. He obtained his bachelor of science in industrial and systems engineering from Georgia Institute of Technology, his master of science in operations research from Stanford University and his doctorate in operations research from Purdue University.

Joshua Tuttle (of the chapter titled Network-Wide Awareness) holds a B.S. degree in computer and network security from Dakota State University. He has worked in security consulting and data management for small and medium sized companies. Over his course of education and professional experience he has gained knowledge of Unix/Linux systems administration, network administration, vulnerability analysis, reverse engineering, offensive and defensive security applications, systems and software development, and digital forensic techniques.

Brian E. Ulicny (of the chapter titled Inference and Ontologies) is chief scientist at VIStology, Inc, in Framingham, MA. Dr. Ulicny is currently leading an effort on semantic information integration in humanitarian assistance/disaster relief situations. He has been PI for various projects funded by ONR, AFRL, MDA, and DARPA, among others. He previously worked at Ask Jeeves and Lycos. Dr. Ulicny completed his Ph.D. at MIT's Department of Linguistics and Philosophy.

Cliff Wang (of the chapters titled Preview and Concluding Thoughts) graduated from North Carolina State University with a Ph.D. in computer engineering in 1996. He has been carrying out research in the area of computer vision, medical imaging, high speed networks, and most recently information security. He has authored around 40 technical papers and 3 Internet standards RFCs. Dr. Wang also served as an editor for nine books and hold three US patents on information security system development. Since 2003, Dr. Wang has been managing extramural research portfolio on information assurance at U.S. Army Research Office. In 2007 he was selected as the director of the computing sciences division at ARO while in the same time managing his program. Dr. Wang also holds adjunct faculty position at both Department of Computer Science and Department of Electrical and Computer Engineering at North Carolina State University.

Peng Xie (of the chapter titled Network-Wide Awareness) received an M.S. degree from Boston University in 2004 and his Ph.D. degree in computer science from the University of Connecticut at Storrs in 2008. Dr. Peng Xie is a lead scientist at IAI and has extensive experience in the areas of virtualization technology and its application to cyber security, cloud computing, trusted computing, security forensic analysis, network security, information theory, and cryptography. Dr. Peng Xie serves as PI and co-PI for several phase I and phase II projects including virtualization based application protection, satellite hypervisor, securing Air-Borne wireless network communication, secure data storage in wireless networks, program behavior characterization and malware detection, extracting and representing knowledge for software protection system, and damage assessment.

Shanchieh Jay Yang (of the chapters titled Impact Assessment and Attack Projection) received his Ph.D. degree in electrical and computer engineering from the University of Texas at Austin. He is currently an associate professor and the department head for the Department of Computer Engineering at Rochester Institute of Technology. Dr. Yang is a codirector of the Networking and Information Processing (NetIP) Laboratory at RIT and an active member of the Center for Multisource Information Fusion based in western New York. His research group has developed several systems and frameworks in the area of network attack modeling for threat and impact assessment. Notably, his team introduced the use of Variable Length Markov Models, Virtual Terrain, and Attack Social Graphs for attack prediction and cyber situation awareness. More recently, an attack obfuscation modeling framework and a semi-supervised coordinated attack learning framework were developed to provide in-depth understanding of sophisticated attack strategies. The above works are complemented with a network attack simulation environment his team is developing, aiming at providing ground truth data for complex and varying attack behaviors. Dr. Yang has published more than 40 papers and worked on numerous research projects. He has served on organizing committees for several conferences and as a guest editor and reviewer for a number of journals. He was a cochair for IEEE Joint Communications and Aerospace Chapter in Rochester NY in 2005, when the chapter was recognized as an Outstanding Chapter of Region 1. He has also contributed to the development of two Ph.D. programs at RIT and received Norman A. Miles Award for academic excellence in teaching in 2007.

John Yen (of the chapter titled Cognitive Process) is University Professor of College of Information Sciences and Technology at the Pennsylvania State University. He received his Ph.D. in computer science from University of California, Berkeley in 1986. Between 1989 and 2001, he was on the faculty of computer science at Texas A&M University. His research interests include artificial intelligence, cognitive modeling, and big data analytics. He has developed a patented multi-agent technology (R-CAST) informed by Recognition-Primed Decision (RPD). He has also developed novel predictive models about the dynamics of networks. He was a 2013 summer faculty fellow at Army Research Laboratory. His research has been supported by NSF, ARL, ARO, ONR, AFOSR, DOE, and others. He has published 3 books and more than 200 referred papers. He received the NSF Young Investigator Award and the IBM Faculty Award. He is a senior member of the Association for the Advancement of Artificial Intelligence (AAAI) and a fellow of IEEE.

Chen Zhong (of the chapter titled Cognitive Process) is a Ph.D. student in the College of Information Sciences and Technology at the Pennsylvania State University. She received her B.S. degree in computer science and technology from Nanjing University in 2011. The goal of her research is to improve our understanding about the analytical reasoning process of cyber analysts to better support cyber defense. Her current research interests include knowledge representation and reasoning, cognitive modeling, human-in-the-loop system development, and quantitative and qualitative data analysis. She has received more than ten awards, including GHC scholarship in 2013, VAST Challenge Honorable Mention in 2013, Outstanding Student Award of Nanjing University in 2010, and National Scholarship of P.R. China in 2008 and 2009.

Preview

Alexander Kott, Cliff Wang, and Robert F. Erbacher

Cyber security has emerged as one of the dominant challenges to our highly networked society. Individuals, corporations and Governments are increasingly concerned about the costs and threats imposed on them by cyber crime, cyber espionage and cyber warfare. Within the field of cyber defense, situational awareness is particularly prominent. It relates to science, technology and practice of perception, comprehension and projection of events and entities in the relevant environment—in our case cyber space. Situational Awareness is difficult to achieve in such fields as aviation, plant operation or emergency management. It is even more difficult—and poorly understood—in the relatively young field of cyber defense where the entities and events are so unlike the more conventional physical phenomena.

We (here and below, "we" refers to all co-authors of this book collectively) begin the book with the chapter titled **Foundations and Challenges**—an overview of how cyber operators develop SA and an analysis of the requirements for supporting SA in cyber operations. Based on the unique challenges in this domain, several key thrusts for research and development are identified that need to be addressed to provide tools that effectively support cyber operator SA and decision making. We explain why the development of cyber situation awareness is critical to effective defense of networks and the assurance of security in cyber operations. A number of factors limit cyber SA in current operations, including: a highly complex and fluid system topology, rapidly changing technologies, a high signal to noise ratio, potentially long durations

A. Kott (✉)
709 Lamberton Drive, Silver Spring, MD 20920, USA

United States Army Research Laboratory, 2800 Powder Mill Rd., Adelphi, MD 20783, USA
e-mail: Alexander.kott1.civ@mail.mil

C. Wang
United States Army Research Office, 4300 S Miami Blvd, Durham, NC 27703, USA

R.F. Erbacher
United States Army Research Laboratory, 2800 Powder Mill Rd., Adelphi, MD 20783, USA

© Springer International Publishing Switzerland 2014
A. Kott et al. (eds.), *Cyber Defense and Situational Awareness*,
Advances in Information Security 62, DOI 10.1007/978-3-319-11391-3_1

between the insertion of an attack and its effect, rapidly evolving and multi-faceted threats, speed of events that exceed human capacity, non-integrated tools that are poorly aligned with SA needs, data overload and meaning underload, and automation challenges.

Although a fairly new topic in the context of cyber security, SA has a far longer history of study and applications in such areas as control of complex enterprises and in conventional warfare. For this reason, far more is known about the SA in conventional military conflicts, or adversarial engagements, than in cyber confrontations. By exploring what is known about SA in conventional—also commonly referred to as kinetic—battles, we may gain insights and research directions relevant to cyber conflicts. This is the topic of the chapter titled **Cyber and Kinetic**, where we discuss the nature of SA in conventional (often called kinetic) conflict, review what is known about such a conventional SA (KSA), and then offer a comparison with what is currently understood regarding the cyber SA (CSA). We find that challenges and opportunities of KSA and CSA are similar or at least parallel in several important ways. With respect to similarities, in both kinetic and cyber worlds, SA strongly impacts the outcome of the mission. Also similarly, cognitive biases are found in both KSA and CSA. As an example of differences, KSA often relies on commonly accepted, widely used organizing representation—such as a map of the physical terrain of the battlefield. No such common representation has emerged in CSA, yet.

Having discussed the importance and key features of CSA, we proceed to explore how it emerges. Formation of Cyber Situational Awareness is a complex process that goes through a number of distinct phases and produces a number of distinct outputs. Humans with widely different roles drive this process while using diverse procedures and computerized tools. The **Formation of Awareness** chapter explores how situational awareness forms within the different phases of the cyber defense process, and describes the different roles that are involved in the lifecycle of situational awareness. The chapter presents an overview of the overall process of cyber defense and then identifies several distinct facets of situational awareness in the context of cyber defense. An overview of the state of the art is followed by a detailed description of a comprehensive framework for Cyber Situational Awareness developed by the authors of this chapter. We highlight the significance of five key functions within CSA: learning from attacks, prioritization, metrics, continuous diagnostics and mitigation, and automation.

In the next chapter—**Network-wide Awareness**—we continue the theme of awareness formation while focusing on a particular type of SA that deals with the holistic, network-wide view of a network. We use the term "macro" SA to refer to the overall dynamics of the network that is seen as a single organism and where individual elements or events are perceived in aggregate. This contrasts with CSA that focuses on individual atomic elements of the network's assets or behaviors, such as an individual suspicious packet, an alert of a potential intrusion, or a vulnerable computer. On the other hand, atomic events can have a broad impact on the operation of the entire network. This means that the scope of CSA must accommodate both "micro and "macro" perspectives. The process of gaining network-wide awareness includes discovery and enumeration of assets and of defense capabilities, along with threat and attack awareness. We argue that effective CSA must focus on improved decision-making, collaboration, and resource management, and discuss approaches to achieving effective network-wide SA.

Because the human cognition—and the technology necessary to support it—are central to Cyber Situational Awareness, they are the foci of the chapter **Cognition and Technology**. To illustrate the challenges and approaches to integration of information technology and computational representations of human situation awareness, the chapter focuses on the process of intrusion detection. We argue that effective development of technologies and processes that produce CAS in a way properly aligned with human cognition calls for cognitive models—dynamic and adaptable computational representations of the cognitive structures and mechanisms involved in developing SA and processing information for decision making. While visualization and machine learning are often seen among the key approaches to enhancing CSA, we point out a number of limitations in their current state of development and applications to CSA. The current knowledge gaps in our understanding of cognitive demands in CSA include the lack of a theoretical model of cyber SA within a cognitive architecture; the decision gap, representing learning, experience and dynamic decision making in the cyberspace; and the semantic gap, addressing the construction of a common language and a set of basic concepts about which the security community can develop a shared understanding.

Accepting that our understanding about the cognitive reasoning process of cyber analysts is rather limited, the next chapter—**Cognitive Process**—focuses on ways to close this knowledge gap. It starts by summarizing the current understanding about the cognitive processes of cyber analysts based on the results of previous cognitive task analyses. It also discusses the challenges and the importance to capture "fine-grained" cognitive reasoning processes. The chapter then illustrates approaches to overcoming these challenges by presenting a framework for non-intrusive capturing and systematic analysis of the cognitive reasoning process of cyber analysts. The framework includes a conceptual model and practical means for the non-intrusive capturing of a cognitive trace of cyber analysts, and extracting the reasoning process of cyber analysts by analyzing the cognitive trace. The framework can be used to conduct experiments for extracting cognitive reasoning processes from professional network analysts. When cognitive traces are available, their characteristics can be analyzed and compared with the performance of the analysts.

In many fields, analyses of complex systems and activities benefit from visualization of data and analytical products. Analysts use images in order to engage their visual perception in identifying features in the data, and to apply the analysts' domain knowledge. One would expect the same to be true in the practice of cyber analysts as they try to form situational awareness of complex networks. Earlier, the Cognition and Technology chapter introduced the topic of visualization: its criticality to the users, e.g., cyber analysts, as well as its pitfalls and limitations. Now, this **Visualization and Analysts** chapter takes a close look at visualization for Cyber Situational Awareness. We begin with a basic overview of scientific and information visualization, and of recent visualization systems for cyber situation awareness. Then, we outline a set of requirements, derived largely from discussions with expert cyber analysts, for a candidate visualization system. We conclude with a case study of a web-based tool that supports such requirements.

The importance of visualization does not diminish the critical role that algorithmic analysis plays in achieving CSA. Algorithms reason about the voluminous observations and data about the network and infer important features of the situation that help analysts and decision-makers form their situational awareness. In order to perform this inference, and to make its output useful to other algorithms and human users, an algorithm needs to have its inputs and outputs represented in a consistent vocabulary of well-specified terms and their relations, i.e., it needs an ontology with a clear semantics and a standard. This topic is the focus of the present chapter titled **Inference and Ontology**. We already touched on the importance of semantics in the Cognition and Technology chapter. Now we discuss in detail how, in cyber operations, inference based on ontology can be used to determine the threat actor, the target and purpose in order to determine potential courses of action and future impact. Since a comprehensive ontology for cyber security does not exist, we show how such an ontology can be developed by taking advantage of existing cyber security related standards and markup languages.

The next chapter—**Learning and Semantics**—further elaborates on the issue of inference by focusing on a particular class of algorithms important for processing of cyber information—machine learning. The chapter also continues the thread of ontology and semantics as it explores the tradeoffs between the effectiveness of an algorithm and the semantic clarity of its products. It is often difficult to extract meaningful contextual information from a machine learning algorithm, because those algorithms that provide high accuracy also tend to use representations less comprehensible to humans. On the other hand, those algorithms that use more human-accessible vocabulary can be less accurate—they produce more false alerts (false positives), which confuse analysts. A related tradeoff is between the internal semantics of the algorithm versus the external semantics of its output. We illustrate this tradeoff with two case studies. Developers of CSA systems must be aware of such tradeoffs, and seek ways to mitigate them.

As the Foundations and Challenges chapter explained, the second level of SA is called comprehension and deals with determining the significance and relations of various elements of the situation to other elements and to the overall goals of the network. It is also often called situation understanding and involves the "so what" of the information that has been perceived. Previous chapters of this book have not focused on this level of SA. Therefore, the next chapter—**Impact Assessment**—elaborates specifically on the comprehension level of CSA. The chapter explains that an effective way to comprehend significant relations between the disparate elements of the situation is to concentrate on how these elements impact the mission of the network. This involves asking and answering questions of how various suspected attacks relate to each other, how they relate to remaining capabilities of the network's components, and how the resulting disruptions or degradation of services impact elements of the mission and the mission's overall goals.

Having discussed the second level of SA, we now proceed to the third level, in the chapter titled **Attack Projection**. The highest level of SA—projection—involves inferring how the current situation will evolve into the future situation and the anticipation of the future elements of the situation. In the context of CSA, particularly important is the projection of future cyber attacks, or future phases of an ongoing cyber attack. Attacks often take a long time and involve multitudes of reconnaissance, exploitations, and obfuscation activities to achieve the goal of cyber espionage or sabotage. The anticipation of future attack actions is generally derived from the presently observed malicious activities. This chapter reviews the existing state-of-the-art techniques for network attack projection, and then explains how the estimates of ongoing attack strategies can then be used to provide a prediction of likely upcoming threats to critical assets of the network. Such projections require analyzing potential attack paths based on network and system vulnerabilities, knowledge of the attacker's behavior patterns, continuous learning or new patterns and the ability to see through the attacker's obfuscations and deceptions.

Discussion of challenges and ways of improving Cyber Situational Awareness dominated our previous chapters. However, we have not yet touched on how to quantify any improvement we might achieve. Indeed, to get an accurate assessment of network security and provide sufficient Cyber Situational Awareness (CSA), simple but meaningful metrics—the focus of the **Metrics of Security** chapter—are necessary. The adage, "what can't be measured can't be effectively managed," applies here. Without good metrics and the corresponding evaluation methods, security analysts and network operators cannot accurately evaluate and measure the security status of their networks and the success of their operations. In particular, this chapter explores two distinct issues: (i) how to define and use metrics as quantitative characteristics to represent the security state of a network, and (ii) how to define and use metrics to measure CSA from a defender's point of view.

As we come to the end of the book, we look at the end-goals of achieving CSA. In the **Mission Resiliency** chapter we explain that the ultimate objective of CSA is to enable situation management, i.e., continuous adjustments of both the network and the mission that the network supports, in order to ensure that the mission continues to achieve its objectives. Indeed, several previous chapters stressed that CSA exists in the context of a particular mission, and serves the purposes of the mission. A mission that is able to absorb the attacks and keep returning to an acceptable level of execution is called a resilient mission. It can be said that the purpose of CSA is to maintain mission resiliency. This chapter explains that mission-centric resilient cyber defense should be based on collective and adaptive behavior of two interacting dynamic processes, cyber situation management in the cyber space, and mission situation management in the physical space. It discusses architecture and enabling technologies of such mutually adaptive processes that keep the mission persisting even if the network that supports the mission may be compromised by a cyber attack.

Foundation and Challenges

Mica R. Endsley and Erik S. Connors

1 Introduction

The proliferation of network-centric warfare capabilities has led to a greater need to define and understand cyber networks. Critical systems and information sources maintained on such networks are lucrative targets for terrorists, foreign governments, criminal organizations, and competitive businesses. The very same technology that enables efficient communications and conduct within military, government and business communities enables hostile individuals and organizations to identify and exploit vulnerabilities within secure computer networks. Protecting and maintaining these networks is inherently more challenging when compared to traditional information and communication networks.

Cyber network threats tend to be highly complex, and attacks may involve internal or external attackers that span varying levels of sophistication—from amateurs to highly organized entities. Cyber networks may be hacked by coordinated, distributed attacks, which are constantly changing to circumvent and exploit cyber defense methodologies. A cyber attack can have severe consequences in a military network (e.g., loss of nodes leading to warfighter fatality or a compromise of security) as well as to civilian network infrastructures (e.g. SCADA systems that control the electrical grid or water processing facilities, banking systems, corporate intellectual property and personal identity information).

M.R. Endsley (✉)
United States Air Force, Pentagon 4E130, Washington, DC 20330, USA
e-mail: mica.endsley@pentagon.af.mil

E.S. Connors
SA Technologies, Inc., 3750 Palladian Village Drive, #600, Marietta, GA 30066, USA
e-mail: erik.connors@satechnologies.com

© Springer International Publishing Switzerland 2014
A. Kott et al. (eds.), *Cyber Defense and Situational Awareness*,
Advances in Information Security 62, DOI 10.1007/978-3-319-11391-3_2

As cyberspace threats continue to increase in sophistication and complexity, new solutions are needed to provide the information and processing necessary to support critical missions during a cyber conflict. For example, networks and systems must be built with the capability to use alternate paths, as well as survivable architectures and algorithms, in order to perform even when attacked in unanticipated ways that attempt to interfere with normal operations. New methodologies and algorithms are needed for the next generation of cyber networks to support situation awareness, node-based assessment of cyber effects, and dynamic and autonomic response to attacks including reconfiguration, recovery, and reconstitution, all while allowing mission-critical systems to continue to function. Before cyber operators can act to defend against these attacks, perform recovery actions, or even retaliate, they must first achieve and maintain a level of situation awareness (SA) that allows them to identify, understand, and anticipate evolving threats.

Successfully achieving SA of the cyber environment has been shown to be quite difficult with today's systems, however. A recent comprehensive study of cyber operations in the U.S. Air Force, for example, concluded that "the Air Force lacks the comprehensive cyber situation awareness that is a pre-requisite for cyberspace assurance" (United States Air Force 2012). Similarly, the U.S. Army lists cyber situation awareness and understanding as one of its top R&D needs (United States Army 2013). Far more than just a military problem, industry, critical transportation systems and public utilities are all vulnerable to cyber attacks. These entities require significant assistance in developing a comprehensive understanding of their systems and the cyber threats against those systems in order to assure the security and integrity of their operations.

Achieving SA for any complex domain is always a unique blend of technology with human cognitive abilities. Establishing effective understanding of the complex and often hidden aspects of the cyberspace domain stresses this human-technology relationship beyond that of typical network operations or military and intelligence applications. The extreme volume of data and the speed at which that data flows rapidly exceeds human cognitive limits and capabilities. Additionally, new methods of attack and exploitation are constantly being developed and permuted in order to circumvent existing cyber defense methodologies. This motivates the development of new technologies that can operate in these extreme conditions to effectively augment human understanding and decision-making.

To ensure that technology developments are appropriately focused, it is first necessary to fully understand the requirements for cyber defense SA. This begins with developing an understanding of the effects of disruptions and information attacks on cyber systems, the information that is required to understand these cyber events and situations, the decisions that operators are required to make, and how technology solutions should be evaluated with respect to their ability to improve SA and the decision making processes. A clear definition of what exactly constitutes SA in cyber environments, the processes used for deriving SA out of the multitude of information that is available about cyber networks and mission operations, and the existing theoretical foundation for building efficient, effective systems for supporting SA is needed. This will provide a better basis for understanding the current state of cyber SA in existing networks as well as provide directions for the research needs going forward.

2 Cyber Situation Awareness (SA)

2.1 Definition of SA

One of the earliest and most widely used definitions of SA was provided by Endsley (1995) who described it as the "perception of the elements in the environment within a volume of time and space, the comprehension of their meaning and the projection of their status in the near future," (p. 36). Based on this definition, SA is comprised of three levels: (1) perception, (2) comprehension, and (3) projection, (Fig. 1), which directly feed into the decision and action cycle.

Level 1 SA, perception, involves the sensory detection of significant information about the system one is operating and the environment it is operating in. For example, cyber operators need to be able to see relevant displays or hear an alarm signal. In the cyber environment, Level 1 SA may include awareness of the state of various system nodes, current protocols, nodes that have been compromised, a history of activities and the IP address of effected systems.

Comprehension, or Level 2 SA, is important because situation awareness encompasses far more than simply perceiving a bunch of data on a series of computer screens. Comprehending the meaning or significance of that information in relation to one's goals is needed. This process includes developing a comprehensive picture of the system—adding 2 and 2 together to get 4—to form a more complete and integrated understanding of what is happening. Level 2 SA is often called situation understanding and involves the "so what" of the information that has been perceived. Thus, cyber operators with good Level 2 SA are able to understand how vulnerable particular nodes are, the signature of an attack, what separate events might be inter-related, the effect of a given event on current mission operations, and the correct prioritization of competing events.

Projection, the highest level of SA, consists of extrapolating information forward in time to determine how it will affect future states of the operating environment. This combines what the individual knows about the current situation (e.g., events and attacks present on the system) with their mental models of the system to predict what is likely to happen next—for example, being able to project the impact of malicious activity on other nodes across the network, or projected avenues for future attacks. Higher levels of SA allow cyber operators to function in a timely and effective manner, even with very complex and challenging tasks.

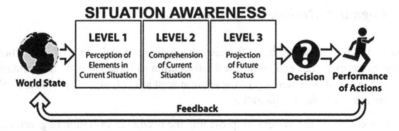

Fig. 1 Situation awareness

Operators will continuously search the environment to build up this constantly evolving picture of the situation, so they may decide to gather more information based on their current understanding of the situation (e.g. to fill in holes or confirm some assessment), or at some point may choose to select a course of action to change the system in some way to align with their goals. Because the state of the environment and the system are constantly changing, there is an ongoing and dynamic need to update SA.

2.2   SA Requirements for Cyber Operations

The specific aspects of the cyber situation that a given individual needs to be aware of depend on the role of that individual in the operation. These SA needs vary considerably between different roles. For example, within an organization involved in cyber defense there may be multiple roles, each of which are focusing on different parts of the network, or who work in conjunction with each other to address different types of threats or different parts of the work flow. Conversely, the commander of an air operations center or the manager of a public utility has a very different set of goals and objectives, but will need to understand the cyber picture at a higher level so that she can understand how the cyber environment may impact a given mission operation.

In that the goals and objectives of these various roles are different, and the decisions they need to make likewise differ, the specific SA needs of each role must be carefully delineated so that the technology solutions developed to support them provide information that is tailored to their needs at all three levels of SA. This analysis has traditionally been performed through a Goal-Directed Task Analysis (GDTA) (Endsley 1993; Endsley and Jones 2012). The GDTA develops a high level goal structure for each role, lists the major decisions to be made by that role, and details the SA requirements at each of the three levels that are needed to support each decision. For example, the GDTA goal tree and a portion of the detailed GDTA SA requirements for a typical cyber operator are shown in Figs. 2 and 3 (Connors et al. 2010). Based on such analyses, not only is it possible to determine the basic data that needs to be provided to a cyber operator, but also the types of integrated information that the system needs to provide, examples of which are shown in Table 1.

2.3   Cognitive Mechanisms for SA

Endsley (1988, 1995) describes a framework cognitive model of SA, showing how human operators gather and understand information to form SA, which is summarized here in Fig. 4. Key features of the environment affect how well people are able to obtain and maintain SA, including:

1. The capability of the system for providing the needed information (e.g. relevant sensors, data transmission capabilities, networking, etc.),

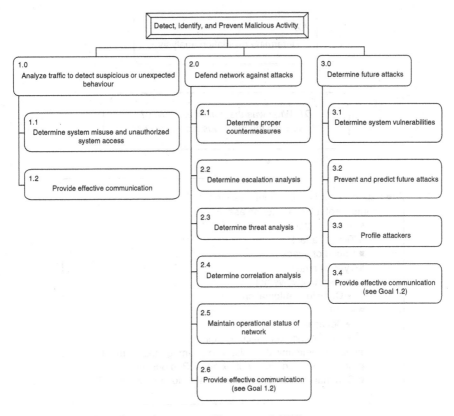

Fig. 2 GDTA goal tree for a cyber operator (Connors et al. 2010)

2. The design of the system interface determining which information is available to the individual along with the format of the displays for effectively transmitting information,
3. System complexity, including number of components, inter-relatedness of those components and rate of change of information, affecting the ability of the individual to keep up with needed information and to understand and project future events,
4. The level of automation present in the system, affecting the ability of the individual to stay "in-the-loop", aware of what is happening and understanding what the system is doing, and
5. Stress and workload that occur as a function of the task environment, the system interface and the operational domain, each of which can act to decrease SA.

In addition to these external factors, the model points out many features of the individual that determine whether a person will develop good SA, given the same environment and equipment as others. In combination, the mechanisms of short-term sensory memory, perception, working memory and long term memory form

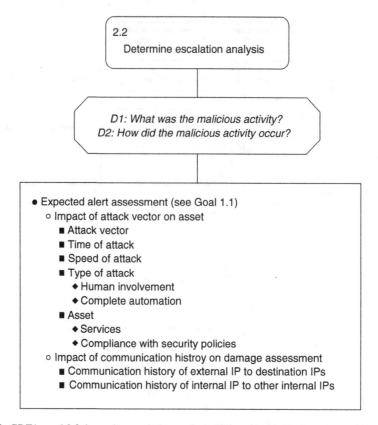

Fig. 3 GDTA: goal 2.2 determine escalation analysis (Connors et al. 2010)

the basic structures on which SA is based. According to this model, elements in the environment (such as the operator's displays) may be initially processed in parallel preattentively where certain emergent properties are detected, such as spatial proximity, color, simple properties of shapes, or movement, providing cues for further focalized attention. Those objects which are most perceptually salient (e.g. based on bright colors or motion) are further processed using focalized attention to achieve perception. Limited attention creates a major constraint on the operator's ability to accurately perceive multiple items in parallel, and, as such, is a major limit on people's ability to maintain SA in complex environments where the amount of data available far exceeds a person's ability to attend to it.

SA is far more complex than simple cue-based perception, however, and also relies on a number of other cognitive mechanisms that significantly augment this simple data driven information flow. First, attention and the perception process can be directed by the contents of both working memory and long-term memory. Advance knowledge regarding the location of information, the form of the information, the spatial frequency, the color, or the overall familiarity and appropriateness of infor-

Table 1 Example SA requirements for a cyber operator

Level 1 SA requirements	Level 2 SA requirements	Level 3 SA requirements
Time	Impact of transcript contents on expected alert assessment	Predicted exploits from known attacks
Signature/packet/protocol	Impact of destination port activity on expected alert assessment	Predicted exploits from new threats
Internal IP address (Destination)	Impact of destination node on expected alert assessment	Predicted vulnerabilities to network
Internal port (Destination port)	Impact of source IP on expected alert assessment	Predicted activities of known attackers
External node IP address (Source)	Impact of recent attacks on reporting	Predicted impact to network from potential attack
Report of attacks	Impact of deviations from expected behavior of destination on expected alert assessment	Predicted mission impact from potential attack
Traffic behavior from controlled activity	Impact of relationships between ports and protocols on expected alert assessment	Expected alert assessment
Information from external sources	Impact of packet payload comparisons on expected alert assessment	Projected new network defense countermeasures
	Impact of malicious activity results on current countermeasures and protection schemes	Projected types of malicious activity escaping real time detection
	Impact of destination IP on determining true source IP	Projected level of information for communication
	Impact of forensic analysis on COA	Projection of the broader implications of related attacks
	Impact of new exploits on mission assets	
	Impact of assets on ongoing missions	
	Impact of attack vector on asset	
	Impact of communication history on damage assessment	
	Impact of time on false alarm frequency	
	Impact of reports on expected alert assessment	
	Impact of correlated attacks on expected alert assessment	
	Impact of unusual behavior on expected alert assessment	
	Impact of compromised nodes on network health	
	Impact of random port openings on network vulnerability	
	Impact of Red Forces on future attacks	
	Impact of system exploits on future attacks	
	Impact of known attacks on potential exploits	
	Impact of potential exploits on threat assessment	
	Impact of attack vector on attacker identity	
	Impact of data payload size on expected alert assessment	
	Impact of packet payloads comparisons on expected alert assessment	

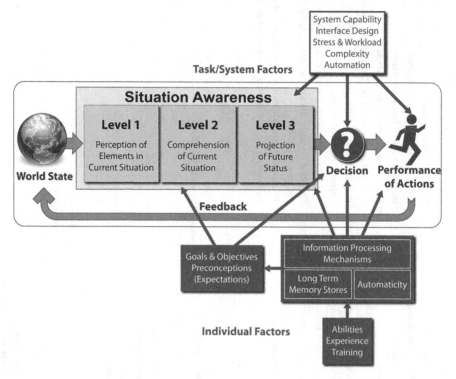

Fig. 4 Model of situation awareness in dynamic decision making (Endsley 1995)

mation all can significantly facilitate perception, for instance. Long term memory also serves to shape the perception of objects in terms of known categories or mental representations. Categorization tends to occur almost instantly. Thus, experienced cyber operators often know where to look for key information and how to interpret it, and can be biased towards looking for information based on their expectations.

For operators who have not developed other cognitive mechanisms (novices and those in novel situations) the perception of the elements in the environment, the first level of SA, is significantly limited by attention and working memory. In the absence of other mechanisms, most of the operator's active processing of information must occur in working memory. New information must be combined with existing knowledge and a composite picture of the situation developed. Projections of future status and subsequent decisions as to appropriate courses of action will occur in working memory as well. Working memory will be significantly taxed with simultaneously achieving the higher levels of SA, formulating and selecting responses and carrying out subsequent actions. Thus novice cyber operators, like those in other domains, are quickly overloaded and unable to effectively process and integrate much of the data that are available. Their overall level of SA tends to be extremely limited in a very complex domain like cyber network operations. For example, a new cyber operator will be able to read available displays and logs, but would not be attuned to realizing the implications of the data, and would be far more likely to not understand that a cyber attack was occurring or its implications for ongoing operations. They would also have a much harder time in determining which data of all that available they should focus more attention on in which circumstances.

In actual practice, however, both goal-directed processing and long term memory mechanisms (in the form of mental models and schema) can be used by more experienced cyber operators to circumvent the limitations of working memory and more effectively direct attention. First, much relevant knowledge about a system is hypothesized to be stored in mental models. Rouse and Morris (1985) define mental models as "mechanisms whereby humans are able to generate descriptions of system purpose and form, explanations of system functioning and observed system states, and predictions of future states".

Mental models are cognitive mechanisms that embody information about system form and function; often they are relevant to some physical system (e.g. a car, computer network, or power plant) or to an organizational system (e.g. how a company, military unit, or cyber attacker works). They typically contain information about not only the components of a particular system, but also how those components interact to produce various system states and events. Cyber operators must develop good mental models of their networks and the various inter-related components to develop an understanding of how it works. Mental models can significantly aid SA as people recognize key features in the world that map to key features in the model. The model then creates the mechanism for determining associations between observed states of components (comprehension) and predictions of the behavior and status of these elements over time. For example, a good mental model of a network and its components can be used to understand its particular vulnerabilities to attack. A mental model of how cyber attackers work can be used to formulate an understanding of attack vectors and projections of likely targets. These mental models can be called upon when examining data of current network events to help interpret observed data and project likely attack progression. Thus mental models can provide for much of the higher levels of SA (comprehension and projection) without loading working memory. Mental models allow experienced cyber operators to comprehend the ultimate meaning of information provided about the state of the network as it relates to their goal of assuring a safe network.

Associated with mental models are also schema—prototypical classes of states the system (e.g. what a particular attack signature looks like, or what typical user behavior consists of). These schema are even more useful to the formation of SA, as these recognized classes of situations provide immediate one step retrieval from memory of the higher levels of SA based on pattern matching between situation cues and known schema in memory. Very often scripts, set sequences of actions, have also been developed for these schema, so that much of the load on working memory for generating alternate behaviors and selecting among them is also diminished. These mechanisms allow the cyber operator to simply execute a predetermined action for a given recognized class of situations (based on their SA). For example, known cyber attack signatures and event types can be easily recognized, with procedures predetermined for how to respond to them. The current situation does not even need to be exactly like one encountered before due to the use of categorization mapping—as long as a close-enough mapping can be made into relevant categories, a situation can be recognized, comprehended in terms of the model, predictions made and appropriate actions selected. In that people have very good pattern matching abilities, this process can be almost instantaneous and produce a much lower load on working memory making high levels of SA possible for experienced personnel, even in very demanding situations. In the cyber environment, where attacks can happen in time frames that exceed human perception and response limitations, this process may be automated for known classes of attacks, however, novel attacks or malware signatures will likely still require human interventions.

Expertise, therefore, plays a major role in the SA process. For novices or those dealing with novel situations, decision making in complex and dynamic systems can be very demanding or impossible to accomplish successfully in that it would require detailed mental calculations based on rules or heuristics, placing a heavy burden on working memory. Where experience has allowed the development of mental models and schema, pattern matching between the perceived elements in the environment and existing schema/mental models can occur on the basis of pertinent cues that have been learned. Thus the comprehension and future projection required for the higher levels of SA can be developed with far less effort and within the constraints of working memory. When scripts have been developed, tied to these schema, the entire decision making process will be greatly simplified. The ability of the system displays to support the operator's need to pattern match between critical cues in the information presented and these mental models is highly important for supporting rapid SA formation and decision making.

The cyber operator's goals also play an important part in the process. These goals can be thought of as ideal states of the system model that the operator wishes to achieve. The cyber operator's goals and plans will direct which aspects of the environment are attended to in the development of SA. Goal-driven or top-down processing is very important in effective information processing and the development of SA. Conversely, in a bottom-up or data-driven process, patterns in the environment may be recognized which will indicate to the operator that different plans will be necessary to meet goals or that different goals should be activated.

An alternating of goal-driven and data-driven is characteristic of much human information processing and underpins much of SA development in complex worlds. People who are purely data driven are very inefficient at processing complex information sets—there is too much information to take so they are simply reactive to which ever cues are most salient. People who have clearly developed goals, however, will search for information that is relevant to those goals, allowing information search to be more efficient and providing a mechanism for determining the relevance of information that is perceived. If one is only goal-driven however, it is likely that key information that indicates a change in goals is needed (e.g. cease with the goal of "determine system vulnerabilities" and activate the goal of "diagnose new event") will be missed. Thus effective information processing is characterized by alternating between these modes—using goal driven processing to efficiently find and process the information needed for achieving goals, and using data driven processing to regulate the selection of which goals should be most important at any given time.

The development of SA is dynamic and on-going process, affected by these key cognitive mechanisms. While it can be very challenging in the cyber domain, with the cognitive mechanisms that can be developed through experience (schema and mental models), we find that people are able to circumvent known limitations (working memory and attention) to develop sufficient levels of SA to function very effectively. Never-the-less, developing accurate SA remains a very challenging feature in complex settings such as cyber operations and demands significant operator time and resources. Thus, developing selection batteries, training program and system designs to enhance SA is a major goal for the cyber domain.

3   Challenges for SA in Cyber Operations

3.1   Complex and Fluid System Topology

First, the sheer size and complexity of computer networks creates a significant challenge for SA. Developing an understanding of the effect of an attack or other event depends on having a good mental model of the system and its components which is inherently difficult the larger the network gets and the more nodes and branches it contains. In addition, those networks can change significantly over the course of days or weeks as new nodes are added or removed, technology is updated, and people join and leave with mobile technologies.

As computer networks have become enormous, with many nodes and components, developing and maintaining an accurate picture of that network has become a seemingly insurmountable challenge in many organizations. Software systems, similarly are composed of long strings of code, often highly nested and complex, making understanding the effects of small changes to that code very difficult to predict. The size and dynamic nature of cyber systems make not only detecting problems challenging, but also create significant difficulty in understanding the impact of potential events on the health of network. People's ability to develop and maintain an accurate mental model of the network is often rapidly exceeded, impacting both SA comprehension and projection without significant aiding.

3.2   Rapidly Changing Technologies

Technologies change very rapidly in the cyber arena. New software, computer systems, routers and other components are introduced on an almost daily basis. Not only does this make it challenging to maintain an accurate understanding of the system topology, but the new and different capabilities introduced by technology evolution can have profound effects on system vulnerabilities and behaviors. This aspect of network architecture seriously taxes SA comprehension and projection. People simply will have a very limited ability to develop and maintain up-to-date and effective mental models upon which to form sufficient understanding of new events in the network and to make accurate and timely predictions.

3.3   High Noise to Signal Ratio

Detecting that the system has come under a cyber attack may also be difficult in many cases. This is because anomalous events are quite common in working with computer networks. Users are quite used to systems not working properly and may easily dismiss nefarious activity as being due to a normal system problem (Endsley and Jones 2001). The noisy background of system failures, software glitches, maintenance updates, forgotten passwords and other disruptions to "normal" all may act to mask the features of an actual cyber attack, Fig. 5. Thus even Level 1 SA, perception of an attack, may be affected.

3.4   Time Bombs and Lurking Attacks

The time frame between an attack and its effect may also be quite distributed. A cyber attack may be injected by code that lies dormant for a long period until a particular time or event triggers it into action. This creates a very poor ability for tying the actions associated with a particular attack to the consequences of those actions. Thus, network operators can go for long periods of time unaware that malicious code already resides in their network.

3.5   Rapidly Evolving and Multi-Faceted Threats

The developers of cyber attacks have a wide range of potential attack vectors that can be used, Fig. 6. And the numbers and types of attack signatures are growing exponentially. One estimate shows that by 2025 there will be roughly 200 million new malware signatures per year (United States Air Force 2012). This means that developing an understanding of the threat and its effects through normal learning and experience will be almost impossible.

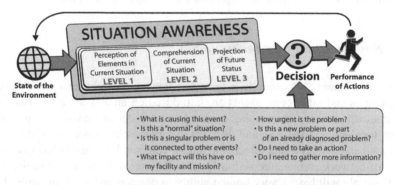

Fig. 5 Decision context for interpreting potential cyber attacks (Endsley and Jones 2001)

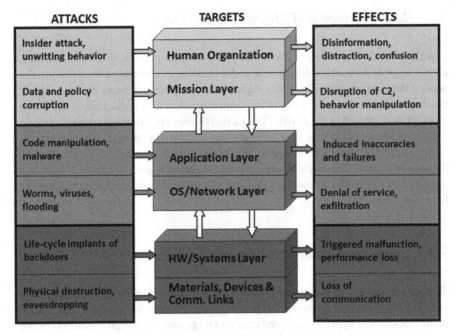

ATTACKS	TARGETS	EFFECTS
Insider attack, unwitting behavior	Human Organization	Disinformation, distraction, confusion
Data and policy corruption	Mission Layer	Disruption of C2, behavior manipulation
Code manipulation, malware	Application Layer	Induced inaccuracies and failures
Worms, viruses, flooding	OS/Network Layer	Denial of service, exfiltration
Life-cycle implants of backdoors	HW/Systems Layer	Triggered malfunction, performance loss
Physical destruction, eavesdropping	Materials, Devices & Comm. Links	Loss of communication

Fig. 6 Elements of a contested cyber environment (United States Air Force 2012)

3.6 Speed of Events

Cyber operations are carried out within a cycle of detecting and understanding events, making decisions and taking actions—often called the Observe-Orient-Decide Act (OODA) loop. A cyber attack can happen in a fraction of a second, however, effectively eliminating the ability of an individual to detect and react to that attack. This has led cyber operators to describe their OODA loop as an OODA point. In such circumstances there is no time for preventing an attack, or reacting to it in real-time. Rather human activity becomes focused on forensic actions to determine what components have been affected by an attack and the impact on operations.

3.7 Non-integrated Tools

Current cyber operations are hampered by the fact that an integrated set of tools to provide the information needed to detect, understand and react to cyber attacks is not present. Rather cyber operators must work with an incomplete set of tools, each of which provides some useful information, but which is not complete in meeting their SA needs (Connors et al. 2010). This creates a highly manually intensive and slow process for finding needed information and mentally integrating it to form a picture of the system and the effects of cyber attacks.

3.8   Data Overload and Meaning Underload

In addition to the high level of overload associated with perceiving data from across a very large and complex network, and the challenges associated with finding the needed data across multiple, non-integrated tools, cyber operators are also highly challenged by the lack of support for comprehension and projection, level 2 and level 3 SA (Connors et al. 2010). That is, individuals are often left to figure out on their own how cyber events may be impacting current operations, or what vulnerabilities may be attacked in future. Given the severe challenges in developing the mental models that would allow people to make such assessments mentally, and the significantly reduced timelines, this lack of support has significant consequences for cyber SA.

3.9   Automation Induced SA Losses

To help overcome the significant challenges with network complexity, change and speed of cyber operations, various types of automated tools for assisting in the automatic detection of cyber attacks, and resultant responses have been developed or are in development. While such tools are likely to be necessary for supporting operations given the limits to human cognition and speed of reaction, they also introduce their own challenge for operator SA. High levels of automation have been found to actually reduce SA by virtue of putting the operator "out-of-the-loop", making it difficult for them to detect and understand system operations and to be able to intervene effectively when the automation encounters new events or situations that it is not programmed to handle (Endsley and Kiris 1995).

3.10   Summary of Cyber SA Challenges

In summary, while the human brain is well designed to derive SA from the world based on a complex set of cognitive processes and mental models and schema learned through experience, the artificial world of cyber operations seriously stresses that process. The combined effects of network complexity and fluidity, combined with a rapidly changing and complex attack vector, events that happen at the millisecond level, high noise to signal ratios, and a very slow linkage between malware introduction and the attack event all conspire to make real-time SA of cyber operations very difficult to achieve. The lack of good integrated tools that help bridge this gap by assisting the operator with an comprehensive set of needed information, transformations of the data to understand the impact of attacks on operations and autonomous actions, and tools to support proactive network defense therefore becomes all the more important. Addressing this gap is critical for developing the necessary cyber SA required for secure operations.

4 Research and Development Needs for Cyber SA

General Keith Alexander, head of the U.S. Defense Department's Cyber Command, has called for the development of a better common operational picture for Cyber. "We must first understand our networks and build an effective cyber situation awareness in real time through a common, sharable operating picture" (Bain 2010). Currently situation awareness of cyber events across networks is often based on forensics generated after an incident has occurred. Cyber operations must move from reactive forensics to a real-time, proactive and preventative counter-cyber operation, with an informed cyber operator acting in concert with effective tools and automated aids.

4.1 The Cyber Common Operating Picture

One of the most direct needs cyber operations is the creation of effective common operating pictures (COP) for cyber networks. The Cyber COP needs to be customized for each of the unique cyber operator positions involved in cyber operations. Further carefully filtered and interpreted versions of cyber information needs to flow into organizational command centers where cyber effects may become integral in the future. Each of these roles has unique needs for perception, comprehension and projection, of which cyber comprises only a portion of this focus, but which must be integrated with their other SA needs.

The situation awareness oriented design (SAOD) process (Endsley and Jones 2012) provides a systematic method for creating role relevant, tailored COPs that are effective for supporting SA based on both an understanding of how the brain forms SA, and some 25 years of research on the topic. SAOD provides a structured approach to the development of COPs and operator displays that incorporates SA considerations into the design process, including a determination of SA requirements, design principles for SA enhancement, and measurement of SA in design evaluation (Fig. 7).

SA requirements analyses are conducted using the GDTA process to identify the goals of a particular role or job class, and to define the decisions and information requirements for meeting each higher goal. This goal-oriented approach moves

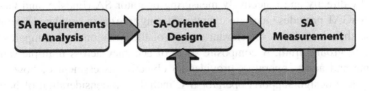

Fig. 7 SA-oriented design (SAOD) is a three-phase methodology for optimizing operator SA (Endsley and Jones 2012)

away from consideration of just task steps or processes (which reflect current technology and processes) and focuses on the operator's cognitive requirements. The GDTA methodology has been used extensively to determine SA requirements in a wide variety of operations including power systems, oilfield services, commercial aviation, and military command and control, as well as for cyber operations, presented previously in this chapter.

The SA design phase starts with an in-depth analysis of SA requirements feeding directly into the design process as a key mechanism for developing information presentations that avoid high workload and maximize SA. By applying the 50 SAOD principles, SA design (1) ensures that the key information needed for high levels of SA is included in each interface, (2) integrates the information in needed ways to support high levels of comprehension and projection of ongoing operations, directly presented on display visualizations, (3) provides big picture integrated information displays to keep global SA high, while providing easy access to details needed for situation understanding, (4) uses information salience to direct the user's attention to key information and events, and (5) directly supports multi-tasking that is critical for SA. This is a significant addition to traditional human factors design principles (which largely address surface features such as legibility, contrast, and readability of information), and human computer interaction principles, which provide effective task interaction mechanisms on computer displays. In addition key principles are provided for dealing with complexity and uncertainty, integrating automation, effective use of alarm systems, and support for shared SA across distributed teams, all of which are highly relevant in cyber operations.

For example, cyber tools could benefit from displays that provide trending information on events and signatures of interest. Tools that allow analysts to keep up-to-date information regarding current, recent and past alerts that support assessment of the significance events across analysts and shifts would also be helpful, as would tools that provide the ability to correlate data and examine patterns across the infrastructure. Overall network health indicators and maps, as well as tools that support impact analysis of key events on current operations are another example of displays needed to support cyber SA.

The third step in the SAOD process involves assessing the effectiveness of the designed system. Depending on project requirements and goals, SA, workload, performance, and usability measures can be used as metrics to evaluate the system. When feasible, objective SA measures provide a proven way to assess operator SA levels and thus system effectiveness. For example, the Situation Awareness Global Assessment Technique (SAGAT) has been successfully used to provide this information by directly and objectively measuring operator SA (Endsley and Garland 2000). SAGAT provides Query to operators during freezes in simulated operations to assess their knowledge of relevant aspects of the situation, and compares their answers to ground truth. A composite score of accuracy across multiple samples over time and across operators provides an objective assessment of how well a given system design supports operator SA, including a consideration of both the adequacy of the system information and how well it is presented to meet human cognitive needs and limitations. A version of SAGAT for measuring SA in cyber operations has been developed (Connors et al. 2010). It includes Query for the operator such as:

- Has the *source IP address* y been involved in suspicious activity previously?
- Is the packet payload for *alert A* unusual for *destination IP address x*?
- What other assets will be impacted if *alert A* occurs and attacks *destination IP address x*?

SAOD can be applied systematically to cyber operations in order to design future Cyber COPs and other mission COPs to support the cyber related decisions that we face, taking advantage of significant work that has been done in this arena.

4.2 Visualization of Large-Scale Complex and Dynamically Changing Networks

Cyber operations provide a unique challenge in terms of the sheer size of the networks involved and their inherent level of dynamics. Understanding the topography of the cyber network is a key component to being able to understand the potential impact of a particular event or attack on a given mission or operation. This has proven to be quite challenging in many cases. New research will be need to help operators to better visualize existing networks, particularly as they change. As we develop networks that dynamically morph as a function of their design, as well as a function of other factors (e.g. computers or software getting added or deleted, mobile users joining the network at various locations and times), the understand-ability of the network will be severely strained. New methods to support operators by mapping system topology to operational decisions are needed. This research will need to address not just abstract visualization, but also the types of display support that are needed for addressing the various types of comprehension and projection needs of operators who are answering very real questions about the system's performance (e.g. see Table 1). For example, displays that assist the operator in assessing the impact of a malicious activity on current protection schemes and needed assets. These sorts of SA requirements have been found to be very poorly supported in many existing tools (Connors et al. 2010).

4.3 Support for Decision Maker SA

It is also recognized that outside of a cyber operations center, most cyber effects will be viewed from the lens of organizational managers who will make decisions about cyber within the context of their mission objectives. In the military domain, commanders will also examine cyber options along with other types of both lethal and non-lethal effects at their disposal. For instance, will it be better to eliminate an enemy command center by attacking it with a conventional kinetic weapon, or by employing a missile that uses microwave energy to knock out its electronic systems, or to use a cyber attack to disable the command and control system? What would be the expected outcomes of these various options, what are the risks, and how long would it take to carry them out? These are the types of realistic questions that will need to be answerable and supported in future military command centers in order for cyber effects to be used within the context of broader mission operations. Future COPs in mission command centers will need to provide the SA needed to address these sorts of questions.

4.4   Synergistic Human-Autonomy Teams

Due to the rapidity of cyber effects, it is widely recognized that automated tools will likely be needed to help detect potential cyber attacks and to respond to them in a timely manner. The speed at which operations can occur in the cyber world significantly outpaces the ability of human operators to perceive and react. Therefore, automated tools in this domain are inevitable.

Automation is not an easy answer, however. Considerable research has shown that the use of automation can render the human operator out-of-the-loop, with a much delayed ability to detect that a problem is occurring and a reduced ability to be able to understand the situation and act in a timely manner (Wickens 1992; Wiener 1988). This out-of-the-loop performance decrement has been shown to be due to lower SA when working with automated systems (Endsley and Kiris 1995). In part this can be due to lower vigilance (automation complacency) or poor design of the interface to support understanding of automation, but fundamentally, even when these two factors are not present, it is because automation makes people passive in the processing of information which inherently lowers SA (Endsley and Kiris 1995). In addition, challenges with poor understanding of system states and modes, and lack of trust in automation have been found to lead to problems in many systems where automation has been implemented, reducing its ultimate effectiveness (Lee and See 2004; Sarter and Woods 1995).

If the automation works perfectly for all cases (which it rarely does), this would not be such a problem. However, in the evolving world of cyber, it is likely that automation will only work well for known classes of problems and new types of attacks the automation is not programmed for would proceed unabated. Therefore, there will always be a need for human operators to understand the basic state of the system and any potential attacks occurring on it. Even with learning algorithms that are envisioned for systems with higher levels of autonomy, the need for operators to interact with the autonomy to deal with novel cyber attacks will be high.

As automation is introduced to take care of more and more of the routine situations, it will be highly incumbent on designers to take care to make sure that the human operator is fully aware of both the state of the automation and the underlying cyber network that it is acting upon. Design principles for supporting the required human-automation synergy for effective teaming include (1) providing for supervised flexible autonomy across various levels of automation, (2) automation transparency supporting the ability to understand both current actions of the autonomy and projected future actions, (3) maintaining the human operator in-the-loop and in control of the functioning of the system, (4) providing support for information integration to provide the needed comprehension and projection for decision making, (5) keeping the system understandable, minimizing modes and making system states salient (Endsley and Jones 2012).

A high degree of shared SA between the autonomy and the human operator will be needed to support goal alignment, task alignment, dynamic function allocation and reallocation and effective performance of both the human and the autonomy. The goal is simple, smooth and seamless transitions between the human operator and the autonomy—requiring high levels of shared SA that will need to be zsupported as we transition to the greater use of autonomy in cyber operations.

4.5 Verification and Validation of Components and Code

Any work on cyber necessitates that a serious, systematic effort be applied to the verification and validation of both the components and the code that are involved. To this end, trust in autonomy will require new verification and validation methods (United States Air Force 2013). Complex adaptive systems with autonomous reconfigurability implies an approach to an infinite state system even for moderate levels of autonomy, exceeding the capabilities of traditional software testing methods based on requirements traceability. Problems are exacerbated by data and communication link losses that may occur. This is an extremely challenging problem, but one that must be addressed to provide the level of trust in autonomous cyber operations that will be needed. Methods for graceful degradation and system safeing need to be considered, along with methods for making systems cyber resistant, cyber tolerant and cyber resilient.

4.6 Proactive Control

In a shift to proactive control, operators will not wait for a cyber attack to occur, but rather will be undertaking activities to cyber-proof the network. This requires tools that will allow them to better understand inherent cyber vulnerabilities and prevent both future attacks of a known type and future attacks that have never occurred before, but which might be possible. They will need tools that will allow them to profile suspected attackers, creating profiles of identities, motives and sponsors that can be used to formulate mission relevant strategies. And they need tools that can help them to share knowledge of potential future attacks and defensive countermeasures. Tools that will better illuminate the impact of possible attacks and potential countermeasures on mission operations will ultimately be needed to support effective decision-making.

5 Summary

Cyber is as significant a change to warfare as the invention of the airplane, and likely to change the face of warfare accordingly. History has not been kind to countries who have ignored technological change and continued to fight in outmoded ways. And it will not be kind to those who fail to grasp the new opportunities and dangers inherent in the cyber world. The development of cyber situation awareness is critical to effective defense of networks and the assurance of security in cyber operations. SA is comprised of three levels: (1) perception, (2) comprehension, and (3) projection, (Fig. 1), which directly feed into the decision and action cycle. The specific aspects of the cyber situation that a given individual needs to be aware of depend on the role of that individual in the operation. The specific SA needs of each role must be carefully delineated so that the technology solutions developed to support them provide information that is tailored to their needs at all three levels of SA. This analysis has traditionally been performed through a Goal-Directed Task Analysis (GDTA) The GDTA develops a high level goal structure for each role, lists the major decisions to be made by that role, and details the SA requirements at each of the three levels that are needed to support each decision. A number of factors act to severely limit cyber SA in current operations, including: a highly complex and fluid system topology, rapidly changing technologies, a high signal to noise ratio, potentially long durations between the insertion of an attack and its effect, rapidly evolving and multi-faceted threats, speed of events that exceed human capacity, non-integrated tools that are poorly aligned with SA needs, data overload and meaning underload, and automation challenges. One of the most direct needs cyber operations is the creation of effective common operating pictures (COP) for cyber networks. The Cyber COP needs to be customized for each of the unique cyber operator positions involved in cyber operations. New research will be needed to help operators to better visualize existing networks, particularly as they change. New methods to support operators by mapping system topology to operational decisions are needed. There will always be a need for human operators to understand the basic state of the system and any potential attacks occurring on it. A high degree of shared SA between the autonomy and the human operator will be needed.

References

Bain, B (2010, June 3) New DOD cyber commander seeks better situational awareness, FCW
Connors, E, Jones, RET, Endsley, MR (2010) A comprehensive study of requirements and metrics for cyber defense situation awareness. SA Technologies, Inc., Marietta, GA
Endsley, MR (1988) Design and evaluation for situation awareness enhancement. In: Proceedings of the Human Factors Society 32nd Annual Meeting, Santa Monica, CA. p 97–101
Endsley, MR (1993) A survey of situation awareness requirements in air-to-air combat fighters. International Journal of Aviation Psychology 3(2): 157–168
Endsley, MR (1995) Toward a theory of situation awareness in dynamic systems. Human Factors 37(1): 32–64

Endsley, MR, & Garland, DJ (Eds) (2000) Situation awareness analysis and measurement. Lawrence Erlbaum, Mahwah, NJ

Endsley, MR, Jones, DG (2001) Disruptions, Interruptions, and Information Attack: Impact on Situation Awareness and Decision Making. In: Proceedings of the Human Factors and Ergonomics Society 45th Annual Meeting, Santa Monica, CA. p 63–68

Endsley, MR, Jones, DG (2012) Designing for situation awareness: An approach to human-centered design (2nd ed) Taylor & Francis, London

Endsley, MR, Kiris, EO (1995) The out-of-the-loop performance problem and level of control in automation. Human Factors 37(2): 381–394

Lee, JD, See, KA (2004) Trust in automation: Designing for appropriate reliance. Human Factors 46(1): 50–80

Rouse, WB, Morris, NM (1985) On looking into the black box: Prospects and limits in the search for mental models (DTIC #AD-A159080). Center for Man–machine Systems Research, Georgia Institute of Technology, Atlanta, GA

Sarter, NB, Woods, DD (1995) "How in the world did I ever get into that mode": Mode error and awareness in supervisory control. Human Factors 37(1): 5–19

United States Air Force (2012) Cyber Vision 2025. United States Air Force, Washington, DC

United States Air Force (2013) Global Horizons. United States Air Force, Washington, DC

United States Army (2013) Army Cyber Command Industry Day http://www.afea.org/events/cyber/13/documents/afceaIndustryOutreachBriefjun13ARCYBER.pdf

Wickens, CD (1992) Engineering psychology and human performance, 2nd edn. Harper Collins, New York

Wiener, EL.(1988) Cockpit automation. In: Wiener, EL & Nagel, DC (Eds), Human Factors in Aviation, Academic Press, San Diego, p 433–461

Kinetic and Cyber

Alexander Kott, Norbou Buchler, and Kristin E. Schaefer

1 Introduction

Although a fairly new topic in the context of cyber security, situation awareness (SA) has a far longer history of study and applications in such areas as control of complex enterprises and in conventional warfare. Far more is known about the SA in conventional military conflicts, or adversarial engagements, than in cyber ones. By exploring what is known about SA in conventional—also commonly referred to as kinetic—battles, we may gain insights and research directions relevant to cyber conflicts. For this reason, having outlined the foundations and challenges on CSA in the previous chapter, we proceed to discuss the nature of SA in conventional (often called kinetic) conflict, review what is known about this kinetic SA (KSA), and then offer a comparison with what is currently understood regarding the cyber SA (CSA). We find that challenges and opportunities of KSA and CSA are similar or at least parallel in several important ways. With respect to similarities, in both kinetic and cyber worlds, SA strongly impacts the outcome of the mission. Also similarly, cognitive biases are found in both KSA and CSA. As an example of differences, KSA often relies on commonly accepted, widely used organizing representation—map of the physical terrain of the battlefield. No such common representation has emerged in CSA, yet.

A. Kott (✉)
United States Army Research Laboratory, 2800 Powder Mill Rd., Adelphi, MD 20783, USA
e-mail: Alexander.kott1.civ@mail.mil

N. Buchler • K.E. Schaefer
United States Army Research Laboratory, Aberdeen Proving Ground, MD 21005, USA
e-mail: norbou.buchler.civ@mail.mil; kristin.e.schaefer2.ctr@mail.mil

© Springer International Publishing Switzerland 2014   29
A. Kott et al. (eds.), *Cyber Defense and Situational Awareness*,
Advances in Information Security 62, DOI 10.1007/978-3-319-11391-3_3

1.1   The Transition from a Conventional to a Virtual Battlefield

The dynamics of conflict continue to evolve over time and are historically punctu-
ated by rapid technological advancements. The grinding attrition of industrial-age
conflict of the past century, whereby interaction occurred face-to-face, is currently
giving way to information-age conflict (Moffat 2006). For reference, some key
characteristics of the prior industrial-age and the current information-age are presented in Fig. 1. Current Information Age conflicts encompass conventional and
virtual battlefields, with perhaps an increasing emphasis on the latter.

In our view, the Information Age battlefield is defined by the rise of networked
forms of organization. In a networked organization, the number of potential collaborators is virtually limitless, as is the availability of information. Operating in
such a broadly collaborative and information-rich environment confers unprece-
dented advantages to a military organization (National Research Council 2005). For
instance, the transformation of U.S. and NATO countries in the late 1990s and early
2000s to networked forms of organization has given rise to large, interacting, and
layered networks of Mission Command personnel communicating and sharing
information within and across various command echelons as well as across joint,
interagency, intergovernmental, and multinational seams and boundaries. Our
dependency upon networked organizations has the consequence that warfare is no
longer limited to the physics of the conventional battlefield. Increasingly, conflicts
are waged purely across networks in virtual cyberspace.

A departure for our comparison is to understand the domain characteristics of
kinetic and cyber operations highlighted in Table 1. This is first seen through the
prominent divergence between kinetic and cyber operations specific to the domain
of threat. Kinetic conflict has occurred for centuries within the immutable physical
world where threat characteristics are physically observable through direct (visual
observation) or augmented (technology assisted) means. However, unlike this
kinetic conflict situation, the cyber domain is highly malleable and prone to deception. For instance, a spoofing attack is a situation in which one person or computer
program successfully masquerades as another by falsifying data and thereby gaining an illegitimate advantage (Gantz and Rochester 2005).

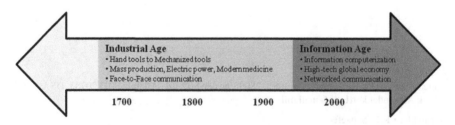

Fig. 1 Characteristics of the industrial age to the information age

Table 1 Comparison of domain characteristics of kinetic and cyber operations

	Kinetic operations	Cyber operations
Domain	Physical world that is largely immutable	Virtual world that is highly malleable and prone to deception
Military doctrine	Defender has the advantage	Attacker has the advantage
Mathematical definition	Force-on-force engagements defined by Lanchester equations[a]	Cyber engagements are potentially scale-free[b]
Requisite resources	Resource intensive, requiring an organization with integrated capabilities (i.e. logistics)	Resource non-intensive; scales down to an individual with few prerequisite capabilities
Threat characteristics	Physically observable	Hidden in network, can take on many forms
Massing of forces	Space and time dependent, advance warning possible	Unconstrained, with little to no advanced warning
Detection	Distributed with many possibilities "hits" from sensors to ISR[c] assets to patrolling units	Dependent on automation and rule-based Intrusion Detection Systems (IDS); analyst combs through huge log files and creates new attack signatures
Big data challenge	Managing data collection. Intelligence analysis	Detection (attack correlation) Forensic analysis
Analytical challenge	Finding insurgent networks among populace	Finding new threats/developing signatures
Attack characteristics	Unfold in space and time	Instantaneous and massively parallel
Effects	Linear effects whose impact is known, immediate, and attributable to an adversary	Non-linear (potentially cascading) effects whose impact may be hidden, unknown, undetected for periods of time, and non-attributable to an adversary
Battle damage assessment	Observable and quantifiable	Some observables with many potentially complex higher-order effects; requires forensics and can take months
Visualization	Common operational picture; counter-insurgency operations require network analyses and dependency graphs	Attack graphs, dependency graphs, and cyber terrain[d]
Deception	Largely at the strategic level, requires substantial planning and is resource intensive	Largely at tactical levels, requires little planning and is not resource intensive

[a]Bowen and McNaught (1996)
[b]Moffat (2006)
[c]Intelligence, surveillance and reconnaissance
[d]Jakobson (2011)

Further, classic military doctrine in which the defender has numerous advantages (e.g. defensive fortifications and advantageous information asymmetries) is completely up-ended in the cyber domain where the attacker is advantaged. The advantages to the cyber-attacker are numerous and include: (1) anonymity: the ability to hide in a global network across national sovereignty and jurisdiction boundaries complicates attack attribution, (2) targeted attacks: adversaries can pick the time, place, and tools, (3) exploitation: global reach to probe weaknesses of the cyber-defense, (4) human weaknesses: trust relationships are susceptible as evidenced in "social engineering" attacks, and (5) forensics: volatile and transient nature of evidence complicates attack analysis, which can be quite cumbersome (Jain 2005). Although there are differences between kinetic and cyber domains, it is likely that many of these challenges to cyber operations can be addressed by applying lessons learned from the successful management of kinetic operations.

1.2   The Importance of Situation Awareness

It is likely that the dynamics of conflict are extensible to the virtual battlefield. Some key concepts with which to compare kinetic and cyber conflicts are derived from a conceptual framework of *network-enabled operations* underlying information-age conflict (Alberts 2002; Alberts et al. 1999). This framework is comprised of four primary tenets (Alberts and Hayes 2003):

1. A robustly networked force improves information sharing and collaboration
2. Such sharing and collaboration enhance the quality of information and shared situational awareness
3. This enhancement, in turn, enables further self-synchronization and improves the sustainability and speed of command
4. The combination dramatically increases mission effectiveness

Many of these payoffs to network-enabled operations are conceptualized at human and organizational levels in terms of maintaining and enhancing SA, which can in turn lead to force-synchronization and increased mission effectiveness. This conceptual framework explicitly assumes that greater information sharing in a networked organization produces better SA. SA is defined as "the ability to maintain a constant, clear mental picture of relevant information and the tactical situation including friendly and threat situations as well as terrain" (Dostal 2007). We subscribe to a theoretical model of SA described by Endsley (1988, 1995) in which SA is the perception of relevant elements (e.g., status, attributes, dynamics) in the environment within a volume of time and space (Level 1), the comprehension or understanding of their meaning (Level 2), and the projection of future actions (Level 3).

The tenets of network-enabled operations are posited to yield cumulative effects to organizational effectiveness in military conflicts. Performance and effectiveness may be limited by a failure or bottleneck at any step in the sequence. For instance, an increase in information available to commanders and their staff is postulated to increase the quality of decision-making due to enhanced SA. There may be situations, however, where increased information sharing increases the *quantity* of available information without a corresponding increase in *quality*. The sheer volume and rapid pace of information received and readily accessible through networked systems can be overwhelming. This presents a challenge to the command staff as there are clear limits to human cognition and how much information can be attended to, processed, and shared in a given amount of time, which can potentially limit situational awareness. The following subsections highlight the importance of SA to conflict-based situation management across kinetic (conventional) and cyber (virtual) battlefields.

1.3   Kinetic SA

On the conventional battlefield, information is largely gathered directly whether by physical sensors, human sensory perception, or tele-operation of unmanned intelligence, surveillance, and reconnaissance platforms. This corresponds to Level 1 situation awareness (SA). The battlefield is physical and immutable and the opposing forces perceive various states of the same physical battlefield and have access to many similar elements of situational information. In kinetic operations, SA is often dependent upon a careful analysis of the geography of the physical terrain (major waterways, roads, etc.) coupled to target sightings and movements, and friendly positions. Developing and maintaining an accurate *analog* model of the physical battlefield is a critical process, whether "sand tables" (prior 1960s), board game varieties (1960–1980s), or maps with digital overlay (since 1990s). Such models are critical for both perception of the battlefield and comprehension by reasoning about it.

However, there is often a tradeoff between data acquisition and comprehension. Additional efforts in data acquisition may provide more information about the battlefield space; however, adding too much data could overwhelm human processing capacities to analyze the information in a timely manner, greatly impacting comprehension of the current situation. A key research question is understanding the limits to human information processing and how they are manifest in complex, information-rich and broadly-collaborative networked operational environments.

1.4   Cyber SA

Technological advancement of the information-age continues to push us towards virtual conflict of networked organizations and individuals. Through mediums such as the Internet, traditional geographical boundaries are subsumed. Thus, a primary goal on the virtual battlefield is to mount a robust cyber-defense. Cyber analysts clamor for advanced capabilities to support their cyber mission and provide better SA. These should include the capabilities that automatically map all paths of vulnerability through networks; correlate and fuse data from a variety of sources; provide visualization of attack paths; automatically generate mitigation recommendations; and ultimately produce analysis of mission impact from cyber attacks (Jajodia et al. 2011).

2   Examples of Research in KSA

In the following sections, we describe a challenge in kinetic warfare, and then attempt to review what is known about related challenges in cyber world. In some cases, we find significant similarities or at least parallels, while in others we find instructive differences. In yet other cases, too little is known yet about challenges—or lack thereof—in cyber situation awareness (CSA), and therefore in such cases we merely point out a potential research direction. We begin by describing two examples of research efforts that quantified and illustrated significant aspects of KSA, particularly the characteristic challenges of KSA experienced by practitioners.

2.1   Example of Research in KSA: The DARPA MDC2 Program

The first of the two examples of KSA research we use in this chapter is the program called Multicell and Dismounted Command and Control (Kott 2008), performed in 2004–2007 by the United States' Defense Advanced Research Programs Agency (DARPA). The main thrust of that research was an experimental exploration of battle command in light-armored, information-rich, distributed networked forces. At the time, the U.S. Army was eyeing the possibility of future combat force based on a combination of fighting units mounted on fast-moving, lightly armored vehicles with large number of sensors—flying drones and autonomous ground sensors—and precise, far-shooting weapons. Such combat units would rely far less on the thickness of their armor than today's ground forces, and far more of their ability to see and destroy the enemy from far away.

In effect, in such a concept, the combat unit was trading the value of heavy armor for the value of advanced information about its enemy. The concern with this concept was whether the human soldiers, the consumers and users of all the rich information that would enable the defectiveness of this hypothetical combat force, would be able to absorb, comprehend and act on this complex and voluminous information. In other words, whether the cognitive challenges imposed by information-rich command environment would prove to be insurmountable.

Since previous battle command systems were not designed to function in such an information-rich environment, a prototype of a new human-machine system was created to translate high-rate inflow of battlespace data into high-quality situation awareness and command decisions. The new prototype system included specially developed situation awareness tools that continuously and autonomously fused all data into a shared situation portrait. Also included were action execution tools that helped human soldiers control intelligence gathering, movements on the battlefield and assessments of results of long-range attacks by precision weapons. Here we start to see some similarities to CSA—very large volume of information and relative absence of direct physical cues.

The research proceeded through a series of intricately organized and rather expensive experiments—simulated battles. In each battle, the Blue Force were U.S. Army soldiers who sat in mock-up battle vehicles equipped with elaborate information systems, and fought a reasonably realistic battle against the well-trained Red Force, portrayed by military professionals. The battle was fought on a simulated battlefield where special simulation software calculated and depicted all physical effects—movements of vehicles, observations of sensors, and shooting of weapons. A set of instrumentation and human observers recorded the state of situation awareness, including the degree of awareness that could be potentially possible given the available information, and the degree of awareness actually exhibited by the soldiers. The actual state of the battle was also recorded for every moment of the battle, e.g., how many Red soldiers were in a particular forest, as opposed to what Blue sensors observed or Blue soldiers recognized. This allowed quantitative tracking of situation awareness overtime, using metrics that combined location, state of health, priority and quantity of opponent's forces. Such metrics could be analyzed also by comparing them with soldiers' understanding of the available information as transpired form their verbal exchanges and actions. In a later section, we continue to discuss the KSA-related findings of this program in comparison with Cyber SA.

2.2 Another Example of Research in KSA: The RAID Program

The research program titled Real-time Adversarial Intelligence and Decision-making (RAID) was sponsored by the United States' Defense Advanced Research Programs Agency (DARPA) during the period of 2004–2008 (Kott 2007; Kott et al. 2011; Ownby and Kott 2006). The objective of the program was to build tools for automated generation of enemy situation estimates and predictions of enemy near-term action (Level 3 SA) in military operations. A part of the program was also to measure the situation awareness of the human soldiers and to compare their awareness with the estimates of the automated tool.

The RAID program focused on an intentionally narrow but still very challenging domain: tactical combat of Blue Force (infantry, supported by armor and air platforms) against the Red Force (an insurgent-like irregular infantry) in an urban terrain. The problem situation may involve the defense of Blue facilities, the rescue of downed aircrew, the capture of an insurgent leader, the rescue of hostages or the reaction to an attack on a Blue patrol.

In planning and executing a battle like this, the company commander, his supporting staff (including possibly the staff at the higher echelon of command) and his subordinate unit leaders would receive and integrate (mentally or with the aid of

Fig. 2 Formation of KSA in
the RAID system

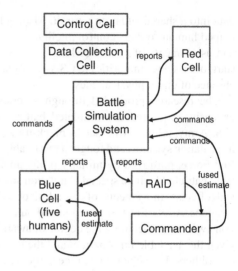

computerized fusion system like RAID) a bewildering array of information (Fig. 2).
For example, information on the Blue force composition and mission plan; detailed
maps of the area, potentially including detailed 3D data of the urban area; known
concentrations of non-combatants such as markets; culturally sensitive areas such
as worship houses; reports of historic and recent prior activities such as explosions
of roadside bombs in the area; continuous updates on the locations and status of the
Blue force as they move before and during the battle.

Using all this information, commander and staff typically produce two types of
output. First is the estimate of the Red force's current situation: estimated actual
locations of the Red force (most of which are normally concealed and are not
observed by the Blue force); the current intent of the Red force, and potential deceptions that the Red force may be performing. The second type of output describes the
estimated future events: Red force's future locations (as a function of time), movements, fire engagements with the Blue force, changes in strengths and intent.

Each of multiple experiments in the RAID program consisted of wargames executed by live Red and Blue commanders in a simulated computer wargaming environment. In half of the wargames the Blue commander received the support of a
human team of competent assistants (staff). Their responsibilities included producing estimates of enemy situation. This set of wargames constituted the control
group. In the other half of wargames Blue commander operated without a human
staff. Instead, he obtained a similar support from the RAID automated system which
produced enemy situation estimates. These wargames constituted the test group.
The data collection and redaction process compared the accuracy of the control
group with the accuracy of the test group. In effect, we were able to compare situation awareness of human staff with that of the automated tool. Like the MDC2
program, the RAID program also yielded observations about KSA which we will
compare with those of CSA in the following section.

3   Instructive Similarities and Formidable Differences Between KSA and CSA

We now turn to selected experimental findings of the two KSA-focused programs introduced above, and compare them to those in CSA. Challenges and opportunities of KSA and CSA are similar or at least parallel in several important ways. In both kinetic and cyber worlds, SA strongly impacts the outcome of the mission. The process of developing effective and efficient SA through information collection (Level 1 SA), organization (Level 2 SA), and sharing (Level 3 SA) is difficult to manage in both KSA and CSA (Kott and Arnold 2013). Effective SA and concurrent decision making can be limited by an individual's cognitive biases. Collaboration for the sake of forming shared SA is another challenge common to both kinetic and cyber worlds. However, the need for collaboration is often a requirement of kinetic conflict, while cyber conflict is often managed at the individual level. Further, collaboration itself is often difficult, particularly because cyber defenders of different roles and backgrounds do not yet share a common set of concepts, terms and boundary objects. These are yet to emerge in this young field. Also, more than in the kinetic world, cyber defenders may need stronger tailored pictures of the same shared model. Table 2 highlights the key similarities and differences that are further discussed in the sections below.

3.1   KSA and CSA Strongly Impact Mission Outcome

The first finding may seem obvious—higher KSA leads to notable increase in mission outcome, such as fewer casualties in the battle as compared to opponent's, or the ability to capture the opponent territory or to defend one's own ground. In fact, it is not an obvious finding, and certainly not a well-quantified one in prior work. It becomes particularly non-trivial when we note the difference between the information available to the soldiers and the level of its comprehension, i.e., the cognitive component of situation awareness. On a more fundamental level, one might wonder whether the intangible benefits of higher SA can possibly compare with mighty effects of such tangible factors as speed and armor of combat vehicles, or range and precision of weapons.

Nevertheless, quantitative experimental findings of MDC2 program were unequivocal—higher SA does translate into significantly better battle outcome. Indeed, it was the difference between the amount of information available to the Blue Force versus the information available to the Red Force (the information that is obtained from various sources such as sensors or scouts, and made available to the commander and staffs) that emerged as a key predictor of battle outcome. Because this difference was so important, the Blue force found (empirically) that limiting Red's ability to see the Blue force was critical to winning the battle. The information available to Red routinely increased during the fight when distances between Red and Blue were small enough that relatively weaker Red sensors became effective. As the Blue detection of the Red's high-priority targets increased, so did the potential for battle outcomes favorable to Blue.

Table 2 Similarities and differences of KSA and CSA

	KSA	CSA	Research direction
Mission outcome	Characterized by quantitative, tangible metrics (e.g., location and number of enemy targets)	Mission-defined metrics are not well understood	Development of CSA metrics related to mission and mission outcome
Representation	Tends to have a commonly accepted, widely used organizing paradigm—the physical terrain of the battlefield (e.g., map)	No map-like common reference has emerged	Development of a shared non-physical network "map"
Information collection, organization, and sharing	Challenged by difficulties with timely processing of large amounts of data about current battle state space (e.g., managing dynamic, moving, and relatively scarce sensors)	Challenged with the organization, coordination, and timely analysis of volumes of heterogeneous information from automated sensors, intrusion detection systems, and correlating analytical reports	Approaches to effective representation and fusion of information at optimal levels of abstraction
Cognitive bias	Largely suffer from confirmation bias and availability heuristic	Some evidence of risk-aversion as well as confirmation bias and availability heuristic	Additional research on the formation and mechanisms related to cognitive bias
Collaboration/ shared SA	Collaboration has to be controlled, encouraged, and synchronized in order to mitigate potential staff tendency to aggravate cognitive biases and to misdirect precious cognitive resources	Task responsibilities are managed at the level of the individual and are often not shared	Given the malleable nature of the cyber domain, a common set of concepts, terms, and boundary objects are critical for developing CSA and should be a priority for research

Similarly, In RAID program, we also found clear statistical evidence that with more accurate estimates of the Red situation (Level-2 SA, comprehension) and intent (Level-3 SA, projection), the Blue commander was more likely to achieve better battle outcome. To measure the accuracy of SA objectively, we used a metric similar to Circular Error Probable (CEP). Roughly speaking, it gives a typical error between the actual location of an opponent entity, and the location as perceived or projected by the Blue commander. The experimental data were very clear—battle outcome (wargame score) improves as the situation assessment becomes more accurate (i.e., CEP decreases).

In literature on cyber security research, there is recognition, but not yet a quantitative evidence of the impact of CSA on metrics of effectiveness and mission outcomes, such as timely detection if a cyber intrusion. Situation awareness is recognized to be limited in the cyber domain: inaccurate and incomplete vulnerability analysis is common as is the failure to adapt to evolving networks and attacks; and the ability of cyber defenders to transform raw data into cyber intelligence remains quite restricted. Cyber researchers argue that advanced capabilities are needed for mission-centric CSA. These should include the capabilities that automatically map all paths of vulnerability through networks; correlate and fuse data from a variety of sources; provide visualization of attack paths; automatically generate mitigation recommendations; and ultimately produce analysis of mission impact from cyber attacks (Jajodia et al. 2011). Such tools would increase CSA, arguably yielding better cyber defense outcomes, as is the case with KSA.

3.2 Cognitive Biases Limit Comprehension of Available Information

Both KSA and CSA may suffer from cognitive biases. The exact manner in which a cognitive bias influences the formation of SA remains a topic for research, in both cyber and kinetic worlds. It cannot be excluded that CSA suffers from different biases than KSA, and perhaps through different mechanisms. In kinetic battles (as found in the MDC2 program), commander and staff surprisingly often dismissed or misinterpreted the available correct information. They also overestimated the completeness and correctness of their KSA, perhaps partly because the advanced sensors and information displays lulled them into false sense of security—"I can see it all." There was an alarming gap between information available to the commander and staff and the KSA they derived from that information: commander's assessment of the available information was correct only approximately 60 % of the time. A cognitive bias—a kind of "belief persistence"—appeared to be a common cause of this inadequacy of comprehension of available information.

In particular, such seeing-understanding gaps often manifested themselves in poor synchronization of information and movements. Commanders frequently overestimated the strength of the threat they faced, or significantly underestimated that strength. Over-estimate of threat resulted in unnecessarily slowing down the advance of the force in order to acquire more information. Under-estimate of threat caused the force enter into the close contact with the enemy while lacking sufficient information and thereby making Blue Force more vulnerable.

In the RAID program, we also found that human KSA was significantly lower or less accurate than what was possible to achieve using all the available information. We compared two assessments of enemy situation and intent: one produced by humans and another one produced by an automated tool. The tool lacked either the experience or intuition of human soldiers. Nevertheless, the error of the tool's estimates was significantly (on average) lower than that of humans. The fact that the automated tool compared well with competent human staff implied that sufficient information was indeed present in the data, but not extracted by staff in order to yield the best possible KSA.

But why were humans' estimates less accurate than tool's? On one hand, SMEs and psychologists found many similarities in reasoning of humans and of the tool.

The difference, however, seemed to be mainly in human cognitive biases. Although such biases are often useful as convenient shortcuts, on balance they lead to reduced accuracy. For example, we often observed a fixation on a presumed pattern or rule: humans estimated the Red situation by applying a previously learned pattern or doctrine. Then, if disconfirming evidence arose, the humans discounted the evidence. When faced with a clever, rapidly innovating Red opponent, such a fixation on previously observed patterns often produced gross errors in Blue's KSA.

Cognitive biases are also widely evident in CSA. Researchers note that cyber defenders exhibit over-reliance on intuition: with few reliable statistics on cyber attacks, decision makers rely on their experience and intuition, fraught with cognitive biases. Such biases are likely to lead to suboptimal decisions. For example, when faced with the trade-off between a certain loss in the present (e.g., investing in improved security) and a potential loss in the future (consequences of a cyber incident), a common risk-aversion bias is toward the second option. In a related observation, cyber defenders tend to believe that their particular organization is less exposed to risks than other parties, particularly if they feel like having a degree of control over the situation—some refer to this as "optimistic bias." Many are more afraid of risks if they are vividly described, easy to imagine, memorable, and they have occurred in the recent past (related to what is called "availability bias").

Further, a common bias is to ignore evidence that contradicts one's preconceived notions, i.e., the confirmation bias (Julisch 2013). With respect to the optimistic bias mentioned above, it is important to note that individuals distinguish between two separate dimensions of risk judgment—personal level and societal level. Individuals display a strong optimistic bias about online privacy risks, judging themselves to be significantly less vulnerable than others to these risks. Internal belief (perceived controllability) and individual difference (prior experience) significantly modulate optimistic bias (Cho et al. 2010). There is a tendency for individuals to interpret ambiguous information or uncertain situations in a self-serving direction. Perceived controllability and distance of comparison target influence this tendency (Rhee et al. 2012).

In summary, although cognitive biases play important roles in both KSA and CSA, the limited available literature does not allow us to determine the degree of similarity in specific mechanisms involved. Research in CSA may benefit from an explicit and systematic investigation of whether the biases affecting KSA also play a key role in CSA.

3.3 Information Collection, Organization and Sharing is Difficult to Manage

Effective situation awareness takes us through a three-phase process of perception of the data collected (Level 1 SA), organizing said data in a way that it becomes useful information (Level 2 SA), which in turn allows us to make and share decisions based on future predictions (Level 3 SA). Yet this process of information collection, organization, and sharing is difficult to manage in both kinetic and cyber conflicts.

For example, in MDC2 experiments, the commander and staff had difficulties tracking the extent and timing of the sensor coverage available in different parts of the kinetic battlefield. In effect, they often did not know what they had seen and what they had not—an inadequate SA of their own information collection assets. Flaws in sensor layering also led to critical gaps in sensor coverage, which commonly went unnoticed by commanders. These gaps were directly tied to poor KSA related to threat location and proximity, and thus increased the likelihood for encountering an ambush by the opponent.

Especially difficult was management of multiple diverse sensors with significantly different capabilities. Not only they differed in capabilities, area of coverage, agility and latency of information, but also in their organizational ownership and rules of who and when was allowed to use or reposition them. As a result, soldiers had to dedicate a large fraction of their available time and attention to issues of information acquisition. In many cases it became the primary concern of the commander who focused on managing sensor assets, and delegated other tasks. Indeed, over 50 % of all decisions were made to acquire information. "Seeing" was considered the hardest task while "shooting" was considered the easiest task. Commander and Staff also found that battle damage assessment has grown as a critical and most demanding task and a key detriment to KSA. Difficulties in assessing the "state" of engaged targets significantly degraded the level of KSA.

Indeed, a major tenet of the U.S. Office of Secretary of Defense's "data to decisions" initiative and a primary challenge for military commanders and their staff is to shorten the cycle time from data gathering to decisions (Swan and Hennig 2012). A key information-age challenge is that the sheer volume of information available constrains military decision-making cycles, so that the staff is stuck in observe-orient, the "seeing" part of the cycle, rather than advancing further into the decide-act, or "shooting" part of the cycle.

These challenges in KSA parallel the challenges of managing information for CSA. Lack of information, such as reliable statistics on the probability and impact of cyber attacks, induce decision makers to rely unduly on their experience and intuition. In acquiring information about the cyber environment, important classes of information include: (a) the probability of particular types of cyber attacks; (b) the effectiveness of existing countermeasures in defending against these attacks; and (c) the impact or cost of attacks (Julisch 2013). Because dynamic cyber intelligence is difficult to acquire, over-reliance on static knowledge versus dynamic intelligence is common.

Other peculiarities of cyber security world add to the complexity of information acquisition, management, and related formation of CSA. Missions are generally defined in terms of abstract resources and not actual systems and devices (making comprehension of relations between missions and tangible systems more difficult); organizations often outsource parts or all responsibility for cyber defense (thereby complicating understanding of responsibilities and correlation of information); resources are managed in a highly dynamic fashion; and increasingly large number of sensors overload human analysts (Greitzer et al. 2011).

Cyber researchers note additional related challenges: information sharing methods are immature, especially as the process of forming CSA is distributed across human operators and technological artifacts operating in different functional areas. Add to this the rapid rate of environmental change, overwhelming volume of information, and lack of physical world constraints. With such ensemble of challenges in information acquisition and management, it is not surprising that CSA is distributed, incomplete, and domain-specific (Tyworth et al. 2012).

3.4 Collaboration Can Be Challenging

The essence of collaborative teamwork within an organization is the ability to efficiently maintain a coherent set of tasks across multiple people and shared assets. It is commonly understood that SA benefits from effective collaboration of participants of the SA-generation process. However, collaboration also can have a dark side and exact a high cost. In MDC2 experiments, we observed on a number of occasions that a commander's KSA degraded as a result of collaborations with subordinates, peers, or higher echelon decision-makers. Collaboration can reinforce an incorrect perception by apparent acquiescence by other decision makers. Information gaps—the importance of which we mentioned earlier in this chapter—are not necessarily appreciated by individual commanders, and collaboration does not help to alleviate that.

As an example, out of seven episodes of collaboration in a particular experiment in the MDC2 program, three episodes produced improved KSA, two collaboration episodes distracted the decision-maker from the more critical focus, and two others led the decision-makers to reinforce the wrong interpretation of the situation. The mechanisms by which collaboration may impose costs on KSA vary: in some cases collaboration tends to reinforce confirmation bias; in other cases collaboration mis-directs the attention away from most critical issues.

In the RAID program, we observed a negative correlation between the number of collaboration events within the staff, and the quality of KSA. This could be explained as follows: more intensive collaboration may lead to greater consumption of cognitive resources, resulting in lower accuracy of KSA and lower battle score.

In the literature on cyber defense, we do not find concerns about a potential negative impact of collaboration on CSA. However, concerns about the difficulties of enabling effective collaboration are common in the world of cyber defense. On one hand, collaboration in cyber security teams can be very effective. Experiments in synthetic IDS environment demonstrate that collaborative teams outperformed individuals on average. However, this appears to apply when the teams focuses on "hard" cases requiring diverse expertise. It is not unlikely that in "easy" cases, collaboration could be counterproductive (Rajivan et al. 2013).

On the other hand, it is argued that in cyber defense, collaboration suffers from the lack of boundary objects (i.e., intermediate products that can be shared—common in more mature fields of practice). CSA tends to be distributed, incomplete, and highly domain-specific. Boundary objects that have emerged in cyber defense are currently limited to reports; these are inadequate and not as effective as boundary objects in other fields. To alleviate the current lack of commonly understood boundary objects, cyber defense may benefit from visualizations capable of presenting cross-domain information for domain specific purposes (Tyworth et al. 2012).

Other cyber researchers highlight the difficulty of assessing trustworthiness in collaborative communications. For example, means for numeric and verbal communication of cybersecurity risks are not yet adequately developed and are poorly understood in cyber defense (Nurse et al. 2011). This is further exacerbated by barriers between individuals of different roles and backgrounds in cyber defense. For example, cyber experts see users both as potential cyber defense resources, but also as sources of accidents and potential threats. Unlike users, experts tend to use probability rather than consequences as a basis for evaluating risk. In addition, experts' lack of detailed knowledge of their users' information security performance complicates effective collaboration (Albrechtsen and Hovden 2009). As a result, CSA suffers.

3.5 Shared Picture Does Not Assure Shared SA

In addition to effective collaboration, shared picture of the situation is often seen as a key to collaborative SA. However, experiments in MDC2 indicated that sharing picture is no substitute for sharing intent. While a commander often thought that his subordinates understood his intent because they could see it all on the screen, the subordinates in fact could not perceive the commanders intent from the picture he shared with them. And when staff members do not share the commander's SA, including an understanding of the commander's intent, they may be less likely to take initiative.

Perhaps this should not be surprising: because different viewers of the same "shared" picture differ significantly in their roles and backgrounds, they should see different, properly tailored pictures in order to arrive to a common SA. Indeed, some cyber researchers argue that the common picture should not be common. Modalities of interaction and information requirements are inherently different for different types of users. One proposed approach is a model-based cyber defense situation awareness: a common model represents the current security situation of all protected resources, updated over time. Based on this common model, different intuitive visualization can be employed for different users (Klein et al. 2010).

4 Summary

By exploring what is known about SA in conventional—also commonly referred to as kinetic—battles, we may gain insights and research directions relevant to cyber conflicts. For the sake of brevity, we use the abbreviation CSA for Cyber Situation Awareness and KSA for Kinetic Situation Awareness. The Information Age is defined by the rise of networked forms of organization and an increase in information available to commanders and their staff is postulated to increase the quality of decision-making due to enhanced situational awareness. However, there are clear limits to human cognition and how much information can be attended to, processed, and shared in a given amount of time, which can potentially limit situational awareness.

Challenges and opportunities of KSA and CSA are similar or at least parallel in several important ways. In both kinetic and cyber worlds, SA strongly impacts the outcome of the mission. In literature on cyber security research there is recognition, but not yet a quantitative evidence of the impact of CSA on metrics of effectiveness and mission outcomes. Researchers and practitioners of KSA have a commonly accepted, widely used organizing representation—map of the physical terrain of the battlefield. Yet no map-like common representation has emerged in CSA. It is likely, although not yet examined, that cognitive biases are general to both KSA and CSA. For example, in KSA, the human tendency to look for confirming evidence has routinely been exploited in intelligence deception. Cognitive biases are also widely evident in CSA, such as "optimistic bias." Limited or incorrect incoming data, such as reliable statistics on the probability and impact of attacks (whether kinetic or cyber), induce decision-makers to rely unduly on their experience and intuition. Collaboration also can have a dark side and exact a high cost. Collaboration may reinforce an incorrect perception by apparent acquiescence by other decision makers.

References

Alberts, D.S., (2002), *Information Age Transformation: Getting to a 21st Century Military*, Washington, D.C., Command and Control Research Program (CCRP) Publications.

Alberts, D.S., Garstka, J.J., & Stein, F.P. (1999). *Network Centric Warfare*. Washington, D.C., Command and Control Research Program (CCRP) Publications.

Alberts, D. S., & Hayes, R. E. (2003). *Power to the Edge: Command and Control in the Information Age*. Washington D.C., Command and Control Research Program (CCRP) Publications.

Albrechtsen, Eirik, and Jan Hovden. "The information security digital divide between information security managers and users." *Computers & Security* 28.6 (2009): 476-490.

Bowen, K.C. & McNaught, K.R, *Mathematics in warfare: Lanchester theory*, The Lanchester Legacy, Volume 3—A Celebration of Genious (N. Fletcher, ed.), Coventry University Press, Coventry, 1996.

Cho, Hichang, Jae-Shin Lee, and Siyoung Chung. "Optimistic bias about online privacy risks: Testing the moderating effects of perceived controllability and prior experience." *Computers in Human Behavior* 26.5 (2010): 987-995.

Dostal, B.C. (2007). Enhancing situational understanding through the employment of unmanned aerial vehicles. *Interim Brigade Combat Team Newsletter*, No. 01–18.

Endsley, M. R. (1988). Design and evaluation for situation awareness enhancement. In Proceedings of the Human Factors Society, 32 (pp. 97-101). Santa Monica, CA: Human Factors Society.

Endsley, M. R. (1995). Toward a theory of situation awareness in dynamic systems. *Human Factors: The Journal of the Human Factors and Ergonomics Society*, *37*(1), 32-64.

Gantz, J., & Rochester, J. B. (2005). Pirates of the Digital Millennium. Upper Saddle River, NJ: Prentice Hall. ISBN 0-13-146315-2.

Greitzer, Frank L., Thomas E. Carroll, and Adam D. Roberts. "Cyber Friendly Fire." *Pacific Northwest National Laboratory, Tech. Rep. PNNL-20821* (2011).

Jain, A. (2005). *Cyber Crime: Cyber crime: issues and threats* (Vol. 2). Gyan Publishing House.

Jajodia, Sushil, et al. "Cauldron mission-centric cyber situational awareness with defense in depth." *MILITARY COMMUNICATIONS CONFERENCE, 2011-MILCOM 2011*. IEEE, 2011.

Jakobson, G. (2011). Mission cyber security situation assessment using impact dependency graphs. *Proceedings of the 14th International Conference on Information Fusion* (pp. 1-8).

Julisch, Klaus. "Understanding and overcoming cyber security anti-patterns." *Computer Networks* 57.10 (2013): 2206-2211.

Klein, Gabriel, et al. "Towards a Model-Based Cyber Defense Situational Awareness Visualization Environment." *Proceedings of the RTO Workshop "Visualising Networks: Coping with Chance and Uncertainty". Rome, NY, USA.* 2010.

A. Kott, Raiding the Enemy's Mind, Military Information Technology, Dec 29, 2007, Vol 11, Issue 11

Kott, Alexander, ed. *Battle of cognition: the future information-rich warfare and the mind of the commander.* Greenwood Publishing Group, 2008.

Kott, Alexander, et al. "Hypothesis-driven information fusion in adversarial, deceptive environments." *Information Fusion* 12.2 (2011): 131-144.

Kott, Alexander, and Curtis Arnold. "The promises and challenges of continuous monitoring and risk scoring." *Security & Privacy, IEEE* 11.1 (2013): 90-93.

Moffat, J. "Mathematical Modeling of Information Age Conflict" *Journal of Applied Mathematics and Decision Sciences* (2006): 1-15.

National Research Council. *Network Science.* Washington, DC: The National Academies Press, 2005.

Nurse, Jason RC, et al. "Trustworthy and effective communication of cybersecurity risks: A review." *Socio-Technical Aspects in Security and Trust (STAST), 2011 1st Workshop on.* IEEE, 2011.

M. Ownby, and A. Kott, Reading the Mind of the Enemy: Predictive Analysis and Command Effectiveness, Command and Control Research and Technology Symposium, San Diego, CA, June 2006

Rajivan, Prashanth, et al. "Effects of Teamwork versus Group Work on Signal Detection in Cyber Defense Teams." *Foundations of Augmented Cognition.* Springer Berlin Heidelberg, 2013. 172-180.

Rhee, Hyeun-Suk, Young U. Ryu, and Cheong-Tag Kim. "Unrealistic optimism on information security management." *Computers & Security* 31.2 (2012): 221-2

Swan, J. and Hennig, J., From Data to Decisions. *Army Acquisition, Logistics & Technology,* January-March 2012.

Tyworth, Michael, Nicklaus A. Giacobe, and Vincent Mancuso. "Cyber situation awareness as distributed socio-cognitive work." *SPIE Defense, Security, and Sensing.* International Society for Optics and Photonics, 2012.

Formation of Awareness

Massimiliano Albanese and Sushil Jajodia

1 Introduction

Having discussed the importance and key features of CSA, both in general and in comparison with a better known Kinetic Situational Awareness, we now proceed to explore how and from where the CSA emerges. Formation of Cyber Situational Awareness is a complex process that goes through a number of distinct phases and produces a number of distinct outputs. Humans with widely different roles drive this process while using diverse procedures and computerized tools. This chapter explores how situational awareness forms within the different phases of the cyber defense process, and describes the different roles that are involved in the lifecycle of situational awareness. The chapter presents an overview of the overall process of cyber defense and then identifies several distinct facets of situational awareness in the context of cyber defense. An overview of the state of the art is followed by a detailed description of a comprehensive framework for Cyber Situational Awareness developed by the authors of this chapter. We highlight the significance of five key functions within CSA: learning from attacks, prioritization, metrics, continuous diagnostics and mitigation, and automation.

The chapter is organized as follows. Section 2 presents an overview of the overall process of cyber defense, whereas Sect. 3 identifies several facets of situational awareness in the context of cyber defense. Section 4 provides an overview of the state of the art. Then, Sect. 5 describes the details of a comprehensive framework for

M. Albanese • S. Jajodia (✉)
George Mason University, Fairfax, VA 22030, USA
e-mail: malbanes@gmu.edu; jajodia@gmu.edu

© Springer International Publishing Switzerland 2014
A. Kott et al. (eds.), *Cyber Defense and Situational Awareness*,
Advances in Information Security 62, DOI 10.1007/978-3-319-11391-3_4

Cyber Situational Awareness developed by the authors of this chapter. Finally, Sect. 6 discusses future research directions and gives some concluding remarks.

2 The Cyber Defense Process

This section provides an overall description of the typical process and organization of cyber defense, which is often quite distributed and involves individuals in several different roles (security analysts, security engineers, security architects, etc.). Five major functions are involved in the cyber defense process and, as we show in the next section, different types of situational awareness form within the domain of each of these functions.

2.1 Today's Cyber Landscape

In today's complex cyberspace, we are constantly facing the risk of massive data losses or data leaks, theft of intellectual property, credit card breaches, denial of service, identity theft and threats to our privacy. As defenders we have access to a wide range of security tools and technologies (e.g., intrusion detection and prevention systems, firewalls, antivirus software), security standards, training resources, vulnerability databases [e.g., NVD (NIST), CVE (MITRE)], best practices, catalogs of security controls [e.g., NIST Special Publication 800-53 (NIST 2013) and CSA Cloud Controls Matrix (Cloud Security Alliance)], and countless security checklists, benchmarks, and recommendations. To help us understand current threats, we have seen the emergence of threat information feeds, reports [e.g., Symantec's Internet Security Threat Report (Symantec Corporation 2014) and Mandiant's APT1 report (Mandiat 2013)], tools (e.g., Nessus, Wireshark), alert services, standards, and threat sharing schemes. And to put it all together, we are surrounded by security requirements, risk management frameworks [e.g., NIST Special Publication 800-37 (NIST 2010)], compliance regimes, regulatory mandates, and so forth. Therefore, there is certainly no shortage of information available to security practitioners on how they should secure their infrastructure.

However, without well-defined processes to integrate all this knowledge in a consistent and coherent manner, all these resources may have the undesired consequence of introducing competing options, priorities, opinions, and claims that can paralyze or distract an enterprise from taking critical actions. In the last decade, threats have evolved dramatically, malicious actors have become smarter, and users have become more mobile. Data is now distributed across multiple platforms and locations, many of which are not within the physical control sphere of the organization. With more reliance on cloud computing platforms, data and applications are becoming more distributed, thus progressively eroding the traditional notion of security perimeter.

2.2 Cyber Defense Process at a Glance

The overall process of cyber defense relies on the combined knowledge of actual attacks and effective defenses, and ideally involves every part of the ecosystem (the enterprise, its employees and customers, and other stakeholders). It also entails the participation of individuals in every role within the organization and this includes threat responders, security analysts, technologists, tool developers, users, policymakers, auditors, etc. Top experts from all these roles can pool their extensive first-hand knowledge in defending against actual cyber-attacks and develop a consensus list of the best defensive techniques to prevent or track them, and effectively respond to and mitigate damage from the most common or the most advanced of those attacks.

Defensive actions are not limited to preventing the initial compromise of systems, but also address detection of already-compromised machines and prevention or disruption of attackers' subsequent actions. The defenses identified deal with reducing the initial attack surface by hardening device configurations, identifying compromised machines to address long-term threats inside an organization's network (such as advanced persistent threats), disrupting attackers' command-and-control of implanted malicious code, and establishing an adaptive, continuous defense and response capability that can be maintained and improved.

Several critical functions need to be guaranteed in order to setup an effective cyber defense framework. Each of these functions relies on different types or components of the overall situational awareness developed within the organization, and involves different groups, such as system administrators, network administrators, cyber analysts, national CERTs, Managed Security Services, forensic consultants, recovery operators, etc. The main five functions can be described as follows:

1. **Learning from attacks**. This function entails using knowledge of actual attacks that have compromised a system to provide the foundation for continually learning from these events in order to build effective, practical defenses.
2. **Prioritization**. This function identifies and gives higher priority to controls that will provide the greatest risk reduction and protection against the most dangerous threat actors, and that can be feasibly implemented in the existing computing environment.
3. **Metrics**. This function is intended to establish common metrics to provide a shared language for executives, IT specialists, auditors, and security officials to measure the effectiveness of security controls within an organization so that required adjustments can be identified and implemented quickly.
4. **Continuous diagnostics and mitigation**. This function consists in carrying out continuous measurement to test and validate the effectiveness of current security controls, and to help drive the prioritization of the next steps.
5. **Automation**. This function aims at automating defenses so that organizations can achieve reliable, scalable, and continuous monitoring of security relevant events and variables, while relieving human analyst from the most labor-intensive and error-prone tasks.

Situational awareness—in different shapes and at different scales—forms in all the functional areas listed above. Specifically, each of these areas involves different roles, some of which may be responsible for generating situational awareness, whereas others may benefit from it while carrying out their own tasks. For instance, with respect to the first function—learning from attacks—forensic specialists and cyber analysts may be responsible for investigating past incidents and deriving information about existing weaknesses as well as knowledge of the attacker's behavior, thus generating situational awareness. On the other hand, network and system administrators may use such knowledge to harden configurations and prevent future occurrences of the same incidents.

2.3   Cyber Defense Roles

New threats and new measures to counter such threats call for a reorganization of cyber defense teams so that they can focus on defending the organization from targeted attacks. In the last decade, most enterprises have established independent security teams to perform a wide range of security-related activities, including: addressing vulnerabilities by deploying and maintaining patches, updating databases of virus signatures, configuring and maintaining firewalls, configuring and maintaining intrusion detection and prevention systems.

To ensure that policies were created and properly enforced, most organizations also created the position of Chief Information Security Officer (CISO) who enacts those policies and becomes responsible for ensuring that the organization is in compliance with applicable standards and regulations. Conversely, to ensure adequate implementation of security policies, standards, and guidelines, a number of more technical roles were defined. The specific responsibilities assigned to each role may vary across organizations, but they can be roughly summarized as follows.

1. **Security Analyst.** A security analyst is responsible for analyzing and assessing existing vulnerabilities in the IT infrastructure (software, hardware, and networks), investigating available tools and countermeasures to remedy identified vulnerabilities, and recommending solutions and best practices. A security analyst also analyzes and assesses damage to either the data or the infrastructure as a result of security incidents, examines available recovery tools and processes, and recommends solutions. Finally, analysts test for compliance with security policies and procedures, and may assist in the creation, implementation, and/or management of security solutions.
2. **Security Engineer.** A security engineer is responsible for performing security monitoring, security and data/logs analysis, and forensic analysis, detecting security incidents, and initiating incident response. A security engineer investigates and utilizes new technologies and processes to enhance security capabilities and implement improvements. An engineer may also review code or execute other security engineering methodologies.

3. **Security Architect.** A security architect is responsible for designing a security system or major components of a security system, and may lead a security design team building a new security system.
4. **Security Administrator.** A security administrator is responsible for installing and managing organization-wide security systems. Security administrators may also take on some of the tasks of a security analyst in smaller organizations.
5. **Security Consultant/Specialist.** Security consultant and security specialist are broad titles that encompass any one or all of the other roles and titles, tasked with protecting computers, networks, software, data, and/or information systems against viruses, worms, spyware, malware, intrusions, unauthorized access, denial-of-service attacks, and an ever increasing list of attacks by malicious users acting as individuals or as part of organized crime or foreign governments.

Despite an organization's best effort to protect their cyber assets, incident will inevitably occur over time. Therefore, no security policy should be considered complete until procedures are put in place that allow for the handling of and recovery from even the most devastating incidents. A possible solution that most organizations have adopted is the creation of a Computer Incident Response Team (CIRT). A CIRT is a carefully selected and well-trained group of professionals whose purpose is to promptly and correctly handle an incident so that it can be quickly contained, investigated, and recovered from. It is usually comprised of members of the organizations, but the actual composition largely depends on the needs and resources of the organization. However, it is critical to the success of the CIRT that individuals in different roles and capacities are included in the team. First of all, it is essential to have a member of upper level management in the team, as this will give the team authority to operate and make critical decisions. Of course, members of the cyber defense team (security analysts, security administrators, etc.) must be included in the team. They will be responsible for assessing the extent of the damage, conducting forensic analysis, containing the incident, and recovering from the incident.

Many organizations are also beginning to utilize IT auditors that are specially trained in the area of computer technology. Their role within the organization is to ensure that procedures are being followed, and to help foster change when current procedures are no longer appropriate. They may also be present during a crisis, but they would not take action at that time. The role of the IT auditor is to observe, learn why the incident occurred, ensure procedures are being followed, and work with IT and security personnel to avoid similar incidents in the future. They are invaluable members of the team when conducting post-incident reviews.

Other roles that may be represented in a CIRT include: (i) physical security personnel, responsible for assessing any physical damage to the facility or to IT gear, collecting and investigating physical evidence, and guarding evidence during a forensics investigation to maintain a chain of custody; (ii) an attorney, useful for providing legal advice in situations where incidents may have legal implications; (iii) Human Resource, which can provide advice as to how best handle situations involving employees; (iv) Public Relations, which can best advise on the type and tone of communications that should emanate from the company during and/or after an incident, so as to preserve the organization's reputation; (v) a financial auditor, who can put a monetary figure on the damage that has occurred as a result of an incident.

A large organization with divisions spread around the globe or separate large business units may well have cyber defense teams deployed in each division with their own leaders who report up to the Chief Information Security Officer.

3   The Multiple Facets of Situational Awareness

The previous section has provided an overview of the overall cyber defense process. In this section we discuss in more detail the process of situational awareness, which, without loss of generality, can be viewed as a three-phase process: situation perception, situation comprehension, and situation projection (Cyber Situational Awareness: Issues and Research 2010). *Perception* provides information about the status, attributes, and dynamics of relevant elements within the environment. *Comprehension* of the situation encompasses how people combine, interpret, store, and retain information. *Projection* of the elements of the environment (situation) into the near future encompasses the ability to make predictions based on the knowledge acquired through perception and comprehension. We examine the process of situational awareness with respect to several key questions security analysts are routinely trying to answer in order to perceive, comprehend and project the cyber situation, and with respect to each of the five functions identified earlier in this chapter. When applicable, we discuss what type of situational awareness is formed within the domain of each of these questions and functions, its temporal and spatial scope, its scale, and its temporal dynamics. We also discuss what metrics can be used to quantify a specific type of situational awareness, what inputs are needed to generate it and what output is generated, how situational awareness generated in one domain relates to situational awareness generated in other domains. Then, in the next section, we will present specific techniques, mechanisms, and tools that can help form specific types of situational awareness. These mechanisms and tools are part of a comprehensive framework for Cyber Situational Awareness (CSA) developed by the authors of this chapter as part of a funded research project. This framework aims at enhancing the traditional cyber defense process we described in the previous section by automating some of the capabilities that have traditionally required a significant involvement of human analysts and other individuals. Ideally, we envision the evolution of the current *human in the loop* approach to cyber defense into a *human on the loop* approach, where human analysts would be responsible for examining and validating or correcting the results of automated tools, rather than combing through daunting amounts of log entries and security alerts.

Among all the cyber defense roles presented earlier in this chapter, the security analyst—or cyber defense analyst—clearly plays a major role in all the operational aspects of maintaining the security of the enterprise. Security analysts are also responsible for studying the threat landscape with an eye towards emerging threats to the organization. Unfortunately, given the current state of the art in the area of automation, the operational aspects of IT security may still be too time-consuming to allow this type of outward looking focus in most realistic scenarios. Therefore, the scenario we envision—were automated tools would gather and preprocess large amounts of data on behalf of the analyst—is a highly desirable one. Ideally, such tools should be able to automatically answer most, if not all, the questions an analyst may ask about the current situation, the impact and evolution of an attack, the behavior of the attackers, the quality of available information and models, and the plausible futures of the current situation. In the following, we define the fundamental questions that an effective Cyber Situational Awareness framework must be able to help answer.

1. **Current situation**. Is there any ongoing attack? If yes, what is the stage of the intrusion and where is the attacker?

   Answering this set of questions implies the capability of effectively detecting ongoing intrusions, and identifying the assets that might have been compromised already. With respect to these questions, the input to the SA process is represented by IDS logs, firewall logs, and data from other security monitoring tools (Albanese et al. 2013b). On the other hand, the product of the SA process is a detailed mapping of current intrusive activities. This type of SA may quickly become obsolete—if not acted upon timely or updated frequently—as the intruder progresses within the system.

2. **Impact**. How is the attack impacting the organization or mission? Can we assess the damage?

   Answering this set of questions implies the capability of accurately assessing the impact (so far) of ongoing attacks. In this case, the SA process requires knowledge of the organization's assets along with some measure of each asset's value. Based on this information, the output of the SA process is an estimate of the damage caused so far by the intrusive activity. As for the previous case, this type of SA must be frequently updated to remain useful, as damage will increase as the attack progresses.

3. **Evolution**. How is the situation evolving? Can we track all the steps of an attack?

   Answering this set of questions implies the capability of monitoring ongoing attacks, once such attacks have been detected. In this case, the input to the SA process is the situational awareness generated in response to the first set of questions above, whereas the output is a detailed understanding of how the attack is progressing. Developing this capability can help address the limitations on the useful life of the situational awareness generated in response to the first two sets of questions.

4. **Behavior**. How are the attackers expected to behave? What are their strategies?

   Answering this set of questions implies the capability of modeling the attacker's behavior in order to understand its goals and strategies. Ideally, the output of the SA process with respect to this set of questions is a set of formal models (e.g., game theoretic, stochastic) of the attacker's behavior. Such behavior may change over time, therefore models need to adapt to a changing adversarial landscape.

5. **Forensics**. How did the attacker create the current situation? What was he trying to achieve?

   Answering this set of questions implies the capability of analyzing the logs after the fact and correlating observations in order to understand how an attack originated and evolved. Although this is not strictly necessary, the SA process may benefit from the situational awareness gained is response to the fourth set of questions when addressing this additional set of questions. In this case, the output of the SA process includes a detailed understanding of the weaknesses and vulnerabilities that made the attack possible. This information can help security engineers and administrators harden system configurations in order to prevent similar incidents from happening again in the future.

6. **Prediction**. Can we predict plausible futures of the current situation?

   Answering this set of questions implies the capability of predicting possible moves an attacker may take in the future. With respect to this set of questions, the input to the SA process is represented by the situational awareness gained in response to the first (or third) and fourth sets of questions, namely, knowledge about the current situation (and its evolution) and knowledge about the attacker's behavior. The output is a set of possible alternative scenarios that may realize in the future.

7. **Information**. What information sources can we rely upon? Can we assess their quality?

   Answering this set of questions implies the capability of assessing the quality of the information sources all other tasks depend upon. With respect to this set of questions, the goal of the SA process is to generate a detailed understanding of how to weight all different sources when processing information in order to answer all other sets of question the overall SA process is aiming to address. Being able to assess the reliability of each information source would enable automated tools to attach a confidence level to each result.

It is clear from our discussion that some of these questions are strictly correlated, and the ability to answer some of them may depend on the ability to answer other questions. For instance, as we have discussed above, the capability of predicting possible moves an attacker may take depends on the capability of modeling the attacker's behavior. A cross-cutting issue that affects all other aspects of the SA process is scalability. Given the volumes of data involved in answering all these questions, we need to define approaches that are not only effective, but also computationally efficient. In most circumstances, determining a good course of action in a reasonable amount of time may be preferable to determining the best course of action, if this cannot be done in a timely manner.

In the following, we describe the situational awareness process with respect to the five major functions described earlier in this chapter. We discuss what type of situational awareness is formed in each of these areas, its scope and scale, and its lifecycle.

1. **Learning from attacks**. With respect to this function, situational awareness is mainly generated through forensic analysis (see the fifth set of questions above), and consists of a deep understanding of how the attack started, evolved, and

eventually reached its goal. This type of situational awareness is usually generated after the fact by security analysts, and it is an invaluable resource in guiding how systems should be upgraded or redesigned in order to prevent similar incidents from occurring again in the future.

2. **Prioritization**. With respect to this function, situational awareness is mostly an input to the prioritization function rather than the outcome of the process itself. In fact, the task of prioritizing resource allocation for prevention and remediation is informed by knowledge of the current situation, the attacker's behavior, and possible evolution of the current situation. A risk analysis framework can be adopted to put all these elements together, and identify the most cost-effective set of preventive and/or corrective actions to take on the system.

3. **Metrics and Continuous diagnostics and mitigation**. With respect to this function, situational awareness is generated by continuously monitoring the system, the environment, and any deployed countermeasure, and assessing them against a set of common metrics that provide a shared language for executives, IT specialists, auditors, and security officials. On the other hand, situational awareness formed through this process can help define effective prevention and mitigation strategies, which will then need to be prioritized as described before.

4. **Automation**. The role of situational awareness with respect to automation is twofold. On one hand, automation is critical for enhancing situational awareness, both in terms of quality and in terms of volume. On the other end, automated situational awareness tools require inputs that may consist of either background knowledge provided by human experts or situational awareness derived by other tools. In addressing the seven classes of questions above, we have illustrated several cases in which answering one specific set of questions relies on the capability of answering other sets of questions.

In conclusion, the situational awareness process in the context of cyber defense entails the generation and maintenance of a body of knowledge that informs and is augmented by all the main functions of the cyber defense process. Situational awareness is generated or used by different mechanisms and tools aimed at addressing seven classes of questions that security analysts may routinely ask while executing their work tasks.

4 State of the Art

Although the ultimate goal of research in Cyber Situational Awareness is to design systems capable of gaining self-awareness—and leveraging such awareness to achieving self-protection and self-remediation capabilities—without involving any humans in the loop, this vision is still very distant from the current reality, and there does not exist yet a tangible roadmap to achieve this vision in a practical way.

For these reasons, in our analysis, we still view human analysts and decision makers as an indispensable *component* of the system gaining situational awareness.

Nonetheless, we show that humans in the loop can greatly benefit from the adoption of automated tools capable of reducing the semantic gap between an analyst's cognitive processes and the huge volume of available fine-grained monitoring data.

Practical cyber situational awareness systems include not only hardware sensors (e.g., a network interface card) and "smart" computer programs (e.g., programs that can learn attack signatures), but also models of the mental processes of human beings making advanced decisions (Gardner 1987; Johnson-Laird 2006). Cyber situational awareness can be gained at multiple abstraction levels: raw data is typically collected at the lower levels, whereas more refined information is collected at the higher levels, as data is analyzed and converted into more abstract information. Data collected at the lowest levels can easily overwhelm the cognitive capacity of human decision makers, and situational awareness based solely on low level data is clearly insufficient.

Cyber situational awareness systems and physical situational awareness systems have fundamental differences. For instance, physical situational awareness systems rely on specific hardware sensors and signal processing techniques, but neither the physical sensors nor the specific signal processing techniques play an essential role in cyber situational awareness systems [although there is research that has looked at applying signal processing techniques to analyze network traffic and trends (Partridge et al. 2002; Cousins et al. 2003)]. Cyber situational awareness systems rely on cyber sensors such as intrusion detection systems (IDS), log files, anti-virus systems, malware detectors, and firewalls: they all produce events at a higher level of abstraction than raw network packets. Additionally, the speed at which the cyber situation evolves is usually orders of magnitude higher than in physical situation evolution.

Existing approaches to automate the process of gaining cyber situational awareness mostly rely on vulnerability analysis (using attack graphs) (Jajodia et al. 2011; Albanese et al. 2011; Ammann et al. 2002; Phillips and Swiler 1998), intrusion detection and alert correlation (Wang et al. 2006), attack trend analysis, causality analysis and forensics (e.g., backtracking intrusions), taint and information flow analysis, damage assessment (using dependency graphs) (Albanese et al. 2011), and intrusion response. However, these approaches only work at the lower (abstraction) levels. Higher level situational awareness analyses are still done manually by human analysts, making the process labor-intensive, time-consuming, and error-prone.

Although researchers have recently started to address the cognitive needs of decision makers, there is still a huge gap between the mental models and cognitive processes of human analysts and the capabilities offered by existing cyber situational awareness tools.

First, existing approaches are not always able to properly handle uncertainty. Uncertainty in observed or perceived data could lead to distorted situational awareness. For instance, most attack graph analysis toolkits are designed to do deterministic attack consequence estimation. When real time capabilities are critical, such consequence estimates could be extremely misleading due to various uncertainties. Similarly, alert correlation techniques cannot handle the inherent uncertainties associated with inaccurate interpretations of reports from intrusion detection sensors. Such inaccurate interpretations can lead to either false positives or false negatives in determining whether an IDS alert corresponds to a real attack.

Second, lack of data and incomplete knowledge may create additional uncertainty management issues. For instance, lack of data may lead to insufficient understanding of the system being defended. Such partial knowledge may be the consequence of different factors, including but not limited to: incomplete information about system configurations, which is possible when no configuration management system is used; incomplete information about vulnerabilities (Albanese et al. 2013a); incomplete sensor deployment, meaning that sensors deployed across the organization's infrastructure are not sufficient to capture all security relevant events. Similarly, incomplete knowledge about the attacker's behavior may lead to the inability of fully comprehending the current situation. In this scenario, it would then be critical to at least isolate what current models are incapable of explaining (Albanese et al. 2014).

Last, existing approaches also lack the reasoning and learning capabilities required to gain full situational awareness for cyber defense. The key capabilities that would enable viable cyber situational awareness—as defined by the seven classes of questions presented in Sect. 3—have been treated as separate problems. However, effective cyber situational awareness requires that all these capabilities be integrated into a holistic approach to the three phases of situational awareness, namely perception, comprehension, and projection. Such a solution is in general still missing, but the framework discussed in Sect. 5 represents a first important step in this direction. Furthermore, looking beyond cyber situational awareness and considering how cyber situational awareness solutions complement other cyber defense technologies, the conclusion is that cyber situational awareness activities need to be better integrated with effect-achieving or environment-influencing activities (e.g., intrusion response activities).

5 A Framework for Situational Awareness

In this section, we present a framework—encompassing a number of techniques and automated tools—for enhancing situational awareness. This framework aims at addressing the limitations of the typical cyber situational awareness process—which tends to be mostly manual—and enhancing the analyst's performance as well as his understanding of the cyber situation. Most of the work presented in this section is the result of research efforts conducted by the authors of this chapter as part of a funded multi-year multi-university research project.

The first step in achieving any level of automation in the situational awareness process is to develop the capability of modeling cyber-attacks and their consequences. This capability is critical to support many of the additional capabilities needed to address the key questions presented earlier in this chapter (e.g., modeling the attacker, predicting future scenarios).

Attack graphs have been widely used to model attack patterns, and to correlate alerts. However, existing approaches typically have two major limitations. First, attack graphs do not provide mechanisms for evaluating the likelihood of each attack pattern or its impact on the organization or mission. Second, scalability of alert correlation has not been fully addressed, and may represent a major impediment to the development of real-time cyber situational awareness systems. In order to address these limitations, we present a framework to analyze massive amounts of raw security data in real time, comprehend the current situation, assess the impact of current intrusions, and predict future scenarios.

The proposed framework is illustrated in Fig. 1. We start from analyzing the topology of the network, known vulnerabilities, possible zero-day vulnerabilities (these must be hypothesized), and their interdependencies. Vulnerabilities are often interdependent, making traditional point-wise vulnerability analysis ineffective. Our topological approach to vulnerability analysis allows to generate accurate attack graphs showing all the possible attack paths within the network. A node in an attack graph represents (depending on the level of abstraction) an exploitable vulnerability (or family of exploitable vulnerabilities) in either a subnet or an individual machine or an individual software application. An edge from a node V_1 to a node V_2 represents the fact that V_2 can be exploited after V_1, and it is labeled with the probability that an occurrence of the attack will exploit V_2 within a given time period after V_1 has been exploited. This approach extends the classical definition of attack graph by encoding probabilistic knowledge of the attacker's behavior. Probabilities and temporal intervals labeling the edges can be estimated by studying the relative complexity of exploiting different vulnerabilities (Leversage and Byres 2008). Information required to perform this task may be derived from available vulnerability databases, such NIST's National Vulnerability Database (NVD) (NIST) and MITRE's Common Vulnerabilities and Exposures (CVE) (MITRE).

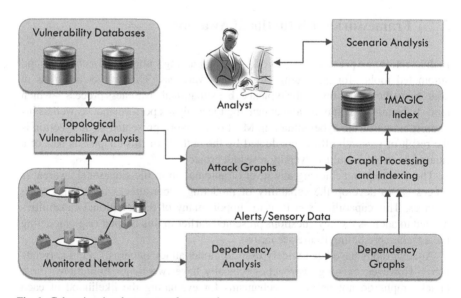

Fig. 1 Cyber situational awareness framework

In order to enable concurrent monitoring of multiple attack types, we merge multiple attack graphs in a compact data structure and define an index structure on top of it to index large amounts of alerts and sensory data (events) in real-time (Albanese et al. 2011). The proposed index structure allows us to solve three important problems:

- **The Evidence Problem.** Given a sequence of events, a probability threshold, and an attack graph, find all minimal subsets of the sequence that validate the occurrence of the attack with a probability above the threshold.
- **The Identification Problem.** Given a sequence of events and a set of attack graphs, identify the most likely type of attack occurring in the sequence.
- **The Prediction Problem.** Identify all possible outcomes of the current situation and their respective likelihood.

We also perform dependency analysis to discover dependencies among services and/or machines and derive dependency graphs encoding how these components depend on one other. Dependency analysis is critical to assess current damage caused by ongoing attacks (i.e., the value or utility of services disrupted by the attacks) and future damage (i.e., the value or utility of additional services that will be disrupted if no action is taken). In fact, in a complex enterprise, many services may rely on the availability of other services or resources. Therefore they may be indirectly affected by the compromise of the services or resources they rely upon (Fig. 2).

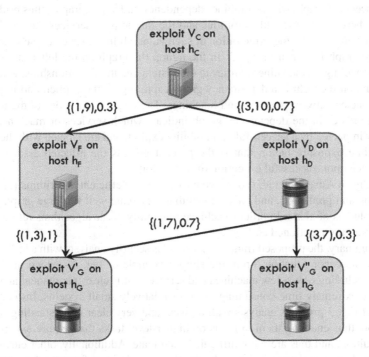

Fig. 2 Example of attack graph

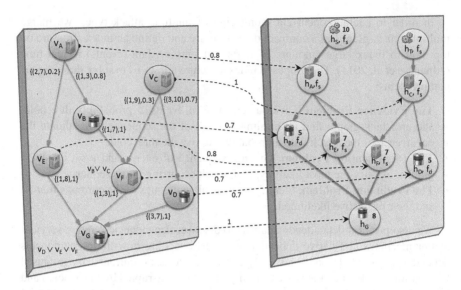

Fig. 3 Example of attack scenario graph

For each possible outcome of the current situation, we can then compute an estimate of future damage that ongoing attack might cause by introducing the notion of attack scenario graph, which combines dependency and attack graphs, thus bridging the gap between known vulnerabilities and the missions or services that could be ultimately affected by the exploitation of such vulnerabilities. An example of attack scenario graph is shown in Fig. 3. In the figure, the graph on the left is an attack graph modeling all the vulnerabilities in the system and their relationships, whereas the graph on the right is a dependency graph capturing all the explicit and implicit dependencies between services and machines. The edges from nodes in the attack graph to nodes in the dependency graph indicate which services or machines are directly impacted by a successful vulnerability exploit, and are labeled with the corresponding exposure factor, that is the percentage loss the affected asset would experience upon successful execution of the exploit.

Finally, in Albanese et al. (2011) we have proposed efficient algorithms for both detection and prediction, and have shown that they scale well for large graphs and large volumes of alerts. In order to achieve scalability, these algorithms rely on the index structure mentioned earlier.

In summary, the proposed framework provides security analysts with a high-level view of the cyber situation. From the simple example of Fig. 3—which models a system including only a few machines and services—it is clear that manual analysis could be extremely time-consuming even for relatively small systems. Instead, the graph of Fig. 3 provides analysts with a visual and very clear understanding of the situation, thus enabling them to focus on higher-level tasks that require experience and intuition, and thus are more difficult to automate. Additionally, other classes of automated analytical processes may be developed within this framework to support the analyst during these higher-level tasks as well. For instance, based on the model of Fig. 3, we could automatically generate a ranked list of recommendations on the best course of actions analysts should take to minimize the impact of ongoing and future attacks [e.g., sets of network hardening actions (Albanese et al. 2012)].

6 Summary

Building on the material presented in previous chapters, we have explored in more detail the process of situational awareness in the context of cyber defense. As we discussed, this process can consists of three phases: situation perception, situation comprehension, and situation projection. Situational awareness is generated and used across these three phases, and we have examined the process of situational awareness with respect to several key questions security analysts are routinely trying to answer, and with respect to each of the five cyber defense functions identified earlier in this chapter. Whenever applicable, we have discussed what type of situational awareness is formed within the domain of each of these functions, its temporal and spatial scope, its scale, and its temporal dynamics.

We have pointed out the major challenges we face when designing systems that can achieve self-awareness, and we have discussed the limitations of current technological solutions to this important problem. We have then proposed an integrated approach to cyber situational awareness, and presented a framework—comprising several mechanisms and automated tools—that can help bridge the gap between the available low-level data and the mental models and cognitive processes of security analysts. Although this framework represents a first important step in the right direction, a lot of work remains to be done for systems to achieve self-awareness capabilities. Key areas that need to be further investigated include adversarial modeling and reasoning under uncertainty, and promising approaches may include game-theoretic and control-theoretic solutions.

References

Albanese, M., Jajodia, S., Pugliese, A., and Subrahmanian, V. S. "Scalable Analysis of Attack Scenarios". In Proceedings of the 16th European Symposium on Research in Computer Security (ESORICS 2011), pages 416-433, Leuven, Belgium, September 12-14, 2011.

Albanese, M., Jajodia, S., and Noel, S. "Time-Efficient and Cost-Effective Network Hardening Using Attack Graphs". In Proceedings of the 42nd Annual IEEE/IFIP International Conference on Dependable Systems and Networks (DSN 2012), Boston, Massachusetts, USA, June 25-28, 2012

Albanese, M., Jajodia, S., Singhal, A., and Wang, L. "An Efficient Approach to Assessing the Risk of Zero-Day Vulnerabilities". In Proceedings of the 10th International Conference on Security and Cryptography, Reykjavík, Iceland, July 29-31, 2013. Best paper award

Albanese, M., Pugliese, A., and Subrahmanian, V. S. "Fast Activity Detection: Indexing for Temporal Stochastic Automaton based Activity Models". In IEEE Transactions on Knowledge and Data Engineering, vol. 25, no. 2, pages 360-373, February 2013.

Albanese, M., Molinaro, C., Persia, F., Picariello, A., and Subrahmanian, V. S. "Discovering the Top-k "Unexplained" Sequences in Time-Stamped Observation Data". IEEE Transactions on Knowledge and Data Engineering, vol. 26, no. 3, pages 577-594, March 2014.

Ammann, P., Wijesekera, D., and Kaushik, S. "Scalable, graph-based network vulnerability analysis," in Proceedings of the 9th ACM Conference on Computer and Communications Security (CCS 2002), pp. 217–224, Washington, DC, USA, November 2002.

Cloud Security Alliance (CSA). "Cloud Controls Matrix Version 3.0", https://cloudsecurity-alliance.org/research/ccm/

Cousins, D., Partridge, C., Bongiovanni, K., Jackson, A. W., Krishnan, R., Saxena, T., and Strayer, W. T. "Understanding Encrypted Networks Through Signal and Systems Analysis of Traffic Timing", 2003.

Gardner, H. "The Mind's New Science: A History of the Cognitive Revolution", Basic Books, 1987.

Jajodia, S., Liu, P., Swarup, V., and Wang, C. (Eds.) "Cyber Situational Awareness: Issues and Research" , Vol. 46 of Advances in Information Security, Springer, 2010.

Jajodia, S., Noel, S., Kalapa, P., Albanese, M., and Williams, J. "Cauldron: Mission-Centric Cyber Situational Awareness with Defense in Depth". In Proceedings of the Military Communications Conference (MILCOM 2011), Baltimore, Maryland, USA, November 7-10, 2011.

Johnson-Laird, P. "How We Reason", Oxford University Press, 2006.

Leversage, D. J., Byres, E. J. "Estimating a System's Mean Time-to-Compromise," IEEE Security & Privacy, vol. 6, no. 1, pp. 52-60, January-February 2008.

Mandiant, "APT1: Exposing One of China's Cyber Espionage Units", 2013

MITRE. "Common Vulnerabilities and Exposures (CVE)", http://cve.mitre.org/.

NIST. "National Vulnerability Database (NVD)", http://nvd.nist.gov/.

NIST. "Guide for Applying the Risk Management Framework to Federal Information Systems", Special Publication 800-37, Revision 1, http://dx.doi.org/10.6028/NIST.SP.800-37r1, February 2010.

NIST. "Security and Privacy Controls for Federal Information Systems and Organizations", Special Publication 800-53, Revision 4, http://dx.doi.org/10.6028/NIST.SP.800-53r4, April 2013.

Partridge, C., Cousins, D., Jackson, A.W., Krishnan, R., Saxena, T., and Strayer, W. T. "Using signal processing to analyze wireless data traffic", In Proceedings of the 1st ACM workshop on Wireless Security (WiSE 2002), ACM, pages 67-76, 2002.

Phillips, C., and Swiler, L. P. "A graph-based system for network-vulnerability analysis," in Proceedings of the New Security Paradigms Workshop (NSPW 1998), pp. 71–79, Charlottesville, VA, USA, September 1998.

Symantec Corporation. "Internet Security Threat Report 2014", Volume 19, April 2014.

Wang, L., Liu, A., and Jajodia, S. "Using attack graphs for correlating, hypothesizing, and predicting intrusion alerts," Computer Communications, vol. 29, no. 15, pp. 2917–2933, September 2006.

Network-Wide Awareness

Nicholas Evancich, Zhuo Lu, Jason Li, Yi Cheng, Joshua Tuttle, and Peng Xie

1 Introduction

In this chapter we continue the theme of awareness formation started in the preceding chapter. Here, however, we focus on a particular type of CSA that deals with the holistic, network-wide view of a network. We use the term "macro" CSA to refer to the overall dynamics of the network that is seen as a single organism and where individual elements or events are perceived in aggregate. This contrasts with CSA that focuses on individual atomic elements of the network's assets or behaviors, such as an individual suspicious packet, an alert of a potential intrusion, or a vulnerable computer. On the other hand, atomic events can have a broad impact on the operation of the entire network. This means that the scope of CSA must accommodate both "micro and "macro" perspectives. The process of gaining network-wide awareness includes discovery and enumeration of assets and of defense capabilities, along with threat and attack awareness. We argue that effective CSA must focus on improved decision-making, collaboration, and resource management, and discuss approaches to achieving effective network-wide SA.

N. Evancich • Z. Lu • J. Li (✉) • Y. Cheng • J. Tuttle • P. Xie
Intelligent Automation, Inc, 15400 Calhoun Dr #190, Rockville, MD 20855, USA
e-mail: nevancich@i-a-i.com; zlu@i-a-i.com; jli@i-a-i.com;
ycheng@i-a-i.com; jtuttle@i-a-i.com; pxie@i-a-i.com

© Springer International Publishing Switzerland 2014   63
A. Kott et al. (eds.), *Cyber Defense and Situational Awareness*,
Advances in Information Security 62, DOI 10.1007/978-3-319-11391-3_5

1.1 Process of Developing Cyber Situational Awareness

The process for developing SA is as follows: (i) define a goal, (ii) gather data, (iii) transform the data into information, and (iv) project a decision from the information.

(i) The user wants to get a defined goal from the SA process. The goal could be answering a question or gaining general knowledge of the network. In CSA, some examples of questions could be finding out what avenues or attacks the network is vulnerable to, or why a switch is dropping packets. The goal of SA is to answer the desired questions.

(ii) The next step of gathering data is the act of collecting the available data, sensor outputs, and user experience. In CSA, this is taking network sensor data (the metrics for this data are described in Sect. 6.1) in order to prepare the data that was collected and applying the user experience and mission/functions to the data, which aids in moving the data from simple data points into information, once context has been overlaid. In an ideal case, the data over-describes the desired goal.

(iii) The data is then translated into contextual information by applying knowledge to the data. The context applied to the data is the domain specific knowledge of the purpose and/or function of the network.

(iv) Finally, the information is used to create a decision about the information, and how it relates to the desired goal.

These steps will be further elaborated in the SA theory (Sect. 1.4).

The three major groups needed for the collection of CSA are network administrators, network defenders, and users. Their roles are described below:

- A network administrator must instrument the network for data collection. When the raw data is collected without context, the throughput (for example) from one network to another is not very comparable without the context or purpose of the network. The context is the operational and historic knowledge about how the network should function, which is often network or mission or application specific. The network administrator is aware of the services and level of service required for their network, and must apply context to the data via mission and operational needs.
- Network defenders are needed in CSA, in order to determine what types of information they require to defend the network. The defender's role in CSA is as a consumer of the SA picture, which shows the available data and contextual information about the network at a point in time. This SA picture may be used to determine what posture changes are needed. The posture change is how the network administrator or defender alters the network to respond to the attack or service level change in the network. A posture change could be disabling a service that is compromised (e.g., like FTP) or moving services to a full operational network element (e.g., in the event of a router that suddenly had a port go bad).
- Finally, users are the last essential element in developing CSA. They act as the source of much of the data, and of problems. Users act like "canaries in the mineshaft" and are often the first to issue a warning about a problem with the network.

1.2 Inputs and Outputs for Cyber Situational Awareness

The inputs, outputs and stages of effort for developing CSA are shown in Fig. 1 (Hoogendoorn et al. 2011).

The process of developing SA is moving from raw data to information that can guide a decision. The inputs to this process are (i) the raw data from the network sensors and user experience, (ii) the context applied to the operation or mission capabilities for the network, and (iii) the model of the network that the network administrator uses. The raw data is processed by observations (which are unsubstantiated guesses about the network), which in turn yield insights about the data. In CSA, the output is the potential change in posture that network administrators should take to ensure network services continue, or the network changes that are needed in order to repair or mitigate an issue.

For example, if a web page is slow to load and the full take packet capture (which is a log of every packet on the network) shows that Domain Name System (DNS) is timing out, the observation could be that the Internet Service Provider's (ISP) DNS is offline. These observations are converted into information by applying context. This process for developing a SA picture was defined by Hoogendoorn et al. (2011). The information becomes a belief, which in this example, is that the DNS is at the root of the problem and the network administrator believes that moving to a different DNS server will correct the issue. The administrator makes the decision and follows that course of action.

These process inputs and outputs map to the theoretical models of SA discussed below.

1.3 Theoretical Models of Situational Awareness

The most commonly used theoretical model of SA was developed by Endsley (1995). This model looks at three stages of developing SA: perception, comprehension, and projection, which are described below.

- Perception involves data gathering and determining the parameters of the environment. The first two steps of data gathering and the initial phase of understanding the data are shown in Fig. 1. Perception will be discussed in the guise of discovery and enumeration of the network and its elements later in Sect. 2).

Fig. 1 SA development

- Comprehension involves aggregating the data and determining the impact of this data on the goals of the system. This will be discussed in terms of awareness for the CSA. This corresponds to the third and fourth steps in Fig. 1.
- Projection involves predicting future actions based on current conditions of the system. When this level of SA is achieved, the SA moves to being effective SA (ESA). This is the last step in Fig. 1 and what makes SA into ESA.

1.4 Gaps in Current Cyber Situational Awareness

Gaps in the current state of CSA include: (i) lack of theoretical modeling with a cyber context, (ii) overabundance of raw sensor data, and (iii) disparate fusion and visualization tools. In addition, the cyber domain also has some specific issues related to the context and data: the speed at which cyber data is collected and events occur, and the continued use of the network during these cyber events.

Though there are theoretical models for SA, applying them within a cyber context is still necessary. There exists a gap between theoretical models for SA with respect to the cyber context, which is the amount of raw data that a network generates. Often SA research has studied SA in low data or limited data contexts like the SA of an airplane, which may have at most a few hundred sources of input and many fewer outputs. A network, on the other hand, will often generate many times what an airplane will and hence the data rate can overwhelm the SA models.

The raw data coming from various network sensors can easily outstrip the full take of the network traffic, which is a log of every packet on the network. The raw data from the network sensors is often the full take of that sensor's data plus some metadata. Storing both full take and all of the raw sensor data easily doubles the data storage requirements. This means more data sifting for the network analysts creating a "needle in a haystack" situation. The network administrator or defender has to sift through the full take of the packet capture returns from the network traffic to correlate packets to events. This prevents cyber defenders and network administrators from having effective SA.

Finally, the fusion and visualization tools do not use a common set of inputs and outputs. Each tool is custom to the network and the mission or operation of that network. Standardization and common metrics are needed.

2   Cyber Situational Awareness in a Network Context

The network context helps to define the scope and issues that are specific to the network for which the SA picture is being developed. In the CSA case, network context is defined as the network and components (users, applications, sensors, etc.) that comprise the network. The issues discussed below are not exhaustive, but cover the major challenges associated with obtaining CSA.

1. **Difficulty in enumeration of a changing network or environment**: Very few networks are truly static. The elements of the network change (e.g. hosts get powered off) and the condition of the network changes (e.g., the load on a specific server will change over time), which makes enumeration of the network a difficult ongoing task. The network needs to be enumerated in order to develop the SA picture. The best SA pictures have the most complete view of the network, including attribution of the assets on the network. The purpose and the value of the asset must be determined in order to evaluate the impact of a state change of that asset.

2. **Wire speed attackers vs. human speed defenders**: Another issue is the capability gap between attackers and defenders. Computer network attacks (CNAs) generally happen at wire speed, which is defined as reaction at the speed of the network as opposed to human reaction times. Wire speed is often several orders of magnitude faster than a human reaction speed. If the attack is new or at least unknown to the defender, the defender does not have wire speed tools, and has only human speed tools to detect and analyze the attack. Network defenders need to realize the scope and intent of the attack, and CSA aids their ability to gain such understanding.

3. **Heterogeneous SA toolset and non-unified or aggregated views**: CSA is sensed by various tools such as intrusion detection system (IDS) and metric captures. Currently, the data is fused outside of these tools and a common SA picture is generated. This, especially with a non-static network, leads to gaps in the SA picture.

In this context, cyber threats or attacks, which include syntactic, semantic, and service attacks, will generally be used interchangeably, unless the type of attack has a specific effect on CSA.

3 Situational Awareness Solutions for Network Operations and Cyber Security

Network operations are "always-on" and need to move at wire speed in a wide range of environments: tactical, operational, and strategic. These environments change the scope of network operations. In a connected and networked world, the network is a service that is expected to be "always-on" and a constantly updating SA picture needs to be created. In order to accomplish this, SA solutions need to:

1. **Scale across the network operations scope and be usable at a "macro" or "micro" level view of the network.** The "macro" scale is the view of the entire network. The "micro" is a view into a single network element or event.

2. **Present views across different time scales.** Current network issues might have had a root cause that happened hours or days ago. The ability to view these different points in time and at different scale levels is important to a complete SA picture.

3. **Offer an impact assessment to defense options.** A SA picture of the network has limited value because most current SA views simply present the current status of the network. Its real value lies in aiding the analyst in making better decisions about the course of action. ECSA provides a type of impact assessment to the analyst, or helps in conjunction with the analyst's knowledge base. The impact assessment details how the operation or mission's effectiveness will be degraded by changing the posture of the network or by deploying different defense options. This will offer predictive scenarios that show network or mission performance vs. resistance to the attack, and give the ability to triage the network. Often the problem cannot be fixed quickly but things can be "patched" in order to have the network operate until the problem can be fully dealt with. Defense measures or postures can be enacted if the network defenders recognize the attack quickly.

4 Situational Awareness Lifecycle

The lifecycle of Cyber Analysts' SA consists of placing the network context into awareness. This lifecycle contains three steps: network, threat or attack, and operational or mission awareness. Awareness in this context is a cognizance of the aspect. It contains both current and historical status and capability.

4.1 Network Awareness

This consists of a current picture of the condition and status of the elements that comprise the network. The elements are everything required for the network to function, such as servers, appliances, power, and cabling. The network needs a proper configuration. Assets often depend on each other and some may have redundancies. The network awareness also includes a recovery time, which includes anything from a reboot to a patch to a hardware failure. The process of gaining network awareness is listed below.

1. **Discovery/enumeration of assets**: The first step in gaining network awareness is discovering the assets. This is difficult to do especially in a very large and complex network. Elements of the network are constantly in flux (patch level, state, etc.), as is the purpose and value of the asset. Running the discovery tools adds an uncertainty to the measurement. By simply measuring the network, the measure degrades the service level of the network and hence alters the data from the ground truth.
2. **Defense capabilities**: Additionally, the defense options for the network need to be determined. The defense capabilities become a set of options for the defenders to use. They can determine what assets can and cannot be taken offline, brought online, or repurposed. This provides the answers the defenders will have to respond to the attack with. The defenders often have the ability to reroute. If they have a good SA picture, they know the network better than the attackers and can turn off or reroute services that are under attack.

4.2   Threat/Attack Awareness

This consists of a current picture of possible attacks and vectors against the network in question. Often this is best accomplished by asking a series of questions.

1. Current attacks: What are the newest set of attacks and how is the network vulnerable to them? Based on the attack traffic and non-traffic attacks (social engineering, for example) what attacks is the network currently experiencing?
2. Historic attacks: Based on network history, what are the likely attacks to be leveled against this network? Are there attacks that occur at a specific time? Has the owner of the network taken any actions that might result in a series of attacks (press-release or insider threat)?
3. Network operation flaws/holes: What are the current flaws of this network? Based on the various exploit repositories like common vulnerabilities and exposures (CVEs), and the network assets, are they any attacks that would be effective against this network? Will there be a configuration change to the network that might expose flaws?

These questions can be answered by combining the knowledge about the network topology and configuration, and the knowledge about vulnerabilities and how attacks may happen in a network setting. In particular, graphical models (Amman et al. 2002; Jajodia et al. 2003; Sheyner et al. 2002) have turned out to be effective in representing potential attack paths in an enterprise network. Given a comprehensive graphical model that captures how exploits may penetrate and propagate in an enterprise network, one can answer the above questions that are related to the current security posture and exploits of interest via running static analysis algorithms on top of the model.

In addition, such graphical models can also enable *dynamic analysis* because (i) current reported alerts can also be incorporated and visualized; (ii) previous events (that might have been omitted by IDS) can be recovered via back-tracking on the graph; and (iii) future potential attacks can be predicted via simulating further propagation on the graph (Xie et al. 2010).

4.3   Operation/Mission Awareness

Operation/Mission Awareness This consists of a picture of how decreased or degraded network operations will affect the mission of the network. Very few networks are built without purpose. Therefore, the network has a "job" or a function, which could be mobile device connectivity or a lab-bench test network or control of critical infrastructure. This is defined as the network's mission. The operational status of the network directly affects the mission readiness, which can be discovered by measuring the value and purpose of the assets.

Overlay of Services vs. Defense Options The network provides services (e.g. email, authentication etc.). Changing the network posture or engaging defenses may affect these services. Defense often comes at the cost of service availability. Knowing this provides mission/operational awareness. Two examples are given below:

1. Suspending port 53 (this is the standard port defined by the DNS standard, RFC-1035) external calls and switching over (for the duration of the attack) to a cached DNS proxy is an example that highlights network agility. CSA will inform the administrator about the potential impacts of making this change. The network becomes agile by being able to move critical services from an offline (or overloaded) host to a host that provides the required critical functionality;
2. Service suspension while crypto keys are being changed is an example that highlights network resiliency. CSA will inform the administrator about the potential impacts of making this change. A resilient network can remain online and provide the critical services during configuration changes to the network.

SA is essential to network security and mission assurance. According to Force (2010), mission assurance in cyberspace needs "measures required to accomplish essential objectives of missions in a contested environment", and "entails prioritizing mission essential functions, mapping mission dependence on cyberspace, identifying vulnerabilities, and mitigating risk of known vulnerabilities This clearly highlights the need for connecting mission dependencies to cyberspace, identifying mission-critical assets, analyzing network vulnerabilities and risks, and mitigating cyber impacts on missions to ensure mission success. Essentially, to answer questions like "who, what, when, where, and how of a cyber-attack and potentially predict and defeat it effectively to reduce the impact, security analysts need to have a robust understanding of their network along with the corresponding cyber activities. Therefore, CSA is critical and extremely important to network security and mission assurance.

Today, most organizations depend heavily on computer networks to execute their daily work and critical operations. Cyberspace also provides adversaries with affordable attack vectors against critical cyber assets and information infrastructure, as well as the business-critical operations carried out in the network. To achieve mission assurance in cyberspace, mission essential functions (MEFs) need to be mapped onto the underlying cyber network, so that critical assets can be identified. In addition, to remediate an asset compromise, analysts need to clearly understand the dependency relationships between the compromised asset and the affected operations.

5   The Need for Effective Cyber Situational Awareness

The current state of the art for CSA in a context of network operations is a collection of dispersed tools, which lack an integrated view. This results in a capability that does not meet current or future needs. The community needs to move to Effective CSA

(ECSA), which is CSA that improves decision-making, collaboration, and resource management. ECSA differs from CSA by providing the defenders intelligence on the network beyond a simple SA picture. The key concepts in ECSA are:

1. **Giving a predicted SA picture based on possible actions**: ECSA will give the defenders the ability to see the likely outcome for various "what if?" scenarios. This will allow defenders to optimize the defense choice. The optimization will be a choice between network service availability and network posture level of protection. This requires a great deal of awareness both current and historic or more simply ECSA.
2. **Integrating sensor data to a unified and current view**: In general, network sensors measure the conditions of the network. The sensor data can be almost anything from a "green-light" informing that power is on, to logs and alerts. This sensor data must be fused into a common operational picture. Seeing how one sensor is reporting in the context of other sensors is the key here.

6   Overview of Effective Cyber Situational Awareness

CSA is difficult due to the dynamic nature of networks. Nodes or elements of the network change very quickly and the level of service to any specific node varies across time and network load. This makes discovery and enumeration more difficult and requires refreshing the network scan. The changing elements in the network are: network assets and the network itself are in flux, attacks are happening at wire speed, and the sensor data is stove-piped. Additionally, the threats brought against the network are changing.

ECSA is greater than monitoring, reporting, and visualization. Moving from CSA to ECSA requires that the picture provided to the analyst helps the analyst to have better intelligence about the status of the network. Figure 2 details the four elements that comprise ECSA which are expanded in Sect. 7.

ECSA should help the analyst to make decisions about actions by providing a picture that broadens the view that the analyst has. This gives them a better world-view, which may highlight actions that are not apparent without the ECSA picture.

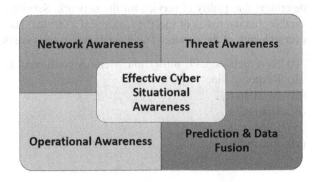

Fig. 2 Effective cyber situational awareness

It also should do more than simply present data. It should provide the ability to run various scenarios and see the mission/operational impact, so that the analyst can assess the impact. These scenarios will also show what services will be impacted by what defense posture and the change in the service level of the network.

Macro vs. *micro* SA represent the different granularities of the picture. *Macro* is the holistic view of the network. It is the entire network, which shows the attacks, the network elements, and defense options. *Micro* focuses on events or hosts, which are the components that the *macro* view is built from. ECSA has the ability to drill down to a micro level and provide insight on a specific event or host. This gives the analysts the ability to see the status of any specific element in the network. It also has the ability to take a "bird's eye" view of the network and see the sum total of hosts and elements on the network and the events.

The purpose of SA is not to simply visualize the network, but rather to provide the analysts and defenders with a tool that improves their ability to defend the network. Thus, the primary purpose of SA is to improve the quality and timeliness of collaborative decision-making regarding the employment, protection, and defense of the network. The goal of CSA is to enable better decision-making; it is an enabling technology. ECSA does not exist just to prove a visualization of the status of the network, but to provide actionable intelligence about the network.

6.1   Instrument the Network to Obtain Data for Effective Cyber Situational Awareness

The data elements that enable ECSA are described here. *Tomography* measures the internals of the network by using information taken from end-to-end link data. The main goal is to limit the uncertainty derived from measuring the network from an external point-of-view. *Route Analytics* is a concept from network monitoring that is used to analyze the routing protocols in a network. It often operates at layer 3 (in the Open Systems Interconnection model), listening to the routing protocols. It uses the "best effort" of IP networks and looks at the control panel to obtain detailed route information. *Protocol Monitoring* looks at the standard protocols (HTTP, FTP, POP3, TCP, SSL, etc.) and checks them for speed and correctness. This is used to determine the quality of service for the network. Service metrics are directly measurable characteristics of specific features of a service. They are used to measure the overall health of the service. The most common ones measured are:

  (i) Host metrics: CPU utilization, Memory consumed, etc.
 (ii) Response time
(iii) Availability
 (iv) Uptime
  (v) Consistency
 (vi) Reliability

IDS is an appliance or application that monitors network or system activities. It scans the activities for malicious events or policy infractions. There are two general classes of IDS: Network IDS (NIDS) and Host IDS (HIDS). NIDS monitors network traffic holistically, and checks the traffic for malicious patterns from alerts/logs. Some NIDS systems have the ability to engage in automated defenses. HIDS runs on hosts on the network, monitors inbounds and outbound packets for hosts, looks for suspicious activity, and sends alerts to a monitoring server. NIDS often has the ability to monitor a host for changes to the files system or running processes.

6.2 Projecting the Current Situational Awareness into the Future

ECSA should give the analyst a view into possible futures based on the actions they might take now. This gives the analyst the ability to quickly see how actions taken now will affect the operational capability of the network and how the threats are likely to respond. Changing postures is often the goal of an attacker and having the ability to see how the threats will act on different postures is a key element of ECSA.

6.3 Potential Approaches to Achieve Effective Cyber Situational Awareness

6.3.1 How to Display the Data

ECSA's data will come from dispersed tools, and needs to be integrated into a holistic view. Disparate visualization that comes from stove-piped tools does not add to ECSA. The various data needs to be fused. Data fusion will happen with like-to-like or similar sensors (this enables different sensors to monitor the same phenomena) and synthesizing data from the measured or observed data, which give the network administrator the ability to create second order data products that are often specific to the network. Additionally, the data shall be displayed in a format that gives a common operating picture. This picture aids the network analyst in making informed choices about the operation of the network. CSA has a unique challenge in data collection since similar sensors might be different but measuring the same type of data, which can yield a different measurement of the same phenomena. One example of this is measuring *goodput* and *throughput*, which are both measures of the service level of the network, but show different scales ("macro" or "micro") and utility. This kind of information from sensors data will be fused and compared. Another source of information is synthesized (and artificial) data, which is data that was not measured, but is a product of a well-instrumented network. An example would be a green light telling the users that all services are active and usable.

6.3.2 How to Keep the SA Updated

The network and the conditions of the network are dynamic, strategies should be employed to ensure that the ECSA has a current and valid picture. The network should be scanned as often as possible without decreasing service. Tools like Nmap (Network Mapper) and ZMap (Zmap—The Internet Scanner), which are described in Sect. 7.2.1, provide effective network scans. The result of the scan needs to be evaluated for legitimate and illegitimate assets on the network.

6.3.3 Inferences and Anti-Inferences

These are two terms used to discuss the context of the cyber event. Both are needed in ECSA as parts of the impact assessment. Changing the defense posture of the network might be a goal of the attacker. Knowing the context or intention of the attack can greatly alter defense response.

Inferences are estimations of the capabilities of an attacker, along with the attacker's intentions. Attackers can have various levels of sufficiation: State Sponsored, Criminal Organization, Hacker Collective, Lone Hacker, and Individual with scripted tools. Figure 3 shows the overlap and resulting abilities of capabilities and intentions.

Also, the intentions can vary from exploration to targeted exfiltration. The intention of the attacker and their capabilities will alter the impact assessment. The intention of the attack is the reason the attack was launched. Intention is mostly a post-event action; it is often difficult to determine what the intent of the attack is while it is in progress. It is usually forensic in nature and the defender cleans up the damage and sees what was accessed. Of course, denial of service attacks or service interruption attacks are different and the intention is usually apparent.

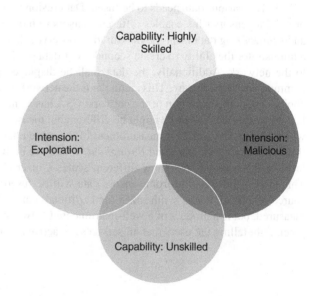

Fig. 3 Inference and anti-inference

Anti-inferences are the tools the defender has to attempt to determine the intentions and capabilities of the attacker. This is not a honey pot that is used to trap traffic. It is a shadow pot that is used to consume traffic, and not give the attacker any additional knowledge. The traffic enters the shadow pot and the attacker does not receive a return. The defender on the other hand sees the techniques that the attacker is using and has the ability to analyze the various attacks.

7 Towards Achieving Effective Cyber Situational Awareness

CSA can be executed by gaining awareness of network, threats, and the mission or operation. Having a current and valid representation of these three items will yield situation recognition. Situation recognition (SR) gives the SA at a specific point in time. The condition of the network, the threats currently being deployed, and finally the current needs of the mission/operation are the elements needed for SA. Collecting enough SR points will yield ECSA (Fig. 4).

The methodology is to gain a deeper SR. The goal is to know as much as possible about the network, which includes the action, reason, intent, and value of the event. If a disk access happened, was that due to a legitimate query? Was it to access data that the process should have access to? Does that process's access carry more value than another?

7.1 Use Case: ECSA

In this section, an operational use case will be outlined using the previously discussed tools and objectives. The first step will be to gather the awareness required and perform the threat analysis. Then, an ECSA picture will be created. Finally, the scenarios will be run through to show the various possible outcomes.

This ECSA will give the analyst the various defense options and the associated impact assessment based on a change in network posture. The impact of the posture change on the operation/mission capabilities will be highlighted. Leads given to the

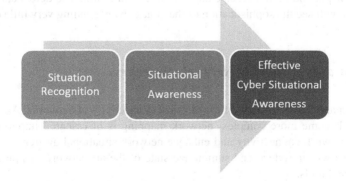

Fig. 4 Towards effective cyber situational awareness

analyst/defender will help them make better choices, or optimize the defense based on mission criteria.

This can be achieved by examining the lifecycle of CSA. The lifecycle of CSA consists of network awareness (discovery and valuation of assets), threat awareness, and network status prediction. Figure 4 shows the generic process flow of this lifecycle.

Discovery is the event where SA is informed about the current elements in the network and their associated status. This act is called enumeration. After enumeration, the current overall status of the network is discovered. This includes things like current attacks and service level. In order to move from SA to ECSA, the analyst needs context. Status context can be achieved by adding historic data to the SA picture. If the network was attacked 2 months ago by attack A, then B, then C, and it is currently being attacked by attack B after attack A has been observed, ECSA will highlight the fact that attack C is likely.

Threat enumeration is the act of applying possible attacks vs. likely attack vs. efficient attacks against the network. These attacks can originate from inside of the network (by disgruntled employee, attacker who has gained physical access, etc.), which is a reason to place more emphasis on ECSA. Most networks have defenses in place to mitigate the majority of the external network threats and attacks which are more common. ECSA is needed for the times that these external attacks cause degradation in network service level or operational readiness.

The final piece of the puzzle is prediction. SA will have the status of the network at the current time. ECSA will give the status of the network in the near and distant futures, which are plotted using likely attacks and likely responses. These views of the current and near future states of the network enable the analysts and defenders to plan posture changes. The far future or post posture change scenario prognosticates the status of the network given these changes, which will finally present the analyst and defender with the best available views to make network changes too.

Additionally, the network defenders have the inferences and anti-inferences tools. While the attack is underway, the defenders can start making inferences of the capabilities and intentions of the attacks. This is used as an input to the impact assessment of the various postures and to predict how the attacker will react to the change in the network's defense. The network can have shadow pots placed in attack pressure points to determine how the attacker reacts to them. This is an imbalanced trade-off for the attacker because they have to expend resources to understand the shadow pot and do not receive any useful data in return. The defenders on the other hand will see the sophistication of the attacks by expending very little effort.

7.2 Towards Achieving Network Awareness

Network mapping is the study of the physical connectivity of networks. As today's networks become more complex, network mapping is of essential importance to discover network connectivity and enhance network situational awareness. In this section, we will introduce and summarize state-of-the-art network mapping technologies and tools.

7.2.1 Review of Current Network Mapping Tool

General-Purpose Network Mapping Tool, Nmap

Nmap (Network Mapper) is a free general-purpose network mapping tool that has been widely used in the network community. Nmap supports a variety of scanning techniques and has been used for recent Internet-wide survey research. Nmap is designed with the following functionalities: (i) Host discovery: Identifying hosts on a network, e.g., listing (the IP address of) hosts that respond to TCP/UDP requests or have a particular port open. (ii) Port scanning: Enumerating the open ports on target hosts, such as port 80 (HTTP) and ports 20/21 (FTP). (iii) Version detection: Interrogating network services on remote devices to determine application name and version number. (iv) Operating system detection: Determining the operating system and hardware characteristics of network devices. In addition, Nmap can provide additional information on a targeted machine, such as device types and MAC-layer addresses.

To reliably detect a host, Nmap maintains a state for the connection to the host, and retransmits a probe packet if the previous one times out. Nmap also adapts its probe packets transmission rate to avoid saturating the upstream or target networks. Such a mechanism in Nmap ensures that it can reliably discover a host, but on the other hand it substantially reduces the scanning speed. It has been shown that Nmap usually spends tens of days to finish scanning all the IPv4 address space in the Internet.

The main focus of Nmap is on probing network hosts. Therefore, it does not provide full-fledged network management functions, such as network topology discovery, network leakage detection, and device profiling.

Nmap initially comes only with console commands. Zenmap is the official Nmap GUI developed for multiple platforms such as Linux, Microsoft Windows, Mac OS and Solaris.

Fast Internet Scanning Tool, ZMap

ZMap (Zmap—The Internet Scanner) is a recent open source network scanner developed by the University of Michigan. Compared with Nmap, ZMap features a much faster IPv4 scanning speed, and is capable of performing a complete scan of the IPv4 address space for a particular port number in under 45 min, approaching the theoretical limit of gigabit Ethernet.

ZMap is designed for fast IPv4 scanning over Linux or Berkeley Software Distribution (BSD). ZMap is stateless compared with Nmap which maintains the state for each connection. ZMap does not initiate a real TCP connection nor does it maintain a state for each probe packet. It simply crafts a TCP connection packet and sends it out immediately to the Ethernet, bypassing the network stack processing in the operating system.

Because of the stateless probing feature, the estimated time for ZMap to execute an Internet-wide scan with two probe packets for each host is 2 h 12 min (Durumeric et al. 2013). Thus, it is an extremely fast tool for network scanning.

It is worth noting that there are two assumptions behind the efficient use of ZMap: (i) No bandwidth limit on upstream networks: ZMap sends probe packets as fast as possible. Thus, it assumes that an upstream network provider can offer or match the network speed that ZMap is sending at. If the network provider imposes a bandwidth limit, ZMap has no way to know whether a large number of probe packets are being dropped by the network provider due to traffic or congestion control. ZMap does provide a rate control interface, through which a user can specify the scanning rate, at the level of Gbps, Mbps, or Kbps. It is assumed that the user must choose a rate that matches the upstream network provider's speed control. (ii) Linux admin privilege: ZMap is currently designed for Linux. Most popular Linux distributions require admin privilege to use raw sockets. Therefore, a user has to be elevated (at least temporarily) to admin to run ZMap in Linux.

The only goal of ZMap is to ensure the fastest scanning in the IPv4 address space in the Internet. It only supports TCP/IPv4 and does not support IPv6, or any network topology discovery or management functions. It cannot find any other information (e.g. fingerprinting) of a host, such as operating system and MAC address.

Commercial Products for Network Mapping

Nmap and ZMap are free network mapping and scanning tools ready for immediate download and use. There are several commercial products with more network management features, including:

- IPsonar: A product suite that is based on technology that first mapped the Internet. IPsonar is meant for large enterprise networks of greater than 5,000 nodes. The patented technology discovers and maps every IP connected device on the network, giving a clear view of risks and policy violations arising from network change.
- SolarWinds: SolarWinds provides a product called Network Topology Mapper (NTM) which automatically discovers every device on the network, including routers, switches, servers, wireless AP's, VoIP phones, desktops, and printers.
- WhatsUpGold: A network management suite with similar capabilities as SolarWinds, WhatsUpGold works at a layer 2 and 3 level and supports discovery of IPv6 devices. It can discover all devices on the network including port-to-port connectivity.
- OpManager: A comprehensive network monitoring software that provides an integrated console for managing routers, firewalls, servers, switches, and printers. Its network scanning is based on either ICMP pings or Nmap.

These commercial products for network mapping offer comprehensive GUIs with an extensive set of network management capabilities for network administers to discover and handle network events. We compare the features of these products in Table 1 in terms of (i) IPv6 support, (ii) reliance on dedicated hardware (for scanning), (iii) virtual device detection, (iv) geo location mapping (that correlates an IP to a geographical location), (v) network topology discovery (that detects the topology of the network where the scanner is), and (vi) reliance on the software (which means that it uses other software to finish the network scanning function).

Table 1 Comparisons of commercial network mapping tools

	Detecting IPv6 devices	Reliance on dedicated hardware	Virtual device detection	Geo location mapping	Network topology discovery	Reliance on other software
IPSonar	Yes	No	Yes	Yes	Yes	No
SolarWinds	Yes	Yes	Yes	Yes	Yes	No
WhatsUpGold	Yes	No	Yes	Yes	Yes	No
OPManager	Yes	No	Yes	Yes	Yes	Yes

From Table 1 we can see that all commercial products support virtual device detection, geo location mapping and network topology discovery. However, IPsonar currently provides less information on IPv6 enabled nodes compared with IPv4 enabled nodes. SolarWinds only runs under Microsoft Windows with dedicated hardware, and its scanning speed is slow. WhatsUpGold supports a variety of functions, but has limited mapping outputs. OpManager's scanning function relies on Nmap.

Network mapping tools are an essential part of network SA toolsets. From such tools, analysts can obtain valuable and updated information about their network assets and connectivity. However, current mapping tools lack in one critical aspect of mapping IPv6 topology and assessing security breaches via comparing IPv6 and IPv4 topologies against pre-defined security policies (which in most cases are determined upon IPv4 configurations).

7.2.2 From Network Mapping to Network Awareness

IPv6 is the next generation protocol designed to replace current IPv4 protocol. However, IPv4 is so successful and widely deployed today that it will take a very long time for IPv6 to replace IPv4 completely. Many IPv6 transition mechanisms are proposed to facilitate the transition to IPv6 protocol. IPv6 transition mechanisms typically adopt dual-stack nodes and various tunneling techniques to enable IPv6 networks to coexist with IPv4 networks. The dual-stack nodes are nodes that support both IPv4 and IPv6 protocols. Tunneling techniques encapsulate IPv6 packets in IPv4 packets for delivery across IPv4 network infrastructure. However, due to the different security assumptions between IPv6 and IPv4 protocols, IPv6 transition mechanisms may generate security problems if configured inappropriately.

IPv6 transition mechanisms may hurt or even nullify the security mechanisms adopted in IPv4 networks. Many security tools were designed for IPv4 networks, and the deployment of dual-stack nodes and tunnels in networks may invalidate the assumptions adopted in these security tools. For example, many IDS systems are deployed in some critical locations in networks to detect port scan attacks against network hosts. If the victim host is a dual-stack node, TCP port scanning packets, such as TCP SYNs, can be sent as IPv6 packets, which are then encapsulated as UDP packets. The UDP packets can pass the IDS for port scan without triggering any alarm. Additionally, the traffic generated by dual-stack nodes and tunnels can penetrate firewalls deployed in networks. Most firewalls, NAT (network address translation) devices or filters do not block UDP traffic initialized by inside hosts. Some IPv6 transition mechanisms, such as the Teredo protocol, encapsulate IPv6 packets in IPv4 UDP packets, which can easily pass these security checks.

Moreover, IPv6 transition mechanisms may also be exploited to evade the security checks in IPv4 networks. For example, the IPv6 routing header, in conjunction with tunneling techniques can be used to evade the IPv4 security checkpoints deployed in networks. The attacker can encapsulate an IPv6 packet within an IPv4 UDP packet and send it to a tunnel-enabled node. UDP traffic can pass most firewalls or NAT devices. Once the tunnel-enabled node receives the packet, it will extract the IPv6 packet and process the IPv6 packet in its IPv6 stack. If the IPv6 packet contains the routing header, then it will be forwarded to the nodes that it is not allowed to visit otherwise.

IPv6 transition mechanisms are ubiquitous and almost inevitable. Many software products already support IPv6 transition mechanisms. If there exists an IPv6 subnet within the organization network, IPv6 transition mechanisms are necessary for these IPv6 subnets to access network services provided by IPv4 networks. Simply shutting down IPv6 transition mechanisms in today's network is not an option. In addition, IPv6 transition mechanisms are easy to configure. Users can configure their computers with some IPv6 transition mechanisms on their own. For example, the tunneling mechanism can be enabled automatically by software installed in the computer or by a mistaken configuration. However, the users may have no authorization or sufficient security knowledge to take the security measures necessary to secure the configured tunneling interface. It is impractical for the network administrator to guarantee that every node in networks is well configured.

It is very difficult to evaluate potential security consequences caused by IPv6 transition mechanisms in networks, due to the following reasons:

1. IPv6 transition mechanisms create a complex network topology. The deployment of IPv6 transition mechanisms in a network generates two topologies: IPv4 topology and IPv6 topology. The tunnel between two dual-stack nodes essentially adds a link between these two nodes in the perspective of IPv6, but does not affect the IPv4 topology at all.
2. The IPv4 topology and IPv6 topology of networks are dynamic. The topology dynamics of networks are caused by many factors. The deployment of dual-stack nodes changes the network topology. The newly deployed dual-stack nodes can potentially communicate with all other dual-stack nodes, and generate more tunnels in the networks, thus changing the IPv6 topology. Software updates may also change the network topology—when a user updates the software to a newer version, the user may inadvertently transform an IPv4-only node into a dual-stack node, thus changing the IPv6 topology.
3. The consequences caused by IPv6 transition mechanisms in networks are not determined only by network topology, but also by the applications running on networks, and/or missions supported by these applications. For example, a web server is usually deployed in a Demilitarized Zone (DMZ) for public access. Generally speaking, it is harmless for the web server to be configured as a dual-stack node.

However, if some application running on the web server is allowed to access a critical database deployed behind a firewall via UDP traffic, then the configuration of such a web server as a dual-stack node can be potentially exploited to set up a tunnel across the DMZ. Validation of IPv6 transition mechanisms and associated risk analysis must be conducted in the context of the network level, application level and mission level.

It is infeasible to assume that the network administrators have enough time, energy and knowledge to handle all these problems. The following approaches can assist in developing capabilities to address these challenging problems:

- Obtain a thorough understanding of the state-of-the-art tools that can be leveraged to obtain accurate and efficient measurement of network topologies, for both IPv4 and IPv6 networks.
- Select and leverage appropriate probing techniques, as much as possible, to detect the connectivity among nodes in various network configurations. Examples of probes include ICMP-based probe packets, TCP-based and UDP-based probe packets. This is important since networking devices and hosts may respond differently (or even not respond) to the same probing packets, and combining different probes increases the hit rate.
- Resolve IP address aliases. A networking device (e.g., a router) in networks may possess multiple IP addresses, called aliases. It is necessary to map the aliases to the physical node in order to generate the correct topology.
- "Fingerprint" the enumerated nodes via leveraging Nmap to obtain system configuration information such as operating system, version number, available services, etc.
- Develop specific techniques to detect the existence of automatically or manually configured tunnels for IPv6 transition mechanisms. For example, intercepting traffic can assist in capturing Teredo packets, generated by the Teredo protocol and detecting automatic tunneling. To detect manually configured tunnels, (specifically crafted) probe packets can be sent into the patch between two IPv6 subnets to check if there exists a configured tunnel.
- Establish a test bed of scale (that is representative of the network in question) to verify that the system can effectively generate network topologies, detect dual-stack nodes and various tunnels.

7.3 Towards Achieving Threat/Attack Awareness

7.3.1 Capturing Threats and Attacks with Graphical Models

In order to effectively evaluate the impacts, and assess the damages of threats and attacks in a network, Attack Graphs (AG) (Amman et al. 2002; Jajodia et al. 2003; Sheyner et al. 2002) have become a widely adopted technology recently in analyzing the casual relationships between attack events and evaluating the potential impact of multi-step attacks. In a typical AG, each node represents a particular state of a host, and each edge represents a possible state transition. The discovered network topologies and node configuration serve as one base to generate such AG models.

However, existing AG techniques have very limited capability in assessing the cyber impacts on a high level mission, as they cannot directly represent the dependency relationship between missions and the corresponding cyber assets. Another limitation of existing AG techniques is that they are not scalable and practical for use with large-scale networks.

To address these limitations, our team has developed an efficient AG model during our previous efforts for Army Research Office (ARO) and Air Force Research Lab (AFRL). The key idea of our AG model lies in the differentiation of the *Type Abstract Graph (TAG)*, the *Network Attack Graph (NAG)*, and the *Real-time Attack Graph (RAG)*. These attack graph models have been developed into a software toolkit, called "NIRVANA" that can automatically generate TAG with the most updated vulnerability entries, and derive network reachability from the imported network configuration files and the firewall rules. Based on TAG and the (computed) network reachability, NIRVANA can automatically generate a corresponding NAG for static security analysis. When a real attack happens, NIRVANA can automatically generate the RAG (triggered by IDS alerts) for dynamic security analysis and damage assessment.[1]

In particular, TAG models the abstract exploit scenarios that include the dependency relationships among prerequisites, exploits, and effects. It is not specific to any network, and serves as a base for generating a network-specific AG. In our team's approach, the TAG is generated by transforming more than 30,000 public CVE records (Common Vulnerabilities and Exposures) into a specific class of generic vulnerability graphical model. Figure 5 shows an example of the generated TAGs.

Given a network setup (for example, the discovered network topologies and configurations), we can create another AG to capture both the exploit dependency and the actual network reachability. Such a derived AG is called a *Network Attack Graph (NAG)*. NAG can be generated through offline operations, by using specific network configurations to instantiate the abstract TAGs. NAG is particularly useful for static security analysis for a given network, which covers most of the needs mentioned in Sect. 4. Figure 6 shows an example of the generated NAGs.

Threat Awareness Based on the NAG, one can answer questions such as whether a particular exploit can exist, the current security posture of the network, the weakest point in the network, and the course of action in terms of which assets to harden first.

Attack Awareness To analyze the received attacks, a RAG can also be generated. In our model, when observed evidence (e.g., IDS alert) is captured, a RAG is triggered to be generated. RAGs are constructed through online operations, which facilitate the (near) real-time security analysis and damage assessment. Figure 7 shows an example the generated RAGs.

---

[1] Patent pending on the process of creation and utilization of TAG, NAG, and RAG.

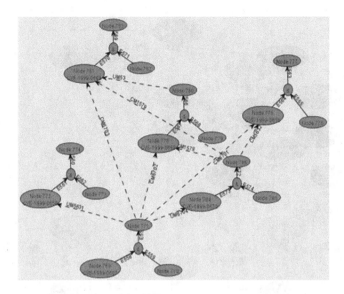

Fig. 5 An example type abstract graph (TAG)

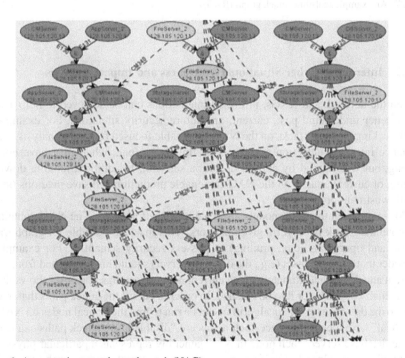

Fig. 6 An example network attack graph (NAG)

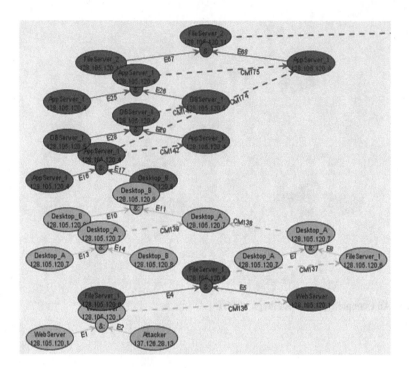

Fig. 7 An example real-time attack graph (RAG)

7.3.2 Interactive Cyber Situational Awareness and Impact Analysis

Given the network and RAGs, informed interactions can be achieved to help analysts better understand past, current, and future security situations. For example, backtracking current attacks on the NAG can enable focused forensics analysis, and enhance intrusion detection accuracy and timeliness (e.g., what must have gone wrong, but was missed by current detection sensors). In addition, looking downstream of current attacks on the NAG can enable prediction and save precious time for downstream protection.

More importantly, such models also enable what-if analysis. The NAG contains all potential attack paths for a given network. This makes it possible for graph traversal and operations (e.g., pruning) to possess security semantics. For example, consider that a critical asset (e.g., the database server) should not be reached from the current attack, but unfortunately given current network settings, the NAG shows that it is actually possible for it to be reached. In order to cut off the attack paths that may lead to the database server, an algorithm can be run to find the critical nodes on NAG. "Critical" here means that once such nodes are "disabled," no attack paths can lead to the database server. Each node in NAG generally represents a particular physical host with some vulnerabilities in some services (e.g., email services, web services).

One can use a software tool (the author team has developed such a tool) to visualize the graphs, and show the effects of "disabling" services on selected nodes, in terms of future potential attack paths.

7.3.3   State and Predictive Scenario Playback

CSA needs the ability to playback various network events by using a saved condition. Additionally, the ability to quickly generate scenarios and test them against each other is needed. The analysts need the ability to preserve the state of the network for running experiments and predicting outcomes of various defense scenarios. Analysts need the ability to look at historic events to determine their applicability to the current situation. The data needs to be presented in a way that is common and customizable to each defender or team. Finally, the ability to quickly generate scenarios and run them is needed.

The authors have developed a software system, called Hermes, which aims to achieve such goals. Since the state of the network is saved at specific points in time, the defenders can go back for "after action" analysis and experiment with different defense postures and examine the resultant ECSA. For example, a good starting place would be to see why the IDS failed to observe the initial infection for some attack scenarios. The details of this software tool are omitted due to space limitation.

7.4   Towards Achieving Mission/Operational Awareness

Essentially, mission decomposition will provide users with an efficient interface to transform a complex mission or operation into a set of specific, more manageable tasks. On the other hand, the mission-to-asset mapping will automatically identify the corresponding network components and cyber assets that are required to carry out the intended mission and tasks.

We assume that a complex global *mission* can be divided into a set of simplified *sub-missions* or *tasks* that have to be performed. If all the specified tasks are performed, it is concluded that the mission has been successfully achieved. Additionally, there are two types of tasks in our model, namely, *compound* and *primitive* tasks. A primitive task is defined as a basic action that a user can perform directly. A compound task, on the other hand, is regarded as a task that is composed of primitive tasks and/or other compound tasks. Additionally, tasks in a mission are interrelated to each other by dependencies and external constraints such as time and resources. It might not be possible to perform a task until some other tasks are completed; that is, the task depends on the completion of other tasks.

Figure 8 illustrates a mission decomposition diagram, in which circles represent the compound tasks, and squares represent the primitive tasks. A compound task is composed of one or more tasks, each of which can also consist of one or more compound or primitive tasks. The root node M0 is regarded as the mission itself. M0

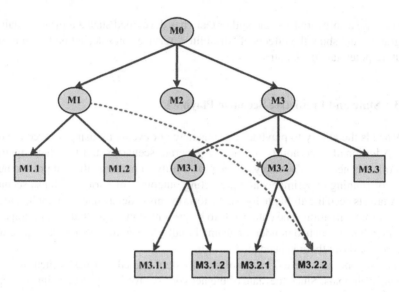

Fig. 8 Mission decomposition diagram

is said to be achieved, if and only if tasks M1, M2, and M3 are completed. In turn, task M3 is completed only if tasks M3.1, M3.2, and M3.3 are completed. In this diagram, dependencies are represented by dashed-arrows in a mission decomposition diagram. Task T1 is said to be dependent on task T2 if there is a dashed arrow drawn from T1 to T2. Taking this notion into account, we can say that in Fig. 8, task M1 depends on task M3.2.2 and task M3.1 depends on task M3.2. This means that task M1 cannot be executed until task M3.2.2 has been executed. Subsequently, task M3.1 cannot be carried out until task M3.2 has been completed. Task dependencies are important aspects that have to be captured in a mission because they represent real-world situations.

7.4.1 Mission Mapping and Integration with Attack Graphs

A mission asset map is designed to capture and represent the dependency between high-level missions and the underlying cyber networks. Generally speaking, each mission carried out in a network depends on certain cyber operations that are further supported by particular network segment and/or cyber assets. In order to identify the specific dependency between a mission and the related cyber assets, we need to decompose a complex mission into a set of manageable tasks which can be directly supported by some network component (e.g., a computer or server) or cyber service (e.g., email, web, FTP). It is clear that different missions have different asset maps.

We briefly classify the cyber assets into three categories: *hosts* (e.g., servers, desktops, hand-held devices), *switches* (e.g., routers, firewalls, VPN equipment, base stations.), and *communication links* (e.g., wired and wireless). Each host or switch can be viewed as an atomic unit of the mission, whose identification (e.g., host name, IP address) and associated information (e.g., location, user) will be marked on the map. Physical connections between hosts are marked as an edge on the map. In addition, each switch could be associated with a connectivity table showing the (allowed) logical connections among various hosts.

Mission asset maps will be used to bridge the gap between mission descriptions and low-level attack events. For this purpose, we need to embed a novel set of information items into mission asset maps, and glue AGs and mission asset maps together.

One of the core requirements is to efficiently and accurately map various cyber assets to the intended missions and tasks. Essentially, to assess the impacts of a compromised/degraded cyber asset, network administrators need to know: (i) Where is the attacked asset? (ii) Whose/what job is relying on the attacked asset? (iii) What organizational mission is impacted? and (iv) What other cyber assets or network capabilities will be affected?

Due to the lack of contextual information, it is hard for today's administrators to answer the above questions. If we assume that some domain knowledge or initial information about the intended mission is present, this information can help us identify some required assets to execute the mission. For instance, mission commanders can briefly divide a complex mission into a set of operational tasks, and give operators an initial asset assignment for each task. Based on such information, we can at least identify some host-level assets required for a mission. For example, if we know that in Mission A, User B needs to contact Customer C via Email, it is not hard to identify that *User B's Computer* and *Email Server* will be required for this mission. Then, from these two assets, we can automatically derive other required host-level cyber assets based on the network topology and reachability analysis.

After identifying the mission-related cyber assets in a network, the next step is to carry out impact assessment and security analysis. In AG models, each node represents a particular state of a host, and each edge represents a possible state transition. This graphical model has limited capability in assessing the cyber impacts on high-level missions. Therefore, we need to find an efficient way to associate the derived mission asset maps (MAP) with the AGs. Essentially, a three-step process can be utilized to glue AGs and associated MAPs together: (i) incorporate MAPs with state information present in the AGs; (ii) incorporate MAPs with exploit event information; and (iii) merge AGs into MAPs. The details of this process are omitted here for brevity.

7.4.2 Mission Awareness via Graphical Models

With integrated missions and attacks, the graphical modes can fundamentally facilitate mission awareness and decision making via graph traversal algorithms. For example, before attacks, analysis algorithms can be carried out on the integrated graphs and answer questions such as:

- What are the weakest security points in my network?
- Which missions could be affected by these weak points?
- If we harden such cyber assets, what benefits will be obtained for mission success?

In addition, given current attacks, the following questions can be answered readily:

- Which applications and missions are affected by the attacks, and how severely?
- What is the overall security and mission assurance posture?

Furthermore, decision support can be provided via what-if analysis throughout the cyber related graphs and the mission graphs, again via graph traversal. For example, expanding the case described in Sect. 7.3.2, one can answer questions regarding the impact of what-if ideas (related to disabling some cyber services) on missions.

Considering all the factors in the attack and mission graphs, and combing cyber asset and policy information, one can formulate decision-making problems and solve such problems with optimal course of action to provide decision support.

7.4.3 Mission Asset Prioritization

To focus limited resources on the most critical cyber assets, network components need to be prioritized based on their criticality in support of mission assurance. The prioritization can be based on the severity analysis of the impacts caused by a cyber-attack. Given the mission asset map and critical values of the assets, many candidate decision algorithms can be used for prioritization. One example is the Analytic Hierarchy Process (AHP) for risk analysis and cyber asset prioritization.

The procedure of the prioritization can be summarized as follows:

1. Model the problem as a hierarchy containing the decision goal, the alternatives, and the criteria.
2. Establish priorities among the elements based on pair-wise comparisons.
3. Synthesize judgments to yield a set of overall priorities for the hierarchy.
4. Check the consistency of the judgments.
5. Come to a final decision.

Figure 9 illustrates a simple example, in which three assets (i.e., desktop A, Router H and Database P) need to be prioritized based on three factors: *mission relevance, attack risk* and *asset value*. Suppose that attack risk and mission relevance are both twice as important as asset value, a pair-wise comparison matrix can be used to decide the proper weights for each factor. In this case, the weights for attack risk and mission relevance are set to 0.4, and the weight for asset value is set to 0.2. Each asset has a vector to specify its relative value corresponding to the three factors, which is used to calculate the asset's criticality based on the weighted factors. Figure 9 shows the prioritizing result of the three assets, in which Database P was the preferred entity, with a priority of 0.715. It was ten times as strong as Desktop A, whose priority was 0.07. Router H fell somewhere in between. Therefore, Database P is the most critical asset in this case, and it should be well protected from potential attacks to assure mission success.

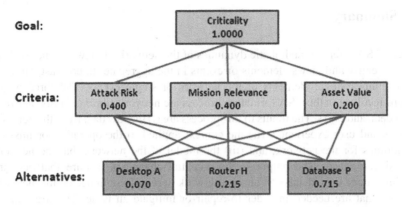

Fig. 9 Prioritization of cyber assets with AHP

8 Future Directions

There are several challenges ahead to realizing ECSA. Three issues at the forefront are: software defined networking (SDN), adoption of encrypted and anonymous services, and contextually aware services.

SDN moves the control panel out of the network's data panel. This enables the network to be altered very quickly. The network's configuration resides on a separate bus, which enables control of the normal processing of the network from outside. This presents several challenges to ECSA: (i) New methods of enumerating the network will need to be developed, as the network can be constantly changing. (ii) Attacks/service interruptions can now happen on two separate panels, which makes troubleshooting more difficult. (iii) Finally, network changes may experience a "butterfly effect." On a positive note, SDN networks can respond to posture changes much more quickly, which will make service levels more robust.

The wide spread adoption of encrypted and anonymous services has become problematic for network operators seeking to limit this type of traffic. The developers of these encrypted and anonymous services are in an arms race with the people attempting to block the service. These services present a challenge to ECSA, because the services are simply unknown. The network does not know if the traffic is malicious or if a user is covering their tracks. ECSA can simply record the relays, bridges, and users, which can be displayed as consumed bandwidth.

Contextually aware services use some derived or calculated data to aid in the richness of the experience delivered to the user. Examples include using the user's current location to serve traffic data or suggesting searches based on open applications. This ubiquitous computing becomes a challenge for ECSA due to the pervasive nature of the data collection. Context aware services often query the device for details about OS version, location, current tasking, etc. This can provide attackers with more knowledge than the network defenders would like exposed.

9 Summary

"Macro" SA refers to the holistic dynamics of the network. It views the network as a single entity and views elements or events in the aggregate. In contrast, "micro" SA examines single elements of the network or single events. The three major groups involved in the CSA formation process are network administrators, network defenders, and users. The inputs to this process are (i) the raw data from the network sensors and user experience, (ii) the context applied to the operation or mission capabilities for the network, and (iii) the model of the network that the network administrator uses. The output is the potential change in posture that network administrators should take to ensure network services continue, or the network changes that are needed in order to repair or mitigate an issue. The lifecycle of Cyber Analysts' SA includes three steps: network, threat or attack, and operational or mission awareness. The process of gaining network awareness includes discovery and enumeration of assets and of Defense capabilities. Threat and attack awareness consists of a current picture of possible attacks and vectors against the network in question. Operation and mission awareness is a picture of how decreased or degraded network operations will affect the mission of the network. Effective CSA (ECSA) is CSA that improves decision-making, collaboration, and resource management. The key concepts in ECSA are giving a predicted SA picture based on possible actions and integrating sensor data to a unified and current view. The elements that enable ECSA include: Tomography measures the internals of the network by using information taken from end-to-end link data; Route Analytics analyzes the routing protocols in a network; and Protocol Monitoring checks the standard protocols for speed and correctness. Inferences are estimations of the capabilities of an attacker, along with the attacker's intentions. Anti-inferences are the tools the defender has to attempt to determine the intentions and capabilities of the attacker. Network mapping is essential to discover network connectivity and enhance network situational awareness. State-of-the-art network mapping technologies and tools, such as Nmap and Zmap, can be useful. Attack graphs underline the models called the Type Abstract Graph (TAG), the Network Attack Graph (NAG), and the Real-time Attack Graph (RAG). These attack graph models have been developed into a software toolkit, called "NIRVANA" that can automatically generate TAG with the most updated vulnerability entries, and derive network reachability from the imported network configuration files and the firewall rules. Based on TAG and the (computed) network reachability, NIRVANA can automatically generate a corresponding NAG for static security analysis. When a real attack happens, NIRVANA can automatically generate the RAG (triggered by IDS alerts) for dynamic security analysis and damage assessment. A mission asset map is designed to capture and represent the dependency between high-level missions and the underlying cyber networks. Network components need to be prioritized based on their criticality in support of mission assurance. The prioritization can be based on the severity analysis of the impacts caused by a cyber-attack. Given the mission asset map and critical values of the assets, an algorithm such as the Analytic Hierarchy Process (AHP) can be applied for risk analysis and cyber asset prioritization.

References

Amman, P., Wijesekera, D., & Kaushik, S. (2002). Scalable, graph-based network vulnerability analysis. *Proc. of 9th ACM Conference on Computer and Communications Security.*

Durumeric, Z., Wustrow, E., & Halderman, J. (2013). ZMap: Fast Internet-wide Scanning and its Security Applications. *Proc. of USENIX Security Symposium.*

Endsley, M. (1995). Toward a theory of situation awareness in dynamic systems. *Human Factors*, 32-64.

Force, D. o. (2010). *Cyberspace Operations (Topline Coordination Draft v4).* Washington: HQ USAF.

Hoogendoorn, M., van Lambalgen, R., & Trur, J. (2011). Modeling Situation Awareness in Human-Like Agents Using Mental Models. *Proceeding of International Joint Conference on Artificial Intelligence.*

Jajodia, S., Noel, S., & O'Berry, B. (2003). Topological analysis of network attack vulnerability. In *Managing Cyber Threats: Issues, Approaches and Challenges.* Kluwer Academic.

Sheyner, O., Haines, J., Jha, S., Lippmann, R., & Wing, J. (2002). Automated generation and analysis of attack graphs. *Proc. of the IEEE Symposium on Security and Privacy*, (pp. 254–265).

Xie, P., Li, J., Ou, X., Liu, P., & Levy, R. (2010). Using Bayesian Networks for Cyber Security Analysis. *Proc of IEEE DSN.*

Cognition and Technology

Cleotilde Gonzalez, Noam Ben-Asher, Alessandro Oltramari, and Christian Lebiere

1 Introduction

As the previous chapters emphasized, the human cognition—and the technology necessary to support it—are central to Cyber Situational Awareness. Therefore, this chapter focuses on challenges and approaches to integration of information technology and computational representations of human situation awareness. To illustrate these aspects of CSA, the chapter uses the process of intrusion detection as a key example. We argue that effective development of technologies and processes that produce CAS in a way properly aligned with human cognition calls for cognitive models—dynamic and adaptable computational representations of the cognitive structures and mechanisms involved in developing SA and processing information for decision making. While visualization and machine learning are often seen among the key approaches to enhancing CSA, we point out a number of limitations in their current state of development and applications to CSA. The current knowledge gaps in our understanding of cognitive demands in CSA include the lack of a theoretical model of cyber SA within a cognitive architecture; the decision gap, representing learning, experience and dynamic decision making in the cyberspace; and the

C. Gonzalez (✉)
Social and Decision Sciences Department, Carnegie Mellon University,
5000 Forbes Ave, Porter Hall 208, Pittsburgh, PA 15213, USA
e-mail: coty@cmu.edu

N. Ben-Asher
Dynamic Decision Making Laboratory, Social and Decision Sciences Department,
Carnegie Mellon University, Pittsburgh, USA
e-mail: noamba@cmu.edu

A. Oltramari • C. Lebiere
Department of Psychology, Carnegie Mellon University, Pittsburgh, USA
e-mail: aoltrama@andrew.cmu.edu; cl@cmu.edu

© Springer International Publishing Switzerland 2014
A. Kott et al. (eds.), *Cyber Defense and Situational Awareness*,
Advances in Information Security 62, DOI 10.1007/978-3-319-11391-3_6

semantic gap, addressing the construction of a common language and a set of basic concepts about which the security community can develop a shared understanding.

Far from being downgraded to interconnected computer technologies that constitute its physical substratum, cyberspace can be seen as a communication infrastructure built by humans to access and share information in real-time by means of a variety of interfaces and languages. In this regard, "cyberspace is defined as much by the cognitive realm as by the physical or digital" (Singer and Friedman 2014). The centrality of cognition in the cyber world is clearly illustrated in the process of detection, where a human analyst (i.e., a defender) is responsible for protecting client networks from illegal intrusions and hostile activity (i.e., cyber attack) that would jeopardize the integrity of its information and infrastructure. The detection process may be seen as analogous to the Data-Information-Knowledge-Wisdom (DIKW) hierarchical model that is central for information and knowledge management (Rowley 2007). In the DIKW model, often depicted as a pyramid, a hierarchical process is proposed where data is transformed into information, information into knowledge, and knowledge into wisdom.

Figure 1 illustrates this process for Detection. The existence of multiple and diverse sensors result in a large amount of network activity data. Cyber security tools (e.g., Intrusion Detection Systems, IDS) are meant to organize and structure network activity to make it relevant, meaningful and useful to support traffic monitoring and to minimize the damage that an attack can cause. Cyber security technologies provide ways to facilitate and protect an analyst from the cognitive challenges that the cyber world presents. For example, it does so by reducing, filtering and organizing large amounts of network events and by preprocessing events to help reduce the information workload of the human analyst. These technologies would help in

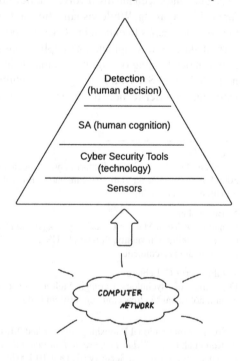

Fig. 1 The detection process

improving the analyst's Situation Awareness (SA): an accurate perception of the elements in the network within a volume of time and space, the comprehension of their meaning, and the projection of their future status (Endsley 1988). However, SA is rarely integrated into technology that would combine information with understanding and capability. Although there are multiple critical technologies to support an analyst in intrusion detection, they are often static and do not adapt to the analyst's state of mind and SA. Furthermore, SA is not an end in itself but rather the means by which analysts can make informed decisions in these complex, fast moving situations. SA is a precondition to make accurate intrusion detection decisions.

To properly design dynamic, adaptive technologies that support the detection process, one needs a strong, quantitative, validated model of the human cognitive processes. Otherwise, the result is often a system that works at counter-purposes with the human user, such as the infamous Microsoft paperclip that constantly changed the ordering of information in menus in a futile attempt to optimize physical movements at the greater cognitive cost to the user of constantly having to relearn a new interface.

Cognitive models are dynamic and adaptable computational representations of the cognitive structures and mechanisms involved in developing SA and processing information for decision making. Cognitive modeling technologies have been developed in the context of the cognitive sciences, which rely on theories of mind that allow for the construction of generative models to be eventually tested against behavioral, physiological, and neural data. The advantage of cognitive models[1] resides in their ability to dynamically learn from experience, to adjust to new inputs, environments, and tasks in similar ways as humans do, and to predict performance in situations that haven't been encountered and for which data is not yet available. In this regard, cognitive models differ from purely statistical approaches, such as machine learning, that are often capable of evaluating only stable, long-term sequential dependencies from existing data but fail to account for the dynamics of human cognition, including learning processes and short-term sequential dependencies (Lebiere et al. 2003; West and Lebiere 2001).

Cognitive models are often built within a cognitive architecture. Cognitive architectures are computational representations of unified theories of cognition (Newell 1990). They represent the invariant mechanisms and structures of cognition, as implemented in the human brain. For example, the well-known ACT-R architecture (Anderson and Lebiere 1998; Anderson et al. 2004), discussed later, is organized as a distributed framework of modules, each devoted to processing a particular kind of information that is integrated and coordinated through a centralized production system module, which may represent the SA and decision making processes. A cognitive model of SA and decision making should represent the perception, comprehension, and projection status of the human mind, which are the preconditions to choice and decision making (Gonzalez et al. 2006). However, to build

---

[1] Note that the distinction between 'model' and 'agent' when dealing with cognitive architectures is a blurred one. In general, an agent can be conceived as a cognitive model that dynamically interacts with the environment.

a cognitive model of cyber SA, more research on the particular cognitive challenges involved in the cyber world is needed.

Research on *cyber* SA is relatively new (Jajodia et al. 2010), and it will require large amounts of collaborative work to determine how much of what is known of SA in the physical world is applicable to the cyber world. The dynamics in the cyber environment do not follow the laws of physics and are not subject to physical constraints. For example, a cyber attack does not utilize physical weapons (a gun, a knife, a bomb) that we can see, touch, or hear and for which we have good established mental models. Cyber attacks use digital weapons that are mostly indiscernible at the human level and for which we often do not have strong intuitions. A cyber attack is not limited by geography and political boundaries. In contrast to physical wars, attacks can be highly distributed, meaning that the attacker can initiate the attack from multiple places at the same time and the same cyber attack can hit multiple targets at once (Singer and Friedman 2014). Furthermore, cyberspace is highly dynamic and it is also a distributed system, "one in which the failure of a computer you didn't even know existed can render your own computer unusable" (Lamport 1987). Thus, the traditional SA triad of perception, comprehension, and projection may have very different meanings in the cyber arena.

This chapter aims at outlining current knowledge gaps in our understanding of cognitive demands in the cyber world; and to present challenges that cognitive architectures and computational approaches face in order to represent and support SA and decision making in the cyber security domain. In what follows, we discuss some particular challenges for obtaining SA and achieving optimal decision making in the cyber world. The gaps identified and discussed in the subsequent sections are: the *cognitive* gap, namely defining a theoretical model of cyber SA within a cognitive architecture; the *decision* gap, representing learning, experience and dynamic decision making in the cyberspace; the *semantic* gap, addressing the construction of a common language and a set of basic concepts about which the security community can develop a shared understanding; the *adversarial* gap, developing ways to represent adversarial behavior; and the *network* gap, scaling up models of human behavior to complex networks and cyber warfare representations. Next, we discuss existing technology developed to support the analyst and recent cognitive models of cyber SA and decision making from which new research may derive.

2 Challenges of the Cyber World and Implications for Human Cognition

In contrast to the physical world, there are many distinct cognitive challenges that a decision maker confronts in the cyber world. First, the amount of data available to the analyst is unusually large and highly diverse. This is due to the relatively inexpensive ways of collecting data (network activity) and to the number and diversity of possible data sources (each network node or piece of equipment can serve as a sensor).

Second, cyber attacks can take many forms, and each form might target different parts or services in the network. As such, an attack might be represented only in one data source or in combinations of several data sources, but not in all the data sources at the same time and in the same manner. Thus, the analyst needs to expend more effort in searching and diagnosing information to achieve the comprehension level of SA.

Third, the cyber world involves rapid and constant change. In normal day-to-day operation, changes like the maintenance of network equipment, the addition of sub-networks, and changes in services or users may be legitimate operations; however, they may also resemble signs of an attack. Furthermore, changes in network behaviors can be abrupt, drastic, and caused by both internal and external factors. For example, a sudden spike in network activity on a retailer network can be caused by an approaching holiday (external), the retailer having a sale (internal), or a cyber attack.

Fourth, the cyber SA of an analyst highly depends on the information coming from sensors (network monitoring equipment, logs, etc.). The analyst needs to constantly determine his level of trust in the sensors and whether to rely on the information coming from them; as it is not possible to directly evaluate the sensors' reliability. For example, an attacker may first compromise sensors to deceive the analyst about the status of the network before and during the attack.

Fifth, cyber attacks are adversarial digital ways of determining who gets power, wealth, and resources. Thus, beyond the SA of one individual, defenders (analysts and end users) in the cyber world need to be aware of cyber attackers. Attackers have one important advantage over defenders: they know their target and decide who, when, and how to attack. Defenders face many difficulties in identifying the origin, attribution, and goal of these attacks. In the cyber world, it becomes very difficult to determine the identity, organizational affiliation, and nationality of those sitting behind a computer with malicious intentions. Furthermore, the defender monitors the network, identifies threats, and repairs each and any vulnerability, while the attacker needs to find a single vulnerability that can be exploited. This simplified view highlights the asymmetric relationship between the defender's SA and the attacker's SA. Cyber SA for a defender, thus, must involve awareness of the attackers' SA and intentions. This is a concept that is not currently well-known in the SA literature. A good amount of research has been devoted to the concept of *Shared SA*, a requirement to perform well in teams and achieve coordination and collaboration among team members (e.g., Gorman et al. 2006; Saner et al. 2009). Shared SA represents the "degree to which team members possess the same SA on shared SA requirements" (Endsley and Jones 2001, p. 48). While the information requirements by one individual that overlap among members of a group are essential elements for shared SA in friendly situations (Saner et al. 2009), the disparity, conflict, and disagreement of information needed to successfully deceive defenders and attackers is one of the most important weapons of agents involved in a cyber war. Thus, a concept of *Adversarial* SA needs to be developed to enhance the theory and models of theory of mind in cyber settings.

In summary, given the challenges of the cyber world and their implications for human cognition outlined above, it is clear that the development of cognitive models and computational approaches to represent and support cyber SA and decision making of the analyst are only in their infancy. In the next section, we review some existing technologies aimed at representing and supporting cyber SA and the detection of cyber attacks. We also introduce the ACT-R cognitive architecture and cognitive models aimed at representing processes involved in cyber defense. In these descriptions, we highlight the current knowledge and outline how cognitive architectures and models can be used to address these gaps.

3 Technology for Supporting an Analyst in Intrusion Detection

A cyber analyst is mainly responsible for reviewing logs from various security tools and network traffic analyzers; they compile information and report incidents based on the intrusions that are detected. Given the cognitive challenges discussed above (e.g., large amounts of raw data collected by network sensors; variable speeds and workloads of events; and complex interrelationships of various elements of a network), the analyst's ability to grasp pieces of information as a coherent *whole* diminishes when dealing with a cyber environment. An important technology that helps support cyber SA and human decision making in the detection of threats and cyber attacks is the Intrusion Detection System (IDS). IDS are relatively well-established technology, and they are widely used in different settings to automatically analyze packets for signs of possible incidents and to highlight those to the human analyst. A comprehensive review of the IDS-based methodologies and technologies that are more commonly used for intrusion detection and prevention are presented by Bernardi and colleagues (2014). IDS and their derivatives are mostly rule-based systems that require knowledge of the vulnerabilities in the networks. Snort (http://www.snort.org/) is probably the most well-known IDS: it is an open source software with millions of users, and it is considered a standard capable of performing packet sniffing and real-time traffic analysis. Snort rules are supported by an active community that improves the rules and the tool's capabilities. Other open source tools such as Bro (https://www.bro.org/) offer faster network capabilities and have also increased in popularity. Bro was developed as a research platform for intrusion detection and is commonly used by the research community.

A main challenge for the analyst is that the IDS generates a large number of false alarms, from which an analyst must identify real threats. IDSs may be used in conjunction with many other tools that help human detection. Of particular interest is the development of correlation models and the estimation of relationships between suspicious events flagged by the IDS, which may help humans detect patterns, the paths of attacks, and the attackers' intentions. Attack graphs have also been widely used to highlight alert correlations and to improve the prediction of the attackers' intentions. These attack graphs highlight the dependencies between network components and known vulnerabilities, and they may be important in providing an analyst with improved SA regarding the possible attack propagation within the network.

Combining attack graphs with dependency graphs, which capture dependencies among assets in the network, can provide the analyst with a more informed decision making process (Albanese et al. 2011).

Another way to support the analyst' cyber SA is with computational assistance tools that filter and visualize data and help prevent "cognitive overload" (Etoty et al. 2014). By and large, as Erbacher (2012) has recently pointed out, the vast majority of these state-of-the art assistance tools are targeted at network analysts with the common function of correlating cyber events within a network topology and facilitating the interpretation of low-level events (where an "anomaly" is essentially a cyber event that violates some pre-defined constraints and deviates from previously observed patterns). This kind of tool (e.g., VisAlert: http://www.visalert.com/, NVisionIP: Lakkaraju et al. 2004, etc.) leverages machine learning and information fusion techniques to extrapolate meaningful structures for the cyber analyst, but they are not designed to either provide a high-level representation of the data (which would include notions like risk management, agility handling tasks, etc.) or to factor into play the distinctive cognitive elements in genuine SA, such as perception, attention, memory, experience, reasoning capabilities, expectations, confidence, performance, etc. Hence, the aim of most existing visualizations tools is to make the data more accessible to the analyst and alleviate some of the effort of the perception phase. Such tools provide less support to the comprehension and projection phases of cyber SA. Furthermore, numerous pitfalls of visualizations can bias the analyst's SA and should be carefully considered when visualizing network data (Tufte and Graves-Morris 1983). For example, visualizations can highlight some data attributes and can lead to over-consideration of these attributes in the decision process while directing less attention to other relevant attributes.

When huge amounts of network traffic need to be analyzed, Machine Learning (ML) methods can provide a means to instantiate IDS processes (Chauhan et al. 2011; Harshna 2013). In general, ML techniques are split into two large groups, namely "classification" and "clustering": the former aims at minimizing the number of false positives (normal events mistakenly classified as attacks) and false negatives (undetected attacks) by using labeled data sets as training examples; the objective of the latter is to extract clusters of similar patterns from a dataset, thus de facto creating multiple data subsets differentiated by some suitable distance measure. The main advantage of clustering is that it does not involve any training phase, which conversely makes classification more effective for a dataset where training data are available, but classification is less reusable across scenarios and less adaptive to novel situations. Among the ML classification techniques used for intrusion detection, we find Inductive Rule Generation (e.g., the Ripper system; Cohen 1995), Genetic Algorithms, Fuzzy Logics, Neural Networks, Immunological-based techniques, and Support Vector Machines. Concerning ML clustering techniques, statistical methods based on Bayes estimators and Markov models represent the most complex frameworks of analysis, where patterns can be computed in a variable time-scale and in a per-host or per-service scale. Overall, ML tools can be very efficient in handling large amounts of data and can provide meaningful insights regarding the state of a network. However, they rely on complex algorithms and intensive computational processes when detecting threats. Eventually, the analyst is provided with a recommendation without the ability to understand the details of the processes that generated that recommendation. Without the ability to acquire the appropriate level of SA, this can expose the analysts to various biases related to trust in automation and eventually harm the comprehension and projection levels of SA.

The technology to support the analyst in intrusion detection is critical to the analyst's acquisition of cyber SA and decision making. But in order to create adaptable technology that accounts for the analyst's mode of thinking, the analyst's cognitive processes and limitations ultimately need to be represented in this technology. Next, we discuss the ACT-R cognitive architecture and the instance-based learning theory (IBLT) (Gonzalez et al. 2003), a theory of decisions from experience in dynamic tasks, which has recently been used to create cognitive models of the intrusion detection process.

4 ACT-R Cognitive Architecture

Cognitive architectures are computational instantiations of unified theories of cognition (Newell 1990). They represent the invariant mechanisms and structures of cognition, as implemented in the human brain. The ACT-R architecture (Anderson and Lebiere 1998; Anderson et al. 2004) is organized as a set of modules, each devoted to processing a particular kind of information that is integrated and coordinated through a centralized production system module (see Fig. 2). Each module is assumed to access and deposit information into a buffer associated with the module, and the central production system can only respond to the contents of the buffers, not the internal encapsulated processing of the modules. Each module and associated buffer has been correlated with activation in particular brain locations (Anderson 2007). The visual module and buffer keep track of objects and locations in the visual field. The manual module and buffer are associated with control of the hands. The declarative module and retrieval buffer are associated with the retrieval of information from long-term declarative memory. The goal buffer keeps track of the goals and the internal state of the system in problem solving, while the imaginal buffer (not pictured) keeps track of problem information. Finally, the procedural module is charged with coordinating the activity of other modules by directing the flow of information between them. That module, implemented as a production system, includes components to pattern matching against buffer contents, to select a single production rule to fire at one time, and to trigger activity in various modules by directing information into their buffer.

The declarative module and procedural module, respectively, store and retrieve information that corresponds to declarative knowledge and procedural knowledge. Procedural knowledge consists of the implicit skills that we display in our behavior, generally without any conscious awareness. Production rules represent procedural knowledge in the form of the strategies and heuristics used to manipulate that information and achieve problem solving. They specify procedures that represent and apply cognitive skill in the current context to retrieve and modify information in the

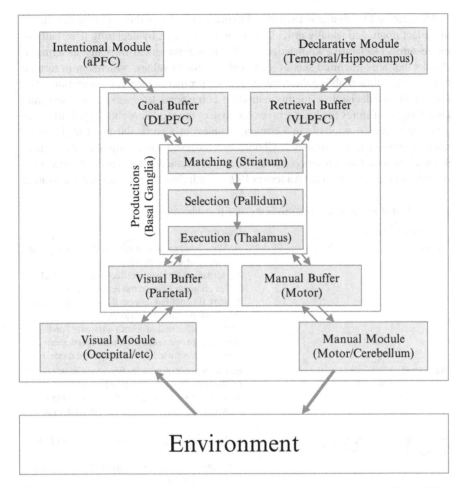

Fig. 2 ACT-R is a production system architecture with multiple modules corresponding to different kinds of perception, action, and cognitive information stores. Modules have been identified with specific brain regions. A central procedural module synchronizes information flow to and from the other modules

buffers and transfer it to other modules. While those procedures could specify expert solutions to the problem, it is generally assumed that achieving expert levels of performance requires up to thousands of hours of experience in the most complex domains. Instead, a common hypothesis in modeling task performance is to assume that individuals rely on direct recognition or recall of relevant experience from declarative memory to guide their solution or, failing that, resort to very general problem-solving heuristics. This compute-vs-retrieve process is a common design pattern used to structure ACT-R models (Taatgen et al. 2006). For instance, it would apply in cyber security when a novice analyst would painstakingly apply a procedure to make a judgment about a new intrusion, while an expert analyst would simply recognize the pattern and make a snap judgment.

Declarative knowledge is the kind of explicit knowledge that a person can attend to, reflect upon, and usually articulate in some way (e.g., by declaring it verbally or by gesture). Declarative knowledge in ACT-R is represented formally in terms of chunks that are structured sets of slots and associated values, which can in turn be other chunks, thus enabling the creation of complex hierarchical representations. The chunks in the declarative memory module correspond to episodic and semantic knowledge that stores the long-term experience of the model. A chunk typically integrates information available in a common context at a particular point in time in a single representational structure. Chunks are retrieved from long-term declarative memory by an activation process (see Table 1 for detailed equations) that reflects the statistics of the environment (Anderson 1993). Each chunk has a base-level activation

Table 1 List of activation mechanisms in the ACT-R architecture

Mechanism	Equation	Description
Activation	$A_i = B_i + S_i + P_i - \varepsilon_i$	B_i: Base-level activation reflects the recency and frequency of use of chunk i S_i: Spreading activation reflects the effect that buffer contents have on the retrieval process P_i: Partial matching reflects the degree to which the chunk matches the request ε_i: Noise value includes both a transient and (optional) permanent component (permanent component not used by the integrated model)
Base-level	$B_i = \ln\left(\sum_{j=1}^{n} t_j^{-d}\right) + \beta_i$	n: The number of presentations for chunk i t_j: The time since the jth presentation d: A decay rate (not used by the integrated model) β_i: A constant offset (not used by the integrated model)
Spreading activation	$S_i = \sum_k \sum_j W_{kj} S_{ji}$	k: Weight of buffers summed over are all of the buffers in the model j: Weight of chunks which are in the slots of the chunk in buffer k W_{kj}: Amount of activation from sources j in buffer k S_{ji}: Strength of association from sources j to chunk i
	$S_{ji} = S - \ln(fan_{ji})$	S: The maximum associative strength (set at 4 in the model) fan_{ji}: A measure of how many chunks are associated with chunk j
Partial Matching	$P_i = \sum_k PM_{ki}$	P: Match scale parameter (set at 2) which reflects the weight given to the similarity M_{ki}: Similarity between the value k in the retrieval specification and the value in the corresponding slot of chunk i The default range is from 0 to -1 with 0 being the most similar and -1 being the largest difference
Declarative Retrievals	$P_i = \dfrac{e^{A_i/s}}{\sum_j e^{A_j/s}}$	P_i: The probability that chunk i will be recalled A_i: Activation strength of chunk i $\sum A_j$: Activation strength of all of eligible chunks j s: Chunk activation noise
Blended Retrievals	$V = \min \sum_i P_i \cdot \left(1 - Sim(V, V_i)\right)^2$	P_i: Probability from declarative retrieval Sim_{ij}: Similarity between compromise value j and actual value i

that reflects its recency and frequency of occurrence, which accounts for the power laws of practice and forgetting that are pervasive in human behavior. Activation spreads from the current focus of attention, including goal and imaginal buffers, through associations among chunks in declarative memory to account for phenomena such as associative priming, in which the context plays an implicit role in our access to information. These associations are built up from experience and they reflect how chunks co-occur in cognitive processing. The spread of activation from one cognitive structure to another is determined by combining the weight of attentional focus from the originating cognitive structure with its associative strength to the other structure. Chunks are compared to the desired pattern specified in the retrieval buffer by using a partial matching mechanism that subtracts its degree of mismatch to the desired pattern from the activation, referred to as similarity. This is done additively for each component of the pattern and corresponding chunk value, weighted by a mismatch penalty factor. This ability to match to imperfect information allows us to deal with changing, approximate, and probabilistic environments. Finally, noise is added to chunk activations to make retrieval a probabilistic process governed by a Boltzmann (softmax) distribution, accounting for the probabilistic nature of human cognition. While the most active chunk is usually retrieved, a blending process (Lebiere 1999) can also be applied; which returns a derived output encoding the consensus value reflecting the similarities between the values of the content of all chunks, weighted by their retrieval probabilities as determined by their activations and partial-matching scores. This blending process is often used to provide a constrained way of making decisions in continuous domains as proposed in IBLT (Gonzalez 2013; Gonzalez and Dutt 2011; Gonzalez et al. 2003), which is described next.

5 Instance-Based Learning Theory and Cognitive Models

The notion that learners have a general-purpose mechanism whereby situation-decision-utility triplets are stored as chunks and later retrieved to generalize solutions to future decisions originates from *instance-based learning theory (IBLT)* (Gonzalez et al. 2003). IBLT is a theory of decisions from experience in dynamic tasks. A simple cognitive model, derived from IBLT, has recently been proposed for representing individual learning and for reproducing choice behavior in repeated binary choice tasks (Gonzalez and Dutt 2011; Lejarraga et al. 2012). This model has shown to be a robust accounting of the choice and learning process in a large variety of tasks and environmental conditions (for a summary, see Gonzalez 2013). Its greatest strength is that it offers a single learning mechanism to account for behavior observable in multiple paradigms and decision making tasks (for a summary, see Gonzalez 2013). However, Gonzalez and colleagues (2003) argue that the strength of IBLT is the explanations of decision making in complex dynamic situations, such as cyber security. With the aim of scaling up from simple binary choice models to the type of complex dynamic tasks that IBLT intended to explain, Gonzalez and colleagues have used the cognitive model for binary choice to represent the detection process in cyber security.

Dutt et al. (2011) proposed an IBL model to study cyber SA. The model represented the cognitive processes of a cyber-security analyst who needs to monitor a computer network and detect malicious network events that constitute a simple island-hopping cyber attack. In this model, the memory of a simulated analyst was pre-populated with instances encoding possible network events, including a set of attributes (e.g., IP address, whether the IDS issued an alert, etc.) that define a network event. An instance also included the analyst's decision regarding that specific combination of attributes, meaning whether the analyst decided that the event (i.e., set of attributes and their values) described malicious network activity or not. Finally, an instance also stored the outcome of that decision, indicating whether the event actually represented a malicious network activity or not. Controlling the representation of the analyst's memory provided the ability to manipulate situation awareness by adjusting the amount of instances in memory that represent malicious network activity. For example, the memory of a very selective analyst had 75 % malicious instances and 25 % non-malicious instances, while a less selective analyst's memory had 25 % malicious instances and 75 % non-malicious instances. When making a decision about whether a new network event is part of a malicious network activity or not, the model retrieved similar instances from memory according to the cognitive judgment mechanisms. Through the process of judging, the modeled analyst accumulated evidence that can indicate if there is an ongoing cyber attack. The risk tolerance parameter of the model governed this accumulation process. The number of malicious network events that the model detected was constantly compared to the analyst's risk tolerance, and once the number of malicious events was equal to or higher than the risk tolerance, the modeled analyst declared that there is an ongoing cyber attack. Thus, risk tolerance served as a threshold for evidence accumulation and risk taking.

The results from simulating different cyber analysts demonstrated that both the risk tolerance level and the past experiences of the analyst affect the analyst's cyber SA, with the effect of experiences (in memory) being slightly more impacting than risk tolerance. This work also highlighted the importance of modeling the adversary's behavior, by comparing the influence of impatient and patient attacker strategies on the performance of the defender. Patient attacker strategy and longer delays between the threat incursions on the network can challenge the security analyst and decrease her ability to detect threats. Thus, the cognitive model was capable of capturing the phenomenon that some attack patterns are more challenging than others to the simulated security cyber analyst.

6 Research Gaps for Understanding the Cognitive Demands of the Cyber World

Many advances need to be made in several research directions to make cognitive models useful and effective in representing and supporting the job of a cyber security analyst. Based on the current state of technology discussed above, we identified five gaps in our understandings of the cognitive demands of the cyber world.

6.1 The Cognitive Gap: Mapping Cognitive Architecture Mechanisms to Cyber SA

The general processes of a cognitive architecture such as ACT-R can be mapped systematically onto the concepts of cyber SA, such that the distinct levels of situation awareness can be related to concrete cognitive mechanisms. This mapping does not take the form of a one-to-one correspondence between cyber SA concepts and cognitive modules, but it instead maps those concepts onto modeling idioms that leverage multiple modules using common patterns. The first level of cyber SA corresponds to the processes involved in the direct acquisition of information from the environment. This perception level can be directly associated with the perceptual modules of the ACT-R cognitive architecture, including the visual and aural modules. However, those modules do not operate on their own, but through the direct supervision and control of the procedural module. Attention is a fundamental construct that reconciles the limited processing resources of our cognitive (including perceptual) modules with the considerable demands arising from the open-ended complexity of the external world. Attentional focus is used to decompose complex external scenes, like a complex cyber security display, into simple components that can be processed directly by our perceptual systems.

The typical flow of control for perception in an ACT-R model (e.g., Anderson et al. 2004) proceeds in a top-down manner. While attention can be directed by external events in the environment, effective performance of complex tasks in information-rich environments typical of cyber security requires structured, goal-directed perceptual processing of information. The first step of perception is therefore a request for a location that matches a specific content condition.[2] This location might already be known if the user is sufficiently familiar with his environment and the environment is stable enough, in which case it will be provided by retrieval from declarative memory. Otherwise, it is directly supplied by a production rule, if sufficient experience has transformed that knowledge into a skill through production compilation. If not, the location will be determined by searching the environment to match the specified condition. Once the location has been obtained, it is supplied to the visual buffer to trigger processing of that area of the visual field in the visual module. This will result in the chunk representing the object recognized at that location to be returned in the same visual buffer. That chunk is then transferred to the imaginal buffer holding the representation of the current situation being elaborated on, which is where the process of comprehension starts. Hence, in the context of cyber SA, this phase correspond to the process through which a cognitive model retrieves and encodes source and destination IP address, protocol type, and other attributes of the network. Comprehension corresponds to the second level of cyber SA, which results in the semantic representation of a perceived situation, a product of the cognitive process known as sensemaking (Klein et al. 2006a). According to Klein et al. (2006b), sensemaking is the process of abstraction that

---

[2]This discussion will be focused on visual attention, though the same principles apply to other perceptual modules such as auditory perception.

maps concrete situations to the general by using mental representations called frames, which correspond to structured conceptual models of the world. Lebiere et al. (2013) describe how sensemaking is fundamentally compatible with IBLT, and more specifically how frames can be mapped onto the chunk representations of situations used in that process. For instance, in the domain of geospatial intelligence, frames correspond to a pattern of input data, aggregating layers of information from independent sensors and associating them with specific hypotheses. "Comprehension" thus corresponds to the process of gradually aggregating the information from perception into hierarchical chunks implementing integrated frames. In the next section, we argue that "ontologies" can enhance this second level of cyber SA by mapping ACT-R declarative chunks to highly expressive semantic structures that formally specify the conceptual models encapsulated in frames. Going back to cyber SA and detection, in this comprehension phase, IP address obtained during the perception phase are organized into categories that reflect whether it is internal or external to the monitored network. This type of reasoning can also bind an event (e.g., an IDS alert) and the reason that the event occurred (e.g., an IDS rule regarding the maximal number of open connections for a communication protocol), thus generating a hypothesis for the observed behavior that will drive further investigations. The third level of cyber SA corresponds to the process of projection, or the generation of expectations about future states of the system. Those changes in system state can result from the actions of the decision maker, from those of an opponent or teammate, or from other independent parts of the system. Projection is essential in evaluating the effect of potential actions by including feedback from the outcome of past actions. Because many cyber security interactions are fundamentally adversarial, it is essential to also being able to generate expectations of the opponent's future actions, encompassing both independent actions and actions taken in response to one's own decisions. Finally, since the actions of third parties, such as system users, also impact the outcome of security measures, generating expectations of their actions is crucial to projecting future system states and effective system control. From the cyber SA perspective, this phase occurs after perceiving an IDS alert and comprehending that it was generated by a rule that limits the number of open connections. Now, when the number of open connections exceeds the limit, projection is used to evaluate whether this is a temporary benign spike in the demand for a service or if it is an indication for a cyber attack. Making such a decision requires integration of additional information that can be perceived and comprehended explicitly from the environment, like the source IP addresses of the connections, as well as consideration of implicit information like the consequence to the network if the number of open connections will continue to increase.

6.2 The Semantic Gap: Integrating Cognitive Architectures with Ontologies of Cyber Security

In the previously mentioned models, modelers themselves directly specified the semantics of the representation. In order to enable full-fledged reasoning capabilities in cognitive architectures, these systems need to incorporate "re-usable declarative representations that correspond to objects and processes of the world" (McCarthy 1980). Similarly, cognitive architectures must provide a way to represent world entities (Sowa 1984), i.e., an "ontology".[3] An ontology is a language-dependent cognitive artifact committed to a certain conceptualization of the world by means of a given language[4] (Guarino 1998). Thus, in broad terms, an ontology corresponds to a semantic model of the world (or of a portion of it, i.e., a "domain"): when the model is simply described in natural language, an ontology reduces to a *dictionary, thesaurus,* or *terminology*; when the model is expressed as an axiomatic theory (e.g., in first order logic), it is called a *formal ontology*. Ultimately, if logical constraints are encoded into machine-readable formats, formal ontologies take the form of *computational ontologies*, and enter de facto in the family of *semantic technologies*, which include search engines, automatic reasoners, knowledge-based platforms, etc. In the context of a cognitive architecture like ACT-R, computational ontologies can extend the semantics of the chunks stored in declarative memory. Although these extensions are not usually required by ACT-R models that perform relatively narrow cognitive tasks, declarative memory should be designed to encompass a rich spectrum of concepts when dealing with decision making in complex scenarios like cyber operations, including classifications of cyber security policies, risks, attacks, system's functionalities, human responsibilities, user's privileges, as well as the mutual connection among them. Widening the scope beyond ACT-R, state of the art work on cognitive architectures has also gone in the direction of mapping ontologies (like Cyc, see Lenat et al. 1985) to declarative memory (see Ball et al. 2004; Best et al. 2010; Emond 2006). It aims to enhance not only the "capability" of representing the available knowledge of a domain but also the functionality of automatically deriving inferences from it, a feature that would also help to increase the "Comprehension" level in cyber SA. In this regard, the role of ontologies in cognitive architectures is to (1) formally characterize chunks in long-term memory that depict conceptual models of situations (frames) and (2) foster *automaticity* of certain cognitive tasks, "that significantly benefit SA by providing a mechanism for overcoming limited attention" and improve the decision making process.

There has been little work on ontologies for cyber security and cyber warfare. An ontology of IDS is discussed by Undercoffer et al. (2003); within a broader paper, there is a brief discussion of an ontology for DDoS attacks (Kotenko 2005); and a general ontology for cyber warfare is discussed in D'Amico et al. (2009). Obrst et al. (2012) provides the best sketch of a cyber warfare ontology, and the scale of the project and its difficulties are discussed by Dipert (2013). With regard to human users and human-computer interface, the most important step in understanding a complex new domain involves producing accessible definitions and classifications of entities and phenomena. Mundie (2013) stressed this point when talking about the Jason Report (The MITRE Corporation 2010). Discussions of cyber warfare often

---

[3] This was the genesis of using the word 'ontology' in AI. Ontology, 'the study of being as such'—as Aristotle named it—originated as a philosophical discipline.

[4] Guarino distinguishes between 'Ontology' as a discipline (with the capital 'o') and 'ontologies' as engineering cognitive artifacts.

begin with the difficulties created by misused terminology (such as characterizing cyber espionage as an "attack"). The Joint Chiefs of Staff created a list of cyber term definitions (Joint Staff Department of Defense 2010) that has been further developed and improved in a classified version. Nevertheless, none of these definitions has been encoded in OWL (Staab and Studer 2003) or in any other computational semantic format, which is a necessary requirement to make them machine-understandable. Likewise, various agencies and corporations (NIST, MITRE, Verizon) have formulated enumerations of types of malware, vulnerabilities, and exploitations, sometimes expressed in XML-based semantics: but without a common vocabulary, their sprawling English descriptions in large, incompatible databases are not directly machine-usable and are nearly impossible to maintain. Efforts that have been made toward developing computational ontologies of cyber security and cyber warfare typically do not work within any standard framework and do not utilize existing military reference ontologies such as UCORE-SL, which define concepts such as the notion of "agent," "organization," "artifact," "weapon," etc.

As a consequence of this general deficiency, one of the first and perhaps most generally useful tasks that will need to be completed to fill the "semantic gap" is to collect definitions of key cyber security concepts that are currently scattered across existing ontologies, controlled vocabularies, doctrines, and other documental resources and to suitably harmonize them in a homogenous computational ontology. As a second step, the capabilities of this cybersecurity ontology will have to be dynamically tested in cognitive models of decision making in cyber operations.

6.3   The Decision Gap: Representing Learning, Experience, and Dynamic Decision Making in the Cyber World

Given the complexity and variability of the cyber environment, there is an ongoing effort to provide decision makers with tools that can support their decision process and provide insights to manage the complex dynamics of the cyber world. To gain and maintain situation awareness, the decision maker is constantly required to make multiple and interdependent decisions in a highly dynamic environment. Dynamic decision making requires an understanding of multiple, interrelated attributes and the ability to anticipate the way that the environment will develop over time. Making the right decision and acting appropriately and in a timely manner can maximize the decision value (Brehmer 1992; Edwards 1962; Gonzalez 2005; Gonzalez et al. 2005).

The modeling of human decision processes in cyber security highlights some important aspects of cyber SA that cognitive models need to account for. For example, pattern recognition under uncertainty represents a defender's attempt to find patterns in the attacker's sequence of actions in order to predict the attacker's next operation and to provide the best response to it. However, if the attacker is aware of these attempts to detect sequential dependencies, one possible path of action is to constantly change the malicious operations and to exploit the sequential dependencies. Cognitive models in ACT-R (Anderson and Lebiere 1998, 2003) and neural networks (West and Lebiere 2001) are capable of accounting for the human ability to detect sequential dependencies, and they use the perceived sequence to project the next action that an opponent will most likely take in a strategic interaction. Through their natural stochasticity, those models can balance the exploitation of the opponent's patterns with some measure of deception and self-protection by avoiding becoming too predictable themselves. Also, cognitive models such as those derived from ACT-R and IBLT provide the capability to learn from experience and the ability to utilize past experiences in novel decision situations.

Human decision makers use the same cognitive system for a vast array of divergent tasks. The underlying cognitive system represents a highly efficient, multipurpose mechanism that has evolved to be as effective as possible across a wide variety situations and conditions (West et al. 2006). Cognitive architectures share the same flexibility and diversity, and as such can efficiently represent and capture human decision making in cyber security. However, continued efforts are needed to maintain and update the formal representation of the cyber environment that the architectures use. This requirement emphasizes the need for cognitive architectures to develop better and more efficient models of perception and information encoding. For cognitive architectures to serve a meaningful role in future cyber security engagements, two main aspects should be carefully developed: the first is the flexibility of reasoning that underlies human adaptivity and the second is the active and efficient perceptual processes that search, detect, and encode information in a dynamic environment.

6.4 The Adversarial Gap: Representing Adversarial Cyber SA and Decision Making

Cognitive architectures provide rich and flexible modeling environment. Using these architectures, it is possible to generate models that represent the analyst' decision making process and SA, as well as models of the adversary. For each of these models, there is a need to define knowledge base, learning processes, and decision making process. Furthermore, the models of the analyst and the adversary interact within a defined environment (i.e., the cyber world) that dictates a set of possible action each model can choose from. Thus, there is a need to define the possible interactions between multiple cognitive models. In addition to defining the possible interactions, there is a need to define how and what kind of feedback the models would receive regarding the outcomes of their combined decision making processes. Issues concerning delayed feedback and incomplete or imperfect feedback are highly relevant when modeling studying decision making and learning in dynamic systems. Therefore, a comprehensive formal representation that can bring together the analyst, the adversary, and the environment in which they interact is needed. Game theory has been successfully used to capture the essence of complex and dynamic situations that involves two or more agents that interact within a well-defined environment. We posit that combining game theoretical perspective and cognitive modeling can provide a controllable, but still ecological valid, representation of interactions in the cyber world and serve as a potent framework for studying cyber SA.

Game theory has been popularized as a potent approach to characterize and analyze decisions in situations that involve social dilemmas and conflict situations. Stackelberg games have been used to model and capture the strategies of defenders and attackers in airport security, as well as for optimizing resources allocation in sensitive settings (Pita et al. 2008). Similarly, game theory has been used for decision making in cyber security (Alpcan and Baar 2011; Grossklags et al. 2008; Lye and Wing 2005; Manshaei et al. 2013; Roy et al. 2010). However, most game-theoretic approaches to security hold some limitations and assume either static game models or games with perfect or complete information (Roy et al. 2010). To some extent, these assumptions misrepresent the reality of the network security context where situations are highly dynamic and the decision maker must rely on imperfect and incomplete information. To overcome this, recent studies that apply game theory to security attempt to account for the bounded rationality of human actors, especially human adversaries (Pita et al. 2012). However, this and other game-theoretic approaches still do not fully address the cognitive mechanisms like memory and learning that drive the human decision making processes and can provide a first-principled predictive account of human performance, including both capabilities and suboptimal biases.

Behavioral Game Theory relaxes some of the constraints of Game Theory with the study of human decision makers and how they interact in strategic situations involving more than one decision maker (Camerer 2003). Using Behavioral Game Theory, it is possible to address some of the limitations imposed by game-theoretic approaches and examine how learning from experience and adaptation to the environment influences decision making and risk taking in cyber security (Gonzalez 2013).

As discussed earlier, ACT-R and IBLT have proven to be highly beneficial to studying the interplay between learning and decision making processes of an individual. One ongoing effort aims at scaling up cognitive models to study interactions between two or more decision makers in social conflicts like the Prisoner's Dilemma (Gonzalez et al. 2014) and the Chicken Game (Oltramari et al. 2013). However, scaling up models of human cognition and SA to cyber worlds with more than two agents involved is still a challenge (Gonzalez 2013). An important issue for all levels of SA is the availability of information regarding the other entities. Recently, cognitive models have been extended to study how the availability of information and the source of the information influence decision making and learning.

Recent studies examine how the availability of descriptive and experiential information influences interactions in social dilemmas (Martin et al. 2013; Oltramari et al. 2013). The key findings of these studies suggest that information is needed for cooperation, and the lack of information fostered situations in which one decision maker tended to exploit the other. Another relevant finding is related to trust and its role in cooperative behavior, indicating that decision makers dynamically weigh the partner's information based on surprise (i.e., the gap between expectations or projections and the observed outcome). Learning models that incorporate surprise into the decision process and combine both descriptive and experiential information can capture the complex dynamics of iterated interaction between two decision makers in conflict situations (Gonzalez et al. 2014; Ben-Asher et al. 2013). Overall, these finding emphasize the interplay between information and cognitive processes in order to achieve SA and finally making a decision.

6.5   The Network Gap: Addressing Complex Networks and Cyber Warfare

Cyber warfare is the extension of the traditional attacker-defender concept that involves multiple units (individual, state-sponsored organizations, or even nations) simultaneously executing offensive and defensive operations through networks of computers. In a cyber war, units can execute attacks against targets in a cooperative and simultaneous manner. Any defending unit can also be attacked by multiple enemies, eventually acting as both attacker and defender at the same time.

The dynamics of a cyber war, which are driven by multiple decision makers making simultaneous decisions, are hard to predict. Achieving and maintaining SA in such an environment is crucial and at the same time challenging. The fact that multiple units operate simultaneously in the environment might imply that a decision maker has to maintain SA in different levels. The decision maker has to perceive, comprehend, and make projections regarding interactions in which the unit itself is involved directly, interactions between other units which do not involve the decision maker directly, and the overall aggregated SA at the environment level. Scaling up cognitive models of SA from the dyad perspective (an analyst and an adversary) to the SA needed in an environment where large networks of units can interact simultaneously requires careful consideration and examination of environmental attributes and their relation to SA. For example, the topology of the network that connects units involved in a cyber conflict has an extensive impact on the availability of information, trust in information, and information propagation.

To support SA and decision making in large scale cyber conflicts, simulations using multiple cognitive models connected in a network can provide predictions and answer what-if questions. Similarly, simulations that combine multiple cognitive models and human decision makers can train humans to acquire and maintain SA in cyber conflicts. Recently, there has been an increasing interest in N-Player models of social conflict that share some similarities with cyber warfare (Kennedy et al. 2010; Hazon et al. 2011). In parallel, there are attempts to study cyber attacks and cyber warfare through multi agent-based modeling (e.g., Kotenko 2005, 2007). However, many of these models use strategic agents and not cognitive models. Such strategic agents are designed to execute an optimal strategy, rather than learn the maximizing strategies from experience; and thus not only fail to replicate SA, human learning, and decision making mechanisms but are fundamentally incapable of coping with fluid, dynamic situations commonly encountered in cyber warfare.

The CyberWar Game (Ben-Asher and Gonzalez 2014) is a multi-player frame-work that aims to capture some of the characteristics and the dynamics of the environment in cyber warfare and aspects of the decision maker. It is inspired by Hazon et al.'s (2011) N-Player model. Considering important aspects of cyber warfare and conflicts in general, the CyberWar Game introduces two relevant concepts that characterize a player: power and assets. In the context of cyber warfare, power represents the ability to successfully accomplish a goal, which for a defender is to block an attack and for an attacker is to accomplish a malicious goal. Power can be seen as a representation of the robustness of cyber security infrastructure and is likely to be a function of investment in cyber security. An asset is an abstraction of what the defender is trying to protect and what the attacker wants to gain. In general, assets are the motivation for building both defense system and attack systems, and selfish assets maximization is the shared goal of all the decision makers in this environment. Power represents the potential of these systems to achieve this goal.

In this paradigm, as illustrated in Fig. 3, several players simultaneously attack each other or defend themselves from attacks. Thus, a player is not assigned to be an attacker or a defender in this game, but it is the players' decision what role they play. Furthermore, this resembles distributed attacks over the network and also incorporates the idea that power can be distributed between multiple goals. A player needs SA and learning processes to identify who might try to attack and who can be a valuable target to attack. For example in Fig. 3, Player 1 and Player 3 are likely to attack Player 2 as she is the weakest player. However, if Player 1 invests all her power in the attacking without defending from Player 3, Player 3 can take advantage and attack only Player 1, who has the highest asset's value. The decision of whether

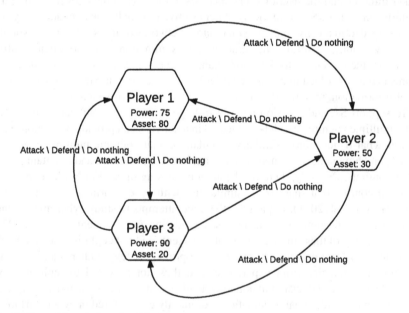

Fig. 3 General description of a CyberWar game

or not to attack an opponent is not straightforward, as the player has to incorporate additional aspects like the cost of attack, the cost of defense, the attack severity (i.e., what percentage of opponent assets it is possible to gain when winning an attack), and the effectiveness of defense. Frameworks like the CyberWar Game allow us to examine the role of SA at the operational level (who to attack and from whom to defend), as well as at the tactical and strategic levels (which coalition to join).

7 Summary

Human cognition is central to our understanding of the challenges of the cyber world. Cyber security is an extremely complex domain that stretches and challenges many of our theories and concepts of situation awareness and decision making. Current theories of SA have been developed for the physical world, and research is needed to determine whether and how much of what we currently know is applicable or useful for cyber security. The process of detection (protecting networks against illegal intrusions) illustrates the challenges involved in cyber security and the need for integration of information technology and computational representations of human situation awareness. Cognitive models are dynamic and adaptable computational representations of the cognitive structures and mechanisms involved in developing SA and processing information for decision making. Cognitive models differ from purely statistical approaches, such as machine learning, that are often capable of evaluating only stable, long-term sequential dependencies from existing data but fail to account for the dynamics of human cognition, including learning processes. An important technology that helps support cyber SA and human decision making is the Intrusion Detection System (IDS). Other assistance tools are targeted at network analysts with the common function of correlating cyber events within a network topology and facilitating the interpretation of low-level events. The aim of most existing visualizations tools is to make the data more accessible to the analyst and alleviate some of the effort of the perception phase. Such tools provide less support to the comprehension and projection phases of cyber SA. Machine Learning (ML) methods can provide a means to instantiate IDS processes and are often divided in two large groups, namely "classification" and "clustering." Eventually, the analyst is provided with a recommendation without the ability to understand the details of the processes that generated that recommendation. Without the ability to acquire the appropriate level of SA, this can expose the analysts to various biases related to trust in automation and eventually harm the comprehension and projection levels of SA. In order to create adaptable technology that accounts for the analyst's mode of thinking, the analyst's cognitive processes and limitations must be represented in a cognitive model. Cognitive models are often built within a cognitive architecture. Cognitive architectures are computational representations of unified theories of cognition and the ACT-R architecture is an example. IBLT is a theory of decisions from experience in dynamic tasks; the strength of IBLT is the explanations of decision making in complex dynamic situations, such as cyber security.

An IBL model to study cyber SA represented the cognitive processes of a cyber-security analyst who needs to monitor a computer network and detect malicious network events that constitute a simple island-hopping cyber attack. When making a decision about whether a new network event is part of a malicious network activity or not, the model retrieved similar instances from memory according to the cognitive judgment mechanisms. The model illustrates how both the risk tolerance level and the past experiences of the analyst affect the analyst's cyber SA. The current knowledge gaps in our understanding of cognitive demands in the cyber world are: the cognitive gap, namely defining a theoretical model of cyber SA within a cognitive architecture; the decision gap, representing learning, experience and dynamic decision making in the cyberspace; the semantic gap, addressing the construction of a common language and a set of basic concepts about which the security community can develop a shared understanding; the adversarial gap, developing ways to represent adversarial behavior; and the network gap, scaling up models of human behavior to complex networks and cyber conflict representations. Together, the descriptions of these gaps present a roadmap for new research and development of cognitive-aware technologies that would support the analyst's cyber SA and decision making process.

References

Albanese M, Jajodia S, Pugliese A, Subrahmanian VS (2011) Scalable analysis of attack scenarios. In: Atluri V, Diaz C (eds.) Lecture notes in computer science, vol. 6879. Springer-Verlag, Berlin, p 415-433

Alpcan T, Basar T (2011) Network security: A decision and game-theoretic approach. Cambridge University Press, New York

Anderson JR (1993) Rules of the mind. Lawrence Erlbaum Associates, Hillsdale, NJ

Anderson JR (2007) How can the human mind occur in the physical universe? Oxford University Press, Oxford

Anderson JR, Bothell D, Byrne MD, Douglass S, Lebiere C, Qin Y (2004) An integrated theory of the mind. Psych Rev 111(4):1036-1060

Anderson JR, Lebiere C (1998) The atomic components of thought. Lawrence Erlbaum Associates, Hillsdale

Anderson JR, Lebiere C (2003) The Newell test for a theory of cognition. Behav Brain Sci 26(5):587-639

Ball J, Rodgers S, Gluck K (2004) Integrating ACT-R and Cyc in a large-scale model of language comprehension for use in intelligent agents. In: Proceedings of the nineteenth national conference on artificial intelligence. AAAI Press, Menlo Park, p 19-25

Ben-Asher N, Dutt V, Gonzalez C (2013). Accounting for integration of descriptive and experiential information in a repeated prisoner's dilemma using an instance-based learning model. In: Kennedy B, Reitter D, Amant RS (eds) Proceedings of the 22nd annual conference on behavior representation in modeling and simulation. BRIMS Society, Ottawa

Ben-Asher N, Gonzalez C (2014) CyberWar Game: A Paradigm for Understanding New Challenges of Cyber War (Under Review)

Bernardi P, McLaughlin K, Yang Y, Sezer S (2014) Intrusion detection systems for critical infrastructure. In: Pathan A-SK (ed) The state of the art in intrusion prevention and detection. CRC Press, Boca Raton, p 115-138

Best BJ, Gerhart N, Lebiere C (2010) Extracting the ontological structure of OpenCyc for reuse and portability of cognitive models. In: Proceedings of the 19th conference on behavior representation in modeling and simulation. Curran Associates, Red Hook, p 90-96

Brehmer B (1992) Dynamic decision making: Human control of complex systems. Acta Psychol 81(3):211-241

Camerer CF (2003) Behavioral game theory: Experiments in strategic interaction. Princeton University Press, Princeton

Chauhan A, Mishra G, Kumar G (2011) Survey on data mining techniques in intrusion detection. Int J Sci Eng Res 2(7):2-4

Cohen, WW (1995) Fast effective rule induction. In: Proceedings of the 12th international conference on machine learning. Morgan Kaufmann, Lake Taho

D'Amico A, Buchanan L, Goodall J, Walczak P (2009) Mission impact of cyber events: Scenarios and ontology to express the relationship between cyber assets. Available online. http://www.dtic.mil/cgi-bin/GetTRDoc?AD=ADA517410

Dipert R (2013) The essential features of an ontology for cyber warfare. In: Lowther A, Yannakogeorgos P (eds) Conflict and cooperation in cyberspace: The challenge to national security. Taylor & Francis, Boca Raton, p 35-48

Dutt V, Ahn Y-S, Gonzalez C (2011) Cyber situation awareness: Modeling the security analyst in a cyber-attack scenario through instance-based learning. In: Li Y. (ed) Lecture notes in computer science, vol. 6818. Springer-Verlag, Berlin, p 281-293

Edwards W (1962). Dynamic decision theory and probabilistic information processing. Hum Factors 4(2):59-73

Emond B (2006) WN-LEXICAL: An ACT-R module built from the WordNet lexical database. In: Fum D, Del Missier F, Stocco A (eds) Proceedings of the seventh international conference on cognitive modeling, University of Trieste, Trieste, 5-8 April 2006

Endsley MR (1988) Design and evaluation for situation awareness enhancement. Hum Fac Erg Soc P 32(2):97-101

Endsley MR, Jones WM (2001) A model of inter- and intrateam situation awareness: Implications for design, training and measurement. In: McNeese M, Salas E, Endsley MR (eds) New trends in cooperative activities: Understanding system dynamics in complex environments. HFES, Santa Monica, p 46-67

Erbacher RF (2012) Visualization design for immediate high-level situational assessment. In: Proceedings of the ninth international symposium on visualization for cyber security. ACM, New York, p 17-24

Etoty RE, Erbacher RF, Garneau C (2014) Evaluation of the presentation of network data via visualization tools for network analysis. Technical Report #ARL-TR-6865, Army Research Lab, Adelphi MD, 20783

Gonzalez C (2005) Decision support for real-time dynamic decision making tasks. Organ Behav Hum Dec 96(2):142-154

Gonzalez C (2013). The boundaries of Instance-based Learning Theory for explaining decisions from experience. In: Pammi VS, Srinivasan N (eds) Progress in brain research, vol. 202. Elsevier, Amsterdam, p 73-98

Gonzalez C, Ben-Asher N, Martin JM, Dutt V (2014) A cognitive model of dynamic cooperation with varied interdependency information. Cognitive Science 1–39

Gonzalez C, Dutt V (2011). Instance-based learning: Integrating decisions from experience in sampling and repeated choice paradigms. Psychol Rev 118(4):523-551

Gonzalez C, Juarez O, Endsley MR, Jones DG (2006). Cognitive models of situation awareness: Automatic evaluation of situation awareness in graphic interfaces. In: Proceedings of the fifteenth conference on behavior representation in modeling and simulation. Simulation Interoperability Standards Organization, Baltimore, p 45-54

Gonzalez C, Lerch JF, Lebiere C (2003) Instance-based learning in dynamic decision making. Cog Sci 27(4):591-635

Gonzalez C, Vanyukov P, Martin MK (2005) The use of microworlds to study dynamic decision making. Comput Hum Behav 21(2):273-286

Gorman JC, Cooke NJ, Winner JL (2006) Measuring team situation awareness in decentralized command and control environments. Ergonomics 49(12-13):1312-1325

Grossklags J, Christin N, Chuang J (2008) Secure or insure? A game-theoretic analysis of information security games. In: Proceedings of the 17th international conference on world wide web. ACM, New York, p 209-218

Guarino N (1998) Formal ontology and information systems. In: Guarino N (ed) Formal ontology in information systems. IOS Press, Amsterdam, p 3-15

Harshna, Kaur N (2013) Survey paper on data mining techniques of intrusion detection. Int J Sci Eng Technol Res 2(4):799-802

Hazon N, Chakraborty N, Sycara K (2011) Game theoretic modeling and computational analysis of n-player conflicts over resources. In: Proceedings of the 2011 IEEE international conference on privacy, security, risk and trust and IEEE international conference on social computing. Conference Publishing Services, Los Alamitos, p 380-387

Jajodia S, Liu P, Swarup V, Wang C (2010) Cyber situational awareness: Issues and research. Springer, New York

Joint Staff Department of Defense (2010). Joint terminology for cyber operations. Available online. http://publicintelligence.net/dod-joint-cyber-terms/

Kennedy WG, Hailegiorgis AB, Rouleau M, Bassett JK, Coletti M, Balan GC, Gulden T (2010) An agent-based model of conflict in East Africa and the effect of watering holes. In: Proceedings of the 19th conference on behavior representation in modeling and simulation. Curran Associates, Red Hook, p 112-119

Klein G, Moon B, Hoffman RR (2006a) Making sense of sensemaking 1: Alternative perspectives. IEEE Intell Syst 21(4):70-73

Klein G, Moon B, Hoffman RR (2006b) Making sense of sensemaking 2: A macrocognitive model. IEEE Intell Syst 21(5):88-92

Kotenko I (2005) Agent-based modeling and simulation of cyber-warfare between malefactors and security agents in internet. In: Merkuryev Y, Zobel R, Kerckhoffs E (eds) Proceedings of 19th European conference on modeling and simulation, Riga Technical University, Riga, 1-4 June 2005

Kotenko I (2007) Multi-agent modelling and simulation of cyber-attacks and cyber-defense for homeland security. In: Proceedings of the 4th IEEE workshop on intelligent data acquisition and advanced computing systems: technology and applications. IEEE, Los Alamitos, p 614-619

Lakkaraju K, Yurcik W, Lee AJ (2004) NVisionIP: NetFlow visualizations of system state for security situational awareness. In: Proceedings of the 2004 ACM workshop on visualization and data mining for computer security. ACM, New York, p 65-72

Lebiere C (1999) The dynamics of cognition: An ACT-R model of cognitive arithmetic. Kognitionswissenschaft 8(1):5-19

Lebiere C, Pirolli P, Thomson R, Paik J, Rutledge-Taylor M, Staszewski J, Anderson JR (2013) A functional model of sensemaking in a neurocognitive architecture. Comp Intell Neurosci 2013: 921695.

Lebiere C, Gray R, Salvucci D, West R (2003) Choice and learning under uncertainty: A case study in baseball batting. In Alterman R, Kirsch D (eds) Proceedings of the 25th annual conference of the cognitive science society. Lawrence Erlbaum Associates, Boston, p 704-709

Lejarraga T, Dutt V, Gonzalez C (2012) Instance-based learning: A general model of repeated binary choice. J Behav Decis Making 25(2):143-153

Lenat DB, Prakash M, Shepherd M (1985). CYC: Using common sense knowledge to overcome brittleness and knowledge acquisition bottlenecks. Artif Intell 6(4):65-85

Lye K-W, Wing JM (2005). Game strategies in network security. Int J Inf Secur 4(1-2):71-86

Manshaei MH, Zhu Q, Alpcan T, Bacsar T, Hubaux JP (2013) Game theory meets network security and privacy. ACM Comput Surv 45(3):25

Martin JM, Gonzalez C, Juvina I, Lebiere C (2013) A description-experience gap in social interactions: Information about interdependence and its effects on cooperation. J Behav Decis Making 27(4):349-362

McCarthy J (1980) Circumscription – A form of non-monotonic reasoning. Artif Intell 13(1-2):27–39

The MITRE Corporation (2010) Science of cyber-security. The MITRE Corporation, McLean, VA, Technical Report.
Mundie D (2013) How ontologies can help build a science of cyber security. Available online. http://www.cert.org/blogs/insider_threat/2013/03/how_ontologies_can_help_build_a_science_of_cybersecurity.html
Newell A (1990) Unified theories of cognition. Harvard University Press, Cambridge
Obrst L, Chase P, Markeloff R (2012) Developing an ontology of the cyber security domain. In: Costa PCG, Laskey KB (eds) Proceedings of the seventh international conference on semantic technologies for intelligence, defense, and security, George Mason University, Fairfax, 23-26 October 2012
Oltramari A, Lebiere C, Ben-Asher N, Juvina I, Gonzalez C (2013) Modeling strategic dynamics under alternative information conditions. In: West RL, Stewart TC (eds) Proceedings of the 12th international conference on cognitive modeling. ICCM, p 390-395
Pita J, Jain M, Marecki J, Ordóñez F, Portway C, Tambe M, Western C, Paruchuri P, Kraus S (2008) Deployed ARMOR protection: The application of a game theoretic model for security at the Los Angeles International Airport. In: Proceedings of the 7th international joint conference on autonomous agents and multiagent systems: industrial track, p 125-132
Pita J, John R, Maheswaran R, Tambe M, Yang R, Kraus S (2012) A robust approach to addressing human adversaries in security games. In: Proceedings of the 11th international conference on autonomous agents and multiagent systems. International Foundation for Autonomous Agents and Multiagent Systems, Richland, p 1297-1298
Rowley J (2007) The wisdom hierarchy: representations of the DIKW hierarchy. J Inf Sci 33(2):163-180
Roy S, Ellis C, Shiva S, Dasgupta D, Shandilya V, Wu Q (2010) A survey of game theory as applied to network security. In: Sprague RH Jr. (ed) Proceedings of the 43rd Hawaii international conference on system sciences. IEEE: Los Alamitos
Saner LD, Bolstad CA, Gonzalez C, Cuevas HM (2009) Measuring and predicting shared situation awareness in teams. J Cog Eng Decis Making 3(3):280-308
Singer PW, Friedman A (2014) Cybersecurity and cyberwar: What everyone needs to know. Oxford University Press, New York
Sowa JF (1984) Conceptual structures: Information processing in mind and machine. Addison Wesley, Reading
Staab S, Studer R (2003) Handbook on ontologies. Springer-Verlag, Berlin
Taatgen N, Lebiere C, Anderson JR (2006) Modeling paradigms in ACT-R. In: Sun R (ed) Cognition and multi-agent interaction: From cognitive modeling to social simulation. Cambridge University Press, New York, p 29-52
Tufte ER, Graves-Morris PR (1983) The visual display of quantitative information, vol. 2. Graphics Press, Cheshire
Undercoffer J, Joshi A, Pinkston J (2003) Modeling computer attacks: An ontology for intrusion detection. In: Vigna G, Kruegel C (eds) Lecture notes in computer science, vol. 2820. Springer-Verlag, Berlin, p 113-135
West RL, Lebiere C (2001) Simple games as dynamic, coupled systems: Randomness and other emergent properties. J Cog Syst Res 1(4):221-239
West RL, Lebiere C, Bothell DJ (2006) Cognitive architecture, game playing, and human evolution. In: Sun R (ed) Cognition and multi-agent interaction: From cognitive modeling to social simulation. Cambridge University Press, New York, p 103-123

Cognitive Process

John Yen, Robert F. Erbacher, Chen Zhong, and Peng Liu

1 Introduction

The previous chapter showed that our understanding about the cognitive reasoning process of cyber analysts is rather limited. Here, we focus on ways to close this knowledge gap. This chapter starts by summarizing the current understanding about the cognitive processes of cyber analysts based on the results of previous cognitive task analyses. It also discusses the challenges and the importance to capture "fine-grained" cognitive reasoning processes. The chapter then illustrates approaches to overcoming these challenges by presenting a framework for non-intrusive capturing and systematic analysis of the cognitive reasoning process of cyber analysts. The framework includes a conceptual model and practical means for the non-intrusive capturing of a cognitive trace of cyber analysts, and extracting the reasoning process of cyber analysts by analyzing the cognitive trace. The framework can be used to conduct experiments for extracting cognitive reasoning processes from professional network analysts. When cognitive traces are available, their characteristics can be analyzed and compared with the performance of the analysts.

Detecting complex multi-step cyber attacks are challenging for cyber analysts for several reasons. First, the alerts received by cyber analysts include false positives. This requires the analyst to filter out false positive alerts in a timely fashion. The false positive alert may mislead the analysts such that their time is wasted on

J. Yen (✉) • C. Zhong • P. Liu
College of Information Sciences and Technology, The Pennsylvania State University,
University Park, PA 16802, USA
e-mail: jyen@ist.psu.edu; czz111@ist.psu.edu; pliu@ist.psu.edu

R.F. Erbacher
The U.S. Army Research Laboratory, Adelphi, MD 20783, USA
e-mail: robert.f.erbacher.civ@mail.mil

© Springer International Publishing Switzerland 2014
A. Kott et al. (eds.), *Cyber Defense and Situational Awareness*,
Advances in Information Security 62, DOI 10.1007/978-3-319-11391-3_7

false alarms, delaying their attention to the alerts related to actual attacks. Second, an alert related to the attack may be missing (i.e., false negative) due to an unknown vulnerability or a new way of exploiting a known vulnerability. Due to missing alerts, analysts may not be able to identify certain attack steps in an attack chain, and hence delay the time to detect the multi-step attack.

One way to deal with false positive alerts and missing alerts is to leverage previous experience (both successful and failure experience) of cyber analysts in handling similar situations. For example, a failure experience associated with a previous false alarm can prevent an analyst from pursuing a similar false alarm. Similarly, a successful experience associated with a previous missing alert can help the analyst to adapt the experience to deal with a similar missing alert in a new cyber attack. A senior analyst, with years of rich experience in cyber analysis, accumulates many experiences of different types. If the cognitive process of these experiences can be effectively captured and analyzed such that they can be aggregated and effectively reused by other analysts, it will provide several important benefits.

Previous Cognitive Task Analyses (CTAs) about cyber defense have provided valuable insights about the high-level cognitive processes of cyber analysts in the real world. Biros and Eppich (2001) identified four cognitive capabilities. D'Amico and Whitley (2008) generated six analysis roles of cyber analysts: **triage analysis, escalation analysis, correlation analysis, threat analysis, incident response**, and **forensic analysis**. We will elaborate on these roles and their relationship with other related cognitive processes. Erbacher et al. (2010a, b) extended the scope of the CTA further to include **vulnerability assessment** and a "big picture" component to highlight the interaction between the tactical-level cyber analysis (e.g., analyzing attacks within an enterprise's regional network) and strategic-level cyber analysis (e.g., detecting attacks involving multiple regions or multiple countries around the globe).

Based on the results of these CTA's, we synthesized and summarized the high-level cognitive processes of cyber analysts and their dependency relationships in Fig. 1. The ovals in the figure represent processes, and the rectangles in the figure represent Data or Information. Because some of the processes are performed by human analysts while some are performed by machine, we distinguish them using solid ovals for cognitive processes of cyber analysts, and white ovals for processes automated by software. For example, "IDS" refers to "intrusion detection system" such as SNORT.

A cyber analysis process transforms a huge amount of raw data in the network (e.g., network packets) and in each computer in the network (e.g., record of system calls such as authentication of a user's password) into decisions about "incident" (which represents a cyber attack that needs to be responded), which lead to response actions (e.g., shutting down a compromised machine) and further actions to mitigate the impact of the incident. This is the tactical level cyber analysis. Cyber analysts also need to correlate related incidents (which may be detected in different regions, different countries, or even possibly far in time) that are parts of a larger attack scheme. This is referred to as the strategic level cyber analysis (D'Amico and Whitley 2008).

The tactical-level cyber analysis also includes vulnerability scanning (typically performed by machine, but can be initiated and scheduled by a human analyst), which perform vulnerability assessment based on known vulnerabilities. Vulnerability of

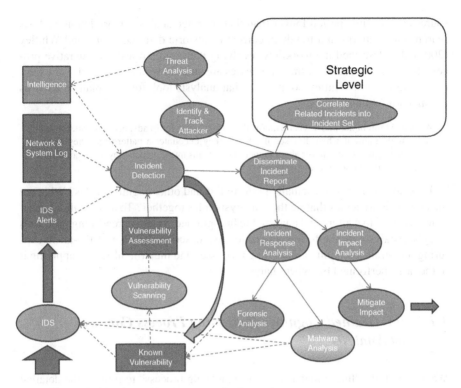

Fig. 1 The tactical-level cognitive processes of cyber analysts

machines often plays a key role for an analyst to confirm an incident. After an incident is detected, a formal report is generated by the analyst and disseminated for four types of further analyses at the tactical level: (1) incident response (for minimizing damage and expedited repairs), (2) impact analysis and mitigation plan (e.g., impacts to the current mission of war fighters), (3) identify and track attackers through threat analysis (i.e., intelligence gathering, analysis, and fusion for identifying the sponsor and the intent of the attack), and (4) forensic and malware analysis to obtain further details about the incident. The fourth step is especially important for a zero-day attack (e.g., an attack exploiting an unknown vulnerability), because they are crucial to identify the "signature" of the attack so that they can be incorporated into IDS for detecting future attacks of the same type.

D'Amico and Whitley (2008) identified six analysis roles that accounted for all the cognitive work performed by cyber analysts: (1) triage analysis, (2) escalation analysis, (3) correlation analysis, (4) threat analysis, (5) incident response, and (6) forensic analysis. While the role of the latter three has been explicitly represented in Fig. 1, the first three cognitive roles are part of Incident Detection and other functions performed by the analysts. Triage analysis filters the large amount of data (e.g., IDS alerts, network or system log) to identify "suspicious activity", which feed to escalation analysis to investigate, interpret, and assemble data from multiple sources over a time period longer than that of triage analysis. Correlation analysis searches for patterns and trends in current or historic data. D'Amico and Whitley (2008) also described the workflow involving these three roles as an iterative process. Some of the details of these processes are still not well understood. For example, D'Amico and Whitley pointed out that analysts look for unexplained patterns during correlation analysis:

> An analyst might not know what patterns they are looking for in advance; instead, the analyst might "know it when they see it". When they encounter a pattern that they cannot explain, they form hypotheses about potential malicious intent, which they try to confirm or contradict via additional investigation.

How do cyber analysts actually perform this and other cognitive roles? What are the cognitive processes that tie these analysis roles together? To answer these questions, we need to capture and analyze the fine-grained cognitive reasoning processes of cyber analysts. In the following section, we describe the state-of-the-art in capturing fine-grained cognitive reasoning processes and the difficulties for applying it to the tasks performed by cyber analysts.

1.1 Fine-Grained Cognitive Reasoning Process Capture and Analysis

We use the term "fine-grained cognitive reasoning process" to refer to the detailed cognitive process that describes individual actions and reasoning steps performed by an analyst and the relationships between these actions and reasoning steps. For example, one or more hypotheses can be formulated by the analyst at a particular point of the reasoning process based on the observations the analyst has made up to that point. These hypotheses can be later refined, rejected, or confirmed by the analyst during his/her reasoning process. For cyber analysts, such detailed cognitive reasoning process can complement the "high-level cognitive processes" described in the previous section in four important ways. First, it will improve our understanding about the difference in the cognitive reasoning processes of the experts and less-experienced analysts. Such an understanding is critically important to facilitate the design of better training tools for cyber analysts. Second, the fine-grained cognitive reasoning process of cyber analysts can provide a unique basis for identifying the opportunities to improve the visualization support for cyber analysts (Erbacher et al. 2010a, b). Third, the analysis of fine-grained cognitive reasoning process can lead to the design of automated cognitive aid tools by reusing and/or aggregating the processes of analysts to enhance the performance of analysts. Finally, the automated capture of the fine-grained cognitive reasoning process of cyber analysts can facilitate the sharing of relevant information and knowledge between cyber analysts, whether they are in different work shifts or in different geographic locations.

Existing methods for capturing fine-grained cognitive reasoning process include (1) talk-aloud protocol, (2) think-aloud protocol, (3) retrospective reports protocol, (4) observational case study, and (5) behavior trace capture. The first three methods are also referred to as types of "verbal protocol analysis" (Ericsson and Simon 1980,

1993). In a verbal protocol analysis, a subject performs a given task while being monitored by experimenters and being recorded (audio or video). In a talk-aloud protocol, the subject is asked to verbally articulate anything that comes to their mind in performing a given mental task. In a think-aloud protocol, the subject is asked to verbally describe anything that comes to their mind as they think to solve a problem. In a retrospective reports protocol, the subject is asked to reflect and articulate their thinking after they solve the problem. Retrospective reports can be combined with one of the first two protocols to validate their completeness (Ericsson and Simon 1993). Protocol analysis is the basis for knowledge acquisition methods, which elicit expert knowledge and encode them in an artificial intelligence system (often referred to as "expert systems", "knowledge-based systems", or "intelligent agents") through interviews and case studies. Due to the complexity of these tasks, the verbal protocol analysis needs to be augmented with an "interviewer" (typically referred to as a "knowledge engineer" due to their familiarity of the target representation language to be used to encode the expertise), who guides the thinking aloud protocol by asking probing questions, and by providing information to simulate the outcome of an action (e.g., test result of a diagnostic task) performed by the subject (Durkin 1994). While this elicitation method is feasible for tasks whose actions generate a limited number of outcomes (e.g., result of a test is positive or negative), it is difficult to apply the method to cyber analysis task whose actions (e.g., filter alerts for a particular port number) can lead to a wide range of possible outcomes.

The fourth method for acquiring fine-grained cognitive reasoning process is observational case study, which observes the subject in performing a task (Bell and Hardiman 1989). This method can be combined with think aloud protocol and/or retrospective report protocol. A case or a scenario is used in observational study to provide a context and relevant information in response to the actions of the subject.

The fifth method for obtaining fine-grained cognitive reasoning process is behavior trace, which transforms the observational data gathered from the subject into a "behavior trace". Tools (such as MacSHAPA) have been developed to facilitate the generation of such behavior trace from observational data (Sanderson et al. 1994). For example, a knowledge/cognitive engineer can use MacSHAPA to encode actions and/or communications captured in the observational data as template or predicate. While this type of tool is useful, it cannot extract the cognitive process that the subject did not explicitly articulate in the think-aloud protocol.

In the rest of this chapter, we first provide a literature review about research related to capturing cognitive process. This is followed by a framework for non-intrusive capturing and analysis of fine-grained reasoning cognitive processes, which includes (1) the Action-Observation-Hypothesis (AOH) conceptual model, (2) the non-intrusive capturing of a cognitive trace of cyber analysts containing a temporal sequence of AOH objects and relationships, and (3) extracting the reasoning process of cyber analysts by analyzing the cognitive trace. Section 4 presents a case study of applying the framework to systematic capturing of the cognitive reasoning process from professional network analysts and the initial results of analyzing the cognitive traces. Finally, we summarize the key contributions of systematic capturing of the cognitive reasoning process of cyber analysts and its critical enabling role toward a more agile cyber defense.

2 Literature Reviews

2.1 *Cognitive Task Analysis*

A cognitive task analysis (CTA) (Crandall et al. 2006) derives the required tasks for highly analytical (cognitive) activities such as decision-making; network analyst determination of network event relevance, importance, and characterization is of particular relevance. More specifically, a CTA attempts to determine what tasks are required to be performed and how the target experts perform said tasks. A cognitive task analysis is critical for developing correct tools and capabilities to improve the effectiveness of the network analyst, such as advanced displays, recommender systems, etc. Three CTAs are particularly relevant to network analysis from existing literature.

- The first CTA (Foresti and Agutter n.d.) examined the tools used by network experts at the time of the CTA as well as the advanced displays that had been developed for use by network experts. The focus of the CTA was to acquire the fundamentals necessary for the development of advanced displays geared towards improving network administrator efficiency. Additionally, results of the CTA identified the temporal organization of decisions and event prioritization through semi-structured interviews.
- The second CTA (D'Amico et al. 2005, D'Amico and Whitley 2008) had three goals. First was to study the set of analyst goals. Second was to identify the needed analyst expertise and their depth. Third was to identify the viability of visual representations and how such visual representations might be used. This study was performed through subject interviews of seven different organizations.
- The third study (Erbacher et al. 2010a, b) performed interviews of individuals with different levels of decision-making responsibility within network operations at Pacific Northwest National Laboratory. In addition to a wide range of requirements, this study generated a cyber command and control task flow diagram with primary tasks including assessment, detailed assessment, response, audit, and big picture, which is shown in Fig. 2.

2.2 *Case-Based Reasoning*

The reuse of cyber analysts' analytical reasoning results has been investigated using case-based reasoning (CBR). Given a problem, a CBR system retrieves a similar problem from a case library (also referred to as case base or knowledge base), modifies its solution for the given problem, and retains the new problem and solution in the case library (Stahl 2004). The original concept of CBR derives from a cognitive model of dynamic memory by Schank (1982), which led to computer-based CBR systems (Kolodner 1983; Lebowitz 1983). The process model of CBR developed by

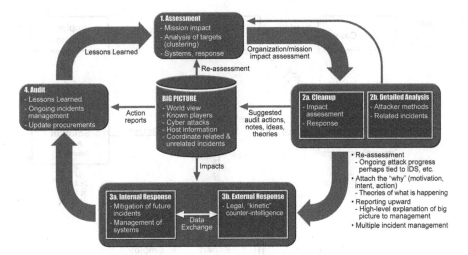

Fig. 2 A cyber command and control task flow (Erbacher et al. 2010a, b)

Aamodt and Plaza (1994), consists of four components: retrieve, reuse, revise, and retain. The model has driven the majority of research and application development in CBR research. Research into each of the four component areas has been extensive resulting in numerous reviews and surveys (De Mantaras et al. 2005). An extension of CBR model, shown in Fig. 3, explicitly includes the generation of incident reports by analysts (Erbacher and Hutchinson 2012).

In operations, a new scenario is matched against the existing scenarios to find the most relevant match, which is then mapped, using a similarity metric, to the new scenario providing an updated solution. Such case-based reasoning has been applied to a wide range of domains including:

- Breathalyzers (Doyle 2005)
- Bronchiolitis (Doyle 2005)
- E-Clinic (Doyle 2005)
- Intelligent tutoring systems (Soh and Blank 2008)
- Help desk systems, i.e. diagnosis (Stahl 2004)
- Electronic commerce product recommendation systems (Stahl 2004)
- Classification, i.e., class membership (Stahl 2004)

The retrieval component of CBR requires a similarity metric between cases. A survey/taxonomy of similarity metrics can be found in Cunningham (2008). Examples of research in retrieval mechanisms include:

- Information theory approaches (Ranganathan and Ronen 2010). This research provides for the identification of similarities between instances in an ontology.
- User defined functions (Sterling and Ericson 2006). The associated patent also covers the representative database issues.

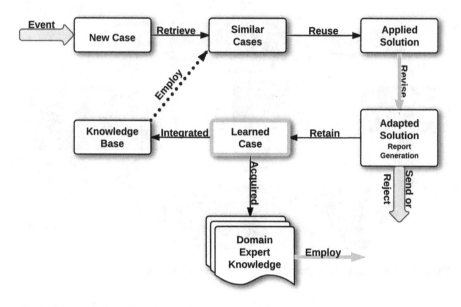

Fig. 3 An extended case-based reasoning process model

- Abduction versus deduction (Sun et al. 2005).
- Fuzzy similarity (Sun et al. 2005).
- Contextual probability (Wang and Dubitzky 2005). This metric integrates probability with distance-based neighborhood weighting and works for both ordinal and nominal data.
- Adaptive similarity (Long et al. 2004). This paradigm allows for specification of new similarity metrics and identification of the similarity metric to be applied in particular scenarios without the need for reprogramming.
- Semantic vs. syntactical similarities (Aamodt and Plaza 1994).
- Models of similarity (Osborne and Bridge 1997). The goal of this work was to identify the primary classes of similarity including absolute and relative similarity metrics.

Specific similarity metrics for categorical data include overlap, eskin, IOF, OF, Lin, Lin1, Goodall1, Goodall2, Goodall3, Goodall4, Smirnov, Burnaby, Anderberg, and Neighborhood Counting Metric (Boriah et al. 2008; Wang and Dubitzky 2005).

Case-based reasoning has been applied to support the reuse of an analyst's "report" that summarizes the analyst's analytical reasoning results regarding previous cyber-attacks so that the efforts of generating reports for a newly detected attack can be reduced significantly (Erbacher and Hutchinson 2012). However, CBR has not been used to capture and reuse the process of the analyst's analytical reasoning process. One of the challenges in applying CBR to retrieving and reusing analytical reasoning processes is a lack of non-intrusive way to capture them.

3   A Systematic Cognitive Reasoning Process Capture and Analysis Framework

To address the challenges of capturing a detailed cognitive process of a cyber analyst, we have developed a framework and associated cognitive trace tool for capturing the cognitive reasoning process of a cyber analyst. The framework not only integrates observational study and behavior trace methods described in Sect. 1.1, but also extends the previous approaches by enabling analysts to record their thinking (as "hypotheses"), and linking them to observations of interests during the observational study. In a way, the framework transforms "think aloud" to "type aloud"— instead of verbally articulating their thinking, analysts record each step of their cognitive reasoning process in a naturalistic way (not necessarily monitored) in the context of solving a given case involving cyber-attacks.

In the rest of this section, we first describe the conceptual model of the framework, which we will refer to as the A-O-H model, named after the three main objects in the framework: **Actions** performed by a subject, **Observations** of interest to the subject, and **Hypothesis** generated by the subject based on the observations. We then introduce the relationship between these objects that forms the analytical reasoning process of cyber analysts. Section 3.3 describes the AOH objects and relationship captured in a non-intrusive way. Finally, we discuss how the reasoning process can be extracted from the cognitive trace to provide the basis for systematic analysis of the cognitive reasoning processes at the individual level as well as across multiple analysts.

3.1   The A-O-H Conceptual Model of an Analytical Reasoning Process

A conceptual model of the analytical process of cyber analysis is informed by cognitive science theories including sense making theory and naturalistic decision making. The sense making theory builds on three key cognitive constructs: **Action, Observation**, and **Hypothesis**. Actions refer to analysts' evidence

Fig. 4 The iterative analytical reasoning process involving action, observation and hypothesis (A-O-H Model) (Zhong et al. 2013)

exploration activities; Observations refer to the observed data/alerts considered relevant by the analysts; Hypotheses represent the analysts' awareness and assumptions in a certain situation. These three constructs iterate and form reasoning cycles. Actions can lead to new or updated observations, which result in new or updated hypotheses, and later subsequent Actions. Not surprisingly, these three constructs, being part of the general sense making theory, naturally map to cognitive activities of cyber analysts. While Actions and Observations in cyber analysis are obvious, Hypotheses are not explicit (i.e., they are "tacit" knowledge) and cannot be fully anticipated due to new attack behaviors (hence needs to be entered by the analyst in a semi-formal representation). Often, a Hypothesis is not known for certain until further evidence (e.g., presence of relevant vulnerability on a node) is gathered to confirm or disconfirm. All the Hypotheses maintained by an analyst are called **"Working Hypotheses"**. We call the instances of Action, Observation and Hypothesis as **"AOH Objects"**.

3.2   The AOH Objects and Their Relationships Can Represent the Analytical Reasoning Processes

In the iterative cycles of analytical reasoning processes, Hypotheses in different sense making cycles be related in important ways. One set of Actions and Observations can lead to a set of disjunctive hypotheses. Therefore, the AOH Objects are connected to each other in an analytical reasoning process. This is illustrated in Fig. 5. Since an Action always results in an Observation, we put Action and Observation in a unit, called "**AO**". The Hypotheses ("**H**"s) being the children of an AO indicates these Hypotheses are generated based on the AO. An AO being a child of an H indicates that this AO is triggered by the H. We can also consider the Hypotheses only. If an H_1 has an AO unit as its child and another H H_2 is a child of AO, we say that H_2 is a child

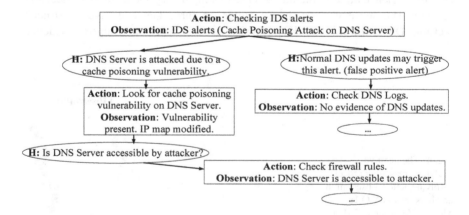

Fig. 5 An analytical reasoning process represented by the AOH objects

hypothesis of H_1. A parent H is connected to its immediate children H showing a conjunctive AND relationship (i.e., refined sub-hypotheses). If an H H_1 and an H_2 have the same AO as their parent, we say that H_2 is a sibling hypothesis of H_1. The sibling Hypotheses have disjunctive OR relationships (i.e., alternative hypotheses). Therefore, the AOH Objects in an analytical reasoning process are interconnected.

3.3 Capturing the Analytical Reasoning Processes

3.3.1 The Representation Indicates What Should Be Captured

We have proposed a model of analytical reasoning processes, which includes the AOH Objects and their relationships. The proposed model supports both a semi-structured representation of interconnected sense making constructs: Actions, Observations, and Hypothesis as well as an AND-OR organization of the Hypothesis. Actions and Observations can be captured in a structured representation, because the analysts' data exploration behaviors and the selected data can be automatically recorded. The Hypothesis constructs can be recorded in free text, which enables a flexible and analyst-friendly representation of analysts' thoughts.

An analyst could conduct various operations on the AOH Objects: the operations on Action could include filtering, searching, inquiring and data selecting; the operations on Observation could be selecting data entries and linking the data; the operations on Hypothesis could be creating a new Hypothesis, modifying an existing Hypothesis, switching the context and confirming/denying an existing Hypothesis. We will describe the operations in detail in Sect. 4. Therefore, we should also record the sequence of an analyst's operations on the AOH Objects in a temporal order.

3.3.2 Non-intrusive Capture

Regarding the importance of tacit knowledge and expertise, we capture the analytical reasoning processes of cyber analysis in a non-intrusive way. A monitoring system is developed to support the construction of AOH Objects, investigation and refinement of Hypotheses. This system audits the analysts' behaviors (e.g. data manipulation, hypothesis creation and refinement) and records them in traces, called "Cognitive Traces". This system would never interrupt the analysts. The Actions and related Observation are automatically tracked as the analysts selected data sources and specific entries of interest from each data source. When the analyst wishes to create a Hypothesis, the previously tracked Observations are automatically included in an initial list to be included as AO (i.e., the action-observation unit). The analyst can choose to modify the list to exclude data entries he/she looked at, but not relevant to the created Hypothesis. After the analyst confirms the captured AO to be associated with a Hypothesis, she/he is presented with a GUI interface to enter a short free-text description of the Hypothesis. Once the analyst completes the entering of Hypothesis description, the newly created AO and Hypothesis and their relationships are recorded to capture the analytic process of the cyber analyst. When the analyst wants to confirm a Hypothesis, he/she can mark the Hypothesis as "True". Alternatively, the analyst can reject a Hypothesis by marking it as "False".

3.4   Reasoning Processes in AOH Representation Can Be Extracted from the Cognitive Traces

Using the proposed representation, an analytical reasoning process is a process of evolving construction of AOH Objects, investigation and refinement of Hypotheses. Since the monitoring system has recorded the analysts' behaviors of construction of AOH Objects, investigation and refinement of the Hypotheses, we can extract the analytical reasoning processes given the captured cognitive traces.

Figure 6 shows the framework of the proposed cognitive tracing analysis. The conceptual AOH model lays the cognitive foundation of our representation of analytical reasoning processes. This representation helps us to capture the analytical reasoning processes in a non-intrusive way. We can then extract the reasoning processes by analyzing the cognitive traces.

By analyzing the cognitive traces, which are generated by cyber analysts and gathered in a non-intrusive way, we can identify gaps and opportunities that lay the foundation for the next generation of cyber defense training, education, and development. More specifically, the results of analyzing analytical reasoning traces of cyber analysts will provide key insights about the differences of analytical reasoning between highly experienced analysts and less-experienced analysts so that opportunities to improve the training of analysts can be identified. Furthermore, the results of the trace analysis will demonstrate the feasibility and the opportunities about leveraging the experience of experienced analysts to support the analytical reasoning of less-experienced analysts. Another important benefit of the results of trace analysis is to

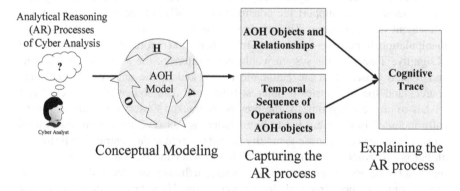

Fig. 6 The framework of the cognitive tracing analysis

demonstrate the opportunities to improve the sharing and communication of knowledge regarding cyber attacks to the decision makers through a systematic construction of "story telling" using the traces. Finally, the results of the trace analysis involving multi-step attacks will identify opportunities for multiple analysts to collaborate and share forensic-sound information to facilitate near real-time cyber forensics to support "fight through" under an asymmetric information environment.

4 A Case Study about Professional Network Analysts

4.1 A Tool for Capturing the Cognitive Traces

We developed ARSCA (Analytical Reasoning Support Tool for Cyber Analysis) toolkit to track the traces of analysts' analytical reasoning processes while they are doing cyber analysis tasks. Figure 7 shows the architecture of ARSCA. ARSCA provides analysts with two main views: Data View and Analysis View. Data View integrates the monitoring data sources, for example, network topology, IDS alerts and firewall logs in this case. The Analysis View enables analysts to create instances of Action, Observation and Hypothesis (i.e. AOH Objects).

Figure 8 shows the interfaces of ARSCA. While an analyst is exploring the monitoring data, the tool automatically captures the activities of data manipulation (for example, searching and filtering) in an emerging Action instance, and also captures the selected data and other information resulting from the previous activities in the emerging Observation instance. ARSCA also enables an analyst to write down their thoughts as a Hypothesis instance and relate it to its corresponding Actions and Observations (Zhong et al. 2013).

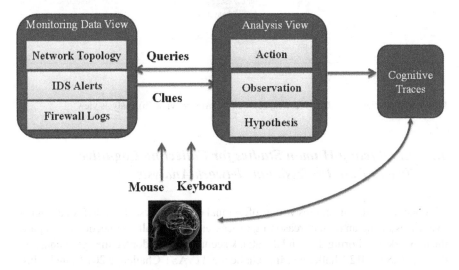

Fig. 7 The architecture of a cognitive trace capture tool

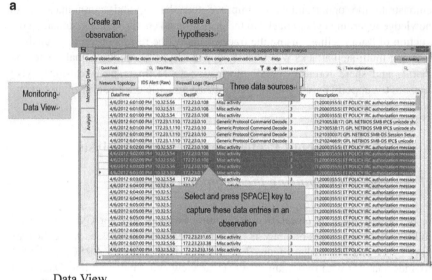

Data View

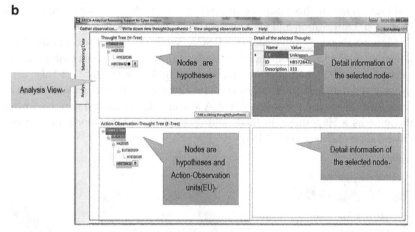

Analysis View

Fig. 8 The interface of ARSCA (Zhong et al. 2013) (**a**) Data view (**b**)Analysis view

4.2 Conducting Human Studies for Collecting Cognitive Traces from Professional Network Analysts

We conducted human studies with professional cyber analysts to gather their cognitive traces of the analytical reasoning processes. First of all, we needed to prepare the network monitoring data and the attack scenarios. We adopted the cyber analysis data of VAST 2012 Challenge Mini-challenge 2 (VAST Challenge 2012), including about 35,000 IDS alerts and 26,000,000 Firewall logs. Figure 9 shows the network

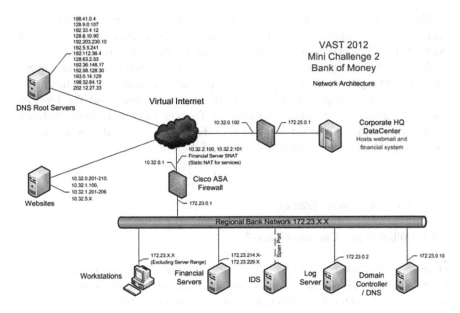

Fig. 9 The network topology of VAST 2012 Mini Challenge 2 (VAST 2012)

	Task	Time period	Raw data size
Table 1 Time period and size of dataset of the tasks	1	4/5 20:18–20:30 (12 min)	IDS: 214 Firewall: 123,133
	2	4/5 22:15–22:26 (11 min)	IDS: 239 Firewall: 115,524
	3	4/6 0:00–0:10 (10 min)	IDS: 296 Firewall: 112, 766
	4	4/6 18:01–18:15 (14 min)	IDS: 252 Firewall: 85,463

topology of the VAST 2012. This dataset implies a multi-step attack that took place over two days (about 40 h). Considering the fact that it is impossible for humans to process such large amounts of data without the help of external data analysis tools in a limited time, we cut out four pieces of the dataset which includes some key attack events and made four tasks using each of them. We made the tasks containing the same number of key attack events occurring in a similar amount of time, and containing a similar amount of network data. Table 1 shows the detailed information about the time period and dataset size of each task. Therefore, we can assume the tasks are at the same level of difficulty.

In collaboration with the U.S. Army Research Laboratory (ARL), the study recruited participants from professional network analysts working at ARL. In each task, analysts were asked to analyze the prepared network monitoring data with the goal of detecting the attack events. We also requested that the analyst use this tool to accomplish the analysis. Therefore, the tool would capture their analytical reasoning traces while they were doing the tasks.

Since the analysts are asked to use our tool, we provided a training session before each task and designed a quiz to test an analyst's proficiency of working with ARSCA. Each subject had to pass the quiz before he/she performs the task.

As a part of the experiment, we also ask subjects to respond to a pre-task questionnaire and a post-task questionnaire. The pre-task questionnaire contains questions about the demographic of the analyst, reasoning style, and the level of knowledge and skills regarding cyber analysis. The post-task questionnaire includes the analyst's retrospective summarization of the key findings and conclusions, as well as their assessment about the usefulness of the tool.

4.3 The Cognitive Traces

4.3.1 What Is in a Cognitive Trace?

Once an analyst completes his/her task, ARSCA generates the analyst's cognitive trace. In the rest of the chapter, we will use one of the subjects, S1, as an example to demonstrate in further detail the cognitive trace captured by ARSCA.

Figure 10 shows the AOH Objects created by subject S1 and their relationships. The ovals are the AO units and the rectangles are Hs. The text in an oval or a rectangle is the ID number for the AOH Object. We refer to the set of Hypotheses that are linked to the same AO (i.e. Action-Observation unit) as Alternative Hypotheses. For example, the Hypotheses in the dotted box in Fig. 10 are Alternative Hypotheses.

The operations on the AOH Objects are recorded in the cognitive trace in the temporal order they were performed by the analyst. Each item in a trace contains a timestamp and an operation on the AOH Objects. These operations can be grouped into three categories: (1) the operations related to Action (i.e. "AOP_Inquring", "AOP_Filtering", "AOP_Searching", and "AOP_Selecting"), (2) the operations

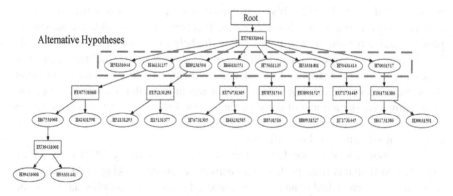

Fig. 10 The AOH objects and their relationships in S1's cognitive trace

Table 2 The description of operations

	Operation	Description
Operation on action	AOP_Filtering	Filter a data source
	AOP_Searching	Search a keyword in a data source
	AOP_Selecting	Select some data entries in a data source
	AOP_Inquiring	Inquire about a port or a term
Operation on observation	OOP_Selected	Generate an observation based on the selected data
	OOP_Linking	Link the selected data
Operation on hypothesis	HOP_New	Create a new hypothesis
	HOP_Add_Sibling	Add an alternative hypothesis
	HOP_SwitchContext	Switch the current focus of attention from one hypothesis to another hypothesis
	HOP_Modify	Modify the content of a hypothesis
	HOP_Confirm/Deny	Confirm/deny a hypothesis

related to Observation (i.e. "OOP_Selected" and "OOP_Linking"), and (3) the operations related to Hypothesis (i.e. "HOP_Confirm/Deny", "HOP_Modify", "HOP_SwitchContext", "HOP_Add_Sibling", and "HOP_New"). Table 2 summarizes these operations.

Figure 11 shows a portion of the file that records the cognitive trace generated by subject S1. Each item in the trace includes a timestamp and an operation. The operations in the trace items shown in Fig. 11 can be explained as follows.

- "FILTERING" (AOP_Filtering): Filtering the data source "Task2IDS" by the condition "SourcePort=6667".
- "SELECTING" (AOP_Selecting): Selecting the data entries in the filtered data set.
- "SELECTED" (OOP_Selected): The selected data entries. Such kind of operations always come in pairs with AOP_Selecting operations.
- "NEW" (HOP_NEW): Creating a new Hypothesis.

4.3.2 Cognitive Trace Analysis

We have conducted a preliminary analysis about the basic features of the collected cognitive traces from ten subjects, denoted by "S1", "S2", "S3", "S4", "S5", "S6", "S7", "S8", "S9", and "S10". Figure 12 shows the number of Action-Observation units and the number of hypotheses in the cognitive traces of these analysts, and the time they took to complete the cyber analysis task (based on VAST 2012). There is a significant differences among the analysts in terms of these three characteristics of their cognitive traces.

We further compared the number and the types of operations for the ten subjects in this case study. As shown in Fig. 13, there is a significant difference among the analysts both in terms of the number of operations and the type of operations

```
<?xml version="1.0" encoding="utf-8"?>
 <Trace ID="TAP84531155">
        ...
   <Item Timestamp="07/31/13 13:01:41">
          FILTERING(
                  SELECT * FROM Task2IDS WHERE SourcePort = '6667',
                  Task2IDS
          )
     </Item>

     <Item Timestamp="07/31/13 13:01:46">
          SELECTING(
                  A[1:2000355:5]-[10.32.5.54]-[172.23.232.252],
                  A[1:2000355:5]-[10.32.5.56]-[172.23.233.59],
                  A[1:2000355:5]-[10.32.5.54]-[172.23.238.124],
                  A[1:2000355:5]-[10.32.5.56]-[172.23.232.55]
                  )
     </Item>

     <Item Timestamp="07/31/13 13:01:46">
          SELECTED(
                  A[1:2000355:5]-[10.32.5.54]-[172.23.232.252],
                  A[1:2000355:5]-[10.32.5.56]-[172.23.233.59],
                  A[1:2000355:5]-[10.32.5.54]-[172.23.238.124],
                  A[1:2000355:5]-[10.32.5.56]-[172.23.232.55]
                  )
     </Item>

     <Item Timestamp="07/31/13 13:04:06">
          NEW (
                  H46131157 The network is not secure,
                  H67531068 IDS IRC Alerts are true: The IDS alerts are showing
                  IRC authorization alerts over tcp/6667. This is the default IRC
                  communication port, and this communication is between the
                  workstation IPs and external resources. In this situation this
                  could indicate that there has been a policy violating because IRC
                  communication on this network isn't allowed. Or this could also
                  be an indicator of compromise because malware can leverage
                  IRC for Command to Control (C2) communication.
                  )
     </Item>
        ...
 </Trace>
```

Fig. 11 An example output file of S1's cognitive trace

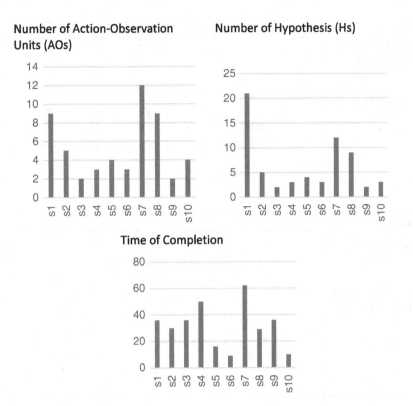

Fig. 12 The number of AOH's in the traces and task completion time

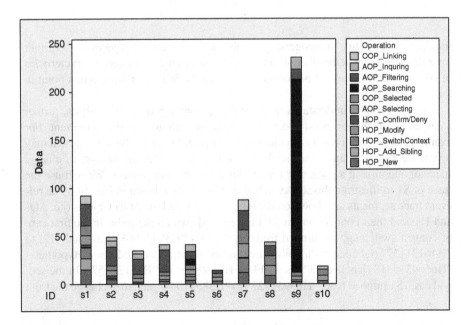

Fig. 13 Comparing the number of operations among ten Subjects (the operations are described in Table 2)

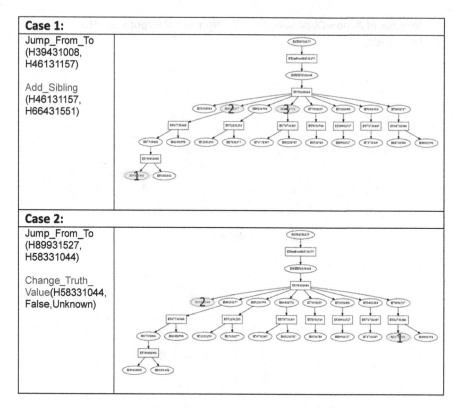

Fig. 14 Two cases of switching to previous hypothesis in S1's trace

they performed. This "heterogeneity" of the cognitive trace motivates us to further investigate to see whether there is any possible relationship between characteristics of cognitive traces and the performance of analysts. We will return to this point in the next section.

To gain a deeper understanding about the reasoning process of analysts, further analyses about the temporal ordering of these operations are also important. For example, switching context is an interesting aspect for trace analysis, because it may reveal the rationale and associated reasoning that enables the analyst to change focus of attention at a particular time in his/her reasoning process. We will use the trace of S1 to illustrate this: S1 switched context twice (shown in Fig. 14). The relevant trace segments are shown on the left of Fig. 14, and the AOH Objects (i.e. AOs and Hs) and their connections in S1's trace are shown on the right. In the first case of context switching, S1 jumped from Hypothesis "H39431008" (labelled "1") to "H46131157" (labelled "2"). Following this operation, S1 created a new Hypothesis "H666431551" (labelled "3") as a sibling Hypothesis of "H46131157". In the second case, S1 jumped from "H89931527" to "H58331044", and then change the truth value of "H58331044" from "Unknown" to "False" (i.e. rejecting it). Even though the analyst S1 switched contexts in both cases, the rationales are quite different. In the first case, S1 went back to a previous hypothesis to create an alternative hypothesis. In the latter case, he/she recalled a previous hypothesis to reject it. This example illustrates the importance in analyzing the temporal sequence of operations to obtain a richer understanding about the reasoning process of the analyst.

4.4 What Are the Characteristics of Cognitive Traces for Different Levels of Performance?

Since the pursuit of our research is to improve the analysts' performance in cyber analysis, we are interested in the analysts' performance in our tasks and the characteristics of cognitive traces for different levels of performance.

The ground truth of our tasks is known, which is the attack scenario of the VAST 2012 Challenge Mini Challenge 2. Therefore, we can evaluate the analyst's performance in a task based on how accurate his/her findings and conclusions are compared to the known ground truth. We conducted two rounds of evaluation to decide a final performance score for each subject, on a scale of 0–5 (with 5 being the best performance). Figure 15 shows the performance score of the ten subjects. Three analysts were rated highest (5 points), four analysts received 4 points, and three analysts were rated lowest (3 points).

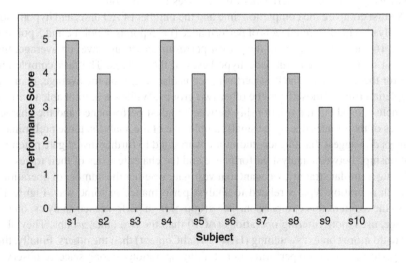

Fig. 15 The performance score of the ten subjects

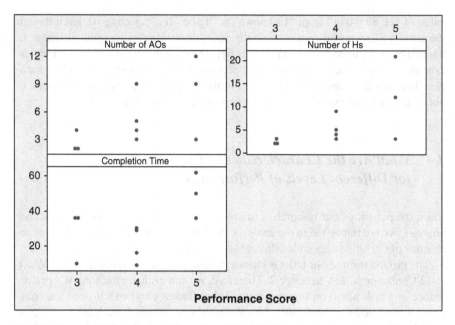

Fig. 16 The completion time and the number of A-O-H objects in the three groups of cognitive traces with different levels of performance scores

Next, we categorize the cognitive traces into three groups according to the performance score (that is, the traces with 3 points, 4 points and 5 points respectively), and investigate the characteristics of these traces in each group.

We first compare the completion time and the number of AO units and hypotheses for analysts with different levels of performance (i.e. 3 points, 4 points, and 5 points). Figure 16 shows that traces in the lowest performance group have, on average, the smallest number of AO units and hypotheses in their traces. The task completion time for the group with the best performance is also larger, on the average, than the completion time of those from the other two groups. While we are not able to arrive at conclusions about the relationship between analyst performance and the characteristics of their traces due to the small sample size of the analysts, these preliminary findings do suggest that further studies are warranted to further investigate potential relationships between analyst performance and the characteristics of their traces.

Using a similar strategy, we want to investigate whether the number of operations for each operation type is related to analyst performance in some way. Figure 17 shows the result of this comparison. The group of high performance analysts, on the average, uses more filtering operations (AOP) than the two other groups. They also tend to do more context switching (HOP SwitchContext) than the others. Finally, the high performance group performs more linking operations among selected observations (OOPLinking). As we mentioned before, more samples and further studies are needed to investigate whether these detailed trace characteristics are correlated with analyst performance in a statistical significant way. These preliminary results, however, do suggest that comparing the characteristics of cognitive traces of analysts with their performance is a promising direction of future research.

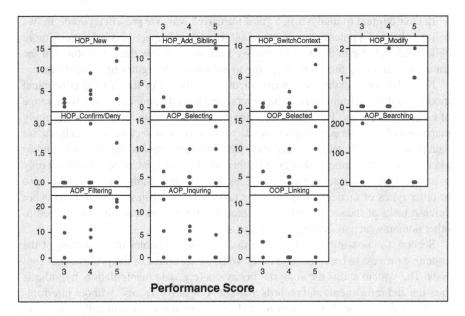

Fig. 17 The number of different types of operations in the cognitive traces at different levels of performance score

5 Summary

As computing devices connected to the internet explode for personal health monitoring and management, environment and physical security surveillance, smart home appliances, smart vehicles, smart energy grid, and ubiquitous computing (e.g., Google Glass), the complexity and the frequency of cyber-attacks faced by cyber defense analysts of governments and business enterprises continue to increase at a rapid speed. The ultimate goal of cyber defense is to increase its agility even for zero-day attacks (e.g., attacks leveraging vulnerabilities that are not known by the cyber defenders), so that the time from detection of attacks to creating automated support tool to enable early and effective detection of future similar attacks is as close to real-time as possible. A critical obstacle on the path to achieving this vision is lacking a systematic framework and supporting methods/tools for capturing the analytical reasoning process of professional cyber defense analysts.

In this chapter, we have described the current understanding about the high-level cognitive process of cyber analysts, based on Cognitive Task Analysis (CTA) conducted previously with professional cyber defense analysts, and the difficulty of capturing fine-grained cognitive reasoning process of analysts using existing methods. To address this difficulty in a way that is well-founded theoretically (for high generality) and, in the same time, practically feasible for being embedded into the work environment of analysts in a "non-intrusive" way, we present a paradigm, we believe, that has a potential to create transformational impacts toward a much more agile cyber defense in the near future. We summarize below the key features of the framework and how they can contribute to enhancing the agility of cyber defense.

First, the sense making cognitive theory foundation of the A-O-H conceptual model enables the framework to be general and broadly applicable to a wide range of tasks and domains. The notion of actions, observations, and hypotheses naturally map to the observable actions performed by the analysts, observations from immense data presented to the analysts, and their hypothesized attack step, sequence, and/or plan. Because the framework is built on the A-O-H model, it can be applied not only to intrusion detection at the tactical level as demonstrated in the case study, but also to other types of tactical cyber analysis tasks (e.g., forensics) as well as to cyber defense tasks at the strategic level. In fact, the framework can also be applied to other domains such as intelligence analysis.

Second, the non-intrusive nature of the framework enables the capturing of the cognitive process to be embedded in the work environment of the professional analysts. The system audits the analysts' behaviors (e.g. data manipulation, hypothesis creation and refinement) and records them in "Cognitive Traces" without interrupting the analysts. The Actions and related Observation are automatically tracked as the analysts selected data sources and specific entries of interest from each data source. When the analyst wishes to create a Hypothesis, the previously tracked Observations are automatically included in an initial list to be included as AO (i.e., the action-observation unit). The non-intrusive capturing of cognitive trace is a key enabler toward a more agile defense because it enables the cognitive trace to be captured at the earliest possible time, and significantly reduce the time and the cost (e.g., due to extra efforts the analysts need to make) it may take to extract reasoning process from the analysts otherwise.

Third, the cognitive traces captured in non-intrusive way, as demonstrated by the case study, provide, for the first time, important characteristics of the reasoning process of analysts and their potential relationship to the performance of analysts. These characteristics and relationship offers promising indication that the analysis of the reasoning process (both at the individual level and at the aggregate level) can be beneficial to the design of training programs and cognitive aids for enhancing the performance of analysts (Zhong et al, 2014).

In summary, this book chapter presents a theoretically well-founded and practical non-intrusive framework for capturing and analyzing the cognitive reasoning processes of professional cyber analysts. It provides important basis for further studies regarding collaboration among analysts (e.g., in two adjacent work shifts), visualization needs and design for supporting analysts, cognitive aids, and training procedures that leverage the reasoning processes captured to assist analysts to perform the cyber defense analysis at hand with higher quality and more efficiency.

References

Aamodt, A. and Plaza, E. (1994) "Case-based reasoning: foundational issues, methodological variations, and system approaches." *AI Commun.* 7, 1, 39–59.

Bell, J., and Hardiman, R. J. (1989) "The third role – the naturalistic knowledge engineer", in *Knowledge elicitation: Principles, Techniques, and Applications*, Dan Diaper (ed.), John Wiley & Sons, New York.

Biros, D., and Eppich, T. (2001) Human Element Key to Intrustion Detection, Signal, p. 31, August.

Boriah, S., Chandola, V., Kumar, V.: (2008) Similarity measures for categorical data: A comparative evaluation. In: SDM, pp. 243–254. SIAM, Philadelphia.

Crandall, B., Klein, G., and Hoffman, R. (2006). *Working minds: A practitioner's guide to cognitive task analysis.* MIT Press.

Cunningham, P., (2008) "A Taxonomy of Similarity Mechanisms for Case-Based Reasoning," University College Dublin, Technical Report UCD-CSI-20080-11, January 6.

D'Amico, A., Whitley, K., Tesone, D., O'Brien, B., and Roth, E., (2005) Achieving Cyber Defense Situational Awareness: A Cognitive Task Analysis of Information Assurance Analysts, in Proceedings of the Human Factors and Ergonomics Society 49th Annual Meeting, 229–233.

D'Amico, A. and Whitley, K. (2008) "The Real Work of Computer Network Defense Analysts," *VizSEC 2007: Proceedings of the Workshop on Visualization for Computer Security*, Springer-Verlag Berlin Heidelberg, pp. 19–37.

De Mantaras, R. L., McSherry, D., Bridge, D., Leake, D., Smyth, B., Craw, S., Faltings, B., Maher, M. L., Cox, M. T., Forbus, K., Keane, M., Aamodt, A., and Watson, I. (2005) Retrieval, reuse, revision and retention in case-based reasoning. *Knowl. Eng. Rev.* 20, 3 (September 2005), 215–240.

Doyle, D. (2005) "A Knowledge-Light Mechanism for Explanation in Case-Based Reasoning," University of Dublin, Trinity College. Department of Computer Science, Doctoral Thesis TCD-CS-2005-71.

Durkin, J. (1994), "Expert Systems: Design and Development", Mamillan, New York, NY.

Erbacher, R. F. and Hutchinson, S. E. (2012) "Extending Case-based Reasoning to Network Alert Reporting", in *Proceedings of 2012 International Conference on Cyber Security*, pp. 187–194.

Erbacher, R. F., Frincke, D. A., Wong, P. C., Moody, S. J., Fink, G. A. (2010a) A multi-phase network situational awareness cognitive task analysis, Information Visualization 9(3): 204–219.

Erbacher, R. F., Frincke, D. A., Wong, P. C., Moody, S. J., Fink, G. A, (2010b) Cognitive task analysis of network analysts and managers for network situational awareness. VDA 2010: 75300

Ericsson, K. A. and Simon, H. A., (1980) "Verbal reports as data", Psychological Review, 87 (3), pp. 215–251.

Ericsson, K. A. and Simon, H. A., (1993) "Protocol analysis", MIT Press, Cambridge, MA.

Foresti, S. and Agutter, J., "Cognitive Task Analysis Report," University of Utah, CROMDI. Funded by ARDA and DOD.

Kolodner, J. (1983) "Reconstructive Memory: A Computer Model," *Cognitive Science* 7 (4), pp. 281–328.

Lebowitz, M. (1983) "Memory-based parsing," *Artificial Intelligence* 21, 4, pp. 363–404.

Long, J., Stoecklin, S., Schwartz, D. G., and Patel, M., (2004) "Adaptive Similarity Metrics in Case-based Reasoning," *The 6th IASTED International Conference on Intelligent Systems and Control* (ISC 2004), August 23–25, Honolulu, Hawaii, pp. 260–265.

Osborne, H. and Bridge, D., (1997) "Models of Similarity for Case-Based Reasoning," *Proc. Interdisciplinary Workshop Similarity and Categorisation*, pp. 173–179.

Ranganathan A., and Ronen, R. (2010) "Information-Theory Based Measure of Similarity Between Instances in Ontology," International Business Machines Corporation, United States Patent #7,792,838 B2.

Sanderson, P., Scott, J., Johnston, T., Mainzer, J., Watanabe, L., and James, J., (1994) "MacSHAPA and the enterprise of exploratory sequential data analysis (ESDA)", *Int. J. Human-Computer Studies*, 41, pp. 633–681.

Schank, R., (1982) *Dynamic Memory: A Theory of Learning in Computers and People* (New York: Cambridge University Press.

Soh, L. K., and Blank, T. (2008) "Integrating Case-Based Reasoning and Meta-Learning for a Self-Improving Intelligent Tutoring System. *Int. J. Artif. Intell. Ed.* 18, 1, 27–58.

Stahl, A. (2004) Learning of Knowledge-Intensive Similarity Measures in Case-Based Reasoning. PHD-Thesis, dissertation.de, Technische Universität Kaiserslautern.

Sterling, W. M., and Ericson, B. J. (2006) "Case-Based Reasoning Similarity Metrics Implementation Using User Defined Functions," NCR Corp., United States Patent # 7,136,852 B1, Nov. 14.

Sun, Z., Finnie, G., and Weber, K. (2005) "Abductive Case Based Reasoning," *International Journal of Intelligent Systems*, 20(9), 957–983.

Wang, H. and Dubitzky, W., (2005) "A flexible and robust similarity measure based on contextual probability." In *Proceedings of the 19th international joint conference on Artificial intelligence* (IJCAI'05). Morgan Kaufmann Publishers Inc., San Francisco, CA, USA, 27–32.

Zhong, C., Kirubakaran, D. S., Yen, J. and Liu, P., (2013) "How to Use Experience in Cyber Analysis: An Analyt-ical Reasoning Support System," in Proc. of IEEE Conf. on Intelligence and Security Informatics (ISI), pp. 263–265.

Zhong, C., Samuel, D., Yen, J., Liu, P., Erbacher, R., Hutchinson, S., Etoty, R., Cam, H., and Glodek, W. (2014) "RankAOH: Context-driven Similarity-based Retrieval of Experiences in Cyber Analysis," in Proceedings of IEEE International Conference on Cognitive Methods in Situation Awareness and Decision Support (CogSIMA 2014) pp. 230–236.

VAST Challenge 2012 http://www.vacommunity.org/VAST+Challenge+2012

Visualizations and Analysts

Christopher G. Healey, Lihua Hao, and Steve E. Hutchinson

1 Introduction

The challenges of CSA discussed in previous chapters call for ways to provide assistance to analysts and decision-makers. In many fields, analyses of complex systems and activities benefit from visualization of data and analytical products. Analysts use images in order to engage their visual perception in identifying features in the data, and to apply the analysts' domain knowledge. One would expect the same to be true in the practice of cyber analysts as they try to form situational awareness of complex networks. Earlier, the Cognition and Technology chapter introduced the topic of visualization: its criticality to the users, e.g., cyber analysts, as well as its pitfalls and limitations. Now, this chapter takes a close look at visualization for Cyber Situational Awareness. We begin with a basic overview of scientific and information visualization, and of recent visualization systems for cyber situation awareness. Then, we outline a set of requirements, derived largely from discussions with expert cyber analysts, for a candidate visualization system.

We conclude with a case study of a web-based tool that supports our requirements through the use of charts as a core representation framework. A JavaScript charting library is extended to provide interface flexibility and correlation capabilities to the analysts as they explore different hypotheses about potential cyber attacks. We describe key elements of the design, explain how an analyst's intent is used to generate different visualizations that provide situation assessment to improve the analyst's situation

C.G. Healey (✉) • L. Hao
Department of Computer Science, North Carolina State University,
890 Oval Drive #8206, Raleigh, NC 27695-8206, USA
e-mail: healey@ncsu.edu; lhao2@ncsu.edu

S.E. Hutchinson
Adelphi Research Center, U.S. Army Research Laboratory,
2800 Powder Mill Road, Adelphi, MD 20783-1138, USA
e-mail: steve.e.hutchinson.ctr@mail.mil

© Springer International Publishing Switzerland 2014
A. Kott et al. (eds.), *Cyber Defense and Situational Awareness*,
Advances in Information Security 62, DOI 10.1007/978-3-319-11391-3_8

awareness, and show how the system allows an analyst to quickly produce a sequence of visualizations to explore specific details about a potential attack as they arise.

Data visualization converts raw data into images that allow a viewer to "see" data values and the relationships they form. The motivation is that images allow viewers to use their visual perception to identify features in the data, to manage ambiguity, and to apply domain knowledge in ways that would be difficult to do algorithmically.

Visualization has a long and rich history, starting with the use of maps and graphs to represent information. In one famous example, John Snow constructed a dot map to identify clusters of victims during a cholera outbreak in central London in 1854. Based on the location of the clusters, Snow hypothesized that contaminated drinking water was the cause of the disease. Disabling a public water pump in the area confirmed this conclusion. Another example occurred during the Crimean War (1853–1856). Florence Nightingale, volunteering as a nurse, observed very poor living conditions for wounded soldiers. This led her to create a multidimensional pie chart, known a Rose or a Coxcomb chart, to document the causes of deaths during the war. She used her charts to highlight that deaths from preventable disease far outnumbered deaths from injury and other non-preventable causes.

Work in visualization continued to expand on these earlier uses. In the area of statistics Bertin presented a theory of graphical symbols used to visually represent information (Bertin 1967). Chernoff proposed the use of facial expression properties (Chernoff faces) to visualize multivariate data (Chernoff 1973). In 1987 the National Science Foundation sponsored a Workshop on Visualization in Scientific Computing. Results were presented to the research community as a foundation for computer-based visualization (DeFanti and Brown 1987). The initial focus was on scientific visualization techniques for data with known spatial embeddings: volume visualization of reconstructed CT or MRI data, terrain visualization of geospatial data, or flow visualization of vector fields representing flow data. Later, the field expanded to include information visualization approaches for more abstract data: text visualization for documents or web pages, level-of-detail visualization for data with hierarchical structures, or multivariate visualizations made up of glyphs that vary their visual appearance to represent multi-valued datasets.

Although scientific and information visualization are seen as two sub-areas, significant overlap exists between them. For example, issues of human perception— how our visual system perceives basic properties of colour, texture, and motion, and how we can use this knowledge to build effective visual representations—apply to both areas. Multivariate data—data elements that encode multiple data attribute values—must be considered in both scientific and information visualization.

The field of visualization has matured significantly since the original NSF workshop. The area of visual analytics was proposed in 2005 to explicitly combine data analytics and visualization for iterative data exploration and hypothesis testing (Thomas and Cook 2005). New research continues in many different directions. Johnson, director of the Scientific Computing and Imaging (SCI) Institute at the University of Utah, published a list of "Top Scientific Visualization Research Problems" (Johnson 2004). Examples include integrating science into visualization, representing error and uncertainty, integrating perception into visualization, taking advantage of novel hardware, and improving human-computer interaction in visualization systems. A more recent report sponsored by the NIH and the NSF on visualization research challenges echoed these suggestions (Johnson et al. 2006). Although nearly 10 years have passed since Johnson's original list, many of these areas continue to generate new research results.

2   Formalizing Visualization Design

Numerous researchers have proposed ways to structure or describe a visualization design, for example, by the data being visualized, by the visual properties being used, or by the tasks the visualization supports.

We present a formalization that describes how data is mapped to visual properties like luminance, hue, size, orientation, and so on. Data passed through this data-feature mapping generates a visual representation—a visualization—that displays individual data values and the patterns they form.

An input dataset D is made up of one or more data attributes $A = \{A_1, \ldots, A_n\}$. Each data element e_i stored in D contains a value for each data attribute, $e_i = \{a_{i,1}, \ldots a_{i,n}\}$. In order to visualize D, a set of n visual features $V = \{V_1, \ldots, V_n\}$ are selected, one for every data attribute in A. Finally, mappings $M = \{M_1, \ldots, M_n\}$ are defined to map the domain of A_i to the range of V_i.

As a simple example, we return to the well-known technique of visualizing data on a map. Consider a temperature map similar to those shown on any weather site. Here, D is made up of three attribute: $A = \{A_1 : longitude, A_2 : latitude, A_3 : temperature\}$. The visual features $V = \{V_1 : x, V_2 : y, V_3 : colour\}$ are used to convert temperature readings throughout the world, stored as data elements $e_i \in D$, into a visual representation. M_1 and M_2 map e_i's longitude and latitude to an absolute x and y location. These can be used to position the map within the visualization window, and to change its size and aspect ratio. M_3 maps temperature values to different colours, often over a discretized rainbow colour scale that mirrors the range of colours seen in a rainbow: violet–indigo–blue–green–yellow–orange–red. This represents cold temperatures with purple and blue, hot temperatures with orange and red, and moderate temperatures with green and yellow, exactly as seen in many temperature maps.

More complicated datasets have more data attributes. For example, suppose we expanded the weather dataset to include not only temperature, but also pressure, humidity, radiation, and precipitation. This requires a visualization design that uses more visual features and data-feature mappings. It quickly becomes difficulty to choose features and mappings in ways that work effectively together. We could also increase the number of weather readings we collect. Even on a high definition display, once the number of data elements exceeds 2.2 million, there are not enough pixels in the display to visualize each element. Introducing additional positional attributes like elevation and time further complicates the visualization's design requirements. Non-numeric data attributes may also exist. Suppose D included an attribute "A_4: forecast" that provides a text description of the current weather conditions, in the context of average and extreme conditions for the given location and time of year. Choosing a visual feature and a mapping to convert text forecasts into visual representations is itself a challenging problem. Researchers in visualization are studying new techniques that are designed to address exactly these types of issues.

Based on this overview, it seems clear that visualization offers the potential for important contributions to cyber situation awareness. Indeed, many existing situation awareness tools use visualization techniques like charts, maps, and flow diagrams to present information to an analyst. It is critical, however, to study how best to integrate visualization techniques into a cyber situation awareness domain. For example, which techniques are best suited to the data and tasks common to this domain? What is the best way to integrate these techniques into an analyst's existing workflow and mental models? How can problems in cyber situation awareness motivate new and novel research in visualization?

3 Visualization for Cyber Situation Awareness

The visualization community has focused recent attention on the areas of cyber security and cyber situation awareness. Early visual analysis of cyber security data often relied on text-based approaches that present data in text tables or lists. Unfortunately, these approaches do not scale well, and they cannot fully represent important patterns and relationships in complex network or security data. Follow-on work applied more sophisticated visualization approaches like node-link graphs, parallel coordinates, and treemaps to highlight different security properties, patterns in network traffic, and hierarchical data relationships. Because the amount of data generated can be overwhelming, many tools adopt a well-known information visualization approach: overview, zoom and filter, and details on demand. This approach starts by presenting an overview of the data. This allows an analyst to filter and zoom to focus on a subset of the data, then request additional details about the subset as needed. Current security visualization systems often consist of multiple visualizations, each designed to investigate different aspects of a system's security state from different perspectives and at different levels of detail.

3.1 Security Visualization Surveys

Visualization for cyber environments has matured to a point where survey papers on the area are available. These papers provide useful overviews, and also propose ways to organize or categorize techniques along different dimensions.

Shiravi et al. presented a survey of visualization techniques for network security (Shiravi et al. 2012). In addition to providing a useful overview of current visualization systems, they define a number of broad categories for data sources and visualization techniques. One axis subdivides techniques by data source: network traces, security events, user and asset context (e.g., vulnerability scans or identity management), network activity, network events, and logs. A second axis considers use cases: host/server monitoring, internal/external monitoring, port activity, attack patterns, and routing behaviour. Numerous techniques are described as examples of different data sources and use cases. The authors specifically address the issue of situation awareness in their future work, noting that many visualization systems try to prioritize important situations and project critical events as ways to summarize the massive amounts of data generated within a network. They distinguish between situation awareness, which they define as "a state of knowledge", and situation assessment, defined as "the process of attaining situation awareness." Converting raw data into visual forms is one method of situation assessment, meant to present information to an analyst to enhance their situation awareness.

Dang and Dang also surveyed security visualization techniques, focusing on web-based environments (Dang and Dang 2013). Dang chose to classify systems based on where they run: client-side, server-side, or web application. Client-side systems are normally simple, focusing on defending web users from attacks like phising. Server-side visualizations are designed for system administrators or cyber security analysts with an assumed level of technical knowledge. These visualizations are usually larger and more complex, focusing on multivariate displays that present multiple properties of a network to the analyst. Most network security visualization tools fall into the server-side category. A final class of system is security for web applications. This is a complicated problem, since it can involve web developers, administrators, security analysts, and end users. Dang also subdivided server-side visualizations by main goal: network management, monitoring, analysis, and intrusion detection; by visualization algorithm: pixel, chart, graph, and 3D; and by data source: network packet, NetFlows, and application-generated data. Various techniques exist at the intersection of each category.

New security and cyber situation visualization systems are constantly being proposed. We present a number of recent techniques, subdivided by visualization type. This offers an introduction to different visualization methods, in the context of the security and situation awareness domains.

3.2   Charts and Maps

As discussed in the overview, charts and maps are two of the most common visualization techniques. Well-known approaches improve a tool's accessibility by reducing the effort needed for analysts to "learn" the visualizations. It is common to present summarizes of data as bar charts, pie charts, scatterplots, or maps. Abstract data like network traffic or intrusion alerts need to be spatially positioned as part of the visualization design. Embedding the data using a chart's axes—for example, a scatterplot that maps IP addresses, $A = \{A_1 : source\ IP, A_2 : destination\ IP,$ to the horizontal and vertical axes, $V = \{V_1 : x, V_2 : y\}$—or assigning a geographic location to each data element—for example, estimating an IP address's longitude and latitude, then converting $A = \{A_1 : longitude, A_2 : latitude\}$ to $V = \{V_1 : x, V_2 : y\}$—are common approaches to positioning data elements.

Roberts et al. proposed the StatVis system, built on stacked bar graphs and geographic heatmaps, to visualize network health over time (Roberts et al. 2012). The graphs and heatmaps are used to present overviews of machine status in different geographic regions. A separate reticle visualization is used to present details about individual machines. The result is a combination of overview and details-on-demand for obtaining real-time situation awareness of a computer network's status.

A similar system called VIAssist visualizes network security data by linking between different charts to present the data from multiple perspectives (Goodall and Sowul 2009). When data elements are selected (or brushed) in one visualization, the same elements are highlighted (or linked) in the others. This identifies how data elements correlate between the visualizations. An overview uses bar and pie charts to visualize the most frequent elements for any data attribute. Coordinated views use various charts and maps to present visualizations that are correlated with one another. This allows analysts to assess different parts of a computer system using different visualization techniques.

3.3 Node-Link Graphs

Another common visualization technique is a node-link graph, where nodes and links correspond to data elements and relationships between the elements. For example, nodes can represent machine clusters and edges network connections between the clusters. Node-link graphs also support the application of graph algorithms to analyze the structure of a network, or the pattern of traffic within the network.

The NetFlow Visualizer uses node-link graphs to display communication as oriented edges between network devices, represented by graph nodes, at different levels of aggregation (Minarik and Dymacek 2008). This allows analysts to build up a situation awareness of the ongoing state of their networks, and to focus on individual flows of interest. The graph visualization is correlated with a spreadsheet containing specific values for individual network properties. Analysts can assign different attributes to control the size and color of the nodes and edges.

3.4 Timelines

Since changes over time are often critical to understanding a dataset, timelines are another common method of visualization for cyber situation awareness. Although timelines are similar to charts—for example, a line chart with $A = \{A_1 : time, A_2 : frequency\}$ mapped to $V = \{V_1 : x, V_2 : y\}$—their specific function is to highlight temporal patterns and relationships in a dataset.

Isis, a system designed by Phan et al. provides two visualizations—timelines and event plots—that are linked together to support iterative investigation of network intrusions (Phan et al. 2007). Isis's timeline presents an overview of temporal sequences of network flows in a histogram chart. The event plot allows an analyst to drill down over a subset of data to reveal patterns in individual events, using a scatterplot with $A = \{A_1 : time, A_2 : IP\ address\}$ mapped to $V = \{V_1 : x, V_2 : y\}$. Markers in the scatterplot represent individual NetFlows. The markers can vary their shape, size, and colour to visualize NetFlow properties.

PortVis also uses a timeline to visualize port-based security events (McPherson et al. 2004). The timeline is ideal for summarizing events over a wide time window (e.g., hundreds of hours). It uses a scatterplot to visualize $A = \{A_1 : port\ number, A_2 : time\}$ mapped to the horizontal and vertical axes, $V = \{V_1 : x, V_2 : y\}$. More detailed visualizations are also available for situation assessment over shorter time windows: a main visualization to investigate activity on individual ports, and a detailed visualization that uses a bar chart to present values for different port attributes.

3.5 Parallel Coordinates

Parallel coordinates (PCs) are a technique for visualizing multivariate data using a set of n vertical axes, one per data attribute in a dataset. Each axis covers the domain of its attribute, from the smallest value at the bottom to the largest value at the top. A data element is represented as positions on each axis defined by the element's attribute values. Positions on neighbouring axes are connected with line segments, visualizing the element as a polyline. An important advantage of PCs is their flexibility in the number and type of data attributes they can represent.

As an example, consider Fisher's Iris dataset, which contains 450 measurements for three species of irises, $A = \{A_1 : type, A_2 : petal\ width, A_3 : petal\ length, A_4 : sepal\ width, A_5 : sepal\ length\}$ Plotting the data using $V = \{V_1 : colour, V_{2-5} : PC\ axis\}$ produces the visualization in Fig. 1. Numerous relationships are visible, for example petal length and width are correlated

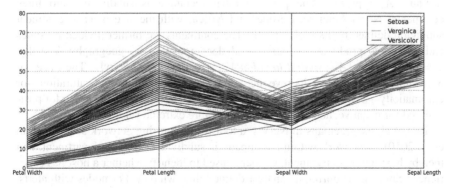

Fig. 1 A parallel coordinates visualization of data from Fisher's Iris dataset

across all three species, as are sepal length and width. Virginica and versicolor irises have similar length and width patterns, but virginica irises have larger petals. Both species have petals that are about the same size as their sepals. Setosa irises, on the other hand, have sepals that are larger than their petals.

Parallel coordinates are used in PicViz to visualize network data (Tricaud et al. 2011). PCs are useful for this type of data, since they can accommodate numbers, times, strings, enumerations, IP addresses, and so on. PicViz is built to investigate correlations across multiple properties of Snort log data. The effectiveness and readability of PCs is often influenced by the ordering of its axes. PicViz supports rapid axis reorganization to determine the best axis sequence for a given investigation. As in Fig. 1, colour is overlaid on an element's polyline to represent an additional user-chosen attribute. This allows for a closer examination of properties of anomalies as they are identified.

A second system, Sol, also uses parallel coordinates, but with horizontal axes (Bradshaw et al. 2012). Sol's Flow Capacitor visualizes NetFlows between two PC axes that represent a flow's source at the top and its destination at the bottom. Common data attributes assigned to the source and destination axes include IP address or geographic location. Small "darts" are shown flowing from the source plane to the destination plane, to visualize the amount of NetFlow activity over a user-defined time window. Users can also insert intermediate axes to visualize additional data properties. This causes the NetFlow darts to pass through multiple states, one per additional data attribute, on their way from source to destination.

3.6 Treemaps

Data with hierarchical structures can be visualized as a treemap, a visualization that recursively subdivides rectangular regions based on the frequency of different data attribute values. Intuitively, a treemap visualizes a multi-level tree as a 2D "map" by embedding leaf nodes within their parent node region.

Consider Fig. 2, which subdivides a dataset with $A=\{A_1 : region, A_2 : parent, A_3 : revenue, A_4 : profit\}$. The parent Global rectangle is subdivided into three continents: North America, Europe, and Africa, with the size of each continent subregion defined by its global profit. The continents are further divided by states and countries, producing a hierarchical decomposition by geography. Visually, $V = \{V_1 : text\ label, V_2 : spatial\ location, V_3 : size, V_4 : chromaticity\}$. The size of each subregion visualizes its revenue, and its combined colour and saturation—or chromaticity—visualize its profit using a double-ended colour scale: green for positive, red for negative, and a stronger hue for more extreme values.

Kan et al. use treemaps in NetVis, a tool for monitoring network security (Kan et al. 2010). A network within a company is subdivided, first by department, and then by host within department. Colour is used to identify whether a host has experienced Snort alerts during an analyst-defined time window. For nodes with alerts, brightness visualizes the number of alerts: brighter for more alerts.

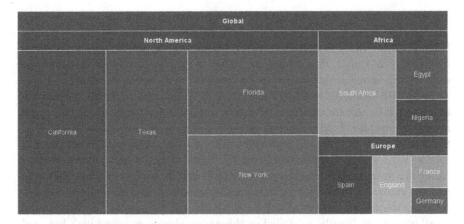

Fig. 2 A treemap of revenue for states and counties in three continents

Mansmann et al. compared treemaps to node-link graphs for network monitoring and intrusion detection (Mansmann et al. 2009). Mansmann's treemap consists of a set of analyst-selected local hosts currently under attack, organized hierarchically by IP address. Attacking hosts are arrayed around the boundary of the treemap, with links from attacker to target identifying where attacks are occurring. The size and colour of each treemap node can be assigned to different variables, including flow counts, packet counts, or bytes transferred. The authors identified numerous advantages and disadvantages of treemaps versus standard node-link graphs, for example, treemaps better emphasize the relationships between external attackers and internal hosts by subnet structure, but edges between attackers and local hosts can obscure the treemap nodes, hiding the information they visualize.

3.7 Hierarchical Visualization

In many cases a dataset can be structured into multiple levels of detail. For example, IPv4 addresses can be represented as an overview by aggregating individual addresses based on their network identifier, and within this as a detail view by including the host identifier. Other common examples include summaries by geographic location, by type of attack, and so on. The ability to visualize this type of contextual structure is useful for a number of reasons. First, overviews can be used to present an intuitive summary of a dataset. Second, a hierarchical visualization helps an analyst to choose subsets of the data that are logically related based on the hierarchy. This fits well with the approach in information visualization of overview, zoom and filter, then details on demand.

Information visualization has studied two related approaches to visualizing large hierarchies: overview+detail and focus+context (Cockburn et al. 2008). Overview+detail combines an overview of a dataset with internal details. Treemaps are an example of this technique. Focus+context presents an overview of a dataset—the context—and allows a user to request additional details at specific locations—the focus. A well-known focus+context approach initially presents an overview of a dataset, then allows an analyst to position a zoom lens within the overview. Data underneath the lens is "zoomed in" to show internal detail.

NVisionIP visualizes NetFlow data at three different levels of detail: an overview of the network state, summaries of groups of suspicious machines, and details on an individual machine (Lakkaraju et al. 2004). A galaxy view provides an overview of the current network state as a scatterplot, with $A = \{A_1 : subnet, A_2 : host\}$ mapped to $V = \{V_1 : x, V_2 : y\}$. Each marker in the scatterplot identifies an IP address participating in a flow. Analysts can select a set of hosts that show signs of abnormal traffic patterns and zoom in to compare traffic across hosts with two histograms: one representing traffic on a number of well-known ports, and the other representing traffic on all other ports. Finally, a detailed machine view visualizes a machine's byte and flow counts for different protocols and different ports for all network traffic over an analyst-chosen time window.

Although these security visualization systems aim to support more flexible user interactivity and to correlate various data sources, many of them still force an analyst to choose from a fairly limited set of static representations. For example, Phan et al. use charts, but with fixed attributes on the x and y-axes. General purpose commercial visualization systems like Tableau or ArcSight offer a more flexible collection of visualizations, but they do not include visualization and human perception guidelines, however, so representing data effectively requires visualization expertise on the part of the analyst. Finally, many systems lack a scalable data management architecture. This means an entire dataset must be loaded into memory prior to filtering, projecting, and visualizing, increasing data transfer cost and limiting dataset size.

4 Visualization Design Philosophy

Our design philosophy is based on discussions with cyber security analysts at various research institutions and government agencies. The analysts overwhelming agreed that, intuitively, visualizations should be very useful. In practice, however, they had rarely realized significant improvements by integrating visualizations into their workflow. A common comment was: "Researchers come to us and say, Here's a visualization tool, let's fit your problem to this tool. But what we really need is a tool built to fit our problem." This is not unique to the security domain, but it suggests that security analysts may be more sensitive to deviations from their current analysis strategies, and therefore less receptive to general-purpose visualization tools and techniques.

This is not to say, however, that visualization researchers should simply provide what the security analysts ask for. Our analysts have high-level suggestions about how they want to visualize their data, but they do not have the visualization experience or expertise to design and evaluate specific solutions to meet their needs. To address these, we initiated a collaboration with colleagues at a major government research laboratory to build visualizations that: (1) meet the needs of the analysts, but also (2) harness the knowledge and best practices that exist in the visualization community.

Again, this approach is not unique, but it offers an opportunity to study its strengths and weaknesses in the context of a cyber security domain. In particular, we were curious to see which general techniques (if any) we could start with, and how significantly these techniques needed to be modified before they would be useful for an analyst. Seen this way, our approach does not focus explicitly on network security data, but rather on network security analysts. By supporting the analysts' situation awareness needs, we are implicitly addressing a goal of effectively visualizing their data.

From our discussions, we defined an initial set of requirements for a successful visualization tool. Interestingly, these do not inform explicit design decisions. For example, they do not define which data attributes we should visualize and how those attributes should be represented. Instead, they implicitly constrain a visualization's design through a high-level set of suggestions about what a real analyst is (and is not) likely to use. We summarized these comments into six general categories:

- **Mental Models.** A visualization must "fit" the mental models the analysts use to investigate problems. Analysts are unlikely to change how they attack a problem in order to use a visualization tool.
- **Working Environment.** The visualization must integrate into the analyst's current working environment. For example, many analysts use a web browser to view data stored in formats defined by their network monitoring tools.
- **Configurability.** Static, pre-defined presentations of the data are typically not useful. Analysts need to look at the data from different perspectives that are driven by the data they are currently investigating.
- **Accessibility.** The visualizations should be familiar to an analyst. Complex representations with a steep learning curve are unlikely to be used, except in very specific situations where a significant cost-benefit advantage can be found.
- **Scalability.** The visualizations must support query and retrieval from multiple data sources, each of which may contain very large numbers of records.
- **Integration.** Analysts will not replace their current problem-solving strategies with new visualization tools. Instead, the visualizations must augment these strategies with useful support.

5 Case Study: Managing Network Alerts

A common task for network security analysts is active monitoring for network alerts within a system. Normally, sets of alerts are categorized by severity—low, medium, and high—annotated with a short text summaries (e.g., a Snort rule), and presented within a web browser every few minutes. The analysts are responsible for quickly deciding which alerts, if any, require additional investigation. When suspicious alerts are identified, additional data sources are queried to search for context and supporting evidence to decide whether the alert should be escalated. Normally, each data source is managed independently. This means results must be correlated manually by the analysts, usually by coordinating multiple findings in their working memory. We were asked to design a system that would support the analysts by: (1) allowing them to identify context more effectively and more efficiently; (2) integrating results from multiple data sources into a single, unified summary; (3) choosing visualization techniques that are best suited to the analysts' data and tasks; but also (4) providing an analyst the ability to control exactly which data to display, and how to present it, as needed.

The analysts' requirements meant that we could not follow a common strategy of defining the analysts' data and tasks, designing a visualization to best represent this data, then modifying the design based on analyst feedback. Working environment, accessibility, and integration constraints, as well as comments from analysts, suggested that a novel visualization with unfamiliar visual representations would not be appropriate. Since no existing tools satisfied all of the analysts' needs, we decided to design a framework of basic, familiar visualizations—charts—that runs in the analysts' web-based environment. We applied a series of modifications to this framework to meet each of the analysts' requirements. Viewed in isolation, each improvement often seemed moderate in scope. However, we felt, and the analysts agreed, that the modifications were the difference between the system possibly being used by the analysts versus never being used. In the end, the modifications afforded a surprising level of expressiveness and flexibility, suggesting that some parts of the design could be useful outside the network security domain.

The configurability, accessibility, scalability, and integration requirements of our design demand flexible user interaction that combines and visualizes multiple large data sources. The working environment requirement further dictates that this happen within the analyst's current workflow. To achieve this, the system combines MySQL, PHP, HTML5, and JavaScript to produce a web-based network security visualization system that uses combinations of user-configurable charts to analyze suspicious network activity.

We adopt Shiravi's definition of situation awareness, "a state of knowledge", and situation assessment, "the process of attaining situation awareness." In this context, the visualization tool is designed to support situation assessment. The expectation is that providing effective situation assessment will lead to an enhanced situation awareness.

5.1 Web-Based Visualization

The visualizations run as a web application using HTML5's canvas element. This works well, since it requires no external plugins and runs in any modern web browser. Network data is visualized using 2D charts (Heyes 2014). Basic charts are one of the most well known and widely used visualization techniques. This supports the accessibility requirement, because: (1) charts are common in other security visualization systems that analysts have seen, and (2) charts are an effective visualization method for presenting the values, trends, patterns, and relationships that analysts want to explore.

5.2 Interactive Visualization

To realize analyst-driven charts, the system provides a user interface with event handling on the canvas element and the jQueryUI JavaScript library for higher-level UI widgets and operations. This design allows for full control over the data attributes assigned to a chart's axes. This capability turns out to be fairly expressive, and can be used by an analyst to generate an interesting range of charts and chart types. Analysts can also attach additional data attributes to control the appearance of the glyphs representing data elements within a chart. For example, a glyph's colour, size, and shape can all be used to visualize secondary attribute values.

5.3 Analyst-Driven Charts

In a general information visualization tool, the viewer normally defines exactly the visualization they want. The current visualization system automatically chooses an initial chart type based on: (1) knowledge about the strengths, limitations, and uses of different types of charts, and (2) the data the analyst asks to visualize. For example, if the analyst asks to see the distribution of a single data attribute, the system recommends a pie chart or bar chart. If the analyst asks to see the relationship across two data attributes, the system recommends a scatterplot or a Gantt chart.

The axes of the charts are initialized based on properties of the data attributes, for example, a categorical attribute on a bar chart's x-axis and an aggregated count on the y-axis. If two categorical attributes like $A = \{A_1 : source\ IP, A_2 : destination\ IP\}$ are selected, the attributes are mapped to a scatterplot's axes as $V = \{V_1 : x, V_2 : y\}$, with markers shown for flows between pairs of addresses (Fig. 3c).

If the attributes were $A = \{A_1 : time, A_2 : destination\ IP\}$, a scatterplot with $V = \{V_1 : x, V_2 : y\}$ would again be used (Fig. 4a). Visualizing netflow properties like $A = \{A_1 : time, A_2 : destination\ IP, A_3 : duration\}$ initially produces a Gantt chart with rectangular range glyphs mapped to $V = \{V_1 : x, V_2 : y, V_3 : width\}$, representing different flows (Fig. 4b). Data elements sharing the same x and y values are grouped together and displayed as a count using additional visual properties. For example, in a scatterplot of traffic between source and destination IPs, the size of each marker indicates the number of connections between two addresses. In a Gantt chart, the opacity of each range bar indicates the number of flows that occurred over the time range for a particular destination IP.

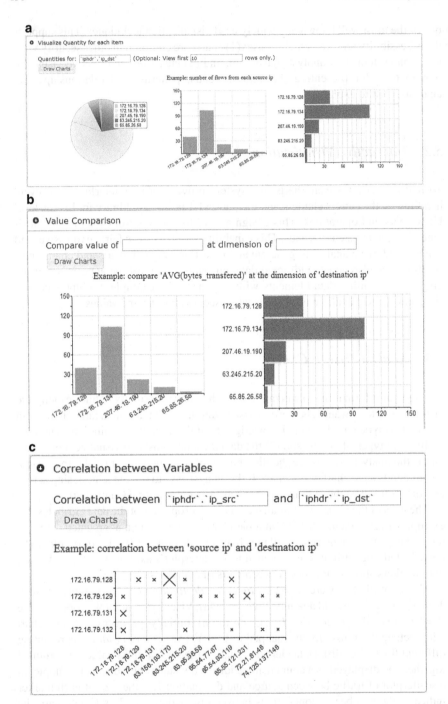

Fig. 3 Charts classified by use case: (**a**) pie and bar chart, analysis of proportion; (**b**) bar chart, value comparison along one dimension; (**c**) scatterplot, correlation analysis

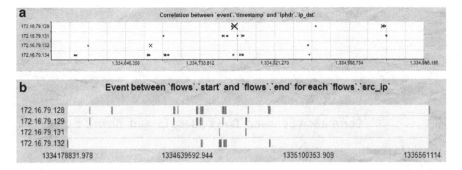

Fig. 4 Scatterplot and Gantt charts: (**a**) connection counts over time by destination IP; (**b**) time ranges for flows by source IP

More importantly, the analyst is free to change any of these initial choices. The system will interpret their modifications similar to the processing we perform for automatically chosen attributes. This allows the analyst to automatically start with the most appropriate chart type (pie, bar, scatterplot, or Gantt) based on their analysis task, the properties of the attributes they assign to a chart's axes, and on any secondary information they ask to visualize at each data point.

5.4 Overview+Detail

The visualization system allows an analyst to focus on a subset of the data, either by filtering the input, or by interactively selecting a subregion in an existing chart to zoom in on. In either case the chart is redrawn to include only the selected elements. For example, consider a scatterplot created by an analyst, where the size of each tick mark encodes the number of flows for a corresponding source and destination IP (plotted on the chart's x and y-axes). Figure 5b is the result of zooming in on the sub-region selected in Fig. 5a. In the original scatterplot the difference between the flow counts for the selected region cannot be easily distinguished. After zooming, the size of the tick marks is re-scaled for the currently visible elements, highlighting differences in the number of flows, particularly for destination IP 172.16.79.132 in the bottom row. The same type of zooming can be applied to Gantt charts (Fig. 5c, d). After zooming into a selected area, the flows that occlude one another in the original chart are separated, helping the analyst differentiate timestamps.

5.5 Correlated Views

Analysts normally conduct a sequence of investigations, pursuing new findings by correlating multiple data sources and exploring the data at multiple levels of detail. This necessitates visualizations with multiple views and flexible user interaction.

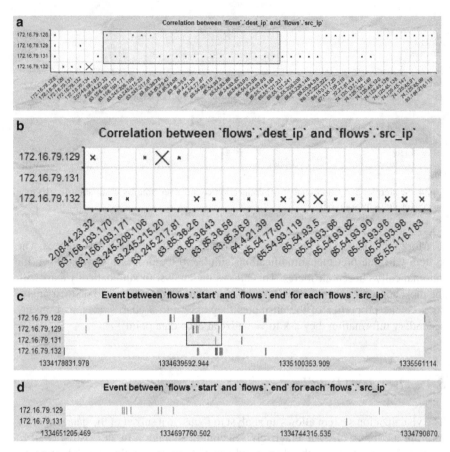

Fig. 5 Chart zooming: (**a**) original scatterplot with zoom region selected; (**b**) zoom result; (**c**) original Gantt chart with zoom region selected; (**d**) zoom results

The system correlates multiple data sources by generating correlated SQL queries and extending the RGraph library to support dependencies between different charts.

As an analyst examines a chart, their situation awareness may change, producing new hypothesis about the cause or effect of activity in the network. Correlated charts allow the analyst to immediately generate new visualizations from the current view to explore these hypotheses. In this way, the system allows an analyst to conduct a series of analysis steps, each one building on previous findings, with new visualizations being generated on demand to support the current investigations.

Similar to zooming, analysts can create correlated charts for regions of interest by selecting the region and requesting a sub-canvas. The system generates a constraint to extract the data of interest in a separate window. The analyst can then select new attributes to include or new tables and constraints to add to the new chart.

5.6 Example Analysis Session

To demonstrate the system, we describe a scenario where it is used to explore trap data being captured by network security colleagues at NCSU. The data was designed to act as input for automated intrusion detection algorithms. This provided a real-world test environment, and also offered the possibility of comparing results from an automated system to a human analyst's performance, both with and without visualization support. Four different datasets were available for visualization: a Netflow dataset, an alert dataset, an IP header dataset, and a TCP header dataset.

An NCSU security expert served as the analyst in this example scenario. Visualization starts at an abstract level with an overview that the analyst uses to form an initial situation awareness. This is followed by explorations of different hypotheses that highlight and zoom into subregions of interest. The analyst generates correlated charts to drill down and analyze data at a more detailed level, and imports additional supporting data into the visualization, all with the goal of improving their situation awareness of specific subsets of the network. Including a new flow dataset extends the analysis of a subset of interest to a larger set of data sources. The visualization system supports the analyst by generating different types of charts on demand, based on the analyst's current interest and needs. This leads the analyst to identify a specific NetFlow that contains numerous alerts. This NetFlow is flagged for further investigation.

The analyst starts by building an overview visualization of the number of alerts for each destination IP, $A = \{A_1 : destination\ IP, A_2 : alert\ count\}$ and using A_1 as the "aggregate for" attribute. Choosing "Draw Charts" displays the aggregated results as pie and bar charts (i.e., using $V = \{V_1 : start\ angle, V_2 : arc\ length\}$ for the pie chart or $V = \{V_1 : x, V_2 : y\text{-}height\}$ for the bar chart, Fig. 6). This provides an initial situation awareness of how many alerts are occurring within the network, and how those alerts are distributed among different hosts. Pie charts highlight the relative number of alerts for different destination IPs, while bar charts facilitate a more effective comparison of the absolute number of alerts by destination IP. The charts are linked: highlighting a bar in the bar chart will highlight the corresponding section in the pie chart, and vice-versa.

The pie and bar charts indicate that the majority of the alerts (910) happen for destination IP 172.16.79.134. To further analyze alerts associated with this destination IP, the analyst chooses "Sub Canvas" to open a new window with the initial query information (the datasets, data attributes, and constraints) predefined. The filter destination IP = 172.16.79.134 is added to restrict the query for further analysis over this target address. This demonstrates how an analyst can continue to add new constraints or data sources to the query as he requests follow-on visualizations to continue his analysis.

Next, the analyst chooses to visualize alerts from different source IPs attached to the target destination IP. He uses destination port to analyze the correlation between source and destination through the use of a scatterplot with $A = \{A_1 : source\ IP, A_2 : port\ number, A_3 : alert\ count\}$ and $V = \{V_1 : x, V_2 : y, V_3 : size\}$.

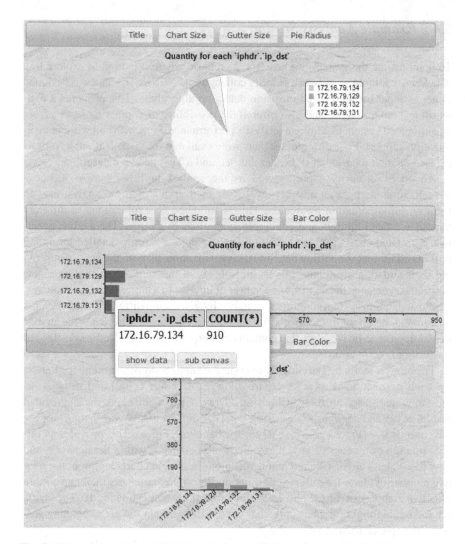

Fig. 6 Aggregated results visualized as a pie chart and horizontal and vertical bar charts

The scatterplot shows there is only one source IP with alerts related to the target destination IP, and that most alerts are sent to port 21. This provides more detailed situation awareness about a specific (source IP, destination IP) pair and port number that the analyst considers suspicious.

The analyst looks more closely at all traffic related to the target destination IP on port 21 by visualizing NetFlows and their associated alerts in a Gantt chart. Here, $A = \{A_1 : \textit{start time}, A_2 : \textit{duration}, A_3 : [\textit{alert times}]\}$ and $V = \{V_1 : x, V_2 : \textit{size}, V_3 : \textit{texture hashes}\}$. Collections of flows are drawn in red with endpoints at the flow set's start and end times. Alerts appear as black vertical bars overlaid on top of the flows at the time the alert was detected. Figure 7a shows most

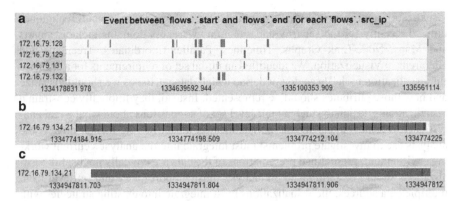

Fig. 7 Gantt chart with alerts for network flows at the destination IP and port of interest: (**a**) two flows; (**b**) zoom on the left flow, showing numerous alerts; (**c**) zoom on the right flow, showing one alert

of the flows are distributed over two time ranges. This further augments the analyst's situation awareness, by point to potential times when attacks may have occurred. By zooming in on each flow separately (Fig. 7b, c), the analyst realizes that the vast majority of the alerts occur in the left flow (Fig. 7b). The alerts in this flow are considered suspicious, and are flagged for more detailed investigation. Later discussion with the author of the datasets confirmed that this set of alerts were meant to simulate an unknown intrusion into the system.

This example demonstrates how the system allows an analyst to follow a sequence of steps based on their own strategies and preferences to investigate alerts. The system supports situation assessment based on the analyst's hypotheses about potential attacks within a system. Effective assessment leads to more and more detailed situation awareness, allowing the analyst to confirm or refute the possibility of an intrusion into the system.

6 Summary

Data visualization converts raw data into images that allow a viewer to "see" data values and the relationships they form. The images allow viewers to use their visual perception to identify features in the data, to manage ambiguity, and to apply domain knowledge in ways that would be difficult to do algorithmically. Visualization can be formalized as mapping: data passed through a data-feature mapping generates a visual representation—a visualization—that displays individual data values and the patterns they form. Many existing situation awareness tools use visualization techniques like charts, maps, and flow diagrams to present information to an analyst. The challenge is to determine how best to integrate visualization techniques into a cyber situation awareness domain. Many tools adopt a well-known information visualization approach: overview, zoom and filter, and details on demand. Techniques utilized recently for the security and situation awareness domains include: Charts and Maps, Node-Link Graphs, Timelines, Parallel Coordinates, Treemaps and Hierarchical Visualization. We identified an initial set of requirements for a successful visualization tool. These do not define which data attributes we should visualize and how those attributes should be represented. Instead, they implicitly constrain a visualization's design through a high-level set of suggestions about what a real analyst is (and is not) likely to use: a visualization must "fit" the mental models the analysts use to investigate problems; must integrate into the analyst's current working environment; pre-defined presentations of the data are typically not useful; visualizations should be familiar to an analyst; must support query and retrieval from multiple data sources; the visualizations must integrate into existing strategies with useful support.We demonstrate a prototype system for analyzing network alerts based on these guidelines.

References

Bertin, J (1967) Sémiologie Graphiques: Les diagrammes, les réseaux, les cartes. Gauthier-Villars, Paris

Bradshaw, J M, Carvalho, M, Bunch, L et al (2012) Sol: An agent-based framework for cyber situation awareness. Künstliche Intelligenz 26(2):127–140

Chernoff, H (1973) The use of faces to represent points in k-dimensional space graphically. Journal of the American Statistical Association 68(342):361–368

Cockburn, A, Karlson, A, and Bederson, B B (2008) A review of overview+detail, zooming, and focus+context interfaces. ACM Computing Surveys 41(1):Article 2

Dang, K T and Dang, T T (2013) A survey on security visualization techniques for web information systems. International Journal of Web Information Systems 9(1):6–31

DeFanti, B H and Brown, T A (1987) Visualization in scientific computing. Computer Graphics 21(6)

Goodall, J and Sowul, M (2009) VIAssist: Visual analytics for cyber defense. Paper presented at the IEEE Conference on Technologies for Homeland Security (HST '09), Boston, MA

Heyes, R (2014) RGraph: HTML5 charts library. http://www.rgraph.net. Accessed 02 May 2014

Johnson, C R (2004) Top scientific visualization research problems. IEEE Computer Graphics & Applications 24(4):13–17

Johnson, C R, Moorehead, R, Munzner, T et al (eds) (2006) NIH/NSF Visualization Research Challenges. IEEE Press

Kan, Z, Hu, C, Wang, Z et al (2010) NetVis: A network security management visualization tool based on treemap. Paper presented at the 2nd International Conference on Advanced Computer Control (ICACC 2010), Shenyang, China

Lakkaraju, K, Yurcik, W and Lee, A J (2004) NVisionIP: Netflow visualizations of system state for security situational awareness. Paper presented at the 2004 ACM Workshop on Visualization and Data Mining for Computer Security (VizSEC/DMSEC '04), Washington, DC

Mansmann, F, Fisher, F, Keim, D A et al (2009) Visual support for analyzing network traffic and intrusion detection events using treemap and graph representations. Paper presented at the Symposium on Computer-Human Interaction for Management of Information (CHIMIT 2009), Baltimore, MD

McPherson, J, Ma, K, Krystosk, P et al (2004) PortVis: A tool for port-based detection of security events. Paper presented at the Workshop on Visualization and Data Mining for Computer Security (VizSEC/DMSEC '04), Washington, DC

Minarik, P and Dymacek, T (2008) NetFlow data visualization based on graphs. In: Visualization for Computer Security, Springer, pp 144–151

Phan, D, Gerth, J, Lee, M, Paepcke et al (2007) Visual analysis of network flow data with timelines and event plots. Paper presented in the Proceedings of the 4th International Workshop on Visualization for Cyber Security (VizSec 2007), Sacramento, CA

Roberts, J C, Faithfull, W J and Williams, F C B (2012) SitaVis—Interactive situation awareness visualization of large datasets. Paper presented in the Proceedings 2012 Conference on Visual Analytics Science and Technology (VAST 2012), Seattle, WA

Shiravi, H, Shiravi, A, and Ghorbani, A A (2012) A survey of visualization systems for network security. IEEE Transactions on Visualization and Computer Graphics 18(8):1313–1329

Thomas, J J and Cook, K A (2005) Illuminating the path: The research and development agenda for visual analytics. National Visualization and Analytics Center

Tricaud, S, Nance, K, and Saade, P (2011) Visualizing network activity using parallel coordinates. Paper presented in the Proceedings of the 44th Hawaii International Conference on System Sciences (HICSS 2011), Poipu, HI

Inference and Ontologies

Brian E. Ulicny, Jakub J. Moskal, Mieczyslaw M. Kokar,
Keith Abe, and John Kei Smith

1 Introduction

The importance of visualization—discussed in the previous chapter—does not diminish the critical role that algorithmic analysis plays in achieving CSA. Algorithms reason about the voluminous observations and data about the network and infer important features of the situation that help analysts and decision-makers form their situational awareness. In order to perform this inference, and to make its output useful to other algorithms and human users, an algorithm needs to have its inputs and outputs represented in a consistent vocabulary of well-specified terms and their relations, i.e., it needs an ontology with a clear semantics and a standard. This topic is the focus of the present chapter. We already touched on the importance of semantics in the Cognition and Technology chapter. Now we discuss in detail how, in cyber operations, inference based on ontology can be used to determine the threat actor, the target and purpose in order to determine potential courses of action and future impact. Since a comprehensive ontology for cyber security does not exist, we show how such an ontology can be developed by taking advantage of existing cyber security related standards and markup languages.

B.E. Ulicny (✉) • J.J. Moskal
VIStology, Inc., Framingham, MA, USA
e-mail: bulicny@vistology.com; jmoskal@vistology.com

M.M. Kokar
Northeastern University, Boston, MA, USA
e-mail: m.kokar@neu.edu

K. Abe
Referentia Systems Incorporated, Honolulu, HI, USA
e-mail: kabe@referentia.com

J.K. Smith
LiveAction, Palo Alto, CA, USA
e-mail: jsmith@liveaction.com

© Springer International Publishing Switzerland 2014
A. Kott et al. (eds.), *Cyber Defense and Situational Awareness*,
Advances in Information Security 62, DOI 10.1007/978-3-319-11391-3_9

The common feature of cyber-security systems is that they need to react very quickly to a dynamic environment that changes its state independently of whether the human or computer agents act on it. The agents want to act on the environment so that its evolution, at least in the area of interest to the agents, leads to the satisfaction of their goals or, more likely, in the case of computer networks the avoidance of certain undesired states: e.g. infiltration, network compromise, and so on. Towards this end, the agents need to collect information about the environment (usually from many different sources), make decisions based on the collected information and their knowledge, act according to their decisions, collect feedback from the environment in response to the actions, and update their knowledge in order to make decisions in the future.

We use the term awareness as described in Kokar et al. (2009), i.e., in order to be aware

> ... one needs to have data pertinent to the objects of interest, some background knowledge that allows one to interpret the collected object data and finally a capability for drawing inferences.

The requirement for the capability of inference comes from such common-sense sources as the Webster's Dictionary: *"awareness implies vigilance in observing or alertness in drawing inferences from what one experiences."*

In cyber systems, where the processing loops (Boyd 1987) are very fast, much of inference must be performed by computers. In other words, automatic inference engines must perform the inference, which in turn requires that the information (facts) to be acted upon by such engines needs to be represented in a language with formal semantics. Inference engines take such facts as input and produce new information.

In the following, we first introduce a malware infection scenario and discuss how a human analyst would deal with the malware detection problem. Then we discuss how an approach that mimics the analyst's process is implemented using ontologies and an inference engine.

2 Scenario

In this chapter we consider a case of malware related to cyber espionage. The following describes significant events in the order of occurrence:

- On 1/1/2012 at 10 am an email message is sent to a particular user account, where the user is associated with a particular laptop (HP-laptop1), via yahoo with a PDF file attached containing malware that exploits a known vulnerability, CVE-2009-0658. This vulnerability causes a buffer overflow in Adobe Reader 9.0 and earlier. It allows remote attackers to execute arbitrary code via a crafted PDF document, related to a non-JavaScript function call and possibly an embedded JBIG2 image stream. This event is captured by Snort - an open source network intrusion prevention and detection system (IDS/IPS) developed by Sourcefire.
- On 1/1/2012 at 11 am a second email message is sent via yahoo with a PDF file attached containing malware that exploits the same vulnerability; the target is the

same HP-laptop1. This event is also captured by Snort. Subsequently the user on HP-laptop1 opens the PDF file and the laptop gets infected.

- On 2/1/2012 the malware now installed on HP-laptop1 sends out a message via getPlunk.com to get the address of the Command and Control (C&C) server—a machine that can support the malware with the attack. GetPlunk.com is an intermediary micro-blogging service. This request is captured by Snort, which provides signature inspection, ID, and network event information.
- On 2/1/2012 the malware then uses the new C&C address to receive commands and exfiltrate data of interest to the attacker. This is captured by Snort based on the signature, ID and network event information.

3 Human Analysis of the Scenario

A human cyber analyst would need to examine network log files in order to detect a malware-supported botnet attack like the one described. In such a situation, a human analyst would need to:

- Detect the events mentioned among the network traffic logs. For example, somehow determine that one of many PDF email attachments that a particular laptop received contained malware.
- Determine that the laptop that opened the infected email attachment had a vulnerability that could be exploited on the basis of the installed software.
- Detect the exchange of messages between the infected laptop and the microblogging service that contains the address of the command-and-control computer address.
- Or, barring that, somehow detect an unusual amount or pattern of traffic between the infected laptop and the command-and-control server, despite the fact that every computer on the network interacts with multiple legitimate servers on a potentially regular basis.

The human analyst could make use of lists of known suspicious domains and IP addresses determined through looking up IP addresses in retracing the laptop's activity once it is discovered that the computer has become infected, by checking every incoming email with a PDF attachment over some period prior to the detection of the infection.

Without tool support, a human analyst would find it very tedious and time-consuming to trace back how a particular laptop came to be infected by malware that allowed the computer to be controlled by an external command-and-control server, if the analyst even became aware that the laptop was being controlled externally at all.

4 An Outline of the Use of Ontologies for Cyber Security

In this section we give a brief introduction to ontologies and automatic inference.

4.1 Ontologies

As used in the knowledge representation domain, the term "ontology" stands for an explicit, formal, machine-readable semantic model that defines the classes, instances of the classes, inter-class relations and data properties relevant to a problem domain (Gruber 2009).

In order for ontologies to be amenable to automatic processing by computers, they need to be represented in a language that has both formal syntax and formal semantics. The syntax must be defined so that computers can recognize whether ontological statements (sentences) are grammatically correct. A formalized semantics means that a machine can judge whether two statements are consistent or not and imply one another or not. A vocabulary without a formalized semantics has at most a syntax: rules constraining what combination or strings of words in that vocabulary are part of that language. This is the case with most of the languages or protocols for exchange of information about the states of networks currently. They are purely syntactic.

For a vocabulary to have a formalized semantics, it must be possible for a computational machine to understand when a statement is true in that vocabulary (model theory), what can be inferred from a set of statements in that vocabulary (inference), and when it is impossible for a set of statements to be jointly true (consistency). An ontology is thus a logical description of a conceptual domain in a vocabulary expressed in a language with both a formal syntax and a formal semantics.

The W3C's (World Wide Web Consortium) Semantic Web activity provides today's most extensive deployment of interoperable vocabularies with semantics in the form of ontologies encoded as OWL (Web Ontology Language) Ontologies. OWL (W3C 2009) is the most commonly used language for expressing ontologies today and has by far the largest developer base. Therefore, we will focus exclusively on OWL ontologies in this discussion.

For our purposes, OWL represents individuals (e.g. elements of the network such as a particular router or a particular user), classes of individuals (e.g. "Router", "Printer", "Authorized User"), properties ("hasIPAddress", "hasPassword", "lastAccessed") that relate individuals either to other individuals ("object properties") or to datatype individuals (e.g. some date expressed as an xsd:dateTime).

The semantics of OWL is based on Description Logics (DL) (Baader et al. 2010), a family of Knowledge Representation (KR) formalisms equipped with a formal, model-based semantics. The architecture of a system based on DL allows for setting up a knowledgebase (KB) and for reasoning about its content. The KB consists of two components, known as the TBox and ABox. In the context of OWL, the TBox introduces axioms defining the ontology classes and properties and their relationship. For example, the TBox asserts relationships between classes. These can be simple class hierarchies (e.g. that every CiscoRouter is a Router) or arbitrary complex logical expressions (e.g. if a single send operation transmits a packet to multiple destinations, then it is a multicast operation). The TBox also enables the ontology to specify the domain and range of properties, cardinality restrictions on properties, property types (symmetric, transitive), property hierarchies, datatype range restrictions, and so on. We cannot provide a complete tutorial on OWL here, but its expressiveness is extremely powerful although not as powerful as that of first-order logic.

The ABox contains assertions about specific named individuals—instances of classes and properties that have been defined in the TBox. In the context of cyber situational awareness, the TBox consists of axioms about the network domain, shared by all instances and states of the network. The ABox, on the other hand, represents facts pertaining to a particular network at particular times.

The logical definitions of the TBox combined with the assertions about particulars in the ABox allow an inference engine to identify new instances of a class by means of the properties it exhibits. Disjointness axioms about classes similarly allow the system to identify inconsistencies according to the ontology. For example, if only users of a certain class are allowed to access certain data, and a particular user is asserted as belonging to a class disjoint with the permitted class, yet there is an assertion that this user accessed that data, then an inconsistency will be detected in the ontology, and OWL inference will halt. A knowledge base must be consistent at all times, since anything can be inferred from an inconsistency.

OWL 2, the most recent version of the standard, defines three subsets, called *language profiles*, which are expressive and tractable, but tailored to specific needs:

- *OWL 2 EL*—terminological/schema reasoning, focused on terminological expressivity used for light-weight ontologies;
- *OWL 2 QL*—query answering via database engines, uses OWL concepts as light-weight queries, allows query answering using rewriting in SQL on top of relational DBs;
- *OWL 2 RL*—reasoning that can be implemented by standard rule engines.

OWL 2 RL, one of the most widely implemented profiles, is a collection of 75 implication and consistency rules. It has desirable characteristics: the set of entailed triples is finite and in PSPACE, and the runtime complexity is in PTIME.

In order to store and exchange OWL ontologies among applications, one of its concrete syntaxes is used. The primary exchange syntax for OWL is RDF/XML, which stems from the fact that the underlying model of OWL is RDF. Since OWL semantics can also be defined in terms of the semantics of RDF (Resource Description Framework), the serialization of OWL is a combination of the serialization of RDF and the additional concepts that are built out of RDF.

RDF's statements (sentences) consist of three elements—subject, predicate and object, collectively called triples. The predicate represents a relation, the subject is an element from the domain of the relation and the object is from the range of the relation. Thus conceptually OWL can also be viewed as a collection of triples.

Other concrete syntaxes, not based on XML, are often used as well, most notably Turtle, OWL XML, and Manchester Syntax (Wang et al. 2007). RDF/XML is the only required syntax to be supported by every OWL compliant tool.

While it may seem that OWL is just another XML language, because it can be expressed in XML, it is important to note that XML is just one of the syntaxes, while OWL has a formal semantics. Semantically equivalent documents in OWL can be expressed in multiple ways, using different syntaxes. Furthermore, because OWL is based on RDF, OWL knowledgebase can be queried with SPARQL, the query language for RDF.

Ontologies can be evaluated for their quality. Various evaluative dimensions are outlined in Brank et al. (2005), Obrst et al. (2007), Shen et al. (2006), Vrandečić (2009). In Ye et al. (2007), the following criteria are proposed:

- Clarity: Concepts in an ontology should be uniquely identified and distinguished from other terms through necessary and sufficient conditions specified in the ontology.
- Coherence: Concepts in an ontology should be defined consistently.
- Ontological commitment: An ontology should be general enough to be usable by any application in that domain. It is advantageous that classes, associated properties, and involved constraints should serve for all of the general problems in the domain.
- Orthogonality: The defined concepts should be mutually exclusive from each other, which makes it easier to share and reuse ontologies.
- Encoding bias: General ontologies should be independent of specific symbol-level encoding. That is, the names of concepts should not favor proprietary- or vendor-specific naming schemes.
- Extensibility: Ontologies should be extensible to allow them to be reused easily by other applications in a specific domain.

As cyber situation awareness ontologies emerge, they can be evaluated and compared along these dimensions.

4.2   Ontology Based Inference

Automatic inference on ontologies expressed in OWL is performed by *inference engines*, or *semantic reasoners*. An inference engine takes a set of facts about a specific domain of interest asserted in OWL and derives other facts using axioms and inference rules. In other words, an inference engine makes explicit the facts that are only implicit in the explicitly represented facts. The derived facts are logical consequences of the facts in a given fact base and ontology that is used to express the facts. Instantiations to any variables that were used in the derivation are also provided.

For instance, if the inference system knows that (in the context of a communication network) a device that routesPackets is a Router and that CiscoRouter routesPackets, then the system can infer that CiscoRouter is a sub-class of Router. While on the surface such an inference is simple and obvious, it is not obvious (although simple) for computers. Also, the derivation of such a fact may have far reaching consequences since now everything that was attributed to Router can be attributed to CiscoRouter as well. Other inferences can derive properties of sub-classes based on the properties of their super-classes (mentioned above), inferring that an individual is an instance of a specific class, and more. All kinds of inference types may be relevant to the case study discussed in this chapter, although the type of inference directly addressed will be the derivation of whether the agent's knowledge entails that a specific situation (malware intrusion) occurs.

OWL's semantics is such that inference is expected to be computationally tractable. OWL inference engines can therefore be guaranteed to make all inferences in a tractable amount of time. Thus, semantic scalability and interoperability can be achieved. The time for processing an OWL ontology depends on the size and the complexity of the axioms in the ontology. However, OWL's semantics guarantees that only valid inferences are drawn, i.e., inference engines are *sound*. At least some OWL profiles are such that *all* inferences can be made (such engines are *complete*) in polynomial time with respect to the ontology size. So the power of formal languages lies in the fact that they are equipped with a formal semantics, which guarantees that inference is sound, possibly complete, and in the case of OWL, tractable.

Several commercial inference engines for making inferences with OWL ontologies (ABox and TBox) are available (OWL/Implementations). Inference engines built to implement the OWL standard will infer all and only the same facts from the same set of given facts. In our project we used the BaseVISor inference engine (Matheus et al. 2006), which is free for research purposes. It allows for including additional inference rules.

4.3 Rules

The expressive power of OWL is relatively high—equivalent to a decidable fragment of complete First Order Logic. The designers of OWL intentionally kept its expressiveness at that level in order to avoid the high computational complexity of inference. However, in many cases more expressive power than can be achieved with OWL is necessary. In such cases OWL can be supplemented with rules.

As an example, consider defining the class of routers that send the same packets. To achieve this, one would need to define this class as a set of pairs of routers, where one of them sends the same packet as the other. While OWL provides capabilities for linking, in this case, packets with routers, e.g., via a sendsPacket property, OWL will not allow to distinguish between the two routers and the two packets that are associated with the routers via this property. To achieve such a goal, variables are needed, a feature that OWL lacks. (For any two specific routers, OWL can be used to express that one router sends all and only the same packets as the second, however.)

The desired result can be easily achieved using rules, however. One can define a rule that would imply that whenever sendsPacket(?R1, ?P1) and sendsSamePacket(?R1, ?R2) then sendsPacket(?R2, ?P1).

Issues with the expressive power of OWL versus rule languages have been long recognized and extensively discussed in the literature (cf. Horrocks and Sattler 2003). In particular, it has been recognized that OWL has serious limitations with handling complex role inclusions. For example, it is not possible to propagate the "ownership" role from an aggregate to its parts (sender of a frame is also the sender of all the packets in that frame). In our approach, we use rules whenever we encounter problems with the expressiveness of OWL alone. It should also be noted that just the use of rules per se does not guarantee the correctness of the solution; one needs to be aware of various pitfalls associated with the use of automatic inference and ensure that the implementation of the rules avoids such problems.

5   Case Study

The first requirement for this study was an ontology for the cyber security domain. Unfortunately, a comprehensive ontology for this domain does not exist. In this section we describe our approach to developing such an ontology. The ontology had to be supplemented with rules, which will be presented next. To demonstrate the usefulness of the ontology based approach to cyber security, a testing environment had to be set up, data collected and then used by an inference engine to infer whether a situation of a specific type of cyber threat is taking place or not.

5.1   Cyber Security Ontologies

An ontology for cyber situational awareness should be expressive enough to capture the classes and properties of individuals involved (e.g. networked devices, the persons or organizations who own, control, or use them), how these classes and properties are related to one another (including membership conditions, property domains and range restrictions, and disjointness axioms), and what elements are networked at particular times and the activities in which they are involved (e.g. message M was sent from element X to element Y at time T). On the basis of this representation of the network in a logical framework, a cyber situational awareness engine needs to characterize the situation as either operating normally or as being under a stage of attack or some otherwise undesirable condition.

Unfortunately, there have been relatively few attempts to develop an ontology to comprehensively encode cyber situation information as an OWL ontology (Swimmer 2008; Parmelee 2010; Obrst et al. 2012; Singhal and Wijesekera 2010), and no comprehensive ontologies have been published. Some design patterns have been published for modeling important network concepts, such as the mereotopology patterns outlined in Dumontier (2013), however.

In our project, various cyber security standards from MITRE (CCE), (CPE), (OVAL), (STIX), NIST (SCAP) and IETF (IODEF) were investigated in representing the various aspects of cyber security. Figure 1 shows the major categories and the standards found in each category. To construct a working ontology for cyber situational awareness, these various standards were converted into OWL versions, in whole or in part. That is, the terms from the various XML-based vocabularies were integrated into an OWL ontology, thus providing them with a computer-processable semantics. Figure 1 lists the standards considered in the project and indicates whether or not they were converted to OWL as part of this effort.

The most relevant standard is a relatively new effort supported by various organizations and managed by MITRE called Structured Threat Information eXpression (STIX). STIX is the most comprehensive effort to unify cyber security information sharing. It is described as "a Structured Language for Cyber Threat Intelligence Information", and it incorporates vocabulary from several other standards. The overall structure is show in Fig. 2. STIX is meant to allow for information sharing

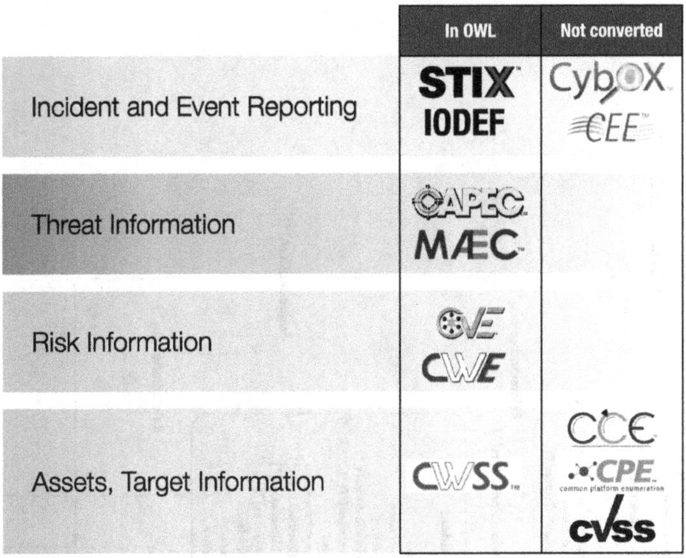

	In OWL	Not converted
Incident and Event Reporting	**STIX**™ **IODEF**	CybOX CEE™
Threat Information	CAPEC MÆC™	
Risk Information	OVE CWE	
Assets, Target Information	CWSS™	CCE CPE common platform enumeration cvss

Fig. 1 Security standards

on cyber threat intelligence. An XML schema for STIX 0.3 was available and used to construct the initial ontology.

STIX captures concepts such as those listed below and provides a high level framework to hold the various cyber intelligence components together. These include:

- Observable and Indicators
- Incident
- Tactics, techniques and procedures of attackers (TTP)
- Exploit Targets
- Courses Of Action
- Campaigns and Threat Actors

The STIX standard helps to glue together the lower level concepts such as events, device and the various other MITRE standards.

5.2 An Overview of XML-Based Standards

In order to reason over statements expressed in all of these vocabularies, we converted the following XML-based cyber standards into OWL ontologies, in whole or part.

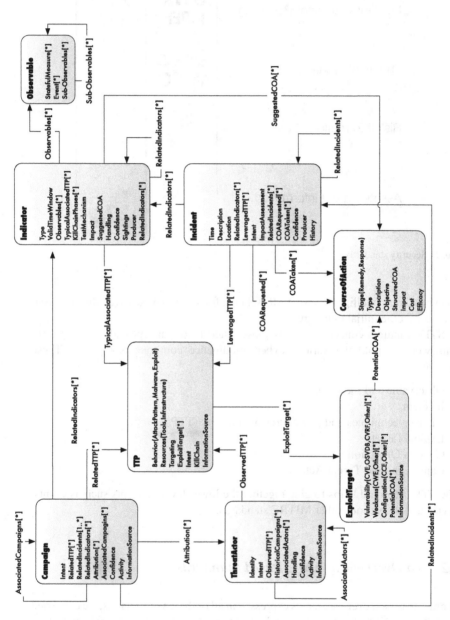

Fig. 2 Structured threat information eXpression (STIX) architecture v0.3 (Structured Threat Information eXpression)

5.2.1 Structured Threat Information eXpression (STIX)

STIX™ is a collaborative community-driven effort to define and develop a standardized language to represent structured cyber threat information. The STIX Language intends to convey the full range of potential cyber threat information and strives to be fully expressive, flexible, extensible, automatable, and as human-readable as possible.

STIX is sponsored by the office of Cybersecurity and Communications at the U.S. Department of Homeland Security.

5.2.2 Common Attack Pattern Enumeration and Classification (CAPEC)

CAPEC™ is international in scope and free for public use. It is a publicly available, community-developed list of common attack patterns along with a comprehensive schema and classification taxonomy. Attack patterns are descriptions of common methods for exploiting software systems. They derive from the concept of design patterns applied in a destructive rather than constructive context and are generated from in-depth analysis of specific real-world exploit examples.

CAPEC is co-sponsored by MITRE Corporation and the office of Cybersecurity and Communications at the U.S. Department of Homeland Security.

5.2.3 Common Vulnerabilities and Exposures (CVE)

CVE is a dictionary of publicly known information security vulnerabilities and exposures. CVE's common identifiers enable data exchange between security products and provide a baseline index point for evaluating coverage of tools and services.

5.2.4 Cyber Observables eXpression (CybOX)

The Cyber Observable eXpression (CybOX) is a standardized schema for the specification, capture, characterization and communication of events or stateful properties that are observable in the operational domain. A wide variety of high-level cyber security use cases rely on such information including: event management/logging, malware characterization, intrusion detection, incident response/management, attack pattern characterization, etc. CybOX provides a common mechanism (structure and content) for addressing cyber observables across and among this full range of use cases improving consistency, efficiency, interoperability and overall situational awareness.

5.2.5 Malware Attribute Enumeration and Characterization (MAEC)

MAEC is a standardized language for encoding and communicating high-fidelity information about malware based upon attributes such as behaviors, artifacts, and attack patterns. By eliminating the ambiguity and inaccuracy that currently exists in malware descriptions and by reducing reliance on signatures, MAEC aims to improve human-to-human, human-to-tool, tool-to-tool, and tool-to-human communication about malware; reduce potential duplication of malware analysis efforts by researchers; and allow for the faster development of countermeasures by enabling the ability to leverage responses to previously observed malware instances.

5.2.6   Common Weakness Enumeration (CWE)

CWE (http://cwe.mitre.org) provides a unified, measurable set of software weaknesses that is enabling more effective discussion, description, selection, and use of software security tools and services that can find these weaknesses in source code and operational systems as well as better understanding and management of software weaknesses related to architecture and design.

5.2.7   Whois and Additional Ontologies

Several additional ontologies were used to represent organizations, whois information, and other data. Whois is a query and response protocol used for querying databases that store the registered users or assignees of Internet resources - domain names, IP address blocks, or autonomous systems. The protocol stores and delivers database content in a human-readable format.

5.3   Lifting Cyber Security XML into OWL

XML schemas merely mandate how information should be structured in conveying a pre-specified set of XML elements from one agent to another. What the various XML elements mean is implicit or, at most, only represented in the XML schema documentation, and implemented in code that inputs and outputs data in that schema, in a manner that is consistent or inconsistent with data encoded by other implementers. That is, following the distinctions outlined in the previous sections, the various XML schemas used to communicate cyber situations currently provide a set of concept names, with distinct URIs, and syntax (message format) but no formal semantics. Hence, they fall short of being ontology and cannot be subject to automatic inference.

The process of transforming XML data to semantic representation (RDF or OWL) is called *lifting*. This process can be largely automated, but with some caveats because not all XML schema constructs have a direct counterpart in OWL. A plethora of research has been conducted in this area (Bedini et al. 2011a; Bikakis et al.; Anagnostopoulos et al. 2013; Ferdinand et al. 2004; Bohring and Auer 2005; Rodrigues et al. 2006).

In converting the XML-based schemas to OWL, we faced the following choices:

- Use a generic XSLT Translation: Since both XSD and OWL are XML-based formats, XSLT can be used to transform XSD to OWL.
- Write a custom XSLT script: This approach requires writing a tailored XSLT script per XSD allowing the resulting OWL to more accurately represent the schema.
- Write custom application: This is a more heavy-duty solution that involves writing a procedural code (Java, C++, etc.) that loads the specific XSD document into memory and generates OWL (possibly using an OWL library).
- Use an external tool: Use one of the tools available on the market, like TopBraid Composer.
- Manual: Manually create the ontology based on the XSD data model using an ontology editor such as Protégé.

The STIX XML Schema is quite complex. It uses many advanced features, like xsd:choice, xs:restriction, xs:extension, xs:enumeration, which often cannot be easily transformed into OWL. Moreover, the model is partitioned into multiple files that not only import each other, but also import additional external schemas. Not surprisingly, the automatic translation offered by generic XSLT scripts or by the third party applications did not yield satisfactory results. The resulting ontology was inconsistent, messy and effectively very hard to use. Enumerations were improperly converted, namespaces were improperly defined, and countless classes and properties that were generated were practically useless, acting as placeholders. Numerous classes and properties were redefined across multiple generated OWL files, which produced inconsistencies. Moreover, the translation did not handle datatypes correctly and generated object properties when it was not necessary, or correct, effectively defining primitive data types as OWL classes, such as String.

In general, since XML Schema is concerned only with message structure, not message meaning, datatype properties such as strings are used to encode entities, making OWL inference impossible over them, since they do not represent entities (i.e. something denoted by a URI/IRI) but only a piece of data. For example, if the country associated with an IP address is represented as a string in OWL (e.g. "Republic of Ireland"), then it is impossible to do geospatial reasoning with this element using an ontology of places and their relations (GeoNames Ontology). In order to reason about something like a region, the entity must be a first-class individual with associated properties (latitude-longitude coordinates, etc.), denoted by an IRI/URI.

Automated translation methods were not yet satisfactory for use in converting the STIX model to OWL. Techniques for such automatic translation in general are still subject of an ongoing research (Bedini et al. 2011b). In general, automated XSD to OWL methods fail because they cannot:

- Distinguish container elements (e.g. Contacts) from singular classes to which a parent class might be related one-to-many (e.g. Contact).
- Distinguish datatype and object-type properties.
- Generate useful object property relation identifiers.

- Produce useful property restrictions between classes (except for cardinality restrictions, which were often accurate).
- Generate domain and range restrictions.
- Generate useful class hierarchies.

Our second approach was to write custom XSLT scripts. However, due to the complexities of the STIX model described above, the result was also far from satisfactory, and we decided to create the STIX ontology by hand, using the XSD model as a guideline. During the manual process we were able to leverage some OWL-specific mechanisms and create an ontology that maintained the intention of the schema, but used slightly different constructs to express it. For instance, in order to associate an indicator with a sequence of observables in XSD, authors of the STIX model created a type stix:ObservablesType, which is a complex type with an unbounded sequence of stix:ObservableType. To represent the same in OWL, only one class is needed, e.g. stix:Observable, whose instances can then be related to instances of a class stix:Indicator using an object property "stix:observable". If we wanted to restrict this relationship, e.g., say that a single Indicator can have only one Observable, we would simply define the "stix:observable" property as a functional property.

Nearly all relationships between XSD elements were expressed as OWL restrictions on classes that represented one of the elements. For instance, in order to express the fact that an instance of stix:Indicator can have a relationship with multiple instances of stix:Observable, we defined a restriction on class stix:Indicator:

```
<owl:Class rdf:about="http://stix.mitre.org/STIX#Indicator">
<rdfs:subClassOf>
<owl:Restriction>
<owl:onProperty rdf:resource="http://stix.mitre.org/STIX#observable"/>
<owl:allValuesFromrdf:resource="http://stix.mitre.org/STIX#Observable"/>
</owl:Restriction>
</rdfs:subClassOf>
</owl:Class>
```

In the end, the resulting ontology reflects the relationships expressed in the original model, yet it is clean, logically consistent and easy to use when writing SPARQL queries or declarative rules.

5.4 STIX Ontology

The resulting STIX OWL ontology that we created on the basis of the STIX XML Schema (XSD) document has the following characteristics (Fig. 3):

The STIX ontology imports the following ontologies, in addition to the multiple STIX ontology files (Fig. 4):

METRICS	
Axiom	527
Logical axiom count	304
Class count	67
Object property count	83
Data property count	33
Individual count	11
DL expressivity	ALUHOQ(D)

CLASS AXIOMS	
SubClassOf axioms count	270
EquivalentClasses axioms count	11
DisjointClasses axioms count	0
GCI count	0
Hidden GCI count	6

Fig. 3 STIX 0.3 ontology metrics

PREFIX	NAMESPACE
Common	*http://cybox.mitre.org/Common#*
capec_v1	*http://capec.mitre.org/capec_v1#*
data-marking	*http://data-marking.mitre.org#*
cybox_v1	*http://cybox.mitre.org/cybox_v1#*
killchain	*http://referentia.com/killchain/*
maec-core-2	*http://maec.mitre.org/XMLSchema/maec-core-2#*

Fig. 4 STIX ontology imports

A high-level overview of the STIX ontology that was produced in this project, is depicted in Fig. 5. The central class is TTP (Tactic, Techniques and Procedure), the instances of which are cyber security exploits. These TTPs may have a variety of subclasses. TTPs are related to instances of AttackPattern, Exploit, ExploitTarget, InformationSource, Infrastructure, Intent, KillChain, KillChainPhase, Identity (of target) and ToolInformation via object properties that further individuate the instances of that class. TTP has subclasses ObservedTTP, RelatedTTP, and LeveragedTTP. Indicators are related to TTP by means of the indicatedTTP object property. Restrictions on the object properties are used to structure the instances of this class, and other classes.

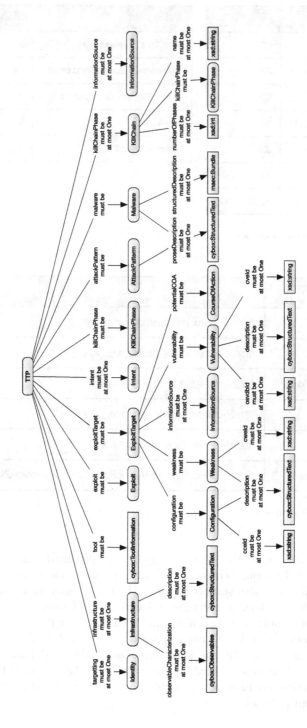

Fig. 5 High-level view of STIX ontology

5.4.1   Populating Vulnerabilities Using the NVDClient

The NVDClient is a tool we have developed that uses the National Vulnerability Database (available from NIST) to fetch data about a particular cyber vulnerability in the CVE (Common Vulnerabilities and Exposures) registry (CVE). The data includes information about the CVE's impact [Common Vulnerability Scoring System (CVSS-SIG)], references to advisories, solutions and tools and a relationship to CWEs. Because they were so numerous, we did not want to first incorporate all the vulnerabilities into an ontology that we would use in inference, since there would be too much information that was not necessary. The information in the CAPEC ontology relates attack patterns to classes of vulnerabilities.

NIST does not provide any web service access to its data; instead, it publishes a data feed, which is regularly updated. The feed is formatted in XML and is rather large (16 MB). Downloading and processing the entire feed is impractical if one is interested in getting information about only a few CVEs at a time. To address this issue, we developed a Java program that scrapes the CVE information directly from its corresponding web page. All CVEs are described on single pages accessible under an HTTP address of the following format:

http://web.nvd.nist.gov/view/vuln/detail?vulnId=<*CVE ID*>

Consequently, the tool downloads the HTML code of the web page describing a particular CVE of interest by supplying appropriate *CVE ID*. Next, using the jsoup library (jsoup), it scrapes useful information about the CVE using a CSS-like syntax to access particular HTML elements on the page.

Once the CVE information is stored in memory, the tool creates a new ontology model in Apache Jena and generates an OWL document representing the CVE. Tools like TopBraid Composer or BaseVISor inference engine can then process the resulting OWL document, which are imported at inference time.

5.5   Other Ontologies

5.5.1   Persons, Groups and Organizations

We used the Friend of a Friend (FOAF) ontology (The Friend of a Friend) to represent persons, groups, and organizations. Additionally, we developed an ontology for WhoIs Internet registration information (WhoIs) in order to associate IP addresses of devices with human agents and organizations. We used a service called whoisxmlapi.com to provide WhoIs information for IP addresses we encountered. This requires two lookups. The first lookup identified a contact email based on the IP address supplied. We then did a DNS lookup on the contact email domain (assuming they would be the same) to get the domain name and other information for the domain that controls that IP address. Similarly, we could look up the registrar name. If the registrar is suspicious, knowing this fact about an IP address is useful for our purposes. Unfortunately, the XML produced by the whoisxmlapi.com service was less useful for foreign IP addresses, because it failed to contain structured information. Relevant information was contained in the record, but it was enclosed just as text strings, often in a foreign language, which would require additional parsing to populate the XML fields and then lifted to OWL. We did not implement a custom parser for accomplishing this.

5.5.2 Threat Representation

For threat representation, the NIST CAPEC classification was used and represented in an ontology. The CAPEC classification provides ways to classify the attacks and used with detected cyber events to understand the CVE vulnerabilities, which were associated with an exploit using a particular CAPEC attack mechanism. This was then used to infer potential effects on the target and future actions the malware may perform.

The MAEC schema was not used as it is typically used to represent the actual malware and this type of data is usually not accessible at various security sites, unless through a paid subscription. CVE and vulnerability information is typically available but not the actual malware data.

5.5.3 Weakness and Risk Representation

The CWE representation that classifies the various types of weaknesses was entirely represented in the ontology with the referenced CAPEC information. CVE vulnerability information was not represented in the ontology, as it is usually part of the signature used in detecting security events. Typically a Snort signature would identify a specific CVE, which would then be used to identify associated CWE and the CAPEC information.

The CWE provides the various weaknesses that may be exploited by malware and can be used to understand the attack and also determine the impact and malware behavior. Figure 6 depicts a portion of the CWE structure; the red boxes represent the CWEs that are being used by the National Vulnerability Database.

5.5.4 Asset and Target Representation

MITRE standards such as CPE, CCE and CVSS were used to represent the target and asset being targeted by malware. The CPE and CCE tend to be more for end host representation of the configuration, operating system and applications but are not used in the ontology, as those concepts already exist. The CVSS information on the vulnerability score will be used for specific attacks to understand the potential impact and severity of the attacks.

Other ontologies that were developed include an ontology of Snort events and similar events, an ontology of part-whole relations, that were used to represent IP domains and sub-domains, and a watchlist ontology. The prototype system was

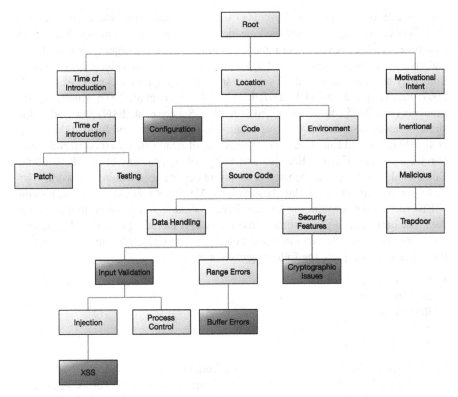

Fig. 6 Portion of the structure of the common weakness enumeration (CWE) (http://nvd.nist.gov/cwe.cfm)

capable of processing events from various sources and converting them into the ontology. For Snort IDS events, the system queried the Snort database and processed the various events. The key Snort field was the classification of the type of event and for known signatures, the CVE code of the exploited vulnerability.

For associating users with entities on the network, an LDAP directory was queried as to domain login and logoff information, which were converted into ontology events.

Netflow events were obtained from an existing netflow collector; since the system was not producing a high level of netflow data, occasional processing of the flow to ontology was done. Performance data of the network was obtained from a network management capability that polled SNMP related statistics and converted it into OWL form.

5.5.5 Kill Chain

Next, we discuss issues related to the modeling of events and situations in an ontology, representing and reasoning about the participation of entities in events and situations as well as mereological, causal, temporal and geospatial relationships between events. An ontology of events or situations treats these entities as individuals that occur or happen. They are considered to be perduring entities that unfold over time, i.e., they have temporal parts. In contrast, material objects such as stones and chairs are said to exist, and all of the parts that they have exist at each point in time; they are called endurants. There are several ontologies for events (Wang et al. 2007; Raimond and Abdallah 2007; IPTC 2008; Doerr et al. 2007; Mueller 2008; Francois et al. 2005; Westermann and Jain 2007; Scherp et al. 2009) and models for situation-awareness that have a close relation to events (Chen and Joshi 2004; Wang et al. 2004; Yau and Liu 2006; Lin 2008), some of which are based on Barwise and Perry's Situation Theory (Barwise and Perry 1983; Matheus et al. 2003, 2005; Kokar et al. 2009) that can be used to represent occurrences within a network.

In our system, an Event class based on the MITRE Common Event Expression (CEE) was used to capture the low level events data that is captured in typical log data. The base ontology uses some of those concepts including time (Hobbs and Pan 2004), priority and other common attributes found in CEE. The ontology was further enhanced to capture the following event subclasses:

- Security Events
- Identity Events
- Reputation Events
- Network Flow
- Network Performance Events

Figure 7 shows the ontology class structure from the ontology tool.

One of the key cyber situational concepts from STIX is the idea of the kill chain, which is a particular type of situation, in which several events of particular types must occur in a specified order. Kill chains as they are related to Advanced Persistent Threats are described in detail in Hutchins et al. (2011). The kill chain model of Advanced Persistent Threats is used to describe the various phases that an adversary would perform as listed below and shown in Fig. 8:

- Reconnaissance
- Weaponization
- Delivery
- Exploitation
- Installation
- C2
- Actions on Objectives

The kill chain referenced in STIX is slightly different than described in the Hutchins paper but similar concepts are expressed. An Intrusion Kill Chain, in our ontology, is a subclass of Kill Chain that contains various associated phases for that type of kill chain (here, Intrusion), which are related to one another by a transitive 'precedes' object property.

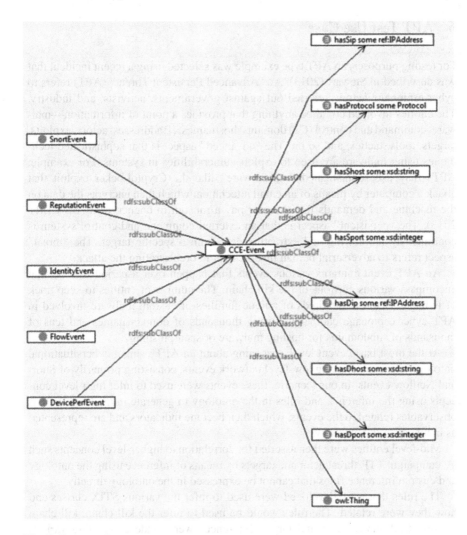

Fig. 7 Event ontology structure

Fig. 8 Kill chain model (Security Intelligence)

6 APT Test Use Case

For testing purposes, an APT type example was selected using a recent incident that was described in Stewart (2013). An "Advanced Persistent Threat" (APT) refers to cyber-espionage activity carried out against governments, activists, and industry. The entities involved could be anything that provides a point of information—malware, command and control (C2) domains, hostnames, IP addresses, actors, exploits, targets, tools, tactics, and so on. The "advanced" aspect is that sophisticated techniques using malware are used to exploit vulnerabilities in systems. For example, APTs may use sophisticated "ransomware" like the CryptoLocker exploit that attack a computer by means of an email attachment which then encrypts the data on the machine and demands that the user pay a ransom to unencrypt it (US-CERT 2013). The "persistent" aspect is that an external command and control system is continuously monitoring and extracting data from a specific target. The "threat" aspect refers to adversarial human involvement in orchestrating the attack.

An APT event contains various events that happen over a period of time that encompass various portions of the kill chain. The number of entities to keep track of is huge: there are hundreds of unique families of custom malware involved in APT cyber-espionage campaigns, using thousands of domain names and tens of thousands of subdomains for hosting malware or spearphishing.

At the most basic event level, reasoning about an APT using a cybersituational ontology requires detecting low-level network events, consisting primarily of Snort and Netflow events. In our scenario, these events were used to infer high-level concepts using the inference and rules in the ontology to generate individuals such as observables related to the events, which then become indicators and are represented as incidents in the ontology.

Mid-level entities were then asserted for correlation to higher-level concepts such as, campaign, TTP, threat actor and targets by means of inference using the ontology and custom inference rules that cannot be expressed in the ontology directly.

The rules that were developed were used to infer the various STIX classes and how they were related. The rules would be used to infer the kill chain, kill chain phases, TTP, threat actor and target. Inferences were made associating various detected events with kill chain stages.

6.1 Test Network

Testing was done on a test network with actual attacks. The network consisted of a hub site connecting to three spoke sites (Fig. 9). There are three potential paths to the spoke sites with various IDS, firewall, router and switches. Various attacks were performed on the network and event information captured and analyzed by the prototype system. The ontology and rules were then used to infer information about the attack and its impacts on the test network. The inference of facts triggered by low-level Snort events to the identification of kill chain elements to the identification of

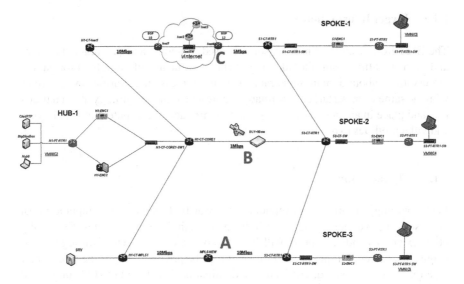

Fig. 9 Test network diagram. Some details are redacted

perpetrators, was done using VIStology's BaseVISor OWL 2 RL forward-chaining inference engine, incorporating the cyber situational ontology produced from the various standards described here.

The inference and rule development consisted primarily of (1) creating the high level STIX incidents from various low level network events, and (2) inferring information as to the state of the network and its paths and potential impacts.

The STIX representation requires development of rules that build out a model of the cyber security state from the network devices, topology, assets with dynamic event information from IDS, NetFlow, network metrics and other event data.

The STIX representation creates STIX incidents, campaign and other high level classes based on individual events. Individual interrelated events such as the CVE Snort based event and the Snort class type were then pieced together to understand the attack type. The IP address from the Snort event was used to infer the identity of the APT threat actor.

6.1.1 Kill Chain

The various low level incidents were correlated as part of a larger kill chain. Looking at the user and target, and correlating the order of various incidents, was used to determine that these events were part of a similar campaign by the same threat actor. The temporal order of the events was then used to classify the nature of the situation. For example, if C2 beaconing occurs before an infected file is downloaded, then this is reversed from the kill chain sequence, so then these two incidents are not stages of the same kill chain, although they may be separate elements of attempts to inject an infected file.

6.1.2   Target Information

The IP address from the Snort sensor was used to understand the targeted devices and user identity from the identity events by means of WhoIs information. Observations about domain registrants were used to associate various cyber events with the same user. As target, information represented in the ontology about a user's role and place in an enterprise can be used to infer actual and potential attack types and vulnerabilities exploited.

6.1.3   Threat Actor

In our ontology, a threat actor reputation list was built based on the reputation list but also from external linkage to WhoIs and domain information sites. Eventually other external incident reports will help to correlate threat actors to larger campaigns that target multiple organizations. It may be possible to infer the threat actor type (e.g. state sponsored, criminal or individual hacker) based on TTP, target and sophistication of attack methods.

Reputation events were researched in conjunction with the Collective Intelligence Framework (CIF) project as a potential source of external IP- and URL-based reputation information. CIF uses data from sites such as the Malware Domain Blocklist, Shadowserver, Spamhaus, and several others, to store and correlate data. For our purposes, we just used Spamhaus (spamhaus.org) reputation lists directly. In the future, the interface to the CIF could be used to get additional information.

6.1.4   Impact Analysis

Rules were developed to infer information about the state of the network and the paths within the network based on the current attacks with respect to impact and mitigation.

In general, our ontology was augmented with some rules used to help infer the more complex APT concepts and to create instances of the STIX representation of the potential attacks. The rules were written in VIStology BaseVISor language and run with the BaseVISor inference engine. The inference engine runs all the rules to infer from the low level events to STIX observables, indicators and incidents in addition to standard OWL 2 RL inference rules for generic inferences about classes and relations. From these low level indicators, a kill chain with a kill chain phase was inferred based on the potential threat actor and target.

SPARQL queries were also used for analysis of impact based on various Snort, reputation and identity events. The Snort events that had a CVE reference were correlated to the CWE and CAPEC associations in the ontology to infer additional network impact scores.

6.2   Rules

In addition to the ontology, a set of rules was developed in order to make the following inferences:

- Tie Snort events to CVEs
- Create an Observable for each Snort or Netflow Event
- Create an Indicator for each Observable
- Extract Kill Chain phase from Snort events to Indicators
- Combine Indicators with the same related CVE
- Combine Indicators with the same signature IDs and source IP
- Combine Indicators with Snort events and NetFlow events of the same source/destination IP and detect time
- Combine indicators with NetFlowEvents matching source/destination but not having a corresponding SnortEvent
- Assert kill chain phase for NetFlow-based Indicators missing a kill chain phase
- Create Incidents for Indicators
- Extract CVSS Base score
- Identify ExploitTarget (destination of Snort event in the user's domain)
- Create a TTP and ThreatActor based on existing ExploitTarget
- Extract AttackPattern from ExploitTarget's CWE to ThreatActor's CAPEC
- Store IP addresses of ThreatActor based on events from ExploitTarget
- Assign indicators as KillChainPhase

These rules were implemented in BaseVISor rule language as Horn clause rules that enable patterns of triples to be expressed using both constants and variables in the body of the rules. The values of variables that are bound to a set of facts that matches the pattern in the body of the rule can then be used to assert new triples in the head of the rule. Additionally, these values can be used as inputs to procedural attachments in the rule head. Such procedural attachments might, for example, call external services to convert a domain name to an IP address or compute the distance between two geospatial points expressed as latitude/longitude pairs.

When security events are found by Snort, if the signature has a CVE associated with it, that information is used as a key to get additional information about the particular vulnerability from the NIST site. The NIST site provides html based data on the CVE but also the association to the CWE, CAPEC and additional information such as CVSS base score, access vector, and so on.

At a basic level, the detected Snort and Netflow events contain CVE signature, host and destination IP address and host information. The events are collected together as observables, which are mapped to indicators by means of the ontology and rules and are then aggregated as Incidents. Snort events with CVE were used to infer which part of the kill chain an event may be characterized as by mapping Snort event classes to kill chain phases in the ontology. Snort events without an associated CVE are correlated with Netflow events to represent their relation. For example command and control traffic may show up as a suspicious event in Snort but with no associated CVE.

Such events can then be correlated with Netflow events on the basis of source and destination information, in order to infer matches to a particular target and threat actors. These mid-level Incidents are then associated with higher-level concepts of a campaign, TTP, threat actor and targets by means of the ontology and rules.

6.3   Inference Based Threat Detection

Rules were used to associate domains or IP addresses with incidents. Multiple events with the same source could then be detected. If the event was characterized as malevolent or part of a kill chain, the domain or IP address could be associated with entries in the reputation ontology derived from the Spamhaus.org entries described previously. In addition, ontology individuals corresponding to countries, organization and Internet registrars allowed the system to characterize domains and IP addresses as more or less suspicious, based on prior activities. Countries can be characterized by their reputation for hosting cyber aggressors, for example. IP addresses can be related to countries by means of WhoIs and DNS lookups, as described previously, as well. Thus, suspicious traffic originating from a known suspicious country would be inferred to be even more suspicious in nature.

7   Other Ontology-Related Efforts for Cyber Security

A number of research papers were found reporting on the use of ontologies in cyber security. First of all there are a number of papers that argue for the need to use ontologies in solving cyber security problems. For instance, in an ARO workshop presentation, Sheth (2007) argued for the use of the Semantic Web techniques and ontologies for cyber situational awareness. Caton (2012) argued for putting the issue of cyber security in a wider context of a more general theory of conflict—going beyond the models of the current situation—to models that include the capabilities of accommodating future developments in the cyberspace warfare. Clearly, this view is in line with the Endsley's model of situation awareness (Endsley 1995) in which the process includes projection in the future. Atkinson et al. (2012) put the problem of cyber security in a wider perspective of social networks and argued for an approach in which the problem is considered as a problem of establishing a cyber-ecology in which means exist for encouraging good behaviors and deterring bad. Their ontological framework includes both the social trust and technological rules and controls.

Ontologies for cyber security go back to the early days of the Semantic Web. For instance, the 2003 paper (Undercoffer et al. 2003) discussed the use of the DAML language (the precursor of OWL) for representing an ontology for the domain of intrusion detection. It compared DAML vs. XML and discussed the inadequacies of the latter. The ontology includes 23 classes and 190 properties/attributes. The 2005 paper (Kim et al. 2005) presented some plans to use ontologies for modeling dependencies between cyber related infrastructures, although no details of the resulting ontology were given. More et al. (2012) describe an experimental system for intrusion detection that uses ontologies and inference. Their ontology is an extension of the one developed by Undercoffer et al. (2003). Okolica et al. (2009) develop a framework for understanding situational awareness in the cyber security domain. They also refer to the ontology developed by Undercoffer et al. (2003).

A large number of papers reported on the use of ontologies for cyber security and situational awareness. However, since the details of the ontologies used are not shown, it was impossible for us to reuse these results. For instance, the paper (Khairkar et al. 2013) mentions a number of research efforts where ontologies were used. It claims that ontologies will resolve many problems with the Intrusion Detection Systems, in particular by classifying malicious activities detected in the logs of network activity, however, it does not show any details of such an approach. The paper (Kang and Liang 2013) discusses an attempt to use an ontology that links security issues to the software development process based on Model Driven Architecture (MDA). In particular, an ontology (which is presented as a collection of the various meta-models) is attributed with the generation of the various MDA models. Unfortunately, the paper does not show any details of how this is achieved. Strassner et al. (2010) discuss an architecture of a system for network monitoring in which ontologies are used. The paper stresses the ability of ontologies to infer facts that are not explicitly represented. But no details of the ontology are shown. Bradshaw and his colleagues (2012) discuss the use of policies and an agent based architecture for the tasks of cyber situational awareness focusing on the human-computer interoperation. Oltramari et al. (2013) discuss the use of ontologies for decision support in cyber operations, however no specific ontology is provided. The paper focuses on the architecture and conceptual justification for the use of cognitive architectures that should include ontologies. The authors of de Barros Barreto et al. (2013) describe a system that uses ontologies. They don't show a new ontology, but rather reuse other existing ontologies.

A number of papers show a (usually graphical) representation of the used ontology. The paper (D'Amico et al. 2010) reports on a workshop in which participants worked on an ontology for capturing relationships between missions and cyber resources. This work is part of the Camus project (cyber assets, missions and users) (Goodall et al. 2009). In Strasburg et al. (2013) a project is described in which an ontology, expressed in OWL, was used to represent the domain of intrusion detection and response. The paper shows only the top level of the ontology. The paper (Bouet and Israel 2011) discusses a system in which an ontology for describing assets and their security information is used. The system works off-line—auditing long files. The paper shows only the top level of the ontology.

By contrast, Fenza et al. (2010) used the Situation Theory Ontology (STO) (Kokar et al. 2009) (which is publicly available) for identifying security issues in the domain of airport security.

Some papers focus on the process of developing ontologies for the cyber security domain. These were of special interest to us since we had to undertake such a task, too. For instance, Wali et al. (2013) describes an approach to developing a cyber security ontology from a cyber security textbook index and an existing ontology (Herzog et al. 2007). The Software Engineering Institute's report (Mundie and McIntire 2013) describes the Malware Analysis Lexicon (MAL)—an initiative influenced by the JASON report (McMorrow 2010).

We close our literature survey with a relatively recent report from MITRE (McMorrow 2010). JASON, an independent scientific advisory group that provided consulting services to the U.S. government on matters of defense science and technology, published a very influential report (McMorrow 2010) in 2010 whose objective was to examine and assess the theory and practice of cyber-security. One of the most important conclusions of this report was:

> The most important attributes would be the construction of a common language and a set of basic concepts about which the security community can develop a shared understanding. Since cyber-security is science in the presence of adversaries, these objects will change over time, but a common language and agreed-upon experimental protocols will facilitate the testing of hypotheses and validation of concepts.

8 Lessons and Future Work

Given the complexity of the current XML-based standards and the state of the art in automatically converting XSD to OWL, the semantic representation of cyber threat information in an interoperable format that can be reasoned over (such as OWL) is difficult. Keeping up with changing and additional standards requires a great deal of manual knowledge representation effort.

In the test scenario described here, the ability of ontologies to represent information and infer additional information was used to identify an advanced persistent threat (APT) whose operation consisted of multiple steps, represented in our ontology as sequential steps in a kill chain. Inference with the ontology was used to understand the threat actor, the target and purpose, which helped to determine potential course of action and future impact.

In general, our experience with using existing terms and concepts implicit in XML-based cyber standards to create an OWL ontology with rules for inferring cyber situational awareness led us to the following conclusions:

- Ontology based analysis is useful for providing cyber situational awareness due to its ability to find patterns and infer new information by integrating information from a number of sources expressed in different standards.
- The ability to tie different event types to infer incident information is promising and could be used to add additional event types in the future.
- Automatically generated ontologies from XML schemas require a lot of massaging to be useful and create a lot of complexity that is difficult to fix.
- The MITRE security standards are helpful in representing concepts in cyber security but are more tailored for XML and must be adapted for ontology use.
- Snort based event information in context with NetFlow information can be used to understand the timing, duration and network characteristics of attacks.

Creating an ontology from real networks is non-trivial. However, ontologies and inference can provide additional insightful information beyond path-based analysis about the network. Ontologies provided an easier framework for incorporating new information and rules compared to traditional Rete based rule engines such as Drools. However, the use of ontologies does require domain knowledge, ontology and software development skills to be successful that are not commonly part of network administration.

The cyber ontologies developed here leveraged various standards developed by MITRE, NIST, USCERT and other organizations. Many of the standards were represented as XML, which was found during the research to be very difficult to automatically convert to an ontology using XML translation rules. The lack of OWL ontologies corresponding to the MITRE standards and other cyber situational standards hinder interoperability and situational awareness because the XML schemas do not have a formal semantics. Thus, information in those standards cannot be combined and used to infer new knowledge. The STIX based ontology developed in this project could be used as a starting point by various organizations that are currently in the process of defining the STIX standards using XML as well as other research organizations. Lessons learned on the conversion process of the MITRE and STIX XML would help others to avoid pitfalls. The STIX ontology could also aid in inter agency and department cyber information sharing as it would help add semantic meaning, but due to the XML usage it may be difficult to get an ontology version that can be kept up to date.

The STIX community has expressed interest in an eventual OWL encoding of its work, but this task is non-trivial. Serious efforts need to begin on constructing interoperable ontologies for cyber situational awareness so that inferences based on shared information can be made in standard, transparent, uniform ways. Since so much valuable work has already gone into developing existing XML-based standards, and each of these has an existing community of users, it makes sense to invest serious effort into developing adequate techniques for lifting XML schemas into OWL ontologies so that machines can share not only common vocabularies, but common meanings for representing and inferring the state of networks.

9   Summary

In cyber systems, where the processing loops are very fast, much of inference must be performed by computers. In other words, automatic inference engines must perform the inference, which in turn requires that the information (facts) to be acted upon by such engines needs to be represented in a language with formal semantics. The term "ontology" stands for an explicit, formal, machine-readable semantic model that defines the classes, instances of the classes, inter-class relations and data properties relevant to a problem domain. In order for ontologies to be amenable to automatic processing by computers, they need to be represented in a language that has both formal syntax and formal semantics. OWL is the most commonly used language for expressing ontologies today and has by far the largest developer base.

Automatic inference on ontologies expressed in OWL is performed by inference engines, or semantic reasoners. An inference engine takes a set of facts about a specific domain of interest asserted in OWL and derives other facts using axioms and inference rules. OWL's semantics is such that inference is expected to be computationally tractable. Several commercial inference engines for making inferences with OWL ontologies are available. The expressive power of OWL is relatively high—equivalent to a decidable fragment of complete First Order Logic. In addition, OWL can be supplemented with rules. There have been relatively few attempts to develop ontology to comprehensively encode cyber situation information as OWL ontology, and no comprehensive ontologies have been published. The most relevant standard is a relatively new effort supported by various organizations and managed by MITRE called Structured Threat Information eXpression (STIX). Other relevant XML schemas exists, however, they merely mandate how information should be structured in conveying a pre-specified set of XML elements from one agent to another. They fall short of being ontology and cannot be subject to automatic inference. Automatic reasoning based on ontologies can support situational awareness in the cyber security domain. An approach that mimics the analyst's process can be implemented using ontologies and an inference engine. A comprehensive ontology for cyber security can be developed by taking advantage of existing cyber security related standards and markup languages.

References

Anagnostopoulos, E. et al. Vol. 418. Studies in Computational Intelligence. Springer Berlin Heidelberg, 2013, pp. 319–360. isbn: 978-3-642-28976-7. doi: 10 . 1007 / 978 - 3 - 642 - 28977 - 4 _ 12. url: http://dx.doi.org/10.1007/978-3-642-28977-4_12

Apache Jena. http://jena.apache.org

Atkinson, S.R., Beaulne, K., Walker, D., and Hossain, L. "Cyber – Transparencies, Assurance and Deterrence", International Conference on Cyber Security, 2012

Baader, F., McGuinness, D. L., Nardi, D., and Patel-Schneider, P. F. (Eds.). (2010) The Description Logic Handbook: Theory, Implementation and Applications. Cambridge University Press.

Barwise, J., Perry, J. (1983) Situations and Attitudes. Cambridge, MA: MIT Press.

Bedini, I. et al. "Transforming XML Schema to OWL Using Patterns". In: Semantic Computing (ICSC), 2011 Fifth IEEE International Conference on. 2011a, pp. 102–109. doi: 10.1109/ICSC.2011.77

Bedini, I., Matheus, C., Patel-Schneider, P. F., and Boran, A. Transforming XML Schema to OWL Using Patterns. ICSC '11 Proceedings of the 2011 IEEE Fifth International Conference on Semantic Computing, Pages 102-109, 2011b.

Bikakis, N. et al. "The XML and Semantic Web Worlds: Technologies, Interoperability and Integration: A Survey of the State of the Art". In: Semantic Hyper/Multimedia Adaptation. Ed. by Ioannis

Bohring, H., and Auer, S. "Mapping XML to OWL Ontologies." In: Leipziger Informatik-Tage 72 (2005), pp. 147–156.

Bouet, M., and Israel, M. "INSPIRE Ontology Handler: automatically building and managing a knowledge base for Critical Information Infrastructure Protection", 12th IFIP/IEEE IM, 2011.

Boyd, J. A discourse on winning and losing. Technical report, Maxwell AFB, 1987.

Bradshaw, J. M., Carvalho, M., Bunch, L., Eskridge, T., Feltovich, P. J., Johnson, M., and Kidwell, D. "Sol: An Agent-Based Framework for Cyber Situation Awareness", Kunstl Intell, 26:127–140, 2012.

Brank, J., Grobelnik, M., and Mladenic, D. A survey of ontology evaluation techniques. In In Proceedings of the Conference on Data Mining and Data Warehouses (SiKDD 2005)

CAPEC – Common Attack Pattern Enumeration and Characterization. http://capec.mitre.org/.

Caton, J. L. "Beyond Domains, Beyond Commons: Context and Theory of Conflict in Cyberspace", 4th International Conference on Cyber Conflict, 2012.

CCE – Common Configuration Enumeration: Unique Identifiers for Common System Configuration Issues. [Online] http://cce.mitre.org/.

Chen, H., and Joshi, A. *The SOUPA Ontology for Pervasive Computing.* Birkhauser Publishing Ltd., April 2004

Common Vulnerability Scoring System (CVSS-SIG). [Online] http://www.first.org/cvss/.

CPE – Common Platform Enumeration. [Online] http://cpe.mitre.org/.

CVE – Common Vulnerabilities and Exposures. [Online] http://cve.mitre.org/.

CWE – Common Weakness Enumeration. National Vulnerability Database, http://nvd.nist.gov/cwe.cfm.

CWE – Common Weakness Enumeration. http://cwe.mitre.org

CybOX – Cyber Observable eXpression. http://cybox.mitre.org

D'Amico, A., Buchanan, L., Goodall, J., and Walczak, P. "Mission Impact of Cyber Events: Scenarios and Ontology to Express the Relationships between Cyber Assets, Missions and Users", International Conference on i-Warfare and Security (ICIW), The Air Force Institute of Technology, Wright-Patterson Air Force Base, Ohio, USA, 2010.

de Barros Barreto, A., Costa, P. C. G., and Yano, E. T. Using a Semantic Approach to Cyber Impact Assessment. STIDS, 2013.

Doerr, M., Ore, C.-E., and Stead, S. The CIDOC conceptual reference model: a new standard for knowledge sharing. In Conceptual modeling, pages 51–56. Australian Computer Society, Inc., 2007. ISBN 978-1-920682-64-4.

Dumontier, M. SemanticScience wiki: ODPMereotopology. https://code.google.com/p/semantic-science/wiki/ODPMereotopology. Updated Nov 27, 2013.

Endsley, M. (1995). "Toward a theory of situation awareness in dynamic systems". Human Factors 37(1), 32-64.

Fenza, G., Furno, D., Loia, V̇., and Veniero, M. "Agent-based Cognitive approach to Airport Security Situation Awareness", International Conference on Complex, Intelligent and Software Intensive Systems, 2010.

Ferdinand, M., Zirpins, C., and Trastour, D. "Lifting XML Schema to OWL". In: Web Engineering. Ed. by Nora Koch, Piero Fraternali, and Martin Wirsing. Vol. 3140. Lecture Notes in Computer Science. Springer Berlin Heidelberg, 2004, pp. 354–358. isbn: 978-3-540-22511-9. doi: 10.1007/978-3-540-27834-4_44. http://dx.doi.org/10.1007/978-3-540-27834-4_44.

Francois, A. R. J., Nevatia, R., Hobbs, J., and Bolles, R. C. VERL: An ontology framework for representing and annotating video events. IEEE MultiMedia, 12(4), 2005.

GeoNames Ontology – Geo Semantic Web. http://www.geonames.org/ontology/documentation.html.

Goodall, J. R., D'Amico, A., and Kopylec, J. K. "Camus: Automatically Mapping Cyber Assetts to Missions and Users", IEEE Military Communications Conference, MILCOM 2009, pp.1-7, 2009.

Gruber, T. Ontology. In Ling Liu and M. Tamer Ozsu, editors, The Encyclopedia of Database Systems, pages 1963–1965. Springer, 2009.

Herzog, A., Shahmehri, N., and Duma, C. "An Ontology of Information Security," IGI Global, 2007, pp. 1-23.

Hobbs, J. R., and Pan, F. An Ontology of Time for the Semantic Web. CM Transactions on Asian Language Processing (TALIP): Special issue on Temporal Information Processing. 2004. Vol. 3, 1, pp. 66-85.

Horrocks, I., and Sattler, U. The effect of adding complex role inclusion axioms in description logics. In Proc. of the 18th Int. Joint Conf. on Artificial Intelligence (IJCAI 2003), pages 343–348. Morgan Kaufmann, Los Altos, 2003.

Hutchins, E. M., Cloppert, M. J., & Amin, R. M. (2011). Intelligence-driven computer network defense informed by analysis of adversary campaigns and intrusion kill chains. Leading Issues in Information Warfare & Security Research, 1, 80.

IODEF – Cover Pages Incident Object Description and Exchange Format. http://xml.coverpages. org/iodef.html.

IPTC International Press Telecommunications Council, London, UK. EventML, 2008. http://iptc.org/. jsoup: Java HTML Parser. http://jsoup.org/

Kang, W., and Liang, Y. "A Security Ontology with MDA for Software Development", International Conference on Cyber-Enabled Distributed Computing and Knowledge Discovery, 2013.

Khairkar, A. D., Kshirsagar, D., and Kumar, S. "Ontology for Detection of Web Attacks", International Conference on Communication Systems and Network Technologies, 2013.

Kim, H. M., Biehl, M., and Buzacott, J. A. "M-CI²: Modelling Cyber Interdependencies between Critical Infrastructures", 3rd IEEE International Conference on Industrial Informatics (INDIN), 2005.

Kokar, M. M., Matheus, C. J., and Baclawski, K. Ontology-based situation aware- ness. Inf. Fusion, 10(1):83–98, 2009. ISSN 1566-2535. doi: http://dx.doi.org/10. 1016/j.inffus.2007.01.004.

Lin, F. *Handbook of Knowledge Representation*, chapter Situation Calculus. El- sevier, 2008

MAEC – Malware Attribute Enumeration and Characterization. http://maec.mitre.org/.

Matheus, C. J., Kokar, M. M., and Baclawski, K. A core ontology for situation awareness; Cairns, Australia. In Information Fusion, pages 545–552, July 2003.

Matheus, C. J., Kokar, M. M., Baclawski, K., and Letkowski, J. An application of semantic web technologies to situation awareness. In International Semantic Web Conference, volume 3729 of LNCS, pages 944–958. Springer, 2005.

Matheus, C., Baclawski, K., and Kokar, M. (2006). BaseVISor: A Triples-Based Inference Engine Outfitted to Process RuleML and R-Entailment Rules. In Proceedings of the 2nd International Conference on Rules and Rule Languages for the Semantic Web, Athens, GA.

McMorrow, D. Science of Cyber-Security. Technical Report, JSR-10-102, The MITRE Corporation, 2010.

More, S., Matthews, M., Joshi, A., Finin, T. "A Knowledge-Based Approach To Intrusion Detection Modeling", IEEE Symposium on Security and Privacy Workshops, 2012.

Mueller, E. T. *Handbook of Knowledge Representation*, chapter Event Calculus. Elsevier, 2008

Mundie, D. A., and McIntire, D. M. "The MAL: A Malware Analysis Lexicon", Technical Note, CMU/SEI-2013-TN-010, Software Engineering Institute, 2013.

NIST. National Vulnerability Database Version 2.2. http:// http://nvd.nist.gov/

Obrst, L., Ceusters, W., Mani, I., Ray, S., and Smith, B. The evaluation of ontologies. In ChristopherJ.O. Baker and Kei-Hoi Cheung, editors, Semantic Web, pages 139–158. Springer US, 2007.

Obrst, L., Chase, P., & Markeloff, R. (2012). Developing an ontology of the cyber security domain. Proceedings of Semantic Technologies for Intelligence, Defense, and Security (STIDS), 49-56.

Okolica, J. S., McDonald, T., Peterson, G. L., Mills, R. F., and Haas, M. W. Developing Systems for Cyber Situational Awareness. Proceedings of the 2nd Cyberspace Research Workshop, Shreveport, Louisiana, USA, 2009.

Oltramari, A., Lebiere, C., Vizenor, L., Zhu, W., and Dipert, R. "Towards a Cognitive System for Decision Support in Cyber Operations", STIDS, 2013.

OVAL – Open Vulnerability and Assessment Language. [Online] http://oval.mitre.org/.

OWL/Implementations. W3C. http://www.w3.org/2001/sw/wiki/OWL/Implementations.

Parmelee, M. *Toward an Ontology Architecture for Cyber- Security Standards.* George Mason University, Fairfax, VA : Semantic Technologies for Intelligence, Defense, and Security (STIDS) 2010

Raimond, Y., and Abdallah, S. The event ontology, October 2007. http://motools.sf.net/event

RDF: Resource Description Framework. W3C. http://www.w3.org/RDF/

Rodrigues, T., Rosa, P., and Cardoso, J. "Mapping XML to Existing OWL ontologies". In: International Conference WWW/Internet. Citeseer. 2006, pp. 72–77.

SCAP – Security Content Automation Protocol. NIST. [Online] http://scap.nist.gov/.

Scherp, A., Franz, T., Saathoff, C., and Staab, S. F–a model of events based on the foundational ontology DOLCE+DnS Ultralight. In Conference on Knowledge Capture, pages 137–144, New York, NY, USA, 2009. ACM. ISBN 978-1-60558-658-8. doi: http://doi.acm. org/10.1145/1597735.1597760.

Security Intelligence. Defining APT Campaigns. SANS Digital Forensics and Incident Response, http://digital-forensics.sans.org/blog/2010/06/21/security-intelligence-knowing-enemy/

Shen, Z., Ma, K.-L., and Eliassi-Rad, T. Visual analysis of large heterogeneous social networks by semantic and structural abstraction. Visualization and Computer Graphics, IEEE Transactions on, 12(6):1427–1439, 2006.

Sheth, A. Can Semantic Web techniques empower comprehension and projection in Cyber Situational Awareness? ARO Workshop, Fairfax, VA, 2007.

Singhal, A., and Wijesekera, D. 2010. Ontologies for modeling enterprise level security metrics. In *Proceedings of the Sixth Annual Workshop on Cyber Security and Information Intelligence Research* (CSIIRW '10), Frederick T. Sheldon, Stacy Prowell, Robert K. Abercrombie, and Axel Krings (Eds.). ACM, New York, NY, USA, Article 58, 3 pages. DOI=10.1145/1852666.1852731 http://doi.acm.org/10.1145/1852666.1852731

Stewart, J. (2013). Chasing APT. Dell SecureWorks Counter Threat Unit™ Threat Intelligence. 23 July 2012. http://www.secureworks.com/research/threats/chasing_apt/

STIX – Structured Threat Information eXpression. "A Structured Language for Cyber Threat Intelligence Information". http://stix.mitre.org

Strasburg, C., Basu, S., and Wong, J. S. "S-MAIDS: A Semantic Model for Automated Tuning, Correlation, and Response Selection in Intrusion Detection Systems", IEEE 37th Annual Computer Software and Applications Conference, 2013.

Strassner, J., Betser, J., Ewart, R., and Belz, F. "A Semantic Architecture for Enhanced Cyber Situational Awareness", Secure& Resilient Cyber Architectures Conference, MITRE, McLean, VA, 2010.

Swimmer, M. Towards An Ontology of Malware Classes. January 27, 2008. http://www.scribd.com/doc/24058261/Towards-an-Ontology-of-Malware-Classes.

The Friend of a Friend (FOAF) project. http://www.foaf-project.org/.

Undercoffer, J., Joshi, A., and Pinkston, J. "Modeling Computer Attacks: An Ontology for Intrusion Detection," in Proc. 6th Int. Symposium on Recent Advances in Intrusion Detection. Springer, September 2003.

US-CERT. (2013) Alert (TA13-309A) CryptoLocker Ransomware Infections. Original release date: November 05, 2013 | Last revised: November 18, 2013 http://www.us-cert.gov/ncas/alerts/TA13-309A

Vrandečić, D. Ontology evaluation. In Stephen Staab and Rudi Studer, editors, Handbook on Ontologies, International Handbooks on Information Systems, pages 293–313. Springer Berlin Heidelberg, 2009.

W3C. OWL 2 Web Ontology Language Document Overview, 2009. http://www.w3.org/TR/owl2-overview/.

Wali, A., Chun, S. A., and Geller, J. "A Bootstrapping Approach for Developing a Cyber-Security Ontology Using Textbook Index Terms", International Conference on Availability, Reliability and Security, 2013.

Wang, X. H., Zhang, D. Q., Gu, T., and Pung, H. K. Ontology based context modeling and reasoning using OWL. In *Pervasive Computing and Communications Workshops*, page 18, Washington, DC, USA, 2004. IEEE. ISBN 0-7695-2106-1

Wang, X., Mamadgi, S., Thekdi, A., Kelliher, A., and Sundaram, H. Eventory – an event based media repository. In Semantic Computing, pages 95–104, Washington, DC, USA, 2007. IEEE. ISBN 0-7695-2997-6.

Westermann, U., and Jain, R. Toward a common event model for multimedia ap- plications. IEEE MultiMedia, 14(1):19–29, 2007.

WhoIs. http://www.whois.com/

Yau, S. S., and Liu, J. Hierarchical situation modeling and reasoning for pervasive computing. In Software Technologies for Future Embedded and Ubiquitous Systems, pages 5–10, Washington, DC, USA, 2006. IEEE. ISBN 0-7695-2560-1.

Ye, J., Coyle, L., Dobson, S., and Nixon, P. Ontology-based models in pervasive computing systems. The Knowledge Engineering Review, 22(4):315–347, 2007.

Learning and Semantics

Richard Harang

1 Introduction

This chapter further elaborates on a topic of the previous chapter—inference—by focusing on a particular class of algorithms important for processing of cyber information—machine learning. The chapter also continues the thread of ontology and semantics as it explores the tradeoffs between the effectiveness of an algorithm and the semantic clarity of its products. It is often difficult to extract meaningful contextual information from a machine learning algorithm, because those algorithms that provide high accuracy also tend to use representations less comprehensible to humans. On the other hand, those algorithms that use more human-accessible vocabulary can be less accurate—they produce more false alerts (false positives), which confuse analysts. A related tradeoff is between the internal semantics of the algorithm versus the external semantics of its output. We illustrate this tradeoff with two case studies. Developers of CSA systems must be aware of such tradeoffs, and seek ways to mitigate them.

Most models of situational awareness (e.g. the widely-cited Endsley 1995) describe the first level of situational awareness (SA) as "perception", defined as the "[perception of] the status, attributes, and dynamics of *relevant* elements in then environment" (emphasis added). While the adaptation of conventional SA models to cyber situational awareness (CSA) is ongoing, it is apparent that this perceptive step, particularly as it pertains to relevance, is made significantly more complex by the overwhelming quantities of benign data flowing across network boundaries. For this reason, current approaches to CSA (see, e.g. D'Amico et al. 2005; Barford et al. 2010a) place greater emphasis on the "detection" or "recognition" of an ongoing incident or attack. The work of D'Amico et al. (2005) presents a cognitive task

R. Harang (✉)
United States Army Research Laboratory, Adelphi, MD, USA
e-mail: richard.e.harang.civ@mail.mil

© Springer International Publishing Switzerland 2014   201
A. Kott et al. (eds.), *Cyber Defense and Situational Awareness*,
Advances in Information Security 62, DOI 10.1007/978-3-319-11391-3_10

analysis of intrusion detection analyst workflows, and divides the process into six tasks, the first of which they term "triage" analysis, the act of weeding out false positives and escalating suspicious activity for further analysis; again emphasizing the role of identifying relevant information. Later stages of analysis rely on and fuse these escalated reports into more complex causal relationships, eventually developing a complete CSA assessment. In a similar vein, the work of Barford et al. (2010a) identifies several key aspect of cyber situational awareness (CSA), the first of which they term "situation recognition," or the realization that an attack is in fact occurring. As with the triage and escalation process in D'Amico et al. (2005), situation recognition is a prerequisite to any additional tactical CSA analysis, such as attribution, impact assessment, and forensic analysis, as well as forming a major component of more strategic CSA analysis such as adversarial activity and prediction.

In both cases, the key input to both situation recognition and triage is not the 'raw' network data—which is generally not amenable to direct human analysis due to both volume and the huge range of protocols, formats, etc.—but the output of network intrusion detection system (NIDS) tools such as Snort (Roesch 1999) or Bro (Paxson 1999), which are generally intended to detect malicious activity and direct the attention of analysts to that activity for further analysis. Such tools typically present analysts with tables of "alerts" which may indicate anything from the presence of exploit signatures in a particular packet of network traffic, to connection abnormalities that could suggest post-compromise activity, to simple statistical summaries of network traffic with outliers along some dimension highlighted. However, as the authors of Barford et al. (2010a) note, despite most NIDS tools ostensibly being designed to detect intrusions, they currently are more accurately understood as serving the role as pre-filters to the vast volume of traffic that flows through a network, attempting to highlight and bring to the attention of human analysts those data that are most likely to be related to an ongoing event, thus assisting in but not removing the need for the 'triage' operation of D'Amico et al. (2005). The actual work of CSA takes place at a human level, fusing the reports from various NIDS tools in a manual process and at human time scales in order to build a comprehensive picture of current situation. Properly facilitating this triage operation is therefore critical; tools that provide sufficient ancillary information to enable rapid triage will allow for more rapid escalation or elimination of alerts, while those that provide little or no ancillary information demand the expenditure of analyst resources to interpret the output of the tool before triage can occur.

The demands placed on such tools will only increase over time due to the exponential increase in total traffic volume year over year. An analysis by Cisco Corporation (2013) concludes that internet traffic is growing with at an annual compound rate of approximately 23 % (doubling roughly every 3.5 years). Increasing the number of NIDS analysts at a comparable rate to keep up with traffic is clearly not sustainable in the long term, leading to the conclusion that CSA synthesis and analysis must be both increasingly tool-facilitated and automated, leaving humans responsible for more and more abstract and high-level tasks centering on verification of the results of the NIDS analysis. Unfortunately, as discussed below, the current generation of NIDS tools are not well-suited to this; either they lack sufficient ability to generalize to novel attacks (or even novel variations on existing attacks), they do not produce information of sufficient reliability to be incorporated into automated analysis, or the transformations that they perform to attain both generalization and reliability are too complex for easy human comprehension and analysis (they suffer from a large semantic gap).

Other automated and semi-automated approaches to enhancing CSA have been proposed. Many efforts completely avoid the question of detection and contextualization of malicious activity, and instead focus facilitating the ability of human analysts to detect malicious behaviors through more natural representations of the available data, usually displaying selected aspects of the entirety of the data in some graphical format, while allowing human operators to manually filter it to components of interest (e.g., Lakkaraju et al. 2004; Yin et al. 2004). While these approaches are promising in the short term, the current rate of growth of internet traffic, as discussed above, suggests that their reliance on humans as the core functional component of the classification engine is not sustainable. Other proposals such as Yegneswaran et al. (2005) (see also closely related work in Barford et al. 2010b) have suggested the use of honeynets to collect data in support of CSA efforts, and reported that such data—particularly in the case of automated activity such as botnet infestations or worm outbreaks—provide useful higher level information of value to CSA analysis. The authors do note that significant analysis was required to render it useful, and focused primarily on and mass-exploitation approaches (scans for misconfigurations, botnet probes, and worms), rendering it more applicable to high level strategic CSA, rather than the more tactical level we consider here.

The remainder of this chapter is organized as follows. We first present a high-level discussion of NIDS tools and machine learning counterparts. Next we discuss the semantics of both the outputs of machine learning tools, as well as their 'internal' semantics: how data is used within machine learning tools to generate decisions or classifications. We provide two concrete examples of machine learning approaches and discuss their output and internal semantics in detail, with emphasis on how to render them useful to human analysts. The final section concludes with recommendations for integrating machine learning tools into the generation of useful cyber situational awareness information.

2 NIDS Machine Learning Tool Taxonomy

NIDS tools are often broadly divided into two broad groups; signature-based intrusion detection systems (often referred to as "misuse" detection) which identify malicious traffic based on matching known examples of malicious traffic, and anomaly-based intrusion detection systems that attempt to characterize normal behavior, and then flag for analysis all abnormal traffic (Sommer and Paxson 2010; Laskov et al. 2005). Signature-based intrusion detection typically focuses on known attacks or malicious behaviors with fairly clearly defined characteristics, either by matching traffic content (Roesch 1999) or behavioral markers (Paxson 1999), while anomaly based intrusion detection systems cast a much broader net, and attempt to characterize "normal" behavior in some fashion, and then flag for inspection any behavior that does not meet that characterization (see Ertoz et al. 2004; Lakhina et al. 2004, 2005; Abe et al. 2006; Zhang et al. 2008; Depren et al. 2005; or Xu et al. 2005), among many others, for examples of the wide range of approaches in this area). Both approaches have their advantages and disadvantages; while signature-based methods perform acceptably on well-known and well-characterized attacks (although rule sets that are not well adapted to the target deployment environment can result in significant errors, see e.g. Brugger and Chow 2007), they fail in the face of novel, uncharacterized, or polymorphic attacks (Song et al. 2009). Anomaly detection methods have the advantage of being able—at least in principle—to detect novel attacks (Wang and Stolfo 2004), however the characterization of 'normal' network traffic and detecting significant novelty has proved to be a significant challenge (Yegneswaran et al. 2005), resulting in extremely high false positive rates (see, e.g., discussion in Sommer and Paxson 2010; Rehak et al. 2008; or Molina et al. 2012).

While the number of cyber attacks continues to grow year over year, this growth is being rapidly outstripped by the total growth of network traffic. The Government Accountability Office analysis of attacks reported to the United States Computer Emergency Readiness Team from 2006 to 2012 shows a roughly linear growth in the number of cyberattacks of approximately 7,180 attacks year over year (Wilshusen 2013), with 48,562 reported in 2012; while as noted above, with the total volume of network traffic has a projected compound annual growth rate of 23 % (Cisco Corporation 2013). Taken in combination, this suggests that the proportion of malicious traffic as a fraction of total traffic received (the "ground truth" positive rate) is low, and will likely fall significantly over the coming years. This extremely low rate renders the usability of a NIDS tool almost entirely dependent on the false positive rate of the system, as discussed in detail by Axelsson (2000). While signature-based NIDS tools typically have a lower false positive rate, and thus may be anticipated perform better in realistic network environments, they do so at the cost of their ability to generalize. Anomaly-based NIDS tools are notoriously susceptible to false positives, which has severely constrained their use in practice. While various attempts to lower the false positive rate of such tools have been made, for example via agent-based fusion of such tools in the CAMNEP project (Rehak et al. 2008), there remain few examples of operationally deployed anomaly-based NIDS tools available in the literature (although see Molina et al. 2012 for a case study involving several anomaly detection tools in a backbone environment).

The primary challenge faced by NIDS tools is then how to achieve some balance between the ability to generalize so that a tool can at least detect variants of known attacks, if not novel attacks, and a usable error rate (dominated by the false positive rate). Various machine learning approaches have been proposed to fill in this gap, with varying degrees of success, however these introduce their own complications for CSA, as we discuss below.

3   Output Versus Internal Semantics in Machine Learning

The use of machine learning in NIDS tools brings with it its own challenges. As noted above, to produce useful CSA, it is necessary that a NIDS tool not only produce alerts when potentially hostile activity is detected, but also provide enough contextual information in some format to allow for the "recognition" or "triage" phase of the situational awareness process to occur. A highly accurate machine learning algorithm that provides little or no contextual information to the user therefore does not enable CSA, regardless of its accuracy, while a less accurate tool that provides a large amount of contextual information may in fact be of significant value in enabling CSA. To examine this concept in more detail, we first provide a brief nontechnical overview of machine learning, and then define and discuss the concepts of "internal" and "output" semantics of a machine learning algorithm.

Machine learning—loosely speaking—concerns the design and analysis of automatic systems that learn from data. While numerous variations exist (see any modern reference such as, e.g., Murphy 2012 for elaboration), the most common approach is to provide the system with a set of "training data," in the form of labeled examples, from which it must learn rules that associate input data to output labels. The aim is to produce a rule that is both accurate in the sense that the output produced by the algorithm reliably matches the desired output, and general in the sense that the algorithm remains accurate even on input data that it has not previously seen. For example, given some set of images of handwritten digits paired with the number they represent, a machine learning algorithm might be expected to determine general rules for labeling never-before-seen images of the same digits (the website at LeCun et al. 2014 maintains state-of-the-art results on this precise problem as of the time of this writing; also see Goodfellow et al. 2013 for a more modern version involving recognizing addresses from street view images).

A wide range of methods can be used to solve this general problem of learning associations based on data; for example, a method as simple as converting the inputs (such as pixel color values) into numbers and then fitting a straight line to those numbers (a 'linear classifier') may produce acceptable results (LeCun et al. 1999). More complex methods, such as building a decision tree from a series of yes-or-no questions, or constructing an artificial neural network consisting of many layers and specialized modules (Goodfellow et al. 2013) may also be used, each with their own time and accuracy tradeoffs. Regardless of the details of the algorithm, however, the data presented to the algorithm must always be converted into some standardized form that the algorithm can process (often referred to as a 'feature vector'), and some useful representation of the output must be selected.

This division between the internal representation and processing of the data and the output format of the data leads to a useful distinction in semantic groupings in machine learning tools. By "output semantics" we refer to the information that is obtainable directly and entirely from the combination of the output of a classifier or decision making tool as well as the question being asked. Even when the output of a classifier contains little information in an absolute sense, such as binary classifier which output a single bit of information at a time, the combination of the output with the problem space (e.g., "is this a picture of a white cat?") can provide significantly more detailed information. By "internal semantics" we refer to the mechanism (or, informally, 'reasoning') by which a classification or decision is arrived at. In the case of linear classifiers, this refers to a point in some topological space residing on one side or the other of a separating hyperplane; for rule-based systems, it indicates which rules were or were not satisfied. For unsupervised learning tools, this typically refers to some measure of quality across clusters, combined with a measure of similarity between the point in question and the remainder of the points.

While traditionally complex pattern recognition tasks have been dominated by humans, machine learning approaches for some tasks, particularly static image analysis tasks such as digit recognition or traffic sign classification, can often meet or exceed human standards of performance (Ciresan et al. 2012), suggesting that the problem of classifying the more complex and heterogeneous temporal data that is associated with network intrusion detection may soon be within reach of machine learning systems. However, to remain useful for CSA, these tools must produce a semantic representation, either internally in or their output, that is sufficiently clear that a human analyst can effectively triage an alert when it is produced by such a tool. The output semantics of such "deep learning" classifiers can be adjusted by using sufficiently detailed classification questions, these models are often expensive to train, and the existence of signature-based tools such as Snort that already provide—in effect—binary classifiers with very clear output semantics makes them less attractive for such purposes. With respect to internal semantics, in order to obtain their best-in-class performances, many machine learning approaches make use of 'black box' models such as deep/convolutional neural networks, that fit tens of thousands to tens of millions of parameters simultaneously, often in manners that defy conventional interpretation. Even significantly simpler machine learning approaches such as support vector machines (Cortes and Vapnik 1995) rely on projection of the observed data into a potentially infinite-dimensional space that can then be (approximately) separated by linear functions defined on that space. When textual or categorical data is involved—or when the dimensionality of the underlying data is extremely high—many approaches (Li and König 2010; Weinberger et al. 2011) rely heavily on various pseudo-random projections, often via hash functions—that are functionally impossible to revert to the original domain.

While the success of machine learning in classification is undeniable, when applying it to a situation in which we wish to obtain some degree of CSA, we must also contend with the need to triage, in order to separate false positives and true positives. In this case, it is not sufficient for a tool to simply report that, e.g., a given connection represents a potential threat; in order for an analyst to efficiently triage such a report, some notion of the reasoning behind that classification must be available. If focus is placed on output semantics, then the more detailed either the classification or the reasoning supporting it are, the more rapidly it can be verified by an analyst.

If the output semantics of a tool are not clear, then the use of internal semantics is required, which (as noted above) is often a much more difficult proposition. Leaving aside the problem of transforming cybersecurity-relevant data (often categorical or textual) into some metric space which can then be measured (see Harang

2014 for more discussion on this point), an analyst who wishes to triage a particular alert based on the internal semantics of a tool must then also contend with whatever transformation the machine learning algorithm required in order to produce its results. When these transformations cannot be easily related back to the original space, or the rationale behind the classification cannot be explained by the algorithm to the analyst in terms of standard attributes that analysts are familiar with, the triage process becomes significantly more difficult, requiring in effect a 'blind' investigation into the potential reasons for the classifier producing such an alert.

When the output semantics of the alert are not clear, triaging a false positive is a particular challenge as it essentially requires one to prove a negative. Without a narrow and readily falsifiable claim made by the machine learning tool (i.e., clear output semantics), or a method by which the machine learning algorithm can explain the reasoning process by which it arrived at the alert to the analyst (i.e., clear internal semantics), the analyst is faced with the unenviable task of asserting that there is no possible threat that could be represented by the datum in question. Note that, when the triage problem is then combined with the base rate fallacy—which demonstrates that the overwhelming majority of errors produced by a classifier in a highly class-imbalanced environment such as cyber security will in fact be false positives—the overall impact can be tremendous.

4 Case Studies: ELIDe and Hamming Aggregation

We present two examples of machine learning approaches to intrusion detection with significantly different internal and output semantics, and examine how their semantics may influence their role in CSA. We first present ELIDe (Extremely Lightweight Intrusion Detection), which acts as a payload-based intrusion detection engine which operates on a high-dimensional transformation of n-grams in packet data, and might be considered the signature-based counterpart to the PAY-L anomaly detection system (Wang and Stolfo 2004). As a binary classifier ELIDe produces an output with (potentially) very clear semantics that can be used for rapid triage, however the internal semantics are essentially intractable to human analysis. On the other extreme we discuss variable Hamming distance alert aggregation, which can be used as an anomaly detection method with extremely clear internal semantics, represented entirely in the terms of the original set of data. Hamming distance alert aggregation, however, when used in an anomaly detection mode, has (like all anomaly detection methods) extremely poor output semantics, and provides no inherent detection capabilities beyond indicating that a subset of the data presented to it appears to be outliers to the rest of the data. These two examples help illustrate some of the tradeoffs and considerations to be made when incorporating machine learning techniques into a CSA process, particularly when considering the effect of semantics on the triage step.

4.1 ELIDe

ELIDe is a linear classifier for intrusion detection that uses histograms of n-grams as features, in an attempt to approximate the capabilities of more complex classifiers with reduced resource requirements. In contrast to earlier n-gram based efforts (such as PAY-L (Wang and Stolfo 2004)), ELIDe can use n-grams with nearly arbitrary lengths due to the use of a "hash kernel" (Shi et al. 2009; Weinberger et al. 2011) (see also Alon et al. 1999) for an earlier appearance of the same idea, there labeled the "tug-of-war" sketch, in a different application domain) which maps the (often intractably large) feature space that large n-grams require into a much smaller one, while approximately preserving inner products. It operates in a supervised learning mode, by training against the output of a reference classifier, such as Snort (Roesch 1999), and updating the weights of the linear classifier through a standard stochastic gradient descent process (Bottou 2010). This combination of longer n-grams with a hash kernel allows for ELIDe to approximate the classification accuracy obtained by working in a high dimensional space, without the excessive cost in both time and memory (exponential in n) incurred by doing computations in that high-dimensional space.

The use of n-grams effectively projects the network packet into a space with highly elevated dimensionality (256^n possible n-grams) where performing linear classification to separate "good" packet data from "suspicious" packet data is reasonably straightforward, at least from a computational point of view. Note, however, that the internal semantics of even this straightforward projection are difficult to interpret, and the computational requirements are prohibitive even for computers, as operating directly on this high-dimensional space requires space (and hence time) exponential in n. N-gram methods that operate directly on byte representations of files (Li et al. 2005) and network packets (Wang and Stolfo 2004) typically use modest values of n, such as 1, where the number of possible distinct n-grams is modest, and perhaps tractable with respect to internal semantics. Even small values of n, however, rapidly render the problem intractable; $n = 3$, for instance, would require approximately 17 million memory locations to store a complete histogram, while large values such as 10 would require roughly 10^{28} memory locations.

However, given the typical maximum transmissible unit limitation of approximately 1500 bytes, in practice the n-gram features in this high-dimensional space will be extremely sparse. While this sparsity does not improve the internal semantics significantly, it does allow for a computational shortcut. The application of a hash kernel allows us to avoid storing the native n-grams in their 256^n space, and instead indexes them by the lower-order bits of their respective hash digests. This effectively re-lowers the dimensionality of the problem space down to the only the size required to represent the truncated hash digests (for example, 2^{10} dimensions for 10-bit hash outputs). The length of the n-gram hash digest output becomes a tuning factor that allows for adjustment of the tradeoff between resource consumption and accuracy. Longer digest sizes allow for more accurate representation of the space and a more complex classifier that will generally have better performance characteristics, while shorter digests allow for lower memory requirements and faster computations. There is also suggestive evidence for the proposition that a reduced hash length, with corresponding loss of total fidelity to the original classifier, will in fact improve the generalization performance of the classifier, allowing it a better chance of classifying variants on existing signatures that a pure signature-matching classifier would miss. Note however that to allow for computational tractability, we have further obscured the (already complex) internal semantics; we have progressed from a high-dimensional representation of the data that is itself difficult to conceptualize in human terms to a pseudo-random projection of the data that—while preserving some mathematical structure—has obliterated any internal semantic content by its randomness.

The effect of the hash size on the speed and accuracy of ELIDe can be visualized in Figs. 1 and 2; an insufficiently high setting for the number of bits results in a testing accuracy that is unacceptably low, while at the same time, raising the length of the hash past roughly 11 bits results in a rapid increase of computation time. However, in the region of 8 to 10 bits, the accuracy approaches 100 % on the training data, while the computation time remains low. We selected 10 bit hash lengths for our final implementation due to the monotonically nondecreasing accuracy with respect to hash length, and the acceptably fast performance at 10 bits. This effectively produces a random projection of our 2^{80} dimensional space onto a 2^{10} dimensional space. While the reduction in dimensionality is significant, visualization and conceptualization of 2^{10} dimensions remains beyond the grasp of most humans, thus rendering the internal semantics of ELIDe of little use in CSA.

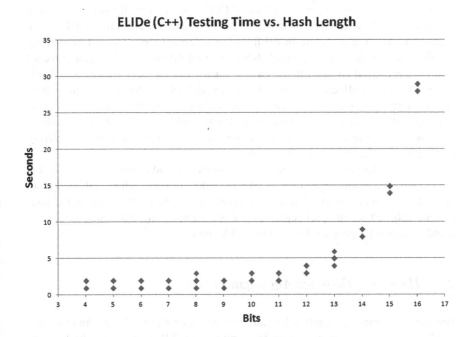

Fig. 1 The effect of low-order bits retained on testing time

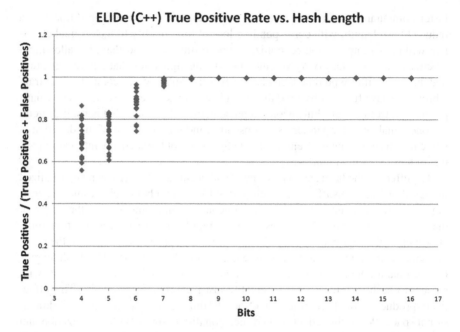

Fig. 2 ELIDe classification results as a function of retained low-order bits

Despite the complexity of the internal semantics of ELIDe, notice that—as a binary classifier—the output semantics of ELIDe are potentially straightforward, and (for correctly selected parameters) the false positive rate is not noticeably worse than the underlying signature-based intrusion detection tool. An alert emitted by ELIDe indicates that with high probability, the tool that was used to train it would also have produced an alert. In the case of a narrowly targeted training set, this is often sufficient to effectively triage the alert with limited additional examination. If, for example, the training set consisted only of rules that related to attacks targeting a specific service, it is straightforward for an analyst to use that information to examine the system identified as the victim, and determine if it is in fact offering that service and hence potentially at risk.

If, on the other hand, the training set is extremely broad or not well-defined, this transfers to the output semantics of ELIDe, reducing their value, and forcing an analyst to rely on the internal semantics. As described above, these internal semantics are difficult to interpret regardless of the training set, and hence would not enable efficient progression through the CSA process.

4.2 Hamming Distance Aggregation

Hamming distance aggregation for intrusion detection alerts (Harang and Guarino 2012) (expanded on significantly in Mell and Harang 2014) attempts to find a high-quality clustering of alerts at some user-defined Hamming distance d, where the

Hamming distance between two alerts is given by the number of fields that do not match. Each cluster constitutes a single meta-alert representing a cluster of alerts all of which are identical on all but d fields; in the event that an alert varies on more than d fields from every other alert in the set, it may be merged with itself to create a meta-alert that covers only that single alert, which we term a "singleton". As the Hamming distance of aggregation increases, these outliers become increasingly significant, and suggest potential targets for further investigation. The output semantics associated with a singleton are somewhat difficult to parse; the fact that an alert does not match any other alert on more than d fields does not immediately suggest a reason why it might not have matched (compare to e.g. ELIDe, where an alert is immediately associated with a policy violation or threat in the training set), however the internal semantics as described below are straightforward.

Table 1 provides a simple example. Notice that alert 5 could either be aggregated to alert 2 (with which it disagrees on column 2) or to alerts 3 and 4 (with which it disagrees on column 3). If we attempt to find a minimum set of meta-alerts covering the largest number of alerts (the clear similarity to the set cover problem is discussed in greater detail in Mell and Harang 2014) then we group alerts 3, 4, and 5 together, and alerts 1 and 2 each form their own meta-alerts. Despite the fact that alert 2 would appear to be an outlier in this case, it was rendered into a single-element meta-alert due to an optimization choice, and so would not be considered a singleton or outlier. By contrast, alert 1 differs on at least 2 columns from all other alerts, and so could not be aggregated with any of them at a Hamming distance of 1; this renders it an outlier of interest, which we may examine in more detail.

While we omit details for space, the work of Mell and Harang (2014) and Mell (2013) presents an efficient hypergraph based algorithm for extracting meta-alerts in $O(n \log n)$ time. If attention is restricted entirely to the construction of the hypergraph and singleton identification, the entire operation can be executed in strictly $O(n)$ time, where n is the number of alerts.

Although Hamming distance aggregation applies well to any NIDS tool that produces a reasonably standardized output (further explored in Mell and Harang 2014), we focused evaluation on a list of Snort alerts containing the following fields: sensor identifier, alert identifier, source/destination Internet Protocol (IP) addresses, receiving/sending ports, associated autonomous system numbers (ASN), and alert date/time stamp. We examine data collected from a mid-size production network using Snort configured with a combination of the Snort ET and VRT rule for several days in February of 2012, aggregated over hours in Table 2, and a single 24 hour period in Table 3. Note that using the algorithm provided in Harang and Guarino (2012),

Table 1 Example alert data

Alert Number	Column 1	Column 2	Column 3
1	A	C	G
2	B	D	K
3	B	F	I
4	B	F	J
5	B	F	K

Table 2 Example meta-alerts at hamming distance 1

	64502 alerts	2 alerts	4 alerts
RuleID	408	402	# 4 distinct values
Ruleset	snort_rules_vrt	snort_rules_vrt	snort_rules_vrt
Rule message	ICMP Echo Reply	ICMP Destination Unreachable Port Unreachable	# 4 distinct values
Sensor	sensor-001	sensor-002	sensor-003
Timestamp	# 366 distinct values	# 2 distinct values	# 24 distinct values
Source IP	10.0.0.1	10.0.0.2	10.0.0.4
Destination IP	# 64502 distinct values	# 2 distinct values	10.0.0.5
Source ASN	0001	0003	0004
Destination ASN	0002	0003	0005
Source country code	A	C	E
Destination country code	B	C	D

Table 3 Example outliers at a hamming distance of 6

	Singleton 1	Singleton 2
RuleID	2406705	2500547
Ruleset	snort_rules_et	snort_rules_et
Rule message	ET RBN Known Russian Business Network IP UDP (353)	ET COMPROMISED Known Compromised or Hostile Host Traffic UDP (274)
Sensor	sensor-003	sensor-002
Timestamp	2012-02-19	2012-02-19
Source IP	10.0.0.7	10.0.0.9
Destination IP	10.0.0.6	10.0.0.11
Source ASN	0004	0003
Destination ASN	0005	0003
Source country code	E	C
Destination country code	D	C

analyzing a complete 24 hours was found to be impractical; later work (Mell and Harang 2014) shows that the algorithm in Harang and Guarino (2012) in addition to having high time complexity, is also in a certain sense suboptimal. We therefore use the later hypergraph-based algorithm to produce the results in Table 3. All alerts have been anonymized with respect to sensitive data.

Some example meta-alerts (first presented in Harang and Guarino 2012) are given in Table 2. Columns 1 and 2 give two examples for aggregation against a single Snort rule; the example in column 1 is from one hour which displayed over 60,000 individual alerts. The aggregation immediately suggests a common root cause (a network scan), and brief inspection into the values for Destination IP are sufficient to clarify that an entire class B subnet generated this alert with a few missed IP addresses. The second column of Table 2 shows a less common alert from the same time period; note here that, despite the fact that the meta-alert covers only 2 alerts, it is not possible (without additional work) to determine whether it is in a grouping of 2 because of its intrinsic rarity, or because other potential candidates for that meta-alert were instead grouped with other meta-alerts. The final meta-alert in Table 2 shows a case where a single IP address was subjected to several repetitions of a set of three alerts. While we do not discuss this possibility in detail, it is clear that this could be used as a building block to determine common attack patterns, and—if the underlying alerts are clear—offers itself to an immediate and straight-forward semantic interpretation.

Singletons, by contrast, have clearer semantics for their classification as single-tons, even as their output semantics are often less clear due to not being correlated to other alerts. If an alert at Hamming distance d is classified as a singleton, then by construction it must differ from every other alert in the entire data set by at least $d+1$ fields. Moreover, as d increases, the likelihood that such a result could be ran-domly obtained reduces sharply. In Table 3 we display the 2 singletons obtained from a complete 24-hour period at a Hamming distance of 6. Note that both rules in this case relate to an observed contact from external IP addresses that were black-listed by the maintainers of the ET ruleset, and in contrast to the bulk scanning or sequential attack activities noted in Table 2, represents potentially more subtle activity that may have been lost in the comparatively large volume of alerts. In addi-tion, as (in this case) the rules are clearly written, further triage of these alerts is straightforward, however they are heavily reliant on the semantics of the underlying alerts to be aggregated.

The relationship for the day under consideration between the number of singletons that could be investigated as anomalous and the Hamming distance is given in Fig. 3.

If singletons are treated as alerts within a CSA context, then while the output seman-tics are not clear—in that there is no direct indication that a singleton is inherently

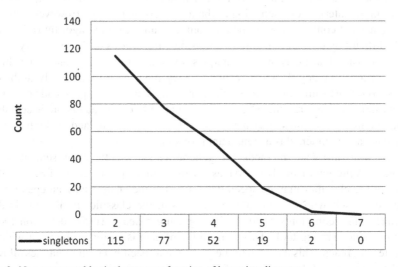

Fig. 3 Non-aggregatable singletons as a function of hamming distance

more alarming or related to a specific attack than a non-singleton—the internal semantics are straightforward: the alert was produced precisely because it differed on at least some clearly defined number of features from any other record produced in the given period of time. This mechanism of raising 'anomalous' records to analyst visibility while at the same time making it clear and immediately understandable why that record was highlighted enables the analyst to make a rapid decision about the significance of the singleton, and thus triage it efficiently, supporting the CSA process.

5 Summary

The first step of building cyber situational awareness has been defined as 'triage' or 'perception': taking network security data and determining which items indicate attacks and which items are safe and can be ignored. The high volume of network traffic means that automated machine learning methods for handling the output of current front-line NIDS tools are of increasing importance to facilitating the job of network security analysts, allowing them to find proverbial needles in an exponentially growing haystack. However this high class asymmetry (very few attacks in a very large amount of benign traffic) results in false positive results being the predominant error that analysts must cope with, which—in the absence of additional information—places an unrealistic burden on them when performing the triage and perception operation that is the foundation of the CSA process.

In order to adequately support the development of full cyber situational awareness, machine learning based NIDS tools must therefore be designed and implemented to provide the required additional information for triage, taking into account the difficult problem posed by high number of false positives. This additional information may be understood in the form of clear semantics, either in the output of the tool or in the internal representation of the tool decision process. However, extracting the needed contextual information from machine learning algorithms is often made difficult by the elaborate high-dimensional transforms or the extremely complex processing that many such techniques rely upon in order to obtain their high classification accuracy. In most scenarios, they must be treated simply as black boxes, producing some form of classification or label based on inputs, and very little further introspection into the process is possible. While this may be an acceptable limitation in other settings, the triage process for cyber security and the high cost of a false negative renders this a significant problem.

Two straightforward methods for generating sufficiently clear semantics to enable CSA present themselves: first, as discussed in the presentation of ELIDe, the target of the classifier may be specific enough that the analyst may independently verify the result with no further need to consult the classifier itself. This is the approach most commonly followed by signature-based intrusion detection tools (and machine learning tools derived from them), and is currently the most widely accepted approach. This use of extremely clear and specific output semantics allows for the analyst to safely reject many false alarms at minimal cost.

The other method, as discussed in our presentation of Hamming distance aggregation, is to explore classifiers that are capable of producing some form of reasoning or explanation for their decision in terms accessible to human analysts, i.e. ones that have extremely clear internal semantics, typically performing simple operations on untransformed versions of the data. Rule-based systems (see discussion and references in Harang 2014) are one example of this approach; however they have not yet achieved the same level of success as signature-based systems. Various visualization techniques and data exploration systems may be viewed as an extreme case of this latter approach, forgoing the generation of alerts altogether, in favor of supporting broad introspection into the entire body of data collected by the network sensors.

Notably, outside of niche applications such as scan detection tools, in which the focused nature of the tool both completely determines and narrows the semantics of the output, the vast majority of anomaly detection methods do not possess clear semantics of either form. They take full advantage of the high dimensional transformations and projections that have been developed to support modern machine learning, obscuring internal semantics, and then attempt to broadly divide traffic into the extremely broad binary categories of 'anomalous' and 'normal', with little clarity in the output semantics. Alerts from such tools cannot be efficiently triaged to determine if they are false positives, and thus the CSA process stalls.

An ideal machine learning approach to network intrusion detection in support of cyber situational awareness would provide both internal and output semantics that were clear and relatively unambiguous: identifying potentially hostile traffic as well as producing a compelling and human-comprehensible defense of its classification. Such a system would allow for immediate triage of alerts, rapidly moving to the next stage of cyber situational awareness as a result. However, such capabilities appear at present to be beyond the reach of machine learning approaches. In the absence of such a system, the careful analysis and construction of internal or output semantics must be considered when designing machine learning NIDS tools to support cyber situational awareness.

References

Abe, N., Zadrozny, B., and Langford, J. "Outlier detection by active learning," in *Proceedings of the 12th ACM SIGKDD international conference on Knowledge discovery and data mining*, New York, NY, USA, 2006.

Alon, N., Gibbons, P. B., Matias, Y., & Szegedy, M. (1999). Tracking join and self-join sizes in limited storage. *Proceedings of the eighteenth ACM SIGMOD-SIGACT-SIGART symposium on Principles of database systems*.

Axelsson, S. "The base-rate fallacy and the difficulty of intrusion detection," *ACM Transactions on Information and System Security (TISSEC)*, vol. 3, no. 3, pp. 186–205, 2000.

Barford, P., Dacier, M., Dietterich, T. G., Fredrikson, M., Giffin, J., Jajodia, S., and Jha, S. "Cyber SA: Situational awareness for cyber defense," in *Cyber Situational Awareness*, Springer, 2010a, pp. 3–13.

Barford, P., Chen, Y., Goyal, A., Li, Z., Paxson, V., and Yegneswaran, V. "Employing Honeynets for network situational awareness," in *Cyber Situational Awareness*, Springer, 2010b, pp. 71–102.

Bottou, L. (2010). Large-scale machine learning with stochastic gradient descent. *Proceedings of COMPSTAT, 2010.*

Brugger, S. T., and Chow, J. "An assessment of the DARPA IDS Evaluation Dataset using Snort," UC Davis department of Computer Science, 2007.

Ciresan, D., Meier, U., and Schmidhuber, J. "Multi-column deep neural networks for image classification," in *IEEE Conference on Computer Vision and Pattern Recognition*, 2012.

Cisco Corporation. "Cisco Visual Networking Index: Forecast and Methodology, 2012–2017," Cisco Corporation, 2013.

Cortes, C., and Vapnik, V. "Support-vector networks," *Machine Learning*, vol. 20, no. 3, pp. 273–297, 1995.

D'Amico, A., Whitley, K., Tesone, D., O'Brien, B., and Roth, E. "Achieving cyber defense situational awareness: A cognitive task analysis of information assurance analysts," in *Proceedings of the Human Factors and Ergonomics Society Annual Meeting*, 2005.

Depren, O., Topallar, M., Anarim, E., and Ciliz, M. K. "An intelligent intrusion detection system (IDS) for anomaly and misuse detection in computer networks," *Expert Systems with Applications*, vol. 29, no. 4, pp. 713–722, nov 2005.

Endsley, M. R. "Toward a theory of situation awareness in dynamic systems," *Human Factors: The Journal of the Human Factors and Ergonomics Society*, vol. 37, no. 1, pp. 32–64, 1995.

Ertoz, L., Eilertson, E., Lazarevic, A., Tan, P.-N., Kumar, V., Srivastava, J., and Dokas, A. P. "MINDS-minnesota intrusion detection system," *Next Generation Data Mining*, pp. 199–218, 2004.

Goodfellow, I. J., Bulatov, Y., Ibarz, J., Arnoud, S., & Shet, V. (2013). Multi-digit Number Recognition from Street View Imagery using Deep Convolutional Neural Networks. *ArXiv/CS, abs/1312.6082.*

Harang, R. "Bridging the Semantic Gap: Human Factors in Anomaly-Based Intrusion Detection Systems," in *Network Science and Cybersecurity*, New York, Springer, 2014, pp. 15–37.

Harang, R., and Guarino, P. "Clustering of Snort alerts to identify patterns and reduce analyst workload," in *MILITARY COMMUNICATIONS CONFERENCE*, 2012.

Lakhina, A., Crovella, M., and Diot, C. "Diagnosing network-wide traffic anomalies," *ACM SIGCOMM Computer Communication Review*, vol. 34, no. 4, pp. 219–230, 2004.

Lakhina, A., Crovella, M., and Diot, C. "Mining anomalies using traffic feature distributions," *ACM SIGCOMM Computer Communication Review*, vol. 35, no. 4, pp. 217–228, 2005.

Lakkaraju, K., Yurcik, W., and Lee, A. J. "NVisionIP: netflow visualizations of system state for security situational awareness," in *2004 ACM workshop on Visualization and data mining for computer security*, 2004.

Laskov, P., Dussel, P., Schafer, C., and Rieck, K. "Learning Intrusion Detection: Supervised or Unsupervised," in *Image analysis and processing*, 2005.

LeCun, Y., Bottou, L., Bengio, Y., & Haffner, P. (1999). Gradient-based learning applied to document recognition. *Proceedings of the IEEE*, 86(11), 2278-2324.

LeCun, Y., Cortes, C., & Burges, C. J. (2014). *MNIST handwritten digit database*. Retrieved April 14, 2014, from http://yann.lecun.com/exdb/mnist/

Li, P., and König, C. "b-Bit minwise hashing," in *ACM Proceedings of the 19th international conference on World wide web*, 2010.

Li, W.-J., Wang, K., Stolfo, S. J., and Herzog, B. "Fileprints: Identifying file types by n-gram analysis," in *Proceedings from the Sixth Annual IEEE SMC Information Assurance Workshop*, 2005.

Mell, P. "Hyperagg: A Python Program for Efficient Alert Aggregation Using Set Cover Approximation and Hamming Distance," National Institute of Standards and Technology, 2013. [Online]. Available: http://csrc.nist.gov/researchcode/hyperagg-mell-20130109.zip.

Mell, P., and Harang, R. "Enabling Efficient Analysts: Reducing Alerts to Review through Hamming Distance Based Aggregation (SUBMITTED)," in *Twelfth Annual Conference on Privacy, Security, and Trust*, Toronto, 2014.

Molina, M., Paredes-Oliva, I., Routly, W., and Barlet-Ros, P. "Operational experiences with anomaly detection in backbone networks," *Computers & Security,* vol. 31, no. 3, pp. 273–285, may 2012.

Murphy, K. P. (2012). *Machine learning: a probabilistic perspective.* MIT Press.

Paxson, V. "Bro: A system for detecting network intruders in real time," *Computer Networks,* vol. 31, no. 23–24, pp. 2435–2463, 1999.

Rehak, M., Pechoucek, M., Celeda, P., Novotny, J., and Minarik, P. "CAMNEP: agent-based network intrusion detection system," in *Proceedings of the 7th international joint conference on Autonomous agents and multiagent systems,* 2008.

Roesch, M. "Snort – lightweight intrusion detection for networks," *Proceedings of the 13th USENIX conference on System administration,* pp. 229–238, 1999.

Shi, Q., Petterson, J., Dror, G., Langford, J., Strehl, A. L., Smola, A. J., and Vishwanathan, S. V. N. "Hash kernels," in *International Conference on Artificial Intelligence and Statistics,* 2009.

Sommer, R., and Paxson, V. "Outside the Closed World: On Using Machine Learning for Network Intrusion Detection," in *2010 IEEE Symposium on Security and Privacy (SP),* 2010.

Song, Y., Locasto, M. E., Stavrou, A., Keromytis, A. D., and Stolfo, S. J. "On the infeasibility of modeling polymorphic shellcode – Re-thinking . . .," *MACH LEARN,* 2009.

Wang, K., and Stolfo, S. "Anomalous payload-based network intrusion detection," in *Recent Advances in Intrusion Detection,* 2004.

Weinberger, K., Dasgupta, A., Langford, J., Smola, A., and Attenberg, J. "Feature hashing for large scale multitask learning," in *Proceedings of the 26th Annual International Conference on Machine Learning,* 2011.

Wilshusen, G. C. "CYBERSECURITY: A Better Defined and Implemented National Strategy Is Needed to Address Persistent Challenges," 2013.

Xu, K., Zhang, Z.-L., and Bhattacharyya, S. "Reducing unwanted traffic in a backbone network," in *USENIX Workshop on Steps to Reduce Unwanted Traffic in the Internet,* Boston, 2005.

Yegneswaran, V., Barford, P., and Paxson, V. "Using honeynets for internet situational awareness," in *ACM Hotnets IV,* 2005.

Yin, X., Yurcik, W., Treaster, M., Li, Y., and Lakkaraju, K. "VisFlowConnect: netflow visualizations of link relationships for security situational awareness," in *2004 ACM workshop on Visualization and data mining for computer security,* 2004.

Zhang, J., Zulkernine, M., and Haque, A. "Random-Forests-Based Network Intrusion Detection Systems," *IEEE Transactions on Systems, Man, and Cybernetics, Part C: Applications and Reviews,* vol. 38, no. 5, pp. 649–659, sep 2008.

Impact Assessment

Jared Holsopple, Moises Sudit, and Shanchieh Jay Yang

1 Introduction

As the Foundations and Challenges chapter explained, the second level of SA is called comprehension and deals with determining the significance and relations of various elements of the situation to other elements and to the overall goals of the network. It is also often called situation understanding and involves the "so what" of the information that has been perceived. Previous chapters of this book have not focused on this level of SA. Therefore, this chapter elaborates specifically on the comprehension level of CSA. The chapter explains that an effective way to comprehend significant relations between the disparate elements of the situation is to concentrate on how these elements impact the mission of the network. This involves asking and answering questions of how various suspected attacks relate to each other, how they relate to remaining capabilities of the network's components, and how the resulting disruptions or degradation of services impact elements of the mission and the mission's overall goals.

J. Holsopple (✉)
Avarint, LLC., New York, USA
e-mail: jared.holsopple@avarint.com

M. Sudit
CUBRC, Inc., New York, USA
e-mail: sudit@cubrc.org

S.J. Yang
Rochester Institute of Technology, New York, USA
e-mail: Jay.Yang@rit.edu

© Springer International Publishing Switzerland 2014
A. Kott et al. (eds.), *Cyber Defense and Situational Awareness*,
Advances in Information Security 62, DOI 10.1007/978-3-319-11391-3_11

1.1   Motivation for Advanced Threat and Impact Assessment

As the need for cyber defense tools has increased, so have the proposed solutions to fill these technology gaps. Today's cyber defense technology typically analyzes network traffic to identify certain possible malicious or anomalous events. Such tools, which we will generally refer to as "sensors" are intrusion detection sensors, intrusion prevention sensors, firewall logs, or software logs. The outputs of these sensors are typically presented in a tabular format (for signature-based approaches) (Snort 2013; Enterasys – Products – Advanced Security Applications 2013) or a graphical format (for statistical-based approaches) (Valdes and Skinner 2001; HP Network Management Center 2013). Enterprise-level cyber defense tools, such as Arcsight (HP Network Management Center 2013), are able to aggregate the outputs of these tools together so that they can be presented in a cohesive manner. At this point, the analysts can then look at the events and determine whether or not they need to be acted upon.

However, this approach can still yield a very large number of events, many of which are false positives. So even with these potential attack indicators, the amount of data analysts need to deal with can still be unwieldy and error prone. As such, research eventually shifted to the problem of alert correlation (Ning et al. 2002; Valdes and Skinner 2001; Bass 2000; Noel et al. 2004; Sudit et al. 2007), where these singleton events were correlated together into "tracks" indicating causal and/ or temporal relationships between events. The goal of these alert correlation techniques is to define one or more tracks representing a single attacker or a group of attackers while ignoring the false positives.

Although cyber sensors and alert correlators are still actively evolving today, research has started to shift some of the focus onto threat and impact assessment approaches attempting to identify the impact to mission and tasks resulting from cyber attacks. The design objective of these tools is to allow the analysts making timely decisions on which impacts, and, thus, attack tracks to address first.

While this has been a logical progression of technology, impact assessment was generally not considered when designing alert correlators. Alert correlators were generally not considered when designing sensors. Alert correlators were designed based on information available from sensors. Impact assessment tools were designed based on information available from alert correlation and knowledge of the mission at hand. As such, there are no common or standard protocols in place for the tools to talk to each other, nor is there a formal set of required, or at least expect, inputs or outputs for each tool. In addition, there are no standard ways to represent a computer network in a data structure useful for alert correlation or impact assessment, so vendor-specific models are being created to model the computer network. In addition, those network models need to be populated by some means, also requiring vendor-specific ways of populating the necessary data structures. Finally, impact assessment techniques can be severely hampered by the current lack of mission modeling capability, which again leads to vendor-specific models being implemented.

Though no formal design approach was taken in this progression of technology, one can argue that the tools were designed using a "bottom-up" approach such that technologies are built to expand or improve upon existing technologies with the ultimate goal of minimizing the response time of analysts to cyber attacks. However, a limiting factor to this approach is that many of the new technologies require more data or information that is not readily available from cyber defense tools. We will therefore explore an alternative "top-down" approach that will allow us to identify existing technology gaps that need to be addressed to allow us to provide more comprehensive cyber defense tools enabling a faster response time.

In attempting to build upon existing detection and alert correlation technologies, some of the research has shifted towards mission impact assessment (Holsopple and Yang 2008; D'Amico et al. 2010; Jakobsen 2011; Argauer and Yang 2008; Grimalia et al. 2008). Grimaila et al. (2008) has motivated the need for mission impact assessment and has identified many of the hurdles such techniques need to address for effective deployment of such tools. As we will see, many of these hurdles are a result of the lack of standardization of data outputs and lack of understanding the information needed by mission impact assessment. As a result, some technology gaps exist preventing the deployment and evaluation of such techniques.

This chapter will consider Holsopple and Yang's top-down information fusion design (Holsopple and Yang 2009) and apply it to the problem of cyber security. As the design process progresses, existing capabilities to fulfill the design requirements as well as technology gaps will be discussed.

1.2 Existing Alert Correlation Research

Bass (2000) is among the first who motivates the research on alert correlation. Up to that point, the focus on cyber defense had been on the development of Intrusion Detection Sensors (IDSs) that try to identify individual exploits or attack events on a computer network. Since cyber attacks rarely are comprised of a single event, Bass motivated the use of information fusion to correlate alerts together to represent unique attacks (i.e. a collection of events) instead of unique events.

In subsequent years, various alert correlation techniques have been proposed. The approach that arguably has generated the most amount of research has been on attack graphs (Noel et al. 2004). Attack graphs are directed graphs that represent logical progressions of a cyber attack through the network. Attack graphs are created based on the topology and vulnerabilities on the targeted computer network, which can be discovered using various network discovery and vulnerability assessment tools. Attack graphs are defined by a list of exploits and security conditions. Each exploit is a triple (vul, src, dest), of a vulnerability, vul, on a host, dest, connected to another host, src. In the case of a local exploit, the src and dest are the same host. Security conditions must be satisfied before an exploit is possible. Intrusion detection alerts typically map directly to the vulnerabilities, so this structure easily allows intrusion alerts to map to the attack graph.

Other alert correlation techniques focus on Bayesian approaches (Phillips and Swiler 1998) that use probabilities to determine the likelihood of exploits occurring. While the Bayesian approaches lend themselves naturally to alert correlated, it is unclear of the best or most effective way to determine the probabilities. Logically, the probabilities will likely vary greatly based on the network topology, attacker ability, and even the importance of the host. This can create a wide variance of probabilities across different networks, making it difficult to find an accurate set of probabilities.

Information Fusion for Real-Time Decision-Making (INFERD) (Yang et al. 2009) is a flexible alert correlation tool that can be defined to reflect varying levels of granularity and facilitate a creation of attack tracks and a resolution of ambiguities. Many alert correlation tools require a specific level of granularity in the definition of the models. While this can create a very effective tool for certain situations with few false positives, the model may be overly restrictive and miss other situations. INFERD attempts to resolve that by using alert categorization and a flexible constraint definition to allow the models to be varied and tweaked to maximize the detection of a multitude of possible attacks using a single model (at the possible expense of higher false positive rate) or focus on a very specific type of situation (at the possible expense of missing more different types of attacks).

Figure 1 illustrates the INFERD architecture. INFERD receives information from a repository of sensor data and processes it in real-time to output a set of attack

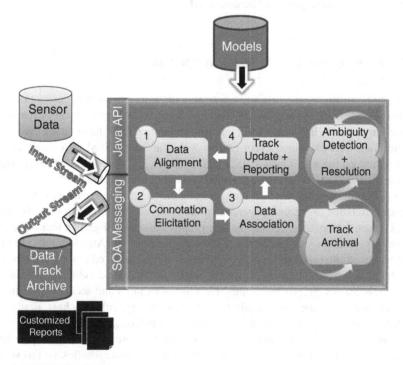

Fig. 1 INFERD Architecture

tracks, which are sequences of events hypothesized to be part of the same attacker. The creation and update of attack tracks is performed using four processes:

(1) Data Alignment—INFERD is able to ingest inputs from different types of sensors, so it needs to align all data into a common format. It should be noted that if a common alert reporting format was widely adopted and consistently used (such as IDMEF or CEF), that this process would not be necessary.
(2) Connotation Elicitation—This process determines the type of event the given observable is. This for example tries to classify the event into categories such as "Recon Scanning", "Intrusion Root", or "DoS". This classification occurs through a set of constraints defined by the model.
(3) Data Association—This process determines whether or not the given event is part of a new track or an existing track. The data association is driven by the constraints defined on the edges of a model.
(4) Track Update and Reporting—Once the data association is performed, the applicable track updates are made and sent as outputs.

There are also some additional background processes that INFERD performs.

(1) Track archival keeps INFERD as a scalable process so as to only keep the relevant tracks available for processing.
(2) Ambiguity Detection and Resolution tries to address any ambiguous data by performing additional processing. It is very possible that the constraints used by the model are insufficient to uniquely correlate an event to an attack track, so this process applies a stronger set of constraints on the events to try to resolve any ambiguities.

Figure 2 shows a simplified INFERD model. The blue circles are known as Template Nodes, which correspond to a high-level concept such as "Recon Scan" (event that scans the network) or "Intrusion Root Internal" (event that gives an attacker root-level access to a computer). Between the template nodes are arcs defining possible transitions. The idea of an INFERD model is that the template nodes and arcs define the level of granularity the alert correlation occurs on. In the example model, the purple box defined for each arc contains a constraint saying that a transition could occur when the target IP address of an event matches either the source or target IP of another connecting event. So if a Recon Scan DMZ occurs on a given host and is followed by a Recon Footprint DMZ on the same host, those two events will be added to the same attack track. It should be noted that in this simple example, IP address is only used for the arcs, so such a model would be subject to errors in the event of IP spoofing. In addition, the model does not take the actual network definition into account. So it is possible that firewalls or intrusion prevention sensors could realistically have thwarted an attack track identified by this model. However, the introduction of such constraints into INFERD could have the unfortunate effect of poor performance. So careful consideration must be taken into how detailed one wishes to make an INFERD model. An INFERD model subject to a large number of false positives could be beneficial if it is able to detect otherwise obscure attacks. In such a case, post-processing of the attack track by another

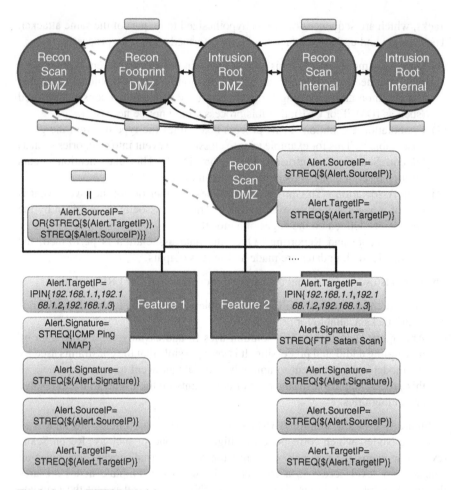

Fig. 2 Sample INFERD Model

process to determine its accuracy (such as the processes discussed regarding the VT) may be able to filter out most of the false positives.

Each template node contains a list of features that ultimately map to a single possible observable with a set of constraints. In the example model, the Recon Scan DMZ has a feature defined for ICMP Ping NMAP and FTP Satan Scan from a Snort sensor including a specific range of IP addresses. Again, this is where the granularity of the model is important. Recall that the hosts on a VT contain services, which ultimately determines the vulnerabilities on a host. The feature constraints in the INFERD model could also utilize these mappings to only classify alerts that a host is vulnerable to. However, this, too, can have a possible negative impact on performance, so it may be beneficial to leave simpler constraints on the INFERD model and use post-processing to resolve the false positives.

1.3   Existing Mission Impact Assessment Research

In the past decade or so, research has focused on modeling the mission dependencies to help facilitate computer-assisted analysis of current missions. D'Amico et al. (2010) focused their research specifically towards computer networks by creating an ontology of the mission dependencies. Their Cyber Assets to Missions and Users (CAMUs) approach assumes that a user uses a cyber capability, whereas a cyber asset provides a cyber capability. This cyber capability in turn supports a mission. Their approach mines existing logs and configurations, such as those from LDAP, NetFlow, FTP, and Unix to create these mission-asset mappings. CAMUs provides a graphical display of the potential missions and capabilities affected by a given cyber alert.

Jakobsen (2011) proposed the use of dependency graphs for cyber impact assessment and a hierarchical time-based approach to mission modeling and assessment. Missions are traditionally thought of as relatively static. However, various aspects of the mission are often important at different times. So it is therefore important for a mission model to be able to incorporate time. The Impact Dependency Graph addresses that by allowing for the mission dependencies to change over time. Their approach is largely focused on assets supporting services, which support missions and tasks. Each of these dependencies can be modeled based on an AND/OR relationship to indicate whether the child components are required for mission success or are redundant of each other. Mission impact scores are driven by the individual asset impacts that are calculated using a logical constraint graph that is tied to the known asset vulnerabilities.

Holsopple and Yang (2013) utilize a tree-based approach to calculate the impact of missions. Their mission tree is a tree-structure that utilizes Yager's aggregators (Yager 2004) to intelligently "roll up" the damage of assets to calculate the impact of each individual mission. This perspective-based approach provides a quick indicator of which missions might need to be addressed by the analysts. The tree structure enables the analyst to "drill down" the tree to determine which assets or missions are causing the impacts. The intent is that the assets will also contain information regarding which events impacted it.

Figure 3 shows the basic structure of the mission tree at a specific point in time. A Mission Tree consists of three different types of nodes—assets, aggregations, and missions. Asset nodes must always be leaf nodes. An aggregation node is a node that performs a mathematical function to calculate the combined impact of all of the children nodes. Finally, the third node type is a mission node. A mission node represents any type of task that needs to be executed either as the primary mission (the root node) or in support of another set of missions.

An asset node is defined by a 3-tuple (i,e,c) for a role r where $i \in [0, 1]$ is the damage score for asset e in support of the parent mission with a criticality c. The damage score can be calculated by a lower level situation estimation process and the process by which the score is calculated is not important so long as the damage score provides a value between 0 (indicating no damage to the asset) and 1 (indicating that

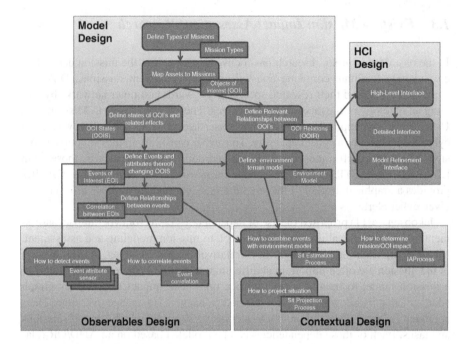

Fig. 3 Mission Tree Structure

the asset's functionality has been completely hampered). The criticality is used to describe the importance of a given node to the parent mission. An asset node must always be a leaf node and have an aggregation node as a parent.

A mission node is also defined by a 3-tuple (i,e,c) such that i is the impact score for mission e in support of the parent mission with a weight c. The weight is used to describe the criticality or importance of a given node to the parent mission. Every mission node must contain a single parent (except for the root) and a single child aggregation node. For a mission node, $i = i(child \ aggregation \ node)$.

An aggregation node calculates the combined impact of all children nodes and is defined by a 3-tuple (i,e,c) where e is an aggregation function with criticality c and $i = f(e)$. Every aggregation node must contain a parent that is either a mission node or an aggregation node. While an aggregation function can be any type of function, we adopt Yager's aggregation functions (Yager 2004) due to their flexibility in defining various logical and mathematical relationships.

Yager's aggregation functions (Yager 2004) use a weighting vector multiplied with a *sorted* vector to perform various mathematical functions, such as maximum, average, and minimum. Due to their flexibility in function definition, they were chosen as the primary calculation means for the aggregation functions.

Each aggregation node is defined by a vector of weights, w, and a sorted vector, v_s, for Yager's aggregation calculations. The sorted vector is a vector sorted in descending order of all $i*c$ (impact multiplied by criticality) values defined by each child. The dot-product of each vector yields the impact score, i, for the node.

The following aggregation functions are supported by the mission tree to enable the modeling of various mission relationships:

(1) And—all children nodes must be functional for the parent mission to be functional. This is represented by a maximum function.
(2) Or—only one of the children nodes needs to be function for the parent mission to be functional (i.e. the perform redundant functions). This is represented by a minimum function.
(3) AtLeastN—at least N of the children nodes need to be functional for the parent mission to be functional. This can be represented by a Yager aggregator.
(4) Threshold—the children are able to exhibit some level of damage before they affect the parent mission. Any damage or impact score below the given threshold will be saturated to 0.

The mission tree is also able to utilize "triggers" to allow the mission tree to dynamically change over time. Various changes to a mission tree include the addition or removal of a mission, a change to criticality, or the re-assignment of an asset. These changes can be triggered in one of three ways:

(1) **Functional Trigger**—These are one-time changes to the mission tree. As business or a particular task evolves, new missions may need to be created or existing missions are deemed unnecessary. These triggers are typically manual changes that must be made in order to accommodate changes that did not have a predictable time at which they became effective.
(2) **Absolute Temporal Trigger**—These are one-time changes that are triggered by a single point in time. These changes typically represent a predictable change to the mission tree, such as a deadline for a given mission. When deadlines for missions have occurred, the mission is permanently removed from the mission tree. In addition, known or planned tasks in support of a mission can be created at the given point in time.
(3) **Cyclical Trigger**—These changes are characterized by a predictable and cyclical change in the mission definition. These changes are typically caused by a business cycle, where certain assets may be more critical during normal business hours. In addition, due to resource availability, assets may only be available within certain timeframe, so there are only specific periods of time at which the assets are able to affect the mission. These changes result in a cyclic change of the mission tree.

1.4   Computer Network Modeling

Philips and Swiler (1998) proposed the use of attack graphs to determine asset vulnerabilities. This approach utilized acyclic graphs to represent the possible attacks on a network. However, the acyclic restriction of their model meant that there was an exponential increase in attack graphs due to bi-directional communication between computers allowing for vulnerabilities to be executed in different directions. Vidalis et al. (2003) proposed the use of vulnerability trees for the purposes of threat assessment. However, the tree structure also makes it difficult to model bi-directional communication leading to the exponential increase of the number of trees needed to model vulnerabilities in a computer network.

While there are a number of vulnerability and network scanning tools, many of them do not provide a comprehensive mapping of the computer network. ArcSight (HP Network Management Center 2013) uses its own tools to scan the network, but it is also a cost-prohibitive tool for many organizations. Such scanners, however, can be useful as tools used to populate a model such as the Virtual Terrain (Holsopple et al. 2008).

The Virtual Terrain (VT) is a security-based representation of a computer network. Its intent is to work towards an open standard for defining a computer network containing the level of information necessary to perform network and impact assessment. Recall from the Mission Modeling section that the developed techniques needed to implement their own methods of scanning for vulnerabilities and network connections. The mission tree was defined independent of the environment model used, but still required inputs regarding the damage to the assets. Defining a common standard for a computer network will not only help to improve all research in cyber network defense, but will also pave the way for public data sets that could be used for the evaluation of more advanced cyber network defense tools.

2 Top-Down Design

Cyber defense systems were built as incremental improvements to existing technologies or analysis approaches. This is a logical way for technology to progress since the lower-level processes (such as attack identification and alert correlation) provide the building blocks for the higher-level processes (such as threat and impact assessment). Since even the lower-level processes are proving to be non-trivial and constantly evolving, the focus has not significantly shifted to the higher-level processes. However, without a coherent architecture in place to design towards, this can lead to fragmented solutions, which can cause more difficult integration tasks between seemingly complementary technologies.

Built upon the exiting works summarized earlier, this section describes a top-down design process to build an architecture for a cyber defense system that minimizes the effort of analysts tracking down and prioritizing malicious threats. This "top-down" design approach is similar to the process discussed by Holsopple and Yang (2009), which focuses on designing an ideal system without assuming any particular technological limitations. With this approach, technology gaps can easily be identified and trigger the development of approaches to address those gaps. However, this approach may identify so many technology gaps that it would be very difficult to develop a complete, coherent system in a reasonable timeframe. Nonetheless, such an approach will identify the ultimate goal for the research and commercial communities to strive towards.

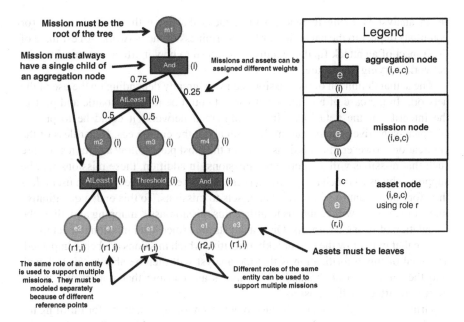

Fig. 4 General Top-Down Design Process

Figure 4 shows Holsopple and Yang's top-down design process (Holsopple and Yang 2009), which is applied to the area of cyber security. The process is segmented into four major components:

(1) Model Design
(2) Human-Computer-Interface (HCI) Design
(3) Contextual Design
(4) Observables Design

While each of these components is defined individually, as with any design process, the components can complement each other and changes to a component may trigger changes in a different component. This is typical of a waterfall design where the individual pieces are continuously refined until the requirements have been fulfilled.

In this chapter we will explore the model design, alert correlation, and how to determine mission impact as a means to demonstrate the top-down design. The next chapter will discuss in detail how to project cyber situations using the design discussed here.

2.1 Model Design—Mission Definition

We first start with the Model Design component. The Model Design component focuses on defining the data that will be needed to be stored or calculated by the system. The ultimate goal of cyber analysts is to identify threats and mitigate them, so an analyst is trying to react to the attacks that have the highest current (or potential) impact to the capability or trustworthiness of the network. An estimate of the impact of an attack fundamentally boils down to how it affects the missions the network is trying to execute.

The actual definition of the missions can vary greatly depending on the use of the network. In the case of a military network, it could be to fight a battle and protect the integrity of the data links. In a commercial network, it could be to protect company-sensitive or personal information about the employees. Regardless of the application, however, the missions will (for the most part) follow a certain structure such that missions will support other missions. In addition, these missions will be supported by assets such as specific servers, computers, services, or even users. It is therefore important to be able to map assets to missions. To this end, a quantitative impact to an asset will enable us to utilize this mission-asset mapping and, thus, the calculation of mission impacts. Once analysts are armed with mission impact information that will allow them to quickly prioritize which missions are being impacted. The goal of this prioritization is that the analyst will then be able to "drill down" into the impacts to understand which assets are causing that impact and which events are affecting those assets.

Grimaila et al. (2008) have discussed how technology is lacking for fulfilling the requirements for Cyber Mission Impact Assessment (CMIA). Determining the impact of an attack to missions can have different meanings:

(1) Ability to perform mission activities
(2) Capabilities of the mission system in general
(3) Achieving specific mission objectives
(4) Information about specific mission instances
(5) Prediction of how mission impact might vary over time
(6) Prediction of how affected resources not currently in use may cause future impact
(7) Prediction of how affected resources may cause impact on future mission instances

Therefore, developing a common language for the effects of a cyber attack is imperative to determining the impact of a cyber attack to one or more missions.

There is currently no existing standard for modeling missions, and those technologies that do exist are more "diagrammatic than computable" (Grimalia et al. 2008). These modeling technologies generally also ignore time, meaning that the importance of assets is assumed to be constant over time, when in reality, the importance should be changing. In addition, existing cyber risk assessment tools are generally offline approaches, meaning that they lack the ability to process data fast enough to provide a timely estimate of current impact – although they are useful for understanding how a network can be affected by future threats. Grimaila et al. (2008) also argues that while there is an abundance of tools that identify the (potentially malicious) activities on a network, none of them attempt to model the *effects* of the cyber attacks, which is necessary for impact assessment.

There are open problems with mission modeling. The problems can be attributed to at least one of the following three issues:

(1) Formal mission modeling for calculating impact, especially for cyber defense, is a very immature field. So all of the known techniques have "holes" preventing them from becoming a complete integrated solution.
(2) Some tools necessary to provide inputs to the mission modeling techniques to calculate impact assessment are not available because they were not necessary prior to considering the problem of impact assessment. This is one of the consequences of the unintentional "bottom-up" design approach that has been taken by cyber defense.
(3) Mission impact assessment is difficult, if not impossible, due to the nature of the problem itself. Providing quantitative evaluations of such tools will be error prone.

CAMUs (D'Amico et al. 2010) uses an ontological structure to model mission information, including cyber capabilities and users. While this approach provides for flexible mission models, this flexibility comes at the cost of not being able to provide impact estimates. As such, the analyst is still tasked with sifting through individual cyber alerts to decide if they are malicious or not. In addition, as we will see with other impact assessment approaches, support for "lower level" cyber defense tools is limited.

The Mission Tree (Holsopple and Yang 2013) approach does not *directly* rely on IDS or System log observables to support their impact calculations; however it does require some sort of pre-processing of observables to provide estimates of damage to the assets. Such pre-processing would need to be implemented for this approach to be viable. The Mission Tree approach, along with the Mission Impact Dependency graph (Jakobsen 2011), also offer no (or very limited) support to actually generate the mission models. Not having an intuitive GUI or integration with certain network discovery tools can lead to error-prone models.

At the time of publication, all of the mentioned techniques were only integrated with a limited set of cyber defense tools, which is due to the immaturity of cyber mission impact assessment research. As these (or future) tools progress, a more complete integration with other cyber defense tools will allow the benefits of these approaches to come to light.

Due to the lack of data to populate the mission impact models, that there are currently no common datasets that can be used to evaluate the effectiveness of such approaches against each other. In addition, none of the listed approaches have been able to reach a high enough maturity to be evaluated in real-time on existing computer networks. So while the utility for mission modeling and impact assessment can be seen at the conceptual level, there is currently no way to determine how heavily it would actually be able to improve the decision-making ability of a cyber analyst.

Even if common data structures are agreed upon by the cyber defense community for mission impact assessment, it will still be challenging to evaluate the effectiveness of mission impact assessment approaches. This is not necessarily just due to the lack of technological innovation or data, but rather the actual problem itself.

As mentioned previously by Grimaila's research (Grimalia et al. 2008), the concept of "impact" can take on different meanings. Therefore, some technologies may focus their assessment on different impact meanings and therefore cannot be adequately compared. Also, any quantitative measurements of impact cannot be known even with a detailed ground truth (e.g., even if a standard impact definition is agreed upon, how can one determine that the actual impact to an asset at a given time is 0.7 instead of 0.65?). Therefore, distance-based comparisons cannot be accurately computed. Another option for evaluating impact accuracy is to "rank" the scores against each other, so only the relative impact scores are important for analysis. However, this gets even more complex, because, the level of impact actually depends on the evaluator's perspective of the situation.

So the "ground truth" impact to an asset must account for:

(1) Who is interested in this assessment and how are they related to the mission(s) being assessed?
(2) Which impact definition(s) is(are) being used for the assessments?
(3) Which parts of the network are being impacted?
(4) When is this assessment valid for?
(5) Which events contributed to this impact?

Being able to account for all of these requirements in ground truth is going to be a subjective process leading to a potential bias in the results. It is therefore, infeasible to try to compare results of impact assessment techniques against a ground truth. The evaluation of such techniques can truly only be done based on the personal utility found by an analyst in using a given tool.

2.2 Model Design—Environment Modeling

Recall that the mission modeling techniques described in the previous section all ultimately relied upon damage estimates to the individual assets. These damage scores can be calculated using the following key pieces of information:

(1) What are the asset vulnerabilities
(2) How the asset is used on the network
(3) How the asset can be access on the network
(4) Which events are potentially targeting the asset

The first three pieces of information can be determined based on knowledge of the computer network, whereas the fourth piece relies on the events that can be detected or correlated on the network. So we will first focus our attention on the first three pieces since the fourth will be addressed as we work our way to the bottom of the design process.

Over the years, various models and tools have been proposed and even implemented to model certain aspects of a computer network. The problem with most of these approaches is that they either do not provide a comprehensive set of data relevant for impact assessment or alert correlation or do not provide automated or convenient ways to populate the model.

The Virtual Terrain (Holsopple et al. 2008) is an XML-based representation using a graph structure that is comprised of the data necessary for impact assessment and other advanced cyber network defense tools. The VT is comprised of multiple components:

(1) **Computer Network**—This contains information about the assets and physical/ virtual connectivity of the network.
(2) **Service-Vulnerability Mapping**—This utilizes the Common Platform Enumeration (CPE) and Common Vulnerabilities and Exposures (CVE) standards to map services to their potential vulnerabilities. Since the CPE and CVE database does not fully support all possible vulnerabilities, there are generalized mappings included to capture more generic events such as pings and port scans.
(3) **Vulnerability-Observable Mapping**—This mapping is dependent on the sensors/loggers being used as inputs. Sensors such as Snort provide a reference to a CVE and other vulnerability databases which can be used to populate this mapping.

The VT is capable of modeling the following aspects of a computer network:

(1) **Hosts, Servers, Clusters, Subnets, etc.**—These are the physical processing components in a computer network that are typically targeted by attackers. The VT generically models all of these components as either a host (a single workstation or server), clusters (multiple hosts of nearly identical configuration), or subnets (a collection of hosts or clusters with identical connectivity). Each of these components contain:

   a. **IP Address, Host name, Domain, etc.**—A set of metadata commonly used to define hosts.
   b. **Service References**—One or more references to services.

(2) **Routers, Switches, Firewalls, Access Points, etc.**—These components all affect the connectivity of a network. These fundamentally all control how traffic is routed or where it is filtered.
(3) **Sensors**—The location and type of sensor is extremely important to being able to filter out false positives and identify true positive alerts. Network-based IDSs typically just process all traffic without much knowledge of the underlying network, which can lead to false positives. For example, a network-based IDS placed outside of a firewall may trigger a number of observables, however, the firewall actually filters out most of that traffic, so those events are not really threats. On the other hand, an observable from a host-based IDS could be treated as more important due to the fact that those hosts are actually receiving the malicious traffic. It is therefore important to know the types and locations of sensors on the network so that asset damage can accurately be estimated.

(4) **Users**—Knowing users and their associated privileges is also important to be able to determine who can access what. Such information could be used to determine users trying to access data they are not supposed to, which is an indicator of an attack.

The intent of breaking down the VT into these three components is to enable the "drill-down" from hosts to services to vulnerabilities to possible observables. This also enables the ability to "roll up" from observables to vulnerabilities to services to hosts, which ultimately is what is needed for advanced cyber network defense. Being able to roll up this information allows for estimates of asset damage to quickly be obtained. For example, if an observable is received indicating a possible Remote Desktop Vulnerability was attempted on a given host, this information can be cross-referenced to quickly see if the targeted host was actually vulnerable to that attack. If the host is vulnerable to the attack, the network connectivity can be checked, along with the sensor types locations, to determine if this detected event damaged the target.

The VT was developed to encompass all necessary information for advanced cyber network defense, but there are some open issues that still need to be addressed:

(1) Integration with existing scanning tools and network components such as firewalls is needed to provide a comprehensive population of information. If a model like the VT were to become a standard, vendors would be able to write their own integration strategies to populate a VT.

(2) An analysis of scalability of the VT. While the concept of host clusters is intended to provide the ability to model hundreds of hosts into a single node, there are still thousands of vulnerabilities and services that need to be mapped. In order to adequately support impact assessment tools, accessing information from the VT must be very fast, so the VT must be evaluated and possibly tweaked for scalability.

(3) The fact that a VT contains a significant amount of information about a computer network is very helpful, but could also be very harmful if it is obtained by an attacker. It is therefore imperative that one or more security protocols be available to encrypt or intelligently distribute the information across the network such that the entire VT is only accessible with the correct security permissions.

2.3 Observables Design

The observables design component focuses on the detection and correlation of events. The topic of cyber detection has been extensively researched and existing commercial, proprietary, and open-source tools are being continuously refined. In this section, we will therefore explore the concept of alert correlation.

Cyber alert correlators generally utilize outputs from intrusion detection sensors and/or system logs to group events through causal and/or temporal relationships into "tracks". Knowledge of the actions taken by a single attack is imperative in understanding the potential or current impact to the missions. An individual event may not cause a significant impact, but the combination of multiple events could create a significant impact.

For example, if it is known that an event has compromised a particular workstation, the impact may be minimal since the threat could be isolated and mitigated easily. However, if it is known that the event was only a small part of a larger attack, a more complex and involved mitigation strategy may need to take place. With respect to asset damage, the meta data for each event in a given track can be used to determine asset damage. The collective set of asset damages for that track will then allow for the collection mission impact to be calculated.

Even though alert correlation is more highly researched that mission impact assessment, it also still suffers the same problem that many of the tools are only integrated with a limited subset of IDSs and other cyber defense tools.

Unlike impact assessment, alert correlation tools are less subjective in their ability to correlate alerts, enabling the use of common data sets to evaluate the performance of the techniques. Salerno has proposed a set of measures of performance to assess cyber alert correlation tools against each other (Salerno 2008). Assuming that a ground truth of activities (tracks) are known for a given data set, They proposed three measures of confidence:

$$Recall = \frac{Correct\ Detections}{Known\ Activities} \tag{1}$$

$$Precision = \frac{Correct\ Detections}{Detected\ Activities} \tag{2}$$

$$Fragmentation = \frac{Number\ of\ results\ that\ identify\ the\ same\ known\ activity}{Detected\ Activities} \tag{3}$$

These three metrics can be used to determine the accuracy of the correlations. Recall calculates how many activities were not detected (higher is better). Precision determines how well each of the detected activities mapped back to their ground truth activity (higher is better). While fragmentation captures how many activities were detected for a single ground truth activity (lower is better).

While the detection accuracy is important, being able to identify the most important activities (i.e. the malicious ones) is even more important. If an alert correlation tool identifies hundreds of different activities, it is infeasible for the analyst to iterate through all of them in a reasonable amount of time. It is therefore necessary for the alert correlation to also rank the activities against each other. Salerno also proposes the Activities of Interest (AOI) score which tries to determine how highly ranked the most important activities were.

One thing these metrics will allow us to evaluate between alert correlation tools is how easily they can detect a diverse array of cyber attacks. Recall that some of the alert correlation approaches require the use of an acyclic directed graph. This is limiting in the sense that this can require a potentially large number of graphs to capture minor variations to the same attack. It is therefore possible that such approaches that model a very specific type of attack will do very well in detecting that type of attack, but perform poorly in variations of that attack and of course other attack types not modeled at all. On the other hand, an alert correlation tool like INFERD (Sudit et al. 2007) is designed to be flexible to detect a wide variance of attacks with a single model. However, this can potentially come at the expense of a large number of false positives. This makes a tool like INFERD very dependent on the rankings of such identified attacks to be a useful tool for cyber defense analysts to use.

3 Summary

Effective mission impact assessment requires a holistic design of intelligent cyber defense systems to efficiently assess or even anticipate the effect of critical attacks to network operations and missions. Such a mission impact assessment system will be a critical component to enable a viable and resilient day-to-day technology enabling cyber situational awareness. Most of current tools were designed using a "bottom-up" approach such that technologies are built to expand or improve upon existing technologies with the ultimate goal of minimizing the response time of analysts to cyber attacks. However, a limiting factor to this approach is that many of the new technologies require more data or information that is not readily available from cyber defense tools. Since cyber attacks rarely are comprised of a single event, information fusion in necessary to correlate alerts together to represent unique attacks (i.e. a collection of events) instead of unique events. Information Fusion for Real-Time Decision-Making (INFERD) is a flexible alert correlation tool that can be defined to reflect varying levels of granularity and facilitate a creation of attack tracks and a resolution of ambiguities. INFERD receives information from a repository of sensor data and processes it in real-time to output a set of attack tracks, which are sequences of events hypothesized to be part of the same attacker. In attempting to build upon existing detection and alert correlation technologies, some of the research has shifted towards mission impact assessment. In the past decade or so, research has focused on modeling the mission dependencies to help facilitate computer-assisted analysis of current missions. Cyber Assets to Missions and Users (CAMUs) approach assumes that a user uses a cyber capability, whereas a cyber asset provides a cyber capability. This cyber capability in turn supports a mission. Computer Network Modeling can benefit from use of attack graphs to determine asset vulnerabilities. ArcSight's tools scan the network and can be useful as tools used to populate a model such as the Virtual Terrain. The Virtual Terrain (VT) is a security-based representation of a computer network. The top-down design process described in this chapter builds architecture for a cyber defense system that minimizes the effort of analysts tracking down and prioritizing malicious threats. The top-down design process is segmented into four major components: Model Design; Human-Computer-Interface (HCI) Design; Contextual Design; Observables

Design. Mission modeling is critical because an estimate of the impact of an attack fundamentally boils down to how it affects the missions the network is trying to execute. However, technology is lacking for fulfilling the requirements for Cyber Mission Impact Assessment (CMIA). E.g., determining the impact of an attack to missions can have different meanings, such as ability to perform mission activities; capabilities of the mission system in general; achieving specific mission objectives, and other. There is currently no existing standard for modeling missions, and those technologies that do exist are not computable. Even if common data structures are agreed upon by the cyber defense community for mission impact assessment, it will still be challenging to evaluate the effectiveness of mission impact assessment approaches. Environment Modeling is important because the mission modeling techniques all ultimately rely upon damage estimates to the individual assets. Much of the assets information can be determined based on knowledge of the computer network. Various models and tools have been proposed and implemented to model certain aspects of a computer network. The Virtual Terrain is an XML-based representation using a graph structure that is comprised of the data necessary for impact assessment and other advanced cyber network defense tools. The observables design focuses on the detection and correlation of events. Cyber alert correlators generally utilize outputs from intrusion detection sensors and/or system logs to group events through causal and/or temporal relationships into "tracks". A process that combines Mission Definition, Environment Modeling, and Observables Design leads to technology architecture supportive of mission impact assessment.

References

Argauer, B., and Yang, S. J. "VTAC: Virtual terrain assisted impact assessment for cyber attacks," in Proceedings of SPIE, Defense and Security Symposium, March 2008.

Bass, T. "Intrusion detection systems and multisensor data fusion," Communications of the ACM, vol. 43, no. 4, Apr. 2000.

D'Amico, A., Buchanan, L., and Goodall, J. "Mission Impact of Cyber Events: Scenarios and Ontology to Express the Relationships between Cyber Assets, Missions, and Users," in Proceedings of 5th International Conference on Information Warfare and Security, April 8–9 2010, Wright-Patterson Air Force Base, OH.

Enterasys – Products – Advanced Security Applications. http://www.enterasys.com/products/advanced-security-apps/index.aspx,2013

Grimalia, M. R. et al. "Improving the cyber incident mission impact assessment (CIMIA) process", Proceedings of the 4th annual workshop on Cyber security and information intelligence research. 2008.

Holsopple, J., and Yang, S. J. "FuSIA: Future Situation and Impact Awareness," in Proceedings of the 11th ISIF/IEEE International Conference on Information Fusion, Cologne, Germany, July 1–3, 2008.

Holsopple, J., Yang, S. J. "Designing a data fusion system using a top-down approach", in Proceedings of Military Communications Conference. Boston, MA. Oct 2009.

Holsopple, J., Yang, S. J. "Handling temporal and function changes for mission impact assessment", in Proceedings of Cognitive Methods in Situation Awareness and Decision Support. San Diego, CA. Feb 2013.

Holsopple, J., Argauer, B., and Yang, S. J. "Virtual terrain: A security based representation of a computer network," in Proceedings of SPIE, Defense and Security Symposium, March 2008.

HP Network Management Center. http://www.hpenterprisesecurity.com/, 2013.

Jakobsen, G. "Mission cyber security situation assessment using impact dependency graphs", in Proceedings of the 14th International Conference on Information Fusion, July 2011.

Ning, P., Cui, Y., and Reeves, D. "Analyzing intensive intrusion alerts via correlation," in Proceedings of the 9th ACM Conference on Computer & Communications Security, 2002.

Noel, S., Robertson, E., and Jajodia, S. "Correlating intrusion events and building attack scenarios through attack graph distances," in Proceedings of ACSAC, December 2004.

Phillips, C., and Swiler, L. P. "A graph-based system for network vulnerability analysis," in Proceedings of the 1998 workshop on New security paradigms. New York, NY, USA: ACM Press, 1998, pp. 71–79.

Salerno, J. "Measuring situation assessment performance through the activities of interest score," in Proceedings of the 11th International Conference on Information Fusion, July 2008.

Snort. http://www.snort.org, 2013

Sudit, M., Stotz, A., and Holender, M. "Situational awareness of a coordinated cyber attack," in Proceedings of International Data Fusion Conference, Quebec City, Quebec, CA, July 2007.

Valdes, A., and Skinner, K. "Probabilistic alert correlation," in Proceedings of the 4th International Symposium on Recent Advances in Intrusion Detection (RAID), vol.2212, pp.54–68, 2001.

Vidalis, S., Jones, A. et al. "Using vulnerability trees for decision making in threat assessment". Technical report. University at Glamorgan, Wales, UK. 2003.

Yager, R. R. Generalized OWA Aggregation Operators, Fuzzy Optimization and Decision Making, 2:93–107, 2004.

Yang, S. J., Stotz, A., Holsopple, J., Sudit, M., and Kuhl, M. "High Level Information Fusion for Tracking and Projection of Multistage Cyber Attacks," Elsevier International Journal on Information Fusion, Special Issue on High-level Information Fusion and Situation Awareness, 10(1):107–121, 2009.

Attack Projection

Shanchieh Jay Yang, Haitao Du, Jared Holsopple, and Moises Sudit

1   Introduction

Having dedicated the previous chapter to the second level of SA, we now proceed to the third level. The highest level of SA—projection—involves envisioning how the current situation may evolve into the future situation and the anticipation of the future elements of the situation. In the context of CSA, particularly important is the projection of future cyber attacks, or future phases of an ongoing cyber attack. Attacks often take a long time and involve multitudes of reconnaissance, exploitations, and obfuscation activities to achieve the goal of cyber espionage or sabotage. The anticipation of future attack actions is generally derived from the presently observed malicious activities. This chapter reviews the existing state-of-the-art techniques for network attack projection, and then explains how the estimates of ongoing attack strategies can then be used to provide a prediction of likely upcoming threats to critical assets of the network. Such projections require analyzing potential attack paths based on network and system vulnerabilities, knowledge of the attacker's behavior patterns, continuous learning or new patterns and the ability to see through the attacker's obfuscations and deceptions.

Cyber attacks to enterprise networks or cyber warfare have moved into an era where both attackers and security analysts utilize complex strategies to confuse and mislead one another. Critical attacks often take multitudes of reconnaissance, exploitations, and obfuscation techniques to achieve the goal of cyber espionage

S.J. Yang (✉) • H. Du
Department of Computer Engineering, NetIP Lab, Rochester Institute of Technology, Rochester, NY, USA
e-mail: jay.yang@rit.edu

J. Holsopple • M. Sudit
Center for Multisource Information Fusion, University of Buffalo, CUBRC, Inc., Buffalo, NY, USA
e-mail: jared.holsopple@avarint.com; sudit@cubrc.org

© Springer International Publishing Switzerland 2014
A. Kott et al. (eds.), *Cyber Defense and Situational Awareness*,
Advances in Information Security 62, DOI 10.1007/978-3-319-11391-3_12

and/or sabotage. The discovery and detection of new exploits, though needing continuous efforts, is no longer sufficient. Imagine a system that can process large volume of sensor observables, some inaccurate, and automatically synthesize relevant events into known or unknown attack strategies; the estimates of ongoing attack strategies can then be used to provide a prediction of immediate threats on critical assets, enabling a **Predictive Cyber Situational Awareness (SA)**. This chapter discusses the current works and opening problems in the area of network attack prediction.

Predicting or projecting multistage network attacks requires the modeling of how an attack might transpire over time. This modeling is broader than the traditional definition of intrusion detection, where the focus is on understanding system vulnerabilities and exploits. In late 1990s, Cohen (1997) provided one of the pioneering network attack modeling frameworks. They used cause-and-effect models to deduce 37 threat profiles (behaviors), 94 attacks (physical and cyber), and 140 defense mechanisms, and reported a set of simulation results (Cohen 1999). Their work, along with several others (Howard and Longstaff 1998; Debar et al. 1999; Chakrabarti and Manimaran 2002) in late 1990s and early 2000s, have provided a comprehensive understanding of the different cyber attack types and their effect to networked systems.

The early works on attack modeling, or more precisely, attack taxonomy, led to the research on alert correlation or attack plan recognition, e.g., (Ning et al. 2002, 2004; Cheung et al. 2003; Valeur et al. 2004; Noel et al. 2004; King et al. 2005; Wang et al. 2006; Stotz and Sudit 2007; Yang et al. 2009). Figure 1 shows an example network with a small set of observed malicious events, some could be unreliable due to obfuscation. This example shows 12 events within ~4 min time frame, and imagine a large number (>10,000) of such events intertwined as a result of many simultaneous attack activities deploying different strategies. Sensor outputs correlated to the same multistage attack can be considered as tracked footprints of an attacker. These footprints and their sequential and causal relationships can be modeled and represented as hypothesized attack strategies, helping analysts to comprehend and manage the situation from overwhelming alerts. The hypothesized attack strategies, as represented in mathematical models, can then be used to project future actions of ongoing attacks.

Time	Source IP	Destination IP	Description
12:56:03	52.2.100.5	100.20.2.15	WEB-MISC Invalid HTTP Version String
12:57:09	211.1.8.10	100.5.11.166	SHELLCODE x86 NOOP
12:58:11	211.1.8.10	100.10.20.4	(http_inspect) BARE BYTE UNICODE ENCODING
12:58:45	100.10.20.4	100.10.20.3	NETBIOS SMB IPC$ unicode share access
12:58:59	100.10.20.3	100.10.20.3	ICMP L3retriever Ping
12:59:37	52.2.100.5	100.10.20.4	WEB-MISC Chunked-Encoding transfer attempt
12:59:37	211.1.8.10	100.10.20.4	(http_inspect) OVERSIZE CHUNK ENCODING
12:59:38	100.10.20.4	100.10.20.4	(http_inspect) BARE BYTE UNICODE ENCODING
12:59:48	92.6.85.103	92.6.85.103	(portscan) TCP Portscan
12:59:50	132.30.8.20	100.5.11.208	ICMP PING NMAP
12:59:57	121.5.1.16	100.10.20.4	WEB-MISC cross site scripting attempt
13:00:21	100.10.20.4	100.10.20.4	(http_inspect) OVERSIZE CHUNK ENCODING

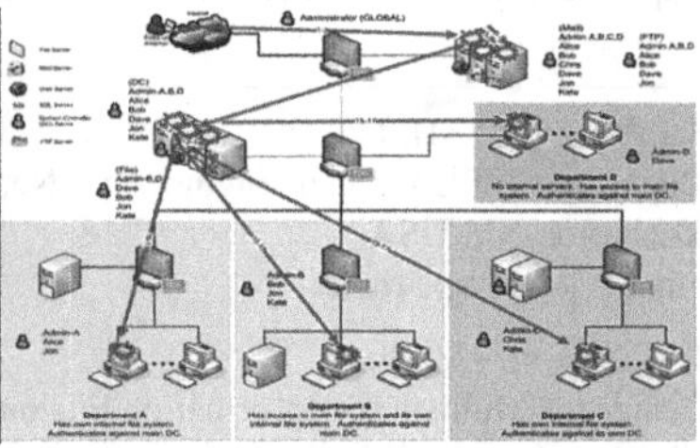

Fig. 1 An example network (*right*) with a small set of observed malicious events (*left*)

This chapter considers a tracked multistage cyber attack $\mathbf{X} = <X_1, X_2, \cdots, X_n>$ as an ordered sequence of observed events where the random variable $X_k \in \Omega$, $k \in \{1, 2, 3, \cdots, N\}$ is defined as the kth action in the sequence. Theoretically, X_k should be defined as a vector with multiple attributes describing the observed event. For ease of illustration within the scope of this chapter, X_k is considered as a random variable unless otherwise noted. In many cases, an attack strategy will be represented as a Lth order Markov model C where

$$P(\mathbf{X} \mid C) = P(X_1, \cdots, X_L) \prod_{k=1}^{N-L} f^C(X_k, \cdots, X_{k+L}). \tag{1}$$

The $P(X_1, \cdots, X_L)$ is the initial distribution of the attack model C, and f^C gives the transition matrix for Lth order model, i.e., $P(X_n \mid X_{n-1}, \cdots, X_{n-L})$. The use of an finite order Markov model is one example of how to represent a hypothesized attack strategy; some of the works reviewed in this chapter use this model while others do not.

Network attack prediction takes many forms, ranging from analyzing potential attack paths based on network and system vulnerabilities (knowledge-of-us) to analyzing the attack behavior patterns (knowledge-of-them). Prediction based on network vulnerabilities gives the advantage of focusing on critical assets and allows an explicit assessment of active defense to prevent further penetration into the network. However, it requires a reasonably up-to-date knowledge of the network, which is challenging in practice. Prediction based on attack behavior patterns does not rely on the knowledge of network and system configurations, but it could mis-predict critical actions due to decoy or obfuscated attacks. The common challenges for these approaches include:

- The network configuration, user accessibility, and system vulnerabilities may not be known accurately or completely a priori at the enterprise network level or higher, not to mention the needs to capture changes and updates in a timely manner. The attack prediction approaches need to be robust to incomplete network information.
- There will be uncertainty due to sensor errors, imperfection on alert correlation, and attack obfuscation. The attack prediction approaches need to be resilient to such uncertainties, or provide an understanding of how they will perform under such uncertainties. As such, it is also beneficial for attack prediction to provide one or more hypothesis for future attacks so that analysts can proactively prepare for a reasonable and manageable set of possible attacks.
- Network attack strategies can be diverse and evolve over time. Attack prediction approaches need to be adaptive and be able to treat unknown attack strategies, preferably in an online manner.

The next section will review and discuss the benefits and limitations of the various current works on network attack prediction, most of which address some of the challenges but not all. Section 3 will discuss the open problems and the preliminary works that provides a better understanding towards an integrated solution that utilizes both the knowledge-of-us and the knowledge-of-them. Finally, Sect. 4 concludes this chapter with a brief summary of the current state-of-the-art and the outlook of Predictive Cyber SA.

2 Network Attack Modeling for Threat Projection

2.1 Attack Graph and Attack Plan Based Approaches

The first set of approaches (Qin and Lee 2004; Wang et al. 2006; Noel and Jajodia 2009) expands from alert correlation. The general idea is that alert correlation creates the hypothesized attack models, also called attack graphs (Wang et al. 2006) or attack plans (Wang et al. 2006; Noel and Jajodia 2009), and prediction can be done by forward analysis using these attack models. A comprehensive review of alert correlation is beyond the scope of this chapter; the following will concentrate on discussing how two predictive analyses expand from their corresponding alert correlation systems, respectively.

Wang et al. (2006) discussed the use of **attack graphs** to correlate, hypothesize, and predict intrusion alerts. The main idea of the attack graph is to provide an efficient representation and algorithmic tools to identify the possible cases system vulnerabilities can be exploited in a network. The approach relies significantly on a reasonably complete and accurate knowledge of the system vulnerabilities and firewall rules in the network. While, ideally, various scanning tools can be used to obtain such information, it is a daunting task for a large-scale enterprise network where multiple system administrators manage different parts of the network. Note that the notion of representing vulnerabilities in a network has also been discussed by others in late 1990s and early 2000s, e.g., (Phillips and Swiler 1998; Tidwell et al. 2001; Daley et al. 2002; Vidalis and Jones 2003). Most of these works revealed the scalability problem when modeling all possible vulnerable paths in a network. The attack graph approach described by Wang et al. (2006) and Noel and Jajodia (2009) has shown ways to alleviate this scalability problem.

Wang et al. (2006) suggested to use Breadth-First Search on the attack graph beginning from the recently received alerts. The search goes forward from the new alerts to find paths satisfying of both security conditions and exploits, without reasoning about the disjunctive and conjunctive relationships between exploits. Essentially, the approach finds *all* possible next attacks from the attack graph. While they discussed the computational and memory usage performance, Wang et al. (2006) did not provide a comprehensive analysis for the prediction performance.

An alternative to the use of attack graph is the use of **Dynamic Bayesian Network (DBN)**. Qin and Lee (2004) were among the first to propose a high-level attack projection scheme. They expanded the use of their alert correlation system, designed to fit sensor observables to pre-defined high level attack structures using

DBNs. This approach allows the definition of causal relationship between observed events, and, more importantly, dynamic learning of transition probabilities through sufficient volume of data. Once learned, the transition probabilities can be used to predict potential future attack actions.

A distinction between the works by Wang et al. (2006) and Qin and Lee (2004) is that the attack graph is more rule-based and the DBN approach is more data-driven and probability-based. Because attack graph is rule-based, it enables specific modeling and analysis of the vulnerabilities and exploits in the network. On the other hand, the use of DBN to model high level attack plans requires a mapping between specific alerts to attack categories, but it allows probability inference and helps reduce from all possible future attack actions to a differentiable list of likely future attacks.

While seemingly promising, The DBN approach discussed by Qin and Lee (2004) is not without limitations. First of all, the high level attack plans need to created a priori by domain experts. It is unclear how a variety of attack plans can be created and updated realistically. It is also not clear how many and how detailed these plans need to be for reasonably good correlation or prediction performance.[1] Second, the transition probabilities need to be learned through a reasonably large amount of data. This means that, for each attack plan, one will need to see sufficiently large number of attack sequences in order to do prediction with high fidelity. This may not be likely in reality because network attack strategies are diverse and evolving in a fast pace. Section 2.3 will discuss a set of approaches that inferences future attack actions without requiring pre-defined attack plans, and, thus, eliminates the need for large volume of data for each attack plan.

2.2 Attack Projection by Estimating Attacker Capability, Opportunity, and Intent

The use of network configurations and vulnerabilities for threat projection can also be applied to the concept of estimating adversary **Capability, Opportunity, and Intent (COI)**, which has been used widely in military and intelligence community for threat assessment (Steinberg 2007). Within the context of *computational techniques* for Cyber SA, this section extends the works by Holsopple et al. (2010) and Du et al. (2010) and presents the following conceptual definition for cyber adversary capability, opportunity, and intent.

Capability Given how difficult it has been to identify the true source of a cyber attack as well as the wide-ranging abilities of attackers, it is challenging to even estimate the set of tools and abilities that can effectively be used by the attacker without a priori knowledge or a learning process. A practical approach is to adopt a probabilistic learning process to infer the set of services each attacker is likely to

---

[1]A discussion of how to assess the similarity/difference between attack models will be presented in Sect. 3.1.

exploit given what he/she has successfully exploited before. Note that we suggest to assess the capability at the service level, e.g., using the Common Platform Enumeration (CPE), as the attackers typically know various exploits for the same service. The probabilistic learning process should account for the skill level required for specific exploits, if such information is available, and the breadth of exploit types across CPE's and Common Weakness Enumerations (CWE's).

Opportunity Assessing cyber attack opportunity can be interpreted as the set of "exposed" systems to each ongoing attack given its current progress in the network. Certainly, if an attacker has insider information of the network configuration or if the network is managed poorly with minimal safeguard, technically or policy-wise, the opportunity assessment will have much less value. Here we assume the network in question is reasonably secured with firewall rules, permission and banned lists, service configurations, etc. to segregate the access domains. The process then is to dynamically identify the reachable next targets from the already exploited or scanned machines or accounts. In a way, the attack graph approach discussed in Sect. 2.1 finds the opportunities for each ongoing observed attack sequence. To differentiate the different exposed targets, a probability-based or weighted approach can be used.

Intent A true adversary intent analysis will require the study of attacker motivation and social influence—a substantial departure from the focus of this chapter. From the technical perspective, one way to infer "worst-case" intent is by assessing the possible impact of next actions, in terms of how the actions may step closer to the critical assets and data in the network. The first step of such analysis is an efficient way to determine the criticality of network assets to the various missions they support, for which one may refer to the impact assessment discussed in the earlier chapter, titled "Top-down Driven Cyber Impact Assessment." From there, one can aggregate the effect of each action over the reachable set of next targets from that action and determine the worst-case intent scenario.

The estimations via Capability, Opportunity and Intent (COI) analysis need to be examined holistically, either through human analytics as traditionally done in military and intelligence communities, or combined via theoretical fusion algorithms, such as Dempster-Shafer combination (Shafer 1976) or Transferable Belief Model (TBM) (Smets 1990).

Very little has been done to show the quantitative benefits of COI analysis. Du et al. (2010) developed an ensemble prediction algorithm that combines capability and opportunity assessments using TBM. They analyzed the performance of the algorithm on two networks, each attacked by 15 attack sequences. Network 1 has four subnets and each subnet has access to two dedicated servers and four shared centralized servers. This is to represent networks with segmented departments. Network 2 has three subnets, each of which can access only one dedicated server but share most others. The subnets in Network 2 are hidden behind layers of tightly controlled firewalls and include a server farm of 10. Table 1 shows the results for the experiment.

The average compromising score (*AvgCS*) shown in Table 1 is the average threat score of entities that are about to be compromised next. Intuitively, a good projection scheme will give high threat score to entities just before they are compromised. Therefore, the higher the *AvgCS*, the better the projection accuracy. Reasonably good

Table 1 Attack projection performance by combining capability and opportunity assessment [reproduced from Du et al. (2010)]

	#Servers	#Subnets	*AvgCS*	*AvgAR*
Network 1	12	4	71.5 %	86.2 %
Network 2	19	3	89.6 %	52.7 %

AvgCS is shown for both networks. Network 1 sees a lower *AvgCS* because the hosts and servers in each subnet are all one server away from the Internet and, thus, are easily susceptible to attacks. This makes it harder to differentiate between more and less severely threatened entities. Network 2, on the other hand, sees close to 90 % *AvgCS*. This exceptional performance is primarily due to the tightly configured server and subnet access of Network 2; only few vulnerable paths are available to attack internal hosts and servers, and the paths can be quite different from one target to another.

The average asset reduction (*AvgAR*) in Table 1 shows the opposite trend as *AvgCS* does. The metric *AvgAR* represents the average percentage of entities the system has reduced for the analysts to focus on. The implemented system only shows analysts the entities that have a threat score no less than 0.5. In other words, for experiments done on Network 1, the analysts only need to focus on 13.8 % of the entities he would have to examine without the proposed system. Network 2 sees a relatively less reduction of 52.7 %. Network 1 sees a better reduction because the subnets are segmented only one server away from the Internet; so the reduction of assessed assets is already high even at the very early stage of an attack.

Network attack projection via COI analysis is at its early stage and much needs to be done to provide a robust system. Particularly, a thorough study is needed to determine how to optimally integrate the estimations from all three aspects of COI. Generally speaking, COI analysis is more effective when applying to tightly secured networks. This approach does not project well for attacks that constantly change the strategy and ignore the exposed systems; such shortcoming can be potentially compensated by assessing the attack behaviors, which will be described in the next section.

2.3   Prediction by Learning Attack Behaviors/Patterns

The network attack prediction approaches discussed in the previous sections assume a good knowledge on either the attack strategies or the network vulnerabilities. In practice, neither of the information can be easily obtained and maintained. In fact, network attack strategies can be diverse and evolving, and so are the network and system configurations. In such cases, network attack prediction will need to dynamically learn about the attack behavior. A few works (Fava et al. 2008; Du and Yang 2011a; Cipriano et al. 2011; Cheng et al. 2011; Soldo et al. 2011) were developed to learn and predict attack behaviors without relying on pre-defined attack plans or detailed network information.

2.3.1   Variable Length Markov Model (VLMM) Attack Prediction

Recognizing the needs to learn and predict ongoing network attacks in an online manner, Daniel et al. (2008) developed an adaptive learning and prediction system using the Variable Length Markov Model (VLMM). While similar machine learning and modeling approaches have been used for anomaly and intrusion detection, e.g., (Lee et al. 1997; Lane and Brodley 1999; Ye et al. 2004), the work by Daniel et al. (2008) was the first that examined the use of VLMM for network attack prediction. The VLMM prediction is a branch of Universal Predictor (Jacquet et al. 2002; Shalizi and Shalizi 2004), originally developed for other applications such as text compression (Bell et al. 1990). VLMM fits well as an online learning system because of its superior computational efficiency over Hidden Markov Model (HMM) and the flexibility over finite (or fixed) order Markov model. The following provides a brief illustration of how VLMM captures attack behavior and its performance in predicting attack actions.

Using the notation defined in Sect. 1, consider an observed attack sequence **X** with a length l. This sequence will contribute to the building of oth order models for $0 \leq o \leq l$. More specifically, this attack sequence will provide one sample to the lth order model, two samples to the $(l-1)$th order model, ..., $l-1$ samples to the 1st order model, and l samples to the 0th order model. One can use a suffix tree or other data structure to store the statistics from these samples from all attack sequences. If a suffix tree is used, it takes $O(l^2)$ time to find the probabilities of next action being X_{l+1} with respect to all models, $P_o(X_{l+1})$, $\forall -1 \leq o \leq l$, where the -1th order model assigns $1/|\Omega|$ to all symbols in the action space Ω to prevent the *zero frequency problem* (Bell et al. 1990). We can then combine the various probabilities to provide a *blended* probability $P(X)$ as follows.

$$P(X_{l+1}) = \sum_{o=-1}^{k} w_o \times P_o(X_{l+1}) = \sum_{o=-1}^{k} w_o \times P(X_{l+1} \mid X_{k-o+1}, \ldots, X_k) \qquad (2)$$

where w_o is the weight associated with the oth order model, and $\sum_{o=-1}^{k} w_o = 1$. Note that finite sequences should be penalized by their rarity and rewarded by their specificity. Examples of the weight functions can be found in Bell et al. (1990). This work considers $w_j = (1-e_j) \times \prod_{k=j+1}^{l} e_k$, $-1 \leq j < l$ where $w_l = (1 = e_l)$, $e_j = 1/(c_j+1)$, and c_j is the number of times the specific pattern has occurred.

A key element in adopting VLMM for attack prediction is the definition of the action space with special symbols to represent new symbols that were not seen before—recall that this is an online attack prediction system. Figure 2 shows the average prediction accuracies achieved by using VLMM as attack events are observed over time. A total of 10,425 attack events from 1,482 attack sources are interleaved, and distinctive attack scenarios with new exploits and target sets are introduced around alerts #3000 and #8000 for a VMWare network. This example shows VLMM prediction performance with respect to two attributes: attack exploits

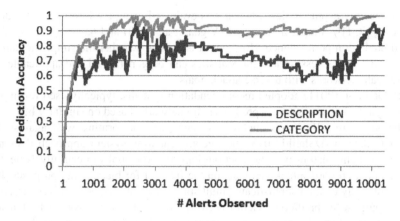

Fig. 2 Average prediction accuracy as alerts are injected to VLMM [reproduced from Fava et al. (2008)]

(Description) and attack effects (Category). The results demonstrate that VLMM not only predicts well but also quickly adapts to new attack scenarios.

The VLMM framework allows us to discover and combine patterns within attack sequences without explicitly defining attack scenarios. In fact, it combines the probabilities associated with all matched patterns in various orders and produce a best guess. An attacker executing few decoy attack sequences should have little impact to dilute the model. In addition, the current work filters back-to-back actions that are identical to explicitly capture the attack transitions, which are often keys to network attack strategies.

A preliminary study was conducted to examine how the location and the occurrence of missing observations will affect the performance of VLMM prediction. The results suggest that, given the same number of missing alerts, spreading the noise throughout the sequences will have a slightly bigger impact to the performance. More importantly, missing events that rarely occur will have a significant impact to VLMM. A comprehensive sensitivity analysis of VLMM with respect to noise or obfuscation will provide a complete understanding of the benefits and limitation of using VLMM for network attack prediction. From there, one may design a resilient VLMM system by combining not only the oth order models but also the potential variations due to the probabilistic noise model.

2.3.2 Other Attack Behavior Learning Approaches

Cipriano et al. (2011) developed a statistical learning system called Nexat. The approach groups intrusion alerts into attack sessions based purely on the source and destination IP addresses recorded in the alerts. Then, statistics are recorded to determine which types of attack actions are more likely to be in the same session. Prediction of future attack actions are, thus, chosen based on the overall statistics given recently captured alerts. Nexat was evaluated using the International Catch-the-Flag (iCTF) competition dataset (Vigna et al. 2013) and has show reasonably good prediction performance. However, it is unclear whether the simplistic definition of the attack session and the statistics can be generalized and applicable for large-scale networks with diverse attack goals.

Soldo et al. (2011) adopted recommendation systems, typically used for movie ranking and shopping sites, to predict victim networks based on similarly behaving malicious source IP. While theoretical sound and performing well against the DShield dataset (DSheild 2013), the recommendation system approach does not provide insights on how the attack actions happen sequentially or causally. Note that DSheild data reports attack incidents on the Internet for blacklisting purposes, but does not really contain sophisticated multistage attack strategies. It serves for a different purpose of predicting victim networks from blacklisted source IP, but not predicting next attack actions among ongoing attacks in enterprise networks.

Cheng et al. (2011) developed a system that measures similarity between attack progressions and project into future actions based on most similar portions of the progressions seen in other attack sequences. The approach is based upon the solution for the classical Longest Common Subsequence problem, and a key novelty lies in the definition of the attack progression as a time-series of three-digit numbers: the first digit indicates the zone distance between the source and destination IP, the second digit stands for the network protocol used, and the third digit reflects the distance between port clusters. From there, an attack sequence becomes a trajectory moving in this three-digit space. While the idea is interesting and unique, the authors evaluated their system against the DARPA Intrusion Detection Dataset (MIT Lincoln Laboratory 2013), which is limited in terms of attack sophistication and certainly not sufficient to demonstrate predictive Cyber SA.

3 Open Problems and Preliminary Studies

The existing works on predicting network attacks have shown some promises, but are still insufficient to provide a resilient solution due to sensor inaccuracy, attack obfuscation, evolving network strategies, and incomplete network information. The following sections will discuss some of the open problems and preliminary works to address these uncertainties, including a brief highlight of the lack of data to validate and assess performance of network attack prediction approaches.

3.1 Impact of Obfuscation on Attack Modeling

Fitting observed attack sequences to attack models is the basis for many attack prediction approaches. These observations, however, are likely to contain noise or obfuscated actions. Little work has been done to systematically analyze the effect of the

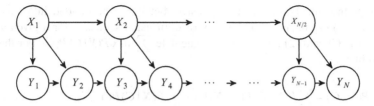

Fig. 3 Attack progression models with noise injection

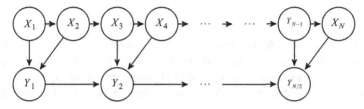

Fig. 4 Attack progression models with trace removal

various obfuscation techniques, e.g., inserting noise, removing traces, altering alerts, on network attack modeling. Du and Yang (2014) have studied the effect of attack obfuscation on classifying attack sequences to attack models. This section expands from that study and discusses how it relates to multistage network attack prediction.

To classify a given attack sequence $\mathbf{X}$ among different models, $C \in \mathscr{C}$, one will need to find

$$\arg\max_C P(C \mid \mathbf{X}) = \arg\max_C \frac{P(\mathbf{X} \mid C)P(C)}{P(\mathbf{X})} = \arg\max_C P(\mathbf{X} \mid C)P(C) \quad (3)$$

Computing the optimal classification rate for a set of attack models $\mathscr{C}$ requires consideration of all possible $\mathbf{X}$'s, which is in the order of $O(|\mathscr{C}| \cdot |\Omega|^N)$ if using a brute-force approach, where Ω is the set of attack actions and N is the observed sequence length.

Now, consider an obfuscated sequence $\mathbf{Y}$, which can be modeled as a transformation of $\mathbf{X}$ given the probabilistic obfuscation model $P(\mathbf{Y}|\mathbf{X})$. The obfuscation model can be as simple as a random change between any possible symbols in Ω, or as complex as changing Y_k depending on all previous actions $\{X_1, \cdots, X_k\}$. Figures 3 and 4 show two example models that represent attack progressions with noise injection and trace removal, respectively.

Similar to those shown in Figs. 3 and 4, a variety of obfuscation techniques can be modeled using the general Dynamic Bayesian Networks (DBNs), also called Statistical Graph Models. From there, one can analyze the impact of matching an obfuscated sequence $\mathbf{Y}$ to the attack model C. Using the Bayesian framework, the optimal classification performance over all possible cases is expressed as follows.

$$\sum_{\mathbf{Y}} P(\mathbf{Y}) \max_C P(C \mid \mathbf{Y}) = \sum_{\mathbf{Y}} \max_C P(\mathbf{Y} \mid C)P(C) \quad (4)$$

Computing Eq. (4) directly is expansive; but it can be divided into two sub-problems: (1) calculate the probability of obfuscated sequence for a given attack model $P(\mathbf{Y}|C)$, and (2) given $P(\mathbf{Y}|C)$, calculate $\sum_{\mathbf{Y}} \max_C P(\mathbf{Y}|C)P(C)$. For the first sub-problem,

$$P(\mathbf{Y}|C) = \sum_{\mathbf{X}} P(\mathbf{X}|C)P(\mathbf{Y}|\mathbf{X},C) = \sum_{\mathbf{X}} P(\mathbf{X}|C)P(\mathbf{Y}|\mathbf{X})$$

$$= \sum_{\substack{\mathbf{X} \\ \mathbf{X}:|\mathbf{Y}-\mathbf{X}|_H = M}} P(X_1, \cdots, X_L) \prod_{k=1}^{N-L} f^C(X_k, \cdots, X_{k+L}) \prod_{\substack{k=1 \\ k:X_k \neq Y_k}}^{N} g(X_k, Y_k) \quad (5)$$

where $|\mathbf{Y} - \mathbf{X}|_H = M$ reflects the number of noise elements that alters from $\mathbf{X}$ to $\mathbf{Y}$. By leveraging the model structure exhibited in DBN, (5) can be solved efficiently with recursion rules similar to those used in Dynamic Programming.

Knowing how to determine $P(\mathbf{Y}|C)$, computing $\sum_{\mathbf{Y}} \max_C P(\mathbf{Y}|C)P(C)$ can be efficiently achieved using Monte-Carlo method. Examining all possible Y requires $O(|\Omega|^N)$ iterations. By randomly sampling sufficient number of $\mathbf{Y}$'s, one can contain the errors based on Hoeffding's bound (Serfling 1974). In the scenarios studied by Du and Yang (2014), only 1,000 samples is required to achieve less than 1% error regardless of $|\Omega|$ or N.

Combining the recursive algorithm and the Monte-Carlo sampling, Du and Yang (2014) developed an efficient algorithm to compute the success rate of which obfuscated sequences are matched to their corresponding attack model. This rate is referred to as the optimal classification rate. Du and Yang's algorithm has been shown to achieve a computational complexity of $\Theta(N \cdot M \cdot |\Omega|^{L+1})$, where L is the order of the finite Markov attack model. Note that L is typically small ($L \leq 3$) as suggested by Fava et al. (2008); when L is small and considered as a constant, the algorithm runs in polynomial time with respect to the attack sequence lengths and the size of the action space.

Figure 5 shows a set of results on the optimal classification rate for a set of distinct attack models, when the observation length N and the obfuscation level increases, respectively. Here the obfuscation level is shown as the ratio of M/N. The classification performance for three scenarios are plotted. *Clean* means no obfuscation is introduced to the observed sequences and the classification is direct based on how X transitions; this scenario represent the best one can ever achieve even with no obfuscation and full knowledge of the attack model. *Noise* means that obfuscation is included but the classification is done without the knowledge of the obfuscation model. The third is a set of experiments when the classification is done for the obfuscated sequences knowing the obfuscation model. The third set consists of five cases, where the estimated obfuscation level equals to the true obfuscation level, 10% more, 20% more, 10% less, and 20% less.

Figure 5 exhibits the significant effect obfuscation can have on the classification performance even though the attack models are quite distinct—the Clean scenario shows mostly 90% or higher classification rate but it drops to mostly 70% without knowing how obfuscation is done. This performance can be brought back to around

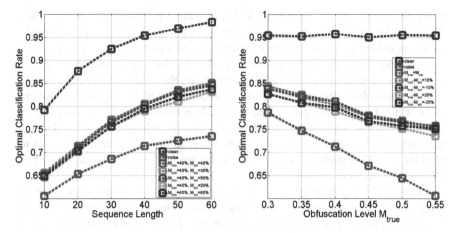

Fig. 5 Optimal classification rate vs. observation length (*left*) and obfuscation level (*right*)

80 % when the obfuscation model is known. Note that imprecise estimation of the obfuscation level does not cause much difference in classification performance. Overall, as expected, the classification performance increases as the observation length increases and when the obfuscation level is lower. The performance improvement is more significant when the observation length is small and when the noise level is high.

The overall framework described above provides a means to systematically and quantitatively assess the impact of obfuscation to attack modeling. Specifically, it assesses:

1. how distinct a set of attack models are with respect to each other,
2. the effect of specific obfuscation techniques and obfuscation level on attack classification, and
3. the effect of observation window length and other operational parameters on attack classification.

Fundamentally, this study offers a theoretical analysis that measures the best one can recover from attack obfuscation or noise, which is inherent in network attack modeling and prediction. Extension of this work includes integrating the obfuscation models directly with the prediction model, and perform similar analytical analysis as the above to estimate the prediction accuracy. At a very minimal, a network prediction solution must be evaluated by taking into account the potentially significant errors in choosing the model for prediction.

3.2 Asset Centric Attack Model Generation

As shown in the last section, there will always be mis-calculation in correlating observables to attack models. In fact, aiming at fitting observables to known models may not be necessarily the best approach, since the dangerous attacks are the ones likely to employ attack strategies deviating from the commonly known ones. Alternatively, one may want to dynamically learn the attack strategies based on the collective evidence that are "relevant" to critical assets in the network. In a way, this approach combines the "knowledge-of-us" and the "knowledge-of-them" without aiming at recovering who did what. In other words, the focus is no longer on determining which observables belong to the same attacker or attacker group and use that to fit or build models for prediction; instead, it is to concentrate on grouping the collective evidence that can lead to the compromise of each critical asset, and simultaneously generate attack behavior models based on the collective evidence. In its ultimate form, this approach shall integrate the benefits of the different attack prediction approaches discussed in Sect. 2.

Strapp and Yang (2014) have developed an online semi-supervised learning framework that aims at simultaneously identifying relevant observables for critical assets and generating attack models based on the collective behaviors exhibited by these observables, even in the presence of IP spoofing. This section will highlight the findings from Strapp and Yang (2014) and discuss how it relates to network attack prediction. Achieving this asset centric attack model generation requires: (1) an appropriate definition of "relevance" in the presence of IP spoofing, and (2) a method to determine whether to match observed events to previously found model or to use them to generate a new model.

To assess the relevance of large-scale malicious events, we first expand the definition of Attack Social Graph (ASG) (Du and Yang 2011b, 2013; Xu et al. 2011), which represents the source-target pairs of cyber attacks in a directed graph.

Definition 1 (Attack Social Graph (ASG)). An ASG $G_\tau(V_\tau, E_\tau)$ is a directed graph representing the malicious events observed within a time interval τ. A vertex $v \in V_\tau$ is a host, and an edge $e_{(u,v)} \in E_\tau$ exists if at least one attack event is observed from u to v during τ. The edge weight, $\mathbf{Z}(u, v, \tau)$, represents the features of attack activities and is a function of the amount and types of observed events from u to v during τ.

Direct use of ASG would implicitly assume the host IP observations are accurate, which is not the case. In fact, multiple attackers may spoof a single IP to perform independent and irrelevant attacks. The proposed method will be able to segment the ASG so that a single attack source IP can exhibit multiple attack behaviors. The only assumption made is that each $\mathbf{Z}(u, v, \tau)$ will represent a single attack behavior for a reasonable τ, because it is unlikely that an IP is spoofed by multiple attackers to perform independent and irrelevant attacks on the same target machine during the same time frame. Such assumption could be relaxed, especially for dormant attacks, to extend from the current work.

Figure 6 shows a small example ASG evolving over time, revealing two attack behaviors exhibited by the same source IP. This is an example extracted from the dataset collected via the Network Telescope project conducted by CAIDA (Aben et al. 2013). The directed edges represent whether the malicious events observed on each source-target pair belong to any model (dashed and solid lines), or not assigned to the incident at the time (dotted lines).

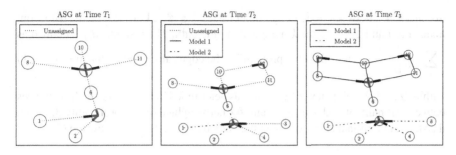

Fig. 6 An example ASG evolving over time

In Fig. 6, Node 6 is in the center of two clusters of attack events; it is unclear whether Node 6 serves a critical role for both, or it is just a result of IP spoofing and the two attack groups should be considered separately. Also notice Nodes 8, 10 and 11. As time goes on, the graph structure suggests this trio is involved in seemingly collaborative attacks for Nodes 7, 9 and 12. While the graph properties signify the relevance of attack sources to one or more incidents, it also requires an examination of how the malicious events occur over time to determine which edges should belong to which incident. To achieve this integrated approach, the Bayesian Classifier is adopted to dynamically create models specified in a feature space, and determine the optimal model M^* for which the events occurring on each edge should best fit. Let $\mathbf{Z}$ represent the features exhibited by the events observed on an edge, and we have

$$M^* = \arg\max_M P(M \mid \mathbf{Z}) = \arg\max_M P(\mathbf{Z} \mid M)P(M) \qquad (6)$$

$P(\mathbf{Z}|M)$ serves to examine the likelihood of each model containing the attack features exhibited by the events on each edge, and $P(M)$ represent the prior signifying the relevance of the model with respect to the graph centered around each critical asset. The following discusses the definition of the relevance prior based on the ASG structure, the attack features, and the use of a generic model to enable the creation of new models in an online manner.

The *graph-based prior*, $P(M)$, is proposed to signify a departure from the frequentist prior in routine Naïve Bayes classification. It utilizes macroscopic information about ASG to determine whether a collective set of evidences is spatially cohesive to infer an attack behavior. The formulation extends the measure of Graph Efficiency defined by Latora and Marchiori (2001), and is similar to the concept of Closeness Centrality (Newman 2001) with an extrapolation to measure the entire graph. The intuition is that a set of observed events is relevant if it is close to the critical asset within the ASG or have a similar behavior to those incident to the asset. From there, a model is more likely to occur if all evidences associated with the model are all cohesively relevant.

Consider a model M and the corresponding subgraph $\mathcal{G}_M$ in the overall ASG. For a given node i, its "position" is determined by the inverse harmonic mean of distances, $d_{i,j}$, between node i to all other nodes $j \in \mathscr{G}_M$. Let $\mathscr{P}_{i,j}$ be the path from nodes i to j and $\mathscr{P}_{i,j}^k$ be the kth edge along the path. The distance $d_{i,j}$ is defined as $\displaystyle\sum_{k \in \mathscr{P}_{i,j}} \frac{1}{P(M \mid \mathscr{P}_{i,j}^k)}$ to reflect the probability the edges along the path between i and j

within $\mathscr{G}_M$. The efficiency $E(\mathscr{G}_M)$ is thus determined by the inverse of the distances between all pairs of nodes in $\mathscr{G}_M$, and further weighted by the probability that both the start and terminal edges between the pairs belong to $\mathscr{G}_M$, as shown in (7).

$$E(\mathscr{G}_M) = \sum_{i \neq j \in \mathscr{G}_M} P(M \mid \mathscr{P}_{i,j}^0) P(M \mid \mathscr{P}_{i,j}^{-1}) \frac{1}{d_{i,j}} \tag{7}$$

The prior probability of each attack model, $P(M)$, is then derived by normalizing over the set of all current attack models. Letting M_{all} be the current set of attack models, the prior probability of each attack model is given by (8).

$$P(M) = \frac{E(\mathscr{G}_M)}{\sum_{M_i \in M_{all}} E(\mathscr{G}_{M_i})} \tag{8}$$

The *attack behavior model* is defined as a collection of feature probability distributions. The probability $P(\mathbf{Z}(u,v,\tau) \mid M)$ can be viewed as the likelihood of Model M exhibiting the attack features $\mathbf{Z}(u,v,\tau)$ shown on the edge $e_{(u,v)}$ during the time interval τ. The following temporal and spatial features are candidates to be incorporated into the overall framework.

Attack Intensity This is a continuous feature showing changes in the attack intensity over time. Time-invariant kernels may be used to define attack intensity as a function of the volume and types of malicious events. This feature can be used to differentiate the overall dynamics of attack activity.

Port Selection Entropy UDP and TCP port numbers reflect the service being or intended to be exploited. The number of feasible port numbers is significant, and focusing on specific port selections may not be necessarily useful in differentiating attack behaviors. Thus, we propose to examine the deterministic versus stochastic behavior of port selection exhibited through observed events. If the set of observed events indicate a certain port is being targeted, i.e., deterministic port selection, the port values can directly be compared to gauge the similarity of attack behavior. On the other hand, a variety of stochastic behaviors (Treurniet 2011; Zseby 2012; Shannon and Moore 2013) may be less obvious to treat: a malicious source may perform a "vertical" scan over many different destination ports; some attacks may randomly select source ports to obscure the behavior profile; "Backscatter" traffic generated from DDoS attacks may also give the appearance of random port selecting. In the case of stochastic port selection, a comparison of the actual port values is unlikely to be meaningful.

Let $\mathscr{P}$ be the random variable on taking a specific port number, $P(D)$ the probability of making a deterministic port selection, and $P(S)$ the probability of making a stochastic port selection. $P(D)$ and $P(S)$ are estimated separately for the source and destination ports, and together fill the hypothesis space for a feature called *port selection entropy* as shown in (9). The formulation is driven by the intuition that the actual value of $\mathscr{P}$ is not important if the port is chosen stochastically.

$$P(\mathscr{P} = X) = P(S) + P(\mathscr{P} = X \mid D)P(D) \tag{9}$$

Graph Position The graph position feature represents the relevance of the malicious activity shown on $e_{(u,v)}$ with respect to each critical asset and the models already identified relevant to the asset. This is the same concept as the relevance defined for $P(M)$ but now for a single edge instead of assessing the entire subgraph associated with a model.

Attack Progression One of the most important features of network attack strategy is how it progresses and utilizes different types of exploits (e.g., CWE) over time. One can adopt the attack models illustrated earlier, e.g., DBN and VLMM, to represent this feature. The challenge is to ensure an efficient computation of $P(\mathbf{Z} \mid M)$. The algorithm discussed earlier in Sect. 3.1 is a likely candidate to be extended for the purpose here.

With the aforementioned spatial priori and attack features, we now turn to the attention on how to introduce new attack models. Bayesian classifier requires a set of hypotheses for the new evidences to be optimally matched to. A requirement here is to be able to recognize and introduce new attack behavior models as new events are observed. A novel *Generic Attack Model* is introduced as a hypothesis to compete against all empirically constructed models during the classification phase. This generic hypothesis intends to fit all behaviors with some modest probability, but not as well as a tailored empirical model. When new events are observed, the generic model is evaluated as a possible class. A higher posterior probability with the generic model suggests that none of the existing empirical models provide a probable explanation, and a new model should be introduced. This also applies to the initial start-up phase whereas the first events observed must be classified to the generic model, and will be used to create a new empirical model. Certainly, if one of the empirical models maximizes the posterior, the new events will be incorporated to update the corresponding empirical model. In effect, the result of unsupervised learning, creating clusters of behaviors based on observed data, has been reproduced with an online supervised approach, resulting in a semi-supervised learning framework.

The work presented by Strapp and Yang (2014) adopts the Generic Attack Model, the Spatial Prior, and the Port Selection Entropy and the Graph Position attack features, along with a few other network protocol oriented features. Figure 7 shows how well the observed events match to the models they are assigned, using a preliminary algorithm called ASMG that realizes part of the aforementioned online semi-supervised learning framework. The performance is plotted for various selections of targets in the CAIDA dataset (Aben et al. 2013). The results show that the framework outperforms a naïve 4-hop method that includes all traffic within a 4-hop perimeter from each target of interest. While this is not surprising, the fact that, in most cases, the observed events match with high 90 % likelihood to the empirically generated models demonstrates the great potential of the framework.

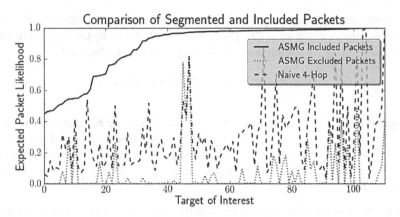

Fig. 7 Performance of ASMG Processing over many targets of interest [reproduced from Strapp and Yang (2014)]

A primary use of the aforementioned attack model generation framework is to reveal immediate threats to the network, based on the collective behaviors exhibited from the relevant events. The synthesized behavior models from the framework are expected to enhance existing threat prediction algorithms because the attack behavior is based on the relevant events leading to and surrounding the critical assets; this shift from an attacker-centric model generation to an asset-centric model generation is expected to reduce the likelihood that the predictions will be diluted by noise or obfuscated malicious activities. An extension of the current work by Strapp and Yang (2014) is to investigate an ensemble prediction based on the empirical models built upon probabilistic measures, including the temporal dynamics in attack intensity (when next batch of attack actions might happen), services targeted (port selection), and types of exploits (attack progression).

3.3   The Need of Data to Evaluate Network
Attack Prediction Systems

Network attack prediction, or more generally, predictive Cyber SA is in great need of data that can be used to evaluate the different prediction systems. Existing data sets, including DARPA Intrusion Detection dataset (MIT Lincoln Laboratory 2013), CAIDA Network Telescope dataset (Aben et al. 2013), the International Catch-the-Flag (iCTF) competition datasets (Vigna et al. 2013), and the DSheild Internet Storm Center data (DSheild 2013) are not suitable for comprehensive assessment of predictive Cyber SA capabilities. Without deviating much from the scope of this chapter, the following lists the requirements for data that can be used to evaluate attack prediction approaches.

- The data should cover a wide variety of attack strategies that employs multitudes of scanning and exploitations for different services.
- The data should reflect up-to-date vulnerabilities in a timely manner.

- The data should reflect a variety of network configurations and scales.
- The data should reflect a wide range of attacker skill set, including the use of various obfuscation techniques and zero-day attacks.

It is clearly not an easy task to produce and maintain real-world data sets that satisfy the above requirements. One solution is to develop a simulation framework that is capable of producing synthetic data based on up-to-date system vulnerabilities, and allows users to specify a spectrum of network configurations, attack behaviors, and skill sets. Limited works on cyber attack simulation were conducted by Cohen (1999), Park et al. (2001), and Kotenko and Man'kov (2003) between late 1990s and early 2000s. It was, however, not until 2007 when Kuhl et al. (2007) proposed a simulation framework for the purpose of generating data for Cyber SA systems. Extending from Kuhl et al. (2007), Moskal et al. (2013, 2014) developed a more completed simulator that consists of an algorithmic core and four context models: Virtual Terrain version 2 (VT.2), Vulnerability Hierarchy (VH), Scenario Guiding Template (SGT), and Attack Behavior Model (ABM). This simulator simultaneously generates multiple attack sequences with user specified network configurations, attack scenarios, and parameterized hacking behaviors. Each attack sequence may contain one or many attack actions, each of which is reported with both the ground truth and sensor reports. One attack action can be associated with zero, one, or multiple observed events, depending on the sensor placement and capabilities, as well as whether the action reflects zero-day attacks. Figure 8 shows the architectural view of the simulator developed by Moskal et al. (2013, 2014).

It is also important to note the difficulty of evaluating prediction algorithms even with a common set of data. Due to the inherent uncertainty in predicting one or more

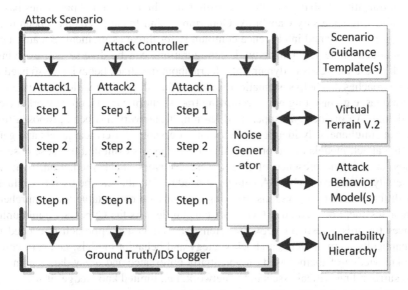

Fig. 8 Architecture of the network attack simulator [reproduced from Moskal et al. (2014)]

future events, the failure to predict a specific event in a single scenario is not necessarily an indicator of poor performance. In addition, an event that actually occurs in the scenario may not necessarily be the most likely to happen either. Therefore, it may be of particular interest to use mission impact assessment techniques in conjunction with the attack prediction algorithms to identify not only the most likely events to occur, but also plausible future events that may have a significant impact.

Additional research is still needed before a fully tested simulator can be used to produce reliable data for evaluating network attack prediction. Nevertheless, simulated/synthetic data seems to be the only viable solution to produce sustainable data year after year to match the fast-pace change of system vulnerabilities and attack strategies.

4 Summary

Cyber Situational Awareness requires anticipation of future attack actions projected from the observed malicious activities. Critical attacks often take multitudes of reconnaissance, exploitations, and obfuscation techniques to achieve the goal of cyber espionage and/or sabotage. The estimates of ongoing attack strategies can be used to provide a prediction of immediate threats on critical assets, enabling a Predictive Cyber Situational Awareness (SA). Network attack prediction takes many forms, ranging from analyzing potential attack paths based on network and system vulnerabilities (knowledge-of-us) to analyzing the attack behavior patterns (knowledge-of-them). Attack graphs can be used to correlate, hypothesize, and predict intrusion alerts. Dynamic Bayesian Network (DBN) allows the definition of causal relationship between observed events, and, more importantly, dynamic learning of transition probabilities through sufficient volume of data. Approaches based on estimating adversary Capability, Opportunity, and Intent (COI) have been used widely in military and intelligence community for threat assessment. Because network attack strategies and network configurations can be diverse and evolving, attack prediction needs to dynamically learn about the attack behavior. Also needed are approaches that help systematically analyze the effect of the various obfuscation techniques, e.g., inserting noise, removing traces, altering alerts, on network attack modeling. An online semi-supervised learning framework has been proposed that aims at simultaneously identifying relevant observables for critical assets and generating attack models based on the collective behaviors exhibited by these observables, even in the presence of IP spoofing. Network attack prediction, or more generally, predictive Cyber SA is in great need of data that can be used to evaluate the different prediction systems. Existing data sets are not suitable for comprehensive assessment of predictive Cyber SA capabilities. As the Cyber SA community moves towards a resilient network defense, an integrated approach is needed to dynamically learn and create attack strategy and behavior models, i.e., estimating the knowledge-of-them, based on potentially obfuscated and noisy data leading to and surrounding critical assets in the network, i.e., limited knowledge-of-us.

References

Aben, E. et al. The CAIDA UCSD Network Telescope Two Days in November 2008 Dataset. (Access Date: Dec. 2013).

Bell, T. C., Cleary, J. G., and Witten, I. H. *Text Compression*. Prentice Hall, 1990.

Chakrabarti, A., and Manimaran, G. Internet infrastructure security: a taxonomy. *IEEE Network*, 16(6):13–21, Nov/Dec 2002.

Cheng, B.-C., Liao, G.-T., Huang, C.-C., and Yu, M.-T. A novel probabilistic matching algorithm for multi-stage attack forecasts. *IEEE Transactions on Selected Areas in Communications*, 29(7):1438–1448, 2011.

Cheung, S., Lindqvist, U., and Fong, M. W. Modeling multistep cyber attacks for scenario recognition. In *Proceedings of DARPA Information Survivability Conference and Exposition*, volume 1, pages 284–292, April 2003.

Cipriano, C., Zand, A., Houmansadr, A., Kruegel, C., and Vigna, G. Nexat: A history-based approach to predict attacker actions. In *Proceedings of the 27th Annual Computer Security Applications Conference*, pages 383–392. ACM, 2011.

Cohen, F. Information system defences: A preliminary classification scheme. *Computers & Security*, 16(2):94–114, 1997.

Cohen, F. Simulating cyber attacks, defences, and consequences. *Computers & Security*, 18(6):479–518, 1999.

Daley, K., Larson, R., and Dawkins, J. A structural framework for modeling multi-stage network attacks. In *Proceedings of International Conference on Parallel Processing*, pages 5–10, 2002.

Debar, H., Dacier, M., and Wespi, A. Towards a taxonomy of intrusion-detection systems. *Computer Networks*, 31(8):805–822, 1999.

DSheild. Internet Storm Center. http://www.dshield.org/. (Access Date: Dec. 2013).

Du, H., and Yang, S. J. Characterizing transition behaviors in internet attack sequences. In *Proceedings of the 20th International Conference on Computer Communications and Networks (ICCCN)*, Maui HI, USA, August 1–4 2011.

Du, H., and Yang, S. J. Discovering collaborative cyber attack patterns using social network analysis. In *Proceedings of International Conference on Social Computing, Behavioral-Cultural Modeling and Prediction*, pages 129–136, College Park MD, USA, March 29–21 2011. Springer.

Du, H., and Yang, S. J. Temporal and spatial analyses for large-scale cyber attacks. In V.S. Subrahmanian, editor, *Handbook of Computational Approaches to Counterterrorism*, pages 559–578. Springer New York, 2013.

Du, H., and Yang, S. J. Probabilistic inference for obfuscated network attack sequences. In *Proceedings of IEEE/ISIF International Conference on Dependable Systems and Networks*, Atlanta, GA, June 23–26 2014.

Du, H., Liu, D. F., Holsopple, J., and Yang, S. J. Toward Ensemble Characterization and Projection of Multistage Cyber Attacks. In *Proceedings of the 19th International Conference on Computer Communications and Networks (ICCCN)*, Zurich, Switzerland, August 2–5 2010. IEEE.

Fava, D. S., Byers, S. R., and Yang, S. J. Projecting cyberattacks through variable-length markov models. *IEEE Transactions on Information Forensics and Security*, 3(3):359–369, September 2008.

Holsopple, J., Sudit, M., Nusinov, M., Liu, D., Du, H., and Yang, S. Enhancing Situation Awareness via Automated Situation Assessment. *IEEE Communications Magazine*, pages 146–152, March 2010.

Howard, J., and Longstaff, T. A common language for computer security incidents. Technical report, Sandia National Laboratories, 1998.

Jacquet, P., Szpankowski, W., and Apostol, I. A universal predictor based on pattern matching. *IEEE Transactions on Information Theory*, 48(6):1462–1472, June 2002.

King, S. T., Mao, Z. M., Lucchetti, D. G., and Chen, P. M. Enriching intrusion alerts through multi-host causality. In *Proceedings of the 2005 Network and Distributed System Security Symposium (NDSS'05)*, Washington D.C., February 2005.

Kotenko, I., and Man'kov, E. Experiments with simulation of attacks against computer networks. In Vladimir Gorodetsky, Leonard Popyack, and Victor Skormin, editors, *Computer Network*

Security, volume 2776 of *Lecture Notes in Computer Science*, pages 183–194. Springer Berlin Heidelberg, 2003.

Kuhl, M. E., Kistner, J., Costantini, K., and Sudit, M. Cyber attack modeling and simulation for network security analysis. In *Proceedings of the 39th Conference on Winter Simulation*, pages 1180–1188. IEEE Press, 2007.

Lane, T., and Brodley, C. Temporal sequence learning and data reduction for anomaly detection. *ACM Transactions on Information and System Security*, 2:295–331, 1999.

Latora, V., and Marchiori, M. Efficient behavior of small-world networks. *Phys. Rev. Lett.*, 87:198701, Oct 2001.

Lee, W., Stolfo, S. J., and Chan, P. K. Learning patterns from Unix process execution traces for intrusion detection. In *Proceedings of the workshop on AI Approaches to Fraud Detection and Risk Management*, pages 50–56, 1997.

MIT Lincoln Laboratory. DARPA intrusion detection data set (1998, 1999, 2000). http://www.ll. mit.edu/mission/communications/cyber/CSTcorpora/ideval/data/. (Access Date: Dec. 2013).

Moskal, S., Kreider, D., Hays, L., Wheeler, B., Yang, S. J., and Kuhl, M. Simulating attack behaviors in enterprise networks. In *Proceedings of IEEE Communications and Network Security*, Washington, DC, 2013.

Moskal, S., Wheeler, B., Kreider, D., and Kuhl, M., and Yang, S. J. Context model fusion for multistage network attack simulation. In *Proceedings of IEEE MILCOM*, Baltimore, MD, 2014.

Newman, M. E. J. Scientific collaboration networks. I. network construction and fundamental results. *Phys Rev E*, 64(1), July 2001.

Ning, P., Cui, Y., and Reeves, D. S. Analyzing intensive intrusion alerts via correlation. In *Lecture notes in computer science*, pages 74–94. Springer, 2002.

Ning, P., Xu, D., Healey, C. G., and Amant, R. S. Building attack scenarios through integration of complementary alert correlation methods. In *Proceedings of the 11th Annual Network and Distributed System Security Symposium (NDSS'04)*, pages 97–111, 2004.

Noel, S., and Jajodia, S. Advanced vulnerability analysis and intrusion detection through predictive attack graphs. *Critical Issues in C4I, Armed Forces Communications and Electronics Association (AFCEA) Solutions Series. International Journal of Command and Control*, 2009.

Noel, S., Robertson, E., and Jajodia, S. Correlating intrusion events and building attack scenarios through attack graph distances. In *Proceedings of 20th Annual Computer Security Applications Conference*, December 2004.

Park, J. S., Lee, J.-S., Kim, H. K., Jeong, J.-R., Yeom, D.-B., and Chi, S.-D. Secusim: A tool for the cyber-attack simulation. In *Information and Communications Security*, pages 471–475. Springer, 2001.

Phillips, C., and Swiler, L. P. A graph-based system for network-vulnerability analysis. In *Proceedings of the 1998 workshop on New security paradigms*, pages 71–79, Charlottesville, Virginia, United States, 1998.

Qin, X., and Lee, W. Attack plan recognition and prediction using causal networks. In *Proceedings of 20th Annual Computer Security Applications Conference*, pages 370–379. IEEE, December 2004.

Serfling, R.J. Probability inequalities for the sum in sampling without replacement. *The Annals of Statistics*, 2(1):39–48, 1974.

Shafer, G., editor. *A Mathematical Theory of Evidence*. Princeton University Press, 1976.

Shalizi, C. R., and Shalizi, K. L. Blind construction of optimal nonlinear recursive predictors for discrete sequences. In *Proceedings of the 20th Conference on Uncertainty in Artificial Intelligence*, pages 504–511, 2004.

Shannon, C., and Moore, D. Network Telescopes: Remote Monitoring of Internet Worms and Denial-of-Service Attacks. Technical report, The Cooperative Association for Internet Data Analysis (CAIDA), 2004. (Technical Presentation - Access Date: Dec. 2013).

Smets, P. The combination of evidence in the transferable belief model. *IEEE Transactions on Pattern Analysis and Machine Intelligence*, 12(5):447–458, May 1990.

Soldo, F., Le, A., and Markopoulou, A. Blacklisting Recommendation System: Using Spatio-Temporal Patterns to Predict Future Attacks. *IEEE Journal on Selected Areas in Communications*, 29(7):1423–1437, August 2011.

Steinberg, A. Open interaction network model for recognizing and predicting threat events. In *Proceedings of Information, Decision and Control (IDC) '07*, pages 285–290, Febuary 2007.

Stotz, A., and Sudit, M. INformation fusion engine for real-time decision-making (INFERD): A perceptual system for cyber attack tracking. In *Proceedings of 10th International Conference on Information Fusion*, July 2007.

Strapp, S., and Yang, S. J. Segmentating large-scale cyber attacks for online behavior model generation. In *Proceedings of International Conference on Social Computing, Behavioral-Cultural Modeling, and Prediction*, Washington, DC, April 1–4 2014.

Tidwell, T., Larson, R., Fitch, K., and Hale, J. Modeling internet attacks. In *Proceedings of the 2001 IEEE Workshop on Information Assurance and Security*, volume 59, 2001.

Treurniet, J. A Network Activity Classification Schema and Its Application to Scan Detection. *IEEE/ACM Tran. on Networking*, 19(5):1396–1404, October 2011.

Valeur, F., Vigna, G., Kruegel, C., and Kemmerer, R.A. A comprehensive approach to intrusion detection alert correlation. *IEEE Transactions on dependable and secure computing*, 1(3):146–169, 2004.

Vidalis, S., and Jones, A. Using vulnerability trees for decision making in threat assessment. Technical Report CS-03-2, University of Glamorgan, School of Computing, June 2003.

Vigna, G. et al. The iCTF Datasets from 2002 to 2010. http://ictf.cs.ucsb.edu/data.php. (Access Date: Dec. 2013).

Wang, L., Liu, A., and Jajodia, S. Using attack graphs for correlating, hypothesizing, and predicting intrusion alerts. *Computer Communications*, 29(15):2917–2933, 2006.

Xu, K., Wang, F., and Gu, L. Network-aware behavior clustering of Internet end hosts. In *Proceedings IEEE INFOCOM'11*, pages 2078–2086. IEEE, April 2011.

Yang, S. J., Stotz, A., Holsopple, J., Sudit, M., and Kuhl, M. High level information fusion for tracking and projection of multistage cyber attacks. *Elsevier International Journal on Information Fusion*, 10(1):107–121, 2009.

Ye, N., Zhang, Y., and Borror, C. M. Robustness of the markov-chain model for cyber-attack detection. *IEEE Transactions on Reliability*, 53:116–123, 2004.

Zseby, T. Comparable Metrics for IP Darkspace Analysis. In *Proceedings of 1st International Workshop on Darkspace and UnSolicited Traffic Analysis*, May 2012.

Metrics of Security

Yi Cheng, Julia Deng, Jason Li, Scott A. DeLoach, Anoop Singhal, and Xinming Ou

1 Introduction

Discussion of challenges and ways of improving Cyber Situational Awareness dominated our previous chapters. However, we have not yet touched on how to quantify any improvement we might achieve. Indeed, to get an accurate assessment of network security and provide sufficient Cyber Situational Awareness (CSA), simple but meaningful metrics—the focus of the Metrics of Security chapter—are necessary. The adage, "what can't be measured can't be effectively managed," applies here. Without good metrics and the corresponding evaluation methods, security analysts and network operators cannot accurately evaluate and measure the security status of their networks and the success of their operations. In particular, this chapter explores two distinct issues: (i) how to define and use metrics as quantitative characteristics to represent the security state of a network, and (ii) how to define and use metrics to measure CSA from a defender's point of view.

Y. Cheng (✉) • J. Deng • J. Li
Intelligent Automation, Inc., 15400 Calhoun Dr., Rockville, MD 20855, USA
e-mail: ycheng@i-a-i.com; hdeng@i-a-i.com; jli@i-a-i.com

S.A. DeLoach • X. Ou
Kansas State University, 234 Nichols Hall, Manhattan, KS 66506, USA
e-mail: sdeloach@ksu.edu; xou@ksu.edu

A. Singhal
National Institute of Standards and Technology, 100 Bureau Dr.,
Gaithersburg, MD 20899, USA
e-mail: anoop.singhal@nist.gov

© Springer International Publishing Switzerland 2014
A. Kott et al. (eds.), *Cyber Defense and Situational Awareness*,
Advances in Information Security 62, DOI 10.1007/978-3-319-11391-3_13

To provide sufficient CSA and ensure mission success in enterprise network environments, security analysts need to continuously monitor network operations and user activities, quickly identify suspicious behaviors and recognize malicious activities, and mitigate potential cyber impacts in a timely manner. However, most existing security analysis tools and approaches focus on system and/or application level. The massive amounts of security-related data make these approaches not only labor intensive, but also prone to error while providing users a "big picture" of their current mission operations, network status, and the overall cyber situation. Security analysts need more sophisticated and systematic methods to quantitatively evaluate network vulnerabilities, predict attack risk and potential impacts, assess proper actions to minimize business damages, and ensure mission success in a hostile environment. As a natural descendant of this requirement, security metrics are—very important for CSA, coordinated network defense, and mission assurance analysis. They can provide a better understanding of the adequacy of security controls, and help security analysts effectively identify which critical assets to focus their limited resources on in order to ensure mission success.

For CSA and mission assurance analysis, security metrics need to be aligned not only with the industry standards for computer and network security management, but also with the overall organizational and business goals in enterprise environments. This chapter discusses the methodology to effectively identify, define, and apply simple but meaningful metrics for comprehensive network security and mission assurance analysis. Focusing on enterprise networks, we will explore security tools and metrics that have been developed, or need to be developed, to provide security and mission analysts the required capabilities to better understand current (and near future) cyber situation and security status of their network and operations. For instance, is there any vulnerability on the system? Is there any (ongoing) attack in the network? What (system/application/service) has been compromised? How can the (potential) risk be measured? What is the most likely consequence of the attack? Can we prevent it? How much (storage/communication/operational) capacity will be lost due to the attack? Is the overall (or a major portion of) mission/task/operation still accomplished? Good defined metrics can help users answer these questions quickly and quantitatively. Users can then focus on the higher-level view of cyber situations, make informed decisions to select the best course of action, effectively mitigate the potential threats, and ensure mission success even in a hostile environment.

2 Security Metrics for Cyber Situational Awareness

2.1 Security Metrics: the What, Why, and How

2.1.1 What Is a "Security Metric"?

As defined by the National Institute of Standards and Technology (NIST), metrics are tools that are designed to facilitate decision-making and improve performance and accountability through collection, analysis, and reporting of relevant performance-related data. Security metrics can be considered as a standard (or system) used for quantitatively measuring an organization's security posture. Security metrics are essential to comprehensive network security and CSA management. Without good metrics, analysts cannot answer many security related questions. Some examples of such questions include "Is our network more secure today than it was yesterday?" or "Have the changes of network configurations improved our security posture?"

The ultimate aim of security metrics is to ensure business continuity (or mission success) and minimize business damage by preventing or minimizing the potential impact of cyber incidents. To achieve this goal, organizations need to take into consideration all information security dimensions, and provide stakeholders detailed information about their network security management and risk treatment processes.

2.1.2 Why Security Metrics for CSA?

We cannot effectively manage or improve CSA if we cannot accurately measure it. Traditional network security management practices mainly focus on the information level and treat all network components equally. Although valuable, these approaches lack meaningful metrics and risk assessment capabilities when applied to comprehensive CSA and mission assurance analysis. Specifically, they cannot quantitatively evaluate or determine the exact impacts of security incidents on the attainment of critical mission objectives. When an attack happens, it is difficult for current solutions to answer mission assurance related security questions such as: "Is there any impact on mission X if host A was compromised?", "Can some portion of mission X still be accomplished?", "What is the probability of successful completion for mission X currently?", or "What can we do to ensure mission X's success?"

To answer these questions, security metrics and advanced mission-to-asset mapping, modeling and evaluation technologies are required. The literature contains several recently proposed metrics for information and network security measurement, such as the number of vulnerabilities or detected cyber incidents in a network, the average response time to a security event, etc. Although these metrics can evaluate network security from certain aspects, they cannot provide sufficient network vulnerability assessment, attack risk analysis and prediction, mission impact mitigation, and quantitative situational awareness, in terms of mission assurance. We argue that to ensure mission survival in a hostile environment, security metrics should be adjusted and tuned to fit a specific organization or situation. In other words, good metrics must be meaningful to specific organizational goals and key performance indicators. Security analysts not only review metrics currently in place, but also need to ensure they are aligned with the specific organizational and business goals.

2.1.3 How to Measure and Model Network Security?

To determine the general security level of an analyzed network, a common process needs to be realized: First, security experts identify what should be measured. Then they organize the involved variables in a manageable and meaningful way. After that, repeatable formulas should be built to illustrate the snapshot status of security and how it changes over time. For network and/or system security measurement, most existing approaches are based on *risk analysis*, in which security risk is expressed as a function of threats, vulnerabilities, and potential impacts (or expected loss).

$$Risk = Threat \times Vulnerability \times Impact \tag{1}$$

Equation 1 is an informal way of stating that security risk is a *function* of threats, vulnerabilities, and potential impact. It is often used in the literature for expressing the necessity and purpose of network security evaluation. When applied to solving a real problem, it is still hard to quantify each variable in Eq. 1 with meaningful values. For example, how should one numerically express a threat? What is the cost of a vulnerability? How should one calculate the impact or expected loss? When we multiply these three variables, how should risk be denoted in a way that can be translated into an action item?

In order to quantify different portions of Eq. 1, Lindstrom (2005) further introduced a number of underlying elements required for general security (risk) analysis. Although they may not completely solve all the problems, these underlying elements still provide security analysts a better understanding and insight to develop meaningful metrics and practical solutions for general network security measurements. Some of the useful elements introduced by Lindstrom (2005) are listed below:

- **Calculation of Asset Value:** Based on the values of different assets (e.g., hardware, software and data), enterprises can focus on their real security needs and allocate adequate resources. As enterprises routinely place values on their information assets, the value of an asset could be defined as the amount of IT spending over a time period (e.g., operations and maintenance) plus the depreciation or amortization value of the assets (hardware and software). For asset value calculation, quantifiable values need to be assigned to each asset for objective evaluation and comparison.
- **Calculation of Potential Loss:** Asset value is linked, but not tied directly to the loss. We need to consider the type of compromise when evaluating the potential losses. Generally there are five distinct types of compromise: *confidentiality breaches, integrity breaches, availability breaches, productivity breaches*, and *liability breaches* (Lindstrom 2005). Note that asset value may not be the only thing that can be lost. Other potential losses, such as the incident costs should also be carefully considered.
- **Measurement of Security Spending:** Although measuring enterprise-wide security spending is difficult, it is important for security management. Security spending is often divided among various business units and departments, as well as being lumped in with network and infrastructure spending. Finding security spending and separating it from other budget items is a daunting task.

- **Attack Risk Analysis:** Defining and modeling risk for an enterprise is another difficult but important task. Lindstrom (2005) lists three common forms of risks: *manifest risk* (the ratio of malicious events to total events), *inherent risk* (the likelihood that system configurations will contribute to a compromise), and *contributory risk* (a measure of process errors or mistakes made during the operations).

None of the above elements is designed to completely answer questions related to security metrics and measurements, but the methodologies outlined here give us a foundation for gathering useful data and applying it to our specific goals and expectations. Based on this basic knowledge, researchers can further define more accurate and complete security metrics, assign proper values to their security formulas, and develop practical evaluation models to quantitatively analyze and measure the security status of their computer network and systems.

2.2 Security Measurement for Situational Awareness in Cyberspace

Generally speaking, security measurement for CSA needs to carefully consider two distinct possible issues: (i) How to define and use metrics as quantitative characteristics to represent the security state of a computer system or network, and (ii) How to define and use metrics to measure CSA from a defender's point of view. This section will briefly review state-of-the-art security metrics and discuss the challenges to define and apply good metrics for comprehensive CSA and mission assurance analysis.

2.2.1 Quantification and Measurement of Traditional Situational Awareness

A general definition of Situational Awareness (SA) is given by Endsley (1988): "SA is the perception of the elements of the environment within a volume of time and space, the comprehension of their meaning, and the projection of their status in the near future." Due to its multivariate nature, a considerable challenge is posed for SA quantification and measurement. Traditional SA measurement techniques can be generally considered either based on "product-oriented" direct measurement (e.g., objective real-time probes or subjective questionnaires assessing perceived SA), or the "process-oriented" inference of operator behavior or performance (Fracker 1991a; b).

According to Bolstad and Cuevas (2010), existing SA measurement approaches can be further classified into the following categories:

- **Objective Measures**: Comparing an individual's perceptions of the situation or environment to some "ground truth" reality (Jones and Endsley 2000). This type of assessment provides a direct measure of SA and does not require operators or observers to make judgments about situational knowledge on the basis of incomplete information. Generally, objective measures can be gathered in three ways: (i) in real-time as the task is completed, (ii) during an interruption in task performance, or (iii) post-test following completion of the task (Endsley 1995).
- **Subjective Measures:** Asking individuals to rate their own or the observed SA of individuals on an anchored scale (Strater et al. 2001). Subjective measures of SA are relatively straightforward and easy to administer, but they also suffer from several limitations. For example, individuals are often unaware of information they do not know, and they cannot fully exploit the multivariate nature of SA to provide detailed diagnostics (Taylor 1989).
- **Performance Measures:** Assuming that better performance usually indicates better SA, performance measures infer SA from performance outcomes. Bolstad and Cuevas (2010) list a set of commonly used performance metrics, including the quantity of output or productivity level, time to perform the task or respond to an event, the accuracy of the response, and the number of errors committed. In addition, good SA does not always lead to good performance, and poor SA does not always lead to poor performance (Endsley 1990). Performance measures should be used in conjunction with other measures for more accurate assessment.
- **Behavioral Measures:** Based on the assumption that good actions usually follow from good SA and vice-versa, behavioral measures infer SA from individuals' actions. Behavioral measures are subjective in nature, as they primarily rely on observer ratings. To reduce this limitation, observers need to make judgments based on good SA indicators that are more readily observable (Strater et al. 2001; Matthews et al. 2000).

Note that the multivariate nature of SA significantly complicates its quantification and measurement. A particular metric may only tap into one aspect of the operator's SA. Durso et al. (1995), Endsley et al. (1998), and Vidulich (2000) also found that different types of SA measures do not always correlate strongly with each other. In this case, multi-faceted approaches that combine distinct but highly related measures should be used for comprehensive SA measurement, as they can take advantage of the strengths of each measure while minimizing the inherent limitations (Harwood et al. 1988).

2.2.2 State-of-the-Art Security Measurement Techniques

Researchers have made many attempts to measure SA in cyberspace over the last few years. NIST provided an overview of existing metrics for network security and SA measurement in Jansen (2009). Hecker (2008) distinguished the lower level metrics (based on well-ordered low-level quantitative system parameters) from the higher level metrics (e.g., conformity distance, attack graph or attack surface based estimations). Meland and Jensen (2008) presented a Security-Oriented Software Development Framework (SODA) to adapt security techniques and filter information. Heyman et al. (2008) also presented their work on using security patterns to combine security metrics.

To define software security metrics, Wang et al. (2009) proposed a new approach based on vulnerabilities in the software systems and their impacts on software quality. They used Common Vulnerabilities and Exposures (CVE) (http://cve. mitre.org/cve/) and Common Vulnerability Scoring System (CVSS) (http://www. first.org/cvss/) in their metric definition and calculation. An attack surface based metric was further proposed by Manadhata and Wing (2011) to measure software security. They formalized the notion of a system's attack surface, and used it as an indicator of the system's security. By measuring and reducing attack surfaces, software developers can effectively mitigate their software's security risks.

Petri nets (PN) have also been discussed as a useful formalism for network security evaluation in literature. The idea of using PN for attack analysis was first introduced by McDermott (2000). Several papers consider the use of Colored PN (CPN) for attack modeling. Zhou et al. (2003) discussed the advantages of CPNs and described a process for mapping an attack tree to a CPN. Dahl (2005) provided a more detailed discussion of the advantages of CPN when it was applied to model concurrency and attack progress.

For CSA and risk assessment in enterprise networks, an ontology-based Cyber Assets to Missions and Users (CAMUS) mechanism was proposed by Goodall (2009). It can automatically discover the relationship between cyber assets, missions and users to facilitate cyber incident mission impact assessment. The basic idea of CAMUS came from the Air Force Situation Awareness Model (AFSAM) (Salerno 2008; Salerno et al. 2005), which described how data is taken to become information and consumed by analysts to further improve the situation management. Tadda et al. (2006) refined the general AFSAM and applied it directly to the cyber domain, resulting in the CSA model. Within the CSA model, the knowledge required for situation management is an accurate understanding of how operations are impacted when there are degradations and compromises in the cyber infrastructure. Grounded in the CSA model, Holsopple et al. (2008) developed a Virtual Terrain that models the network by manually taking mission context into account.

Grimaila et al. (2008) shifted their focus to information asset situation management. They proposed a Cyber Damage Assessment Framework that requires the manual definition and prioritization of both operational processes and information assets. Gomez et al. (2008) proposed an approach for automated assignment of intelligence, surveillance and reconnaissance (ISR) assets to specific military missions. Their Missions and Means Framework (MMF) ontology includes similar concepts in CAMUS, such as missions, operations, tasks, capabilities and systems. Lewis et al. (2008) also proposed a mission reference model to tackle the mapping of cyber assets to missions, based on a mathematical constraint satisfaction approach.

To support enterprise level security risk analysis, Singhal et al. (2010) provided a security ontology framework as a portable and easy-to-share knowledge base. Based on this framework, analysts will know which threats endanger which assets and what countermeasures can lower the probability of the occurrence of an attack. Alberts et al. (2005) proposed a risk-based assessment protocol, called Mission Assurance Analysis Protocol (MAAP), to qualitatively evaluate current conditions and determine whether a project or process is on track for success. MAAP can produce a rich, in-depth view of current conditions and circumstances affecting a project's potential success, but its risk assessment is a complex and time-consuming process. Watters et al. (2009) proposed a Risk-to-Mission Assessment Process (RiskMAP) to connect business objectives to network nodes. RiskMAP first models key features of a corporation (from business objectives, operational tasks, information assets, to network nodes that store, send and make the information available), and then uses the same model to map network level risks to the upper level business objectives for risk analysis and impact mitigation.

Musman et al. (2010) gave an outline of the technical roadmap for mission impact assessment in a MITRE report. They focused on cyber mission impact assessment (CMIA) and tried to link network and information technology (IT) capabilities to an organization's business processes (missions). Grimaila et al. (2009) discussed general design concepts of a system that provides the decision makers with notifications on cyber incidents and their potential impacts on missions. Several approaches based on attack graphs were also investigated for automated attack detection and risk analysis (Noel et al. 2004; Qin and Lee 2004; Cheung et al. 2003).

Jakobson (2011) further proposed a logical and computational attack model for cyber impact assessment. In his framework, a multi-level information structure, called "cyber-terrain," was introduced to represent cyber assets, services, and their inter-dependencies. The dependencies between the cyber terrain and missions are represented by an impact dependency graph. Using these graphical models, both direct impacts and the propogation of cyber impacts on missions through the inter-connected assets and services can be calculated. In Kotenko et al. (2006), the authors proposed a new approach for network security evaluation, based on comprehensive simulation of malefactors' actions, construction of attack graphs, and computation of different security metrics. A software tool was offered for vulnerability analysis and security assessment at various stages of a life cycle of computer networks.

2.2.3 Security Measurement for Enterprise CSA: Challenges & Potential Solutions

State-of-the-art technologies provide useful descriptive information on security analysis, mission modeling, and situation management. While they are quite valuable for security measurement in various situations, existing approaches still face several challenges when applied to CSA and mission assurance assessment in enterprise network environments, due to the lack of meaningful security metrics and efficient evaluation methods.

Briefly speaking, existing methods have suffered from the following limitations that reduce their usefulness and effectiveness for CSA and mission assurance analysis:

- Lack of real-time CSA
- Lack of understanding of impacts of cyber events on high level mission operations
- Lack of quantitative metrics and measures for comprehensive security assessment
- Lack of incorporating human (analyst) cognition into cyber-physical situational awareness
- Lack of mission assurance policy

Table 1 compares current technologies and systems developed for mission asset mapping and modeling, cyber-attack and intrusion detection, risk analysis and prediction, as well as for damage assessment and mission impact mitigation. Each method has its own strength and limitations. When applied for enterprise network CSA, mission assurance assessment and coordinated network defense, advance technologies, mathematical models and evaluation algorithms are still required to answer the following questions:

- How to identify and represent mission composition and dependency relationships?
- How to derive the dependency relationships between mission elements and cyber assets?
- As a single vulnerability may enable widespread compromises in an enterprise, how to quickly identify the start point of an attack and predict its potential attack path?
- How to assess the direct impact and propagation of cyber incidents on high level mission elements and operations?
- How to systematically represent and model the identified inter- and intra- dependency relationships between major elements or components involved in cyber mission assurance?
- How to define and develop quantitative metrics and measures for meaningful cyber situational awareness, enterprise security management and mission assurance analysis?

Table 1 State-of-the-art approaches for CSA

Approach	Technology Strength	Developer	Limitations
CAMUS	Ontology fusion based cyber assets to missions and users mapping	Applied Visions, Inc.	Centralized approach
			Lack of cyber impact assessment
			Lack of mission asset prioritization
MAAP	Mission assurance and operational risk analysis in complex work processes	Carnegie Mellon University	Centralized approach
			Focus on operational risk analysis
			Lack of mission asset dependencies
RiskMAP	Risk-to-mission assessment at network and business objectives levels	MITRE	Centralized approach
			Lack of mission asset dependencies
Ranked Attack Graph	Identifying critical assets based on page rank and reachability analysis on attack graphs	Carnegie Mellon University	Lack of mission models
			Cannot analyze cyber impacts on high level missions
CMIA	Cyber mission impact assessment based on military mission models	MITRE	Centralized approach
			Lack of cyber impact analysis
			Lack of mission asset prioritization

To address these challenges, key technologies such as quantitative and meaningful security metrics, efficient mission-to-asset mapping and modeling methods, and the corresponding risk assessment and impact mitigation mechanisms, need to be further investigated and developed. In this chapter, we will introduce some potential solutions and results of our initial study that leverages and extends recent advances in CSA, mission assurance, common vulnerability assessment, and enterprise security management. As a starting point, our study focuses on developing an integrated framework for real-time CSA and mission assurance analysis in enterprise environments. To achieve this objective, a group of simple but meaningful metrics and corresponding evaluation methods were investigated for three specific use cases: (i) network vulnerability and attack risk assessment, (ii) cyber impact and mission relevance analysis, and (iii) asset criticality analysis and prioritization.

Table 2 lists a set of security and performance metrics, mainly focusing on network vulnerability assessment, attack risk evaluation, and mission impact analysis. Each metric defined in Table 2 attempts to answer a specific question related to computer/network security, system performance, or mission assurance. For instance, the *Vulnerable Host Percentage* (*VHP*) metric tries to answer how many hosts could be compromised in the worst case. The *Average Length of Attack Paths* (*ALAP*) metric attempts to answer the typical effort required for an attacker to violate a security policy. Obviously, each metric has shortcomings if only used by itself for network security analysis. For example, the *Shortest Attack Path* (*SAP*) metric ignores the number of ways an attacker may violate a security policy; the *ALAP*

Table 2 Common security and performance metrics for CSA

Metric	Acronym	Description	Score/Value
Asset capacity	AC	The (remained) capacity of a cyber asset (after being attacked or compromised)	[0, 1]: 0 means not operational; 1 means fully operational
Average length of attack paths	ALAP	The average effort to penetrate a network, or compromise a system/ service; evaluated by attack graphs	n: the average length of potential attack paths
Compromised host percentage	CHP	The percentage of compromised hosts in a network at time t	[0, 1]: 0 means no compromise; 1 means all compromised
Exploit probability	EP	How easy (or hard) to exploit a vulnerability? Could be measured by CVSS exploitability sub-score	[0, 1]: 0 means hard to exploit; 1 means easy to be exploited
Impact factor	IF	The impact level of a vulnerability after being exploited, could be measured by CVSS impact sub-score	[0, 1]: 0 means no impact; 1 means totally destroyed
Number of attack paths	NAP	The number of potential attack paths in a network, could be evaluated based on attack graphs	n: the number of potential attack paths
Network preparedness	NP	Is a network ready to carry out a mission? E.g., all required services are supported by available cyber assets	[0, 1]: 0 means not ready; 1 means fully ready
Network zresilience	NR	The percentage of compromised systems/services that can be replaced/ recovered by backup/alternative systems/services	[0, 1]: 0 means cannot recover; 1 means can be fully recovered
Operational capacity	OC	The (remained) operational capacity of a system/service (after being affected by a direct attack or indirect impact)	[0, 1]: 0 means not operational; 1 means fully operational
Resource redundancy	RR	Is there any redundant (backup) resources assigned or allocated for a critical task/operation?	0 or 1: 0 means no backup system; 1 means at least 1 backup system
Service availability	SA	The availability of a required service to support a particular mission, task, or operation	0 or 1: 0 means not available; 1 means service is available
Shortest attack path	SAP	The minimal effort to penetrate a network, or compromise a system or service, evaluated by attack graphs	n: the shortest length of potential attack paths
Severity score	SS	The severity/risk of a vulnerability if it was successfully exploited, could be measured based on CVSS score	[0, 1]: 0 means no risk; 1 means extremely high risk
Vulnerable host percentage	VHP	The percentage of vulnerable hosts in a network	[0, 1]: 0 means no vulnerable host; 1 means all hosts are vulnerable

metric fails to adequately account for the number of ways an attacker may violate a security policy; while the *Number of Attack Paths* (*NAP*) metric ignores the effort associated with violating a security policy. Therefore, multiple security metrics must be used together to provide users with a comprehensive view and understanding of cyber situational awareness and mission assurance.

Note that the security and performance metrics, as well as the corresponding evaluation mechanisms, introduced in this chapter are not trying to completely solve enterprise CSA quantification and measurement problems. The objective here is to help security analysts to have a better understanding and insight to further develop their own good and meaningful metrics, as well as practical solutions, for their specific questions related to CSA, mission assurance, or enterprise network security defense.

3 Network Vulnerability and Attack Risk Assessment

Although the ultimate goal for enterprise network security is to identify and remove all network and host vulnerabilities, it is infeasible to achieve this goal in practice. For instance, if an organization leverages Commercial-Off-the-Shelf (COTS) software to operate its network, it will expose itself to the vulnerabilities that the software possesses. Issues such as slow and unstable released patches may cause the organization to operate its network with known vulnerabilities. Through these vulnerabilities, attackers may successfully compromise a particular system via a single attack action, or penetrate a network via a series of attack actions. Therefore, network vulnerability and attack risk assessment is the first step for enterprise security management and cyber situational awareness.

3.1 Security Metrics for Vulnerability Assessment

3.1.1 Common Vulnerability Assessment on Computer System

In literature, the Common Vulnerability Scoring System (CVSS) (http://www.first. org/cvss/) has been widely adopted as the primary method for assessing the severity of computer system security vulnerabilities. As an industry standard, CVSS ensures repeatable accurate measurement. It also enables users to see the underlying vulnerability characteristics that were used in its quantitative models to generate the scores. CVSS attempts to establish a measure of how much concern a vulnerability warrants compared to other vulnerabilities. It is composed of three metric groups: *Base*, *Temporal*, and *Environmental*. Each group consists of a set of metrics, as shown in Fig. 1.

In particular, base metrics define criticality of the vulnerability, temporal metrics represent urgency of the vulnerability that changes over time, and environmental

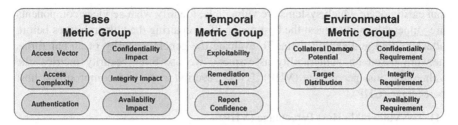

Fig. 1 CVSS metric groups (http://www.first.org/cvss/cvss-guide)

metrics represent the characteristics of a vulnerability that are relevant and unique to a particular user's environment. Each group produces a numeric score (ranging from 0 to 10) and a compressed textual representation that reflects the values used to derive the score. The CVSS complete guide (http://www.first.org/cvss/cvss-guide) gives the detailed descriptions of these metric groups:

- **Base:** representing "intrinsic and fundamental characteristics of a vulnerability that are constant over time and user environments,"
- **Temporal:** representing "characteristics of a vulnerability that change over time but not among user environments," and
- **Environmental:** representing "characteristics of a vulnerability that are relevant and unique to a particular user's environment."

Basically, for each metric group, a particular equation is used to weigh the corresponding metrics and produce a score (ranged from 0 to 10) based on a series of measurements and assessments by security experts, with the score 10 representing the most severe vulnerability. Specifically, when the base metrics are assigned values, the base equation calculates a score ranging from 0 to 10, and creates a vector. This vector is a text string that contains the values assigned to each metric, and facilitates the "open" nature of the framework. Users can understand how the score was derived and, if desired, confirm the validity of each metric. More details on base, temporal and environmental equations, as well as the calculation methods, can be found in the CVSS complete guide (http://www.first.org/cvss/cvss-guide).

3.1.2 General Metrics for Network Vulnerability Assessment

The National Vulnerability Database (NVD) (http://nvd.nist.gov/) provides CVSS scores for almost all known vulnerabilities. Various open source or commercial vulnerability scanners, such as the Nessus Security Scanner (http://www.tenable.com/products/nessus), the Open Vulnerability Assessment System (OpenVAS) (http://www.openvas.org/), and the Microsoft Baseline Security Analyzer (MBSA) (http://www.microsoft.com/en-us/download/details.aspx?id=7558), can be used to feasibly identify vulnerabilities in a network. Regularly and periodically performing vulnerability scan and assessment is critical for enterprise security management, as it can easily locate which systems are vulnerable, identify what services/components are vulnerable, and suggest the best method for repairing the vulnerabilities before attackers find and exploit them. To evaluate the general security of an enterprise network based on vulnerability assessment, we use three security metrics: the vulnerable host percentage (VHP), CVSS severity score, and compromised host percentage (CHP).

(1) The Vulnerable Host Percentage (VHP)

This metric represents the overall security level of a network. The number of vulnerable hosts can be obtained by periodically scanning a network via vulnerability scanning tools such as Nessus. The equation for this metric is given below, where G represents an intended network, V is the set of vulnerable hosts, and H is the set of all hosts in the network.

$$VHP(G) = 100 \times \frac{\sum\limits_{v \in V \subseteq H} v}{\sum\limits_{h \in H} h} \qquad (2)$$

(2) Severity Score of a single vulnerability i (SS_i)

After identifying vulnerabilities that exist in a network, we need to know the severity score of each identified vulnerability based on CVSS. As shown in Table 3, this metric indicates the severity of a certain vulnerability, and how to handle it accordingly.

(3) Compromised Host Percentage (CHP)

This metric indicates the percentage of hosts that have been compromised in a network. Here, a host compromise is defined as the attacker having obtained user- or administrator- level privilege on the intended host. A higher CHP value means more hosts are compromised. Our general goal is to minimize the CHP metric. For instance, an organization should have stricter firewall rules and user access policies so that it is hard to exploit the vulnerabilities (from both outside and inside). The equation for this metric is given below, where C is the set of compromised hosts.

$$CHP(G) = 100 \times \frac{\sum\limits_{c \in C \subseteq H} c}{\sum\limits_{h \in H} h} \qquad (3)$$

Table 3 Severity levels of vulnerabilities

CVSS score	Severity level	Guidance
7.0 through 10.0	High severity	Must be corrected with the highest priority
4.0 through 6.9	Medium severity	Must be corrected with high priority
0.0 through 3.9	Low severity	Encouraged, but not required, to correct these vulnerabilities

3.1.3 Attack Graph Based Network Vulnerability Assessment

In cyberspace, attackers may successfully compromise a particular system via a single attack action or penetrate a network via a series of attack actions. A series of attack actions is usually referred to as a multi-step attack or chained exploit. A multi-step attack leverages the interdependencies among multiple vulnerabilities to violate a network's security policy. In the literature, the multi-step attack can be feasibly represented and modeled via various attack graph models (Ou et al. 2006; Sheyner et al. 2002; Ammann et al. 2002). Attack graphs is a widely adopted technology in analyzing the causal relationships between cyber-attack events in which each node represents a particular state of a cyber asset in a network and each edge represents a possible state transition. In our framework, attack graph based metrics are also defined for network-level vulnerability assessment.

(1) The Number of Attack Paths (NAP)

This metric indicates how many ways an attacker can penetrate the network or compromise a critical system. The equation for this metric is given below, where AG represents network attack graphsand P is the set of all potential attack paths in the corresponding attack graph.

$$NAP(AG) = \sum_{p \in P \subseteq AG} p \tag{4}$$

(2) The Average Length of Attack Paths (ALAP)

This metric represents the average amount of effort that an attacker needs to take in order to penetrate the network or compromise a critical system. The equation for this metric is given below, where $L(p)$ represents the length of attack path p.

$$ALAP(AG) = \frac{\sum_{p \in P \subseteq AG} L(p)}{\sum_{p \in P \subseteq AG} p} \tag{5}$$

(3) The Shortest Attack Path (SAP)

This metric indicates the least amount of effort that an attacker can take to penetrate the network or compromise a critical system. The metric is given below.

$$SAP(AG) = \min\{L(p) \mid p \in P \subseteq AG\} \tag{6}$$

3.2 Modeling and Measurement of Attack Risk

3.2.1 Attack Risk Prediction

To quantitatively evaluate cyber impacts on high level missions, mission related elements such as cyber assets, hardware devices, and mission tasks should be added to the risk analysis model. Leveraging the basic analysis method and evaluation

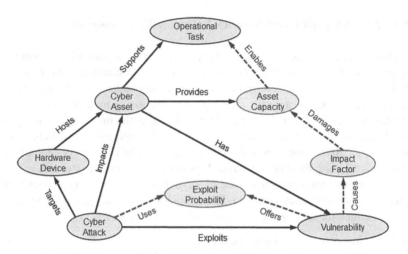

Fig. 2 Attack risk prediction model for mission impact analysis

process proposed by Jakobson (2011), we extend our attack risk prediction model with cyber assets, hardware devices, and mission elements in our initial study. We believe this model can be used to quantitatively evaluate the severity of an identified vulnerability and analyze the consequence if a mission critical asset was attacked or compromised. Using our initial study as the starting point, more complete and concrete analysis models can be further developed.

Our initial study focused on modeling (i) the logical relations that allow us to model the propagation of the impacts through the network and (ii) the computational relations that allow us to calculate the level of those impacts. The conceptual structure of the extended attack model is illustrated by Fig. 2. It contains eight conceptual nodes: *Cyber Attack, Hardware Device, Cyber Asset,* (Asset) *Vulnerability, Operational Task, Asset Capacity, Exploit Probability* and *Impact Factor* (of Vulnerability), as well as the corresponding relations among them.

As pointed by Jakobson (2011), the *Exploit Probability* (*EP*) and *Impact Factor* (*IF*) of the vulnerability, as well as the *Asset Capacity* (*AC*) of the asset, are important parameters in our attack risk analysis model. Specifically, *EP* is a measure defined in an interval [0, 1], which indicates to what degree the vulnerability can be exploited to compromise the attacked asset. For instance, *EP* = 0 means that this vulnerability is effectively impossible to exploit, and so the attack has no impact on the target asset. Conversely, *EP* = 1 means that it is easy to exploit the vulnerability to compromise the intended asset. The *Impact Factor* (*IF*), on the other hand, indicates how much damage can be caused by an attack. It is also a measure defined in an interval [0, 1]. *IF* = 0 means that the attack has no impact on an asset, while *IF* = 1 means that an asset can be totally destroyed (i.e., lose all of its capacity).

3.2.2 Damage Assessment

The *Asset Capacity* (*AC*) is another important measure to characterize the operational capacity of a cyber asset. It indicates how much capacity an asset can still provide to fulfill its function after being attacked. In our model, *AC* can be measured in an interval [0, 1]. Value 0 means the asset is not operational at all; while value 1 means that the asset is fully operational. Note that the computational relation between *EP*, *IF* and *AC* allows us to calculate and measure how the capacity of an asset could be affected by an attack, which further enables the quantitative analysis of the mission impacts caused by the attack.

According to Jakobson (2011), the general calculation of mission impacts should contain the following steps:

(1) **Attack Start Point Detection:** The first step is to identify the start point of an attack. Currently, we use leaf nodes in our attack graphs as the start points.
(2) **Direct Impact Assessment:** The next step is to determine the direct impact of an attack on the targeted asset. We follow the extended attack model in Fig. 2 and calculate the direct impact based on CVSS.
(3) **Propagation of Cyber Impacts Through the Network:** In this step, we calculate the potential impacts on cyber capacities of all mission-related assets along the attack paths derived from our attack graphs.
(4) **Mission Impact Assessment:** After knowing the current capacities of all assets involved in a mission, we can further calculate the potential impacts on the high level missions based on mission asset dependency relationships derived by our logical mission models.

It should be noted that figuring out how to assign the proper value to *EP* and *IF* could be a critical task that requires analysis of historical attack data as well as consultation with cyber security experts. In our initial study, the *Exploitability Score* (*ES*) and *Impact Score* (*IS*) in CVSS have been used as our starting point to calculate *EP* and *IF*. As both *ES* and *IS* range from 0 to 10 in CVSS, we calculate these two parameters by: $EP = ES/10$, and $IF = IS/10$.

4 Cyber Impact and Mission Relevance Analysis

Impact assessment is important for mission assurance analysis in cyberspace, where critical mission elements must rely on the support of the underlying cyber network and compromised assets may have significant impacts on a mission's accomplishment. As described in previous sections, for cyber mission assurance assessment, we need practical analysis models to effectively represent a complex mission and the dependency relationship between high level mission elements and the underlying cyber assets. We also need to build a mission impact propagation model to investigate the direct and indirect consequences caused by malicious cyber incidents on high level mission elements and tasks. In addition, quantitative metrics and measures are required for meaningful mission assurance and cyber situational awareness analysis.

Attribute	Example Value
Node ID	Task 2013-10-3
Task Description	Have a teleconference with client A
Node Level	Root/Leaf/Intermediate Node
Node Type	Composition/Conjunctive/Disjunctive Node
Target Value	50
Priority/Weight	0.2
Accomplishment Status	Not yet start/In progress/Completed/Terminated
Progress Status	70%
Triggered by	Task 2013-10-1
Precedes	Task 2013-10-5
Parent Node	Task 2013-10
Child Node	Task 2013-10-3-1, Task 2013-10-3-2, Task 2013-10-3-3
Start Time	October 1, 2013 at 8:30:00 AM EDT
End Time	October 1, 2013 at 10:30:00 AM EDT

Fig. 3 VGM node attributes

4.1 Mission to Asset Mapping and Modeling

To efficiently represent and model the dependency relationships between high level mission elements and the underlying computer network and cyber assets, a Logical Mission Model (LMM) is developed in our framework. Essentially, the LMM is a hierarchical graphical model for mission planning, decomposition, modeling, and asset mapping, which is further composed of a Value-based Goal Model (VGM) and a Logical Role Model (LRM). The VGM captures the composition, temporal, and dependency relationships among different tasks/subtasks in a complex mission, as well as their relative importance to the overall mission. The LRM, on the other hand, is used to capture the physical or cyber functions required to achieve a particular goal (or successfully carry out a task). Based on this comprehensive LMM, users can feasibly model a complex mission, identify the criticality of each task/subtask, and evaluate the cyber resilience during the mission planning phase.

Value-Based Goal Model Each node in VGM represents a task or goal that has to be achieved or maintained to ensure that the entire mission is accomplished. A higher level task (or goal) is represented as the parent node of multiple lower level subtasks (or sub-goals). Each node has a number of attributes to represent its current status as shown in Fig. 3. For example, each task is associated with a pre-assigned *Target Value* that represents its contribution to the overall accomplishment of its parent node, and the *Priority/Weight* attribute indicates the relative importance (criticality)

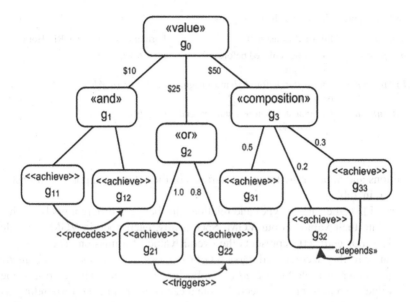

Fig. 4 An example of VGM

of this node to its parent node. In our model, two other important attributes are *Accomplishment Status* and *Progress Status*. During the mission execution phase, these two attributes are periodically measured to evaluate the progress status of a mission task.

In our initial study, we identified three main entities for our VGM model: *goals*, *events*, and *parameters*. Specifically, a *goal* is an observable desired state of a mission/task, while an *event* is an observable phenomenon that occurs during the execution. *Parameters* of a goal or event provide the detailed information about the goal or the specific event. In our VGM, a complex mission is first decomposed into a set of simplified explicit tasks and the corresponding sub-tasks, and then represented by a hierarchical goal tree.

As illustrated in Fig. 4, upper level goals (*parent nodes*) can be decomposed into (also need to be supported by) a number of lower level sub-goals (*child nodes*). Each node (i.e., goal) has a pre-assigned value to represent its contribution to the overall mission. In addition, each parent goal's accomplishment relies on the accomplishment of its child nodes' goals, following the rules specified by mission commanders or Subject Matter Experts (SMEs). In our initial study, the achievement conditions for a parent node include *conjunctive*, *disjunctive*, and *composition* conditions. As shown in Fig. 4, the achievement condition and the value of a goal are represented via «and», «or», «composition», and «value» decorations of a node respectively.

As a starting point, we initially focused on modeling three temporal relationships between goals in the VGM, including *precedes*, *triggers*, and *subgoal* relationship. According to the ORD-Horn subclass defined in (Nebel et al. (1995), the formal

Table 4 Temporal relationships between goals

Condition	Informal Constraint	Formal Constraint in ORD-Horn
$(a,b) \in precedes$	a must be achieved before b can begin	$(a^+ \leq b^-) \wedge (a^+ \neq b^-)$
$(a,b) \in triggers$	a must start before b; b must begin before a ends	$(a^- \leq b^-) \wedge (a^- \neq b^-) \wedge (b^- \leq a^+) \wedge (b^- \neq a^+)$
$(a,b) \in subgoal$	b cannot start before a starts or end before a ends	$(a^- \leq b^-) \wedge (b^+ \leq a^+)$

definitions and appropriate timing constraints of these three temporal relationships are listed in Table 4.

Table 5 lists the various types and relationships between different goals and how to calculate their values in our VGM. Specifically, each node in VGM is a value goal. The *root goal*, $g0$, represents the overall value of a mission. The root value goal can be further decomposed into a set of *Composition, Conjunctive, Disjunctive goals* (as shown in Table 5), or *Leaf goals*. Each goal (i.e., node) has a pre-assigned "maxValue" to represent the expected value it can achieve if the corresponding task can be accomplished successfully. In our model, leaf goals have no subgoals. They directly contribute to the overall goal based on their parent's type. Additionally, in VGM, only leaf goals are actively maintained by the system and need to be supported by the underlying cyber assets. As the leaf goal maintains (or fails), the overall value of a mission is aggregated based on the parent goals' type, until the final goal is achieved (or aborted).

Logical Role Model The LRM is designed to effectively capture corresponding cyber capabilities or functionalities required to achieve (or maintain) a particular task or goal. Working as an intermediate layer, our LRM maps the higher level logical mission elements onto the underlying network and cyber assets. By combining LRM with VGM, analysts will have a complete overview of the goals being pursued, the logical roles being performed to achieve those goals, and the corresponding network resources being used to carry out those roles. In our model, the logical dependency relationships are maintained at both mission planning and execution phases; not only for mission impact analysis, but also to improve the system's resilience (e.g., alternative goals or redundant resources could be suggested or pre-assigned for critical tasks or mission elements, so that mission success can still be achieved even in the worst cases).

When modeling roles, the objective is to identify all the roles in the system as well as their interactions with each other. Given a valid VGM, we follow the following major steps to generate the corresponding LRM:

(1) Create a role for each leaf-level goal in the goal model
(2) If there are multiple ways to achieve a single goal, create a separate role for each approach and quantify the "goodness" of each approach (ranging from 0 to 1).
(3) Identify information flows between the various roles

Table 5 Goals defined in VGM

Node type	Definition	Value	Calculation
Value goal	Each node in VGM is a value goal, and assigned with an associated value	Target Value	$maxValue(g) = \sum_{(g,g')\in subgoal} maxValue(g')$
		Current Value	$currentValue(g) = \sum_{(g,g')\in subgoal} currentValue(g')$
Composition goal	Each subgoal contributes a percentage to its overall value, the total contributions must equal to 1	Target Value	$composition(g)\left(\sum_{(g,g')\in subgoal} contribution(g') \middle| \sum_{(g,g'')\in subgoal} contribution(g'')\right) = 1$
		Current Value	$currentValue(g) = maxValue(g) * \sum_{\substack{(g,g')\in subgoal \\ (g,g'')\in maintained)}} contribution'(g')$
Conjunctive goal	All subgoals have to be maintained; failure of any subgoal will reduce the parent's value to zero	Target Value	$conjunctive(g)(g,g'')\in subgoal\ maxValue(g') = maxValue(g)$
		Current Value	$currentValue(g) = maxValue(g) \times \prod_{(g,g')\in subgoal} \frac{currentValue(g')}{maxValue(g)}$
Disjunctive goal	Value maintained if any subgoal is maintained, each subgoal has an associated contribution value	Target Value	$disjunctive(g)(g,g'')\in subgoal\ maxValue(g') = maxValue(g) * contribution(g')$
		Current Value	$currentValue(g) = max(\{currentValue(g')|(g,g')\in subgoal\})$

(4) If two roles are tightly coupled, consider to combine them into a single role
(5) Define the capabilities required to carry out each role
(6) Determine the appropriate timing values associated with each role

Generally, to create a valid LRM, the first step is to create a single role for each leaf goal in the VGM. However, if we provide multiple ways to achieve a goal, the overall system resilience will increase. Documentation of the alternative approaches for each critical goal hence becomes very beneficial to mission assurance.

Once the roles have been identified, cyber capabilities required to carry out those roles can be further specified. In our model, cyber capabilities can be defined in terms of processing power, communication bandwidth, software and/or hardware specifications or requirements. The information flows between different roles can be used to implicitly define the communication capabilities for the logical roles. For example, if role A has to communicate with role B, the asset assigned for role A must be able to send/receive information to/from the asset assigned to role B. After assigning proper assets, specific communication and routing equipment can be further identified for the logical roles to provide the required communication capabilities.

Note that to maintain and update information about currently available capabilities for supporting logical roles, real-time network monitoring and asset criticality analysis are required. In our framework, a cyber capability model (CCM) is designed to maintain the available capabilities of each cyber asset in a network, such as the current status (e.g., available, occupied, reserved), asset value, and dependency relationships. Other important information that should be maintained in the CCM includes host dependency, service map, and network topology. This knowledge can be directly derived by parsing the outputs of network monitoring and protocol analysis tools, such as Nmap (http://nmap.org/) and Wireshark (http://www.wireshark.org/), or leveraging state-of-the-art automated service discovery mechanisms developed by Tu et al. (2009) and Natarajan et al. (2012) into our framework.

4.2 Cyber Impact Analysis on Mission

After deriving the complete mission-to-asset dependency relationships via our logical mission models, the next step is to evaluate the potential impact of the lower level cyber incidents on the higher level mission elements. Following the same analysis method proposed by Jakobson (2011), the mission impact assessment process includes three major steps: (i) direct impact analysis of cyber incidents, (ii) cyber impact propagation analysis, and (iii) impact assessment on high level mission elements.

4.2.1 Direct Impact of Cyber Incidents

The *direct impact* can be defined as the loss of the *Asset Capacity* (*AC*) of an asset that is a direct target of an attack. As an internal feature of an asset, *AC* stays unchanged for the asset until its value is further reduced by another direct attack, or adjusted by external (human) operations (e.g., network operators may reset AC to 1 by recovering the damaged system). In our basic model, only software assets can be targets of direct attacks, and the initial value of AC is 1 (i.e., we assume that each asset is fully operational before it was attacked).

Particularly, if asset A does not depend on any other assets, then after it was directly attacked by attack X, its asset capacity can be expressed as follows:

$$AC_A\left(t^*\right) = Max\left[\ AC_A\left(t\right) - EP_A\left(t^*\right) \times IF_X\left(t^*\right),\ 0\right] \tag{7}$$

In Eq. 7, $AC_A(t)$ is the capacity of asset A at time t, $EP_A(t^*)$ is the exploit probability of the corresponding vulnerability on asset A at time t^*, $IF_X(t^*)$ is the impact factor of attack X at time t^*, and $AC_A(t^*)$ is the remained capacity of asset A at time t^*, given $t^* > t$.

Note that in a network environment, an asset could also be affected by the other assets it depends on. In this case, its AC will be determined by the combined effect of the other assets and the direct attack on it. For instance, if asset A depends on asset B and was a direct target of attack X, after being attacked its asset capacity should be:

$$AC_A\left(t^*\right) = Min\left[Max\left[\ AC_A\left(t\right) - EP_A\left(t^*\right) \times IF_X\left(t^*\right),\ 0\right],\ AC_B\left(t^*\right)\right] \tag{8}$$

In Eq. 8, $AC_A(t)$ is the capacity of asset A at time t, $EP_A(t^*)$ is the exploit probability of the corresponding vulnerability on asset A at time t^*, $IF_X(t^*)$ is the impact factor of attack X at time t^*, $AC_B(t^*)$ is the capacity of asset B at time t^*, and $AC_A(t^*)$ is the remained capacity of asset A at time t^*, given $t^* > t$.

4.2.2 Propagation of Cyber Impact

In order to calculate the propagation of a direct impact through a network via the derived dependency relationships, we follow the same analysis method proposed by Jakobson (2011) and consider each asset as a generic node in a dependency graph, along with two kinds of specific "AND" and "OR" nodes to represent the logical dependency relationships between different elements. In this propagation model, the "AND" node defines that a parent node needs to depend on all of its children nodes, while the "OR" node defines that a parent node depends on the presence of at least one child node. Note that the "OR" dependency in our model is introduced to achieve better resilience, by providing redundant system, alternative functionality or performance to support a critical mission, task or operation. During the propagation of an attack, the capacities of all generic nodes in the attack path could be affected, either by a direct attack on it, or from a compromised child node it depends on.

To characterize the operational quality of each component or element at different levels in a mission-to-asset dependency graph, we further introduce the *Operational Capacity* (OC) as a universal measure in our model. The *Asset Capacity*

(AC) presented previously is a specific form of the operational capacity provided by cyber assets. Similar to AC, OC is also measured in an interval [0, 1]. It indicates how much operational capacity that a cyber asset, service, task, or mission element can still provide after it was compromised or affected by an attack (directly or indirectly). Value 0 means that a component was totally destroyed (e.g., not operational), while value 1 means that it is still fully operational.

In our basic propagation model, the operational capacities of the "AND" and "OR" nodes are calculated as follows:

$$OC_{OR}(t) = \omega_i * OC_i(t) | \omega_1 * OC_1(t), \omega_2 * OC_2(t), \ldots, \omega_n * OC_n(t)(1 \le i \le n) \quad (9)$$

$$OC_{AND}(t) = Min(\omega_1 * OC_1(t), \omega_2 * OC_2(t), \ldots, \omega_n * OC_n(t))(1 \le i \le n) \quad (10)$$

In Eqs. 9 and 10, $OC_{OR}(t)$ is the operational capacity for an "OR" node at time t, $OC_{AND}(t)$ is the operational capacity for an "AND" node at time t. $OC_1(t)$, $OC_2(t)$, ..., $OC_n(t)$ are operational capacities of the child nodes for the intended "OR" or "AND" nodes. ω_i is the pre-defined weight for each child node, based on its criticality to the parent node. Recursively applying Eqs. 9 and 10 for all the nodes involved in the attack path, analysts can identify not only which asset could be affected, but also how much capacity will be lost due to the attack.

4.2.3 Impact Assessment on High Level Mission Elements

According to Jakobson (2011), during the mission execution stage, the real-time mission impact assessment depends on two major factors: (i) the impact that can be caused by the attacks, and (ii) in which state (e.g., planned, ongoing, or completed) of a mission or task.

For example, suppose that an attack X happened at time t^* (as shown in Fig. 5), and it could impact assets and services that support Tasks A through E. If those tasks have already been completed at time t^*, then those impacts should be irrelevant to the intended mission. If Task F is currently being executed, it can be affected if it relies on assets or services that can be impacted by attack X. Obviously, any other planned tasks that have not started yet but will depend on assets and services that could be impacted by attack X will probably be affected if no further countermeasures were taken.

Note that the planned tasks, such as Task G in Fig. 5, need to be analyzed carefully. As they have not yet been undertaken, their OC will not be accounted in the calculation of the overall OC of the intended mission. However, based on the (planned) mission asset mapping during the mission planning stage, we can calculate the potential impacts on those mission tasks, which could happen if we stick to the original asset mapping and network/system configurations. One advantage of our approach is that based on this real-time mission impact analysis, we can either reconfigure the corresponding network and systems, or replace a planned task with an alternative task to prevent or avoid the coming impacts and ensure a mission's success.

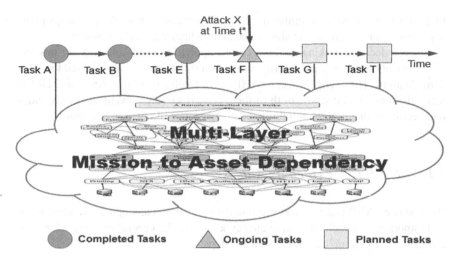

Fig. 5 Temporal relations between mission tasks

In this mission impact analysis model, the execution of a mission is a process that unfolds step-by-step as time progresses. The initial operational capacity value of a mission or task is set as $OC = 1$. This value could be steadily decreasing depending on the operational capacities of its executed stages and whether the corresponding assets and services were impacted by cyber attacks.

The calculation of the overall operational capacity of a mission will be calculated using Eqs. 7–10 accordingly for each potential attack path in our mission asset map, considering both dependency and temporal relationships. To achieve mission resilience, in the mission planning stage, we need to evaluate and compare different mission asset mapping and network configurations. For each mission asset mapping and network configuration, we calculate the operational capacity for both overall mission and the critical tasks. In this manner, we can find the best mapping and configuration to achieve the optimum value. In addition, to achieve better mission resilience, we can intentionally allocate/reserve redundant resources for critical leaf tasks and make critical task nodes as "*OR*" nodes (by adding alternative or backup tasks).

5 Asset Criticality Analysis and Prioritization

To identify the most critical cyber assets in supporting a critical task or operation, an effective measurement method is required for asset criticality ranking and prioritization. In our initial study, we prioritize asset criticality based on the cyber impact, mission relevance, and asset value analysis. In particular, the cyber impact and mission relevance can be evaluated by our attack risk prediction and impact propagation models described in Sects. 3 and 4. The asset value, in general, can be estimated by experienced network administrators, based on the amount of IT spending and the depreciation or amortization value of the assets (hardware and software).

Various decision making methods can be applied in our framework for mission asset criticality analysis and prioritization. As a starting point, we selected the standard Analytic Hierarchy Process (AHP) and Decision Matrix Analysis (DMA) methods in our initial study. Both of them can effectively prevent subjective judgment errors to increase the reliability and consistence of our analysis results.

5.1 AHP Based Criticality Analysis

We first used AHP and pair-wise comparison matrix to calculate the relative value and importance of each mission related cyber asset. The general procedure for asset criticality analysis includes the following steps:

(1) Modeling the problem as a hierarchy containing the decision goal, the alternatives for reaching it, and the criteria for evaluating the alternatives.
(2) Establishing priorities among the elements of the hierarchy by making a series of judgments based on pair-wise comparisons of the elements. For example, when comparing asset value, network administrators might prefer database server over web server, and web server over desktop.
(3) Synthesizing these judgments to yield a set of overall priorities for the hierarchy. This would combine network administrators' judgments about different factors (such as asset value, potential loss, attack risk, and vulnerability severity) for different alternatives (e.g., Desktop A, Router H, Database P, etc.) into overall priorities for each asset.
(4) Checking the consistency of the judgments.
(5) Coming to a final decision based on the results of this process.

Figure 6 shows a simple example of this process, in which three assets (i.e., desktop A, Router H and Database P) need to be prioritized based on three factors: *mission relevance*, *cyber impact* and *asset value*. In this example, we assume that cyber impact and mission relevance are both two times as important as asset value, and use a pair-wise comparison matrix to decide the proper weights for each factor.

As illustrated in Fig. 6, the weights of cyber impact and mission relevance are both 0.4, and the weight of asset value is 0.2. Additionally, each asset has a value vector to specify its relative value corresponding to the three factors, which will be used to calculate the asset's criticality (priority) based on the three weighted factors. Fig. 6 shows the prioritizing result of the three assets, in which Database P was the preferred entity, with a priority of 0.715. It was ten times as strong as Desktop A, whose priority was 0.07. Router H fell somewhere in between. Therefore, Database P is the most critical asset in this example, and it has to be well-protected from potential cyber attacks to assure mission success.

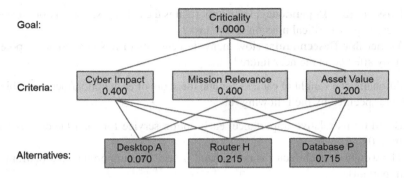

Fig. 6 Prioritization of cyber assets with AHP

5.2   Grid Analysis Based Prioritization

Grid analysis, also known as Decision Matrix Analysis, is another useful technique for making a decision among several options while taking many different factors into account. As the simplest form of Multiple Criteria Decision Analysis (MCDA) (http://en.wikipedia.org/wiki/Multi-criteria_decision_analysis), grid analysis is particularly powerful where users have a number of good alternatives to choose from and many different factors to take into account. To use grid analysis technique for decision making, first we need to list all the available options (*alternatives*) as rows on a table, and the factors (*criteria*) need to be considered as columns in the table. Then, we score each option/factor combination, weight the score, and add these scores up to give an overall score for each option in the table.

The step-by-step process of grid analysis technique can be illustrated as follows:

(1) List all of the available options (*alternatives*) as the row labels on a table, and list the factors (*criteria*) as the column headings in the table.
(2) Specify the relative importance of each factor, ranging from 0 (absolutely unimportant) to 5 (extremely important).
(3) For each column, score each option/factor combination from 0 (poor) to 5 (very good), based on how well it possesses the corresponding factor.
(4) Then, multiply each score from step 3) by the relative importance derived from step 2). This will give users weighted scores for each option/factor combination.
(5) Finally, add up the corresponding weighted scores for each option. Options with higher scores are more important than the options with lower scores.

In our study, we initially considered the following factors to help security analysts decide which cyber asset or network service is more important than others:

- **Asset Value:** How important are the files and data stored in a host or server?
- **Cyber Severity:** What is the severity of a vulnerable service? This value can be derived from the CVSS score.

- **Mission/Task Dependency:** How important is the cyber asset or network service regarding to a critical mission and/or task?
- **Vulnerable Descendants:** How many descendants of this host could be potentially affected in the near future?

Additionally, the weight of each factor and the score of each option/factor combination are specified by the following rules:

- Based on its relative importance, each option service for each factor is scored from 0 to 5.
- The weight of each factor is normalized from 0 (not important) to 5 (extremely important).

Table 6 shows a simple example of grid analysis, in which a number of cyber assets and network services are listed. Specific weights have been assigned for four factors (*Asset Value, Cyber Severity, Mission/Task Dependency,* and *Vulnerable Descendants*). Each option/factor combination is assigned a particular value based on its relative importance decided by security analysts or domain experts.

The total score for each option is calculated and listed in the last column of Table 6. The "Desktop_B" (which is currently running "LICQ" service) has the highest score, which means it is the most important asset in supporting an intended mission. To protect "Desktop_B" from potential attacks, sufficient security resources or countermeasures should be applied. For instance, network administrators may shut down the vulnerable "LICQ" service to prevent the potential attacks. Note that we can virtually "shut down" a vulnerable service to demonstrate the corresponding consequences on the high level mission elements based on our logical mission models. If there is no big impact on the intended mission, or we can mitigate impact by reallocating alternative resource or goals, cyber resilience can be achieved to ensure mission assurance.

6   Future Work

Further investigation and research are still required, especially in the flowing fields:

- Efficient analytical models for mission-to-asset mapping (e.g., how to decompose a complex mission into a set of explicit tasks, identify mission-to-asset dependency, and allocate reliable cyber assets for critical tasks or mission elements.)
- Accurate network vulnerability and attack risk analysis models (e.g., how to configure/reconfigure a network to reduce aggregated network vulnerabilities; how to quickly detect and/or predict attack and attack path.)
- Practical mission impact assessment models (e.g., how to accurately model the direct impact of a cyber incident on a mission element; how to calculate the effect of a compromised cyber asset or failed mission element on the accomplishment of other mission elements.)

Table 6 Grid analysis for mission asset prioritization

Host	IP address	User	Vulnerable services	Factor					Total score
				Asset value	Cyber severity	Mission dependency	Vulnerable descendants		
Weight				3	1	5	5		
Desktop_B	128.105.120.8	Jack	LICQ	1	2	5	3		45
AppServer_1	128.105.120.4	Mike	WebSphere	3	2	2	4		41
DBServer_1	128.105.120.5	John	Oracle DBMS	4	2	0	5		39
Desktop_C	128.105.120.14	Bob	Sysmgr GUI	2	0	1	2		21
Desktop_F	128.105.120.17	Mark	DCOM	2	0	2	1		21
Desktop_O	128.105.120.18	Bill	MySQL 5.1.x	2	0	0	0		6

- Multi-layer graphical models (or a common operational picture) to effectively represent and display various inter- and intra- dependency relationships between different elements and components involved in CSA assessment
- Simple but meaningful metrics and corresponding evaluation algorithms or mechanisms for specific or general network security analysis

Note that the achievement of CSA rests in the ability to judiciously balance the above capabilities to handle the complexities of defensive operations. An integrated framework or software tool that leverages well-defined and developed technologies can significantly improve CSA and network security modeling, analysis, measurement, and visualization capabilities for security and mission analysts in enterprise network environments.

7 Summary

Without meaningful metrics, we cannot quantitatively evaluate and measure the operational effectiveness and system performance of our network. This chapter discussed how to effectively identify good metrics and evaluation methods for enterprise network situational awareness (SA) quantification and measurement. Metrics are tools that are designed to facilitate decision-making and improve performance and accountability through collection, analysis, and reporting of relevant performance-related data. Security measurement for CSA needs to carefully consider two distinct possible relationships: (i) How to define and use metrics as quantitative characteristics to represent the security state of a computer system or network, and (ii) How to define and use metrics to measure CSA from a defender's point of view. The multivariate nature of SA significantly complicates its quantification and measurement. State-of-the-art technologies provide useful descriptive information on security analysis, mission modeling, and situation management. The Common Vulnerability Scoring System has been widely adopted as the primary method for assessing the severity of computer system security vulnerabilities. The National Vulnerability Database provides CVSS scores for almost all known vulnerabilities. To evaluate the general security of an enterprise network based on vulnerability assessment, three security metrics are proposed: the vulnerable host percentage (VHP), CVSS severity score, and compromised host percentage (CHP). Attack graph based metrics can also be defined for network-level vulnerability assessment, such as the Number of Attack Paths, the Average Length of Attack Paths, and the Shortest Attack Path. Useful metrics can also be based on modeling (i) the logical relations that allow us to model the propagation of the impacts through the network, and (ii) the computational relations that allow us to calculate the level of those impacts. Users can feasibly model a complex mission, identify the criticality of each task/ subtask, and evaluate the cyber resilience during the mission planning phase. After deriving the complete mission-to-asset dependency relationships via our logical mission models, the next step is to evaluate the potential impact of the lower level cyber incidents on the higher level mission elements. Using the real-time mission impact analysis, network operators can either reconfigure the corresponding network and systems, or replace a planned task with an alternative task to prevent or avoid the coming impacts and ensure a mission's success. AHP and pair-wise comparison matrix can help calculate the relative value and importance of each mission related cyber asset. Effectively identifying the right metrics to measure security preparedness and awareness within an organization is a hard and complicated problem. To be valuable, security metrics must be meaningful to organizational goals or key performance indicators. Security analysts should review their specific metrics currently in place and ensure they are aligned with the overall industry standards and their particular organizational and business goals.

References

Alberts C., et al. (2005). *Mission Assurance Analysis Protocol (MAAP): Assessing Risk in Complex Environments. CMU/SEI-2005-TN-032.* Pittsburgh, PA: Carnegie Mellon University.

Ammann P., et al. (2002). Scalable, Graph-based Network Vulnerability Analysis. *the 9th ACM Conference on Computer and Communications Security.*

Bolstad C. and Cuevas H. (2010). Integrating Situation Awareness Assessment into Test and Evaluation. *The International Test and Evaluation Association (ITEA),* 31: 240–246.

Cheung S., et al. (2003). Modeling Multi-Step Cyber Attacks for Scenario Recognition. *the 3rd DARPA Information Survivability Conference and Exhibition.* Washington D. C.

Dahl, O. (2005). *Using colored petri nets in penetration testing. Master's thesis.* Gjøvik, Norway: Gjøvik University College.

Durso F., et al. (1995). Expertise and chess: A pilot study comparing situation awareness methodologies. *In experimental analysis and measurement of situation awareness,* (pp. 295–303).

Endsley, M. R. (1988). Situation awareness global assessment technique (SAGAT). *the National Aerospace and Electronics Conference (NAECON).*

Endsley, M. R. (1990). Predictive utility of an objective measure of situation awareness. *the Human Factors Society 34th Annual Meeting,* (pp. 41–45).

Endsley, M. R. (1995). Measurement of situation awareness in dynamic systems. *Human Factors,* 37(1), 65–84.

Endsley, M. R., et al. (1998). A comparative evaluation of SAGAT and SART for evaluations of situation awareness. *the Human Factors and Ergonomics Society Annual Meeting,* (pp. 82–86).

Fracker, M. (1991a). Measures of situation awareness: Review and future directions (Report No. AL-TR-1991-0128). Wright-Patterson Air Force Base, OH: Armstrong Laboratories.

Fracker, M. (1991b). Measures of situation awareness: An experimental evaluation (Report No. AL-TR-1991-0127). Wright-Patterson Air Force Base, OH: Armstrong Laboratories.

Gomez M., et al. (2008). *An Ontology-Centric Approach to Sensor-Mission Assignment.* Springer.

Goodall J., et al. (2009). Camus: Automatically Mapping Cyber Assets to Missions and Users. *IEEE Military Communications Conference.* Boston MA.

Grimaila M., et al. (2008). Improving the Cyber Incident Mission Impact Assessment Processes. *the 4th Annual Workshop on Cyber Security and Information Intelligence Research.*

Grimaila M., et al. (2009). Design Considerations for a Cyber Incident Mission Impact Assessment (CIMIA) Process. *the 2009 International Conference on Security and Management (SAM09).* Las Vegas, Nevada.

Harwood K., et al. (1988). Situational awareness: A conceptual and methodological framework. *the 11th Biennial Psychology in the Department of Defense Symposium*, (pp. pp. 23–27).

Hecker, A. (2008). On System Security Metrics and the Definition Approaches. *the 2nd International Conference on Emerging Security Information, Systems and Technologies.*

Heyman T., et al. (2008). Using security patterns to combine security metrics. *the 3rd International Conference on Availability, Reliability and Security.*

Holsopple J., et al. (2008). FuSIA: Future Situation and Impact Awareness. *Information Fusion.*

Jakobson G. (2011). Mission Cyber Security Situation Assessment Using Impact Dependency Graphs. *the 14th International Conference on Information Fusion (FUSION)* (pp. 1–8). Chicago, IL: IEEE.

Jansen, W. (2009). *Directions in Security Metrics Research.* National Institute of Standards and Technology, Computer Security Division.

Jones D. and Endsley M. R. (2000). Examining the validity of real-time probes as a metric of situation awareness. *the 14th Triennial Congress of the International Ergonomics Association.*

Kotenko I., et al. (2006). Attack graph based evaluation of network security. *the 10th IFIP TC-6 TC-11 international conference on Communications and Multimedia Security*, (pp. 216–227).

Lewis L., et al. (2008). Enabling Cyber Situation Awareness, Impact Assessment, and Situation Projection. *Situation Management (SIMA).*

Lindstrom, P. (2005). Security: Measuring Up. Retrieved from http://searchsecurity.techtarget. com/tip/Security-Measuring-Up

Manadhata P. and Wing J. (2011). An Attack Surface Metric. *Software Engineering, IEEE Transactions on*, vol. 37, no. 3, pp. 371–386.

Matthews M., et al. (2000). Measures of infantry situation awareness for a virtual MOUT environment. *the Human Performance, Situation Awareness and Automation: User-Centered Design for the New Millennium.*

McDermott, J. (2000). Attack net penetration testing. *Workshop on New Security Paradigms.*

Meland P. and Jensen J. (2008). Secure Software Design in Practice. *the 3rd International Conference on Availability, Reliability and Security.*

Musman S., et al. (2010). *Evaluating the Impact of Cyber Attacks on Missions.* MITRE Technical Paper #09-4577.

Natarajan A., et al. (2012). NSDMiner: Automated discovery of network service dependencies. *INFOCOM* (pp. 2507–2515). IEEE.

Nebel B., et al. (1995). Reasoning about temporal relations: a maximal tractable subclass of Allen's interval algebra. *Journal of the ACM (JACM)*, vol. 42, no. 1, pp. 43–66.

Noel S., et al. (2004). Correlating Intrusion Events and Building Attack Scenarios through Attack Graph Distance. *the 20th Annual Computer Security Conference.* Tucson, Arizona.

Ou X., et al. (2006). A Scalable Approach to Attack Graph Generation. *the 13th ACM Conference on Computer and Communication Security (CCS)*, (pp. 336–345).

Qin X. and Lee W. (2004). Attack Plan Recognition and prediction Using Causal Networks. *the 20th Annual Computer Security Applications Conference.*

Salerno J., et al. (2005). A Situation Awareness Model Applied to Multiple Domains. *Multisensor, Multisource Information Fusion.*

Salerno, J. (2008). Measuring situation assessment performance through the activities of interest score. *the 11th International Conference on Information Fusion.*

Sheyner O., et al. (2002). Automated Generation and Analysis of Attack Graphs. *the 2002 IEEE Symposium on Security and Privacy*, (pp. 254–265).

Singhal A., et al. (2010). Ontologies for modeling enterprise level security metrics. *the 6th Annual Workshop on Cyber Security and Information Intelligence Research.* ACM.

Strater L., et al. (2001). *Measures of platoon leader situation awareness in virtual decision making exercises (No. Research Report 1770).* Army Research Institute.

Tadda G., et al. (2006). Realizing Situation Awareness within a Cyber Environment. *Multisensor, Multisource Information Fusion: Architectures, Algorithms, and Applications* (p. 1–8). Orlando: SPIE Vol.6242.

Taylor, R. (1989). Situational awareness rating technique (SART): The development of a tool for aircrew systems design. *the AGARD AMP Symposium on Situational Awareness in Aerospace Operations, CP478.*

Tu W., et. al. (2009). Automated Service Discovery for Enterprise Network Management. Stony Brook University. Retrieved May 8, 2014, from http://www.cs.sunysb.edu/~live3/research/asd_ppt.pdf

Vidulich M. (2000). Testing the sensitivity of situation awareness metrics in interface evaluations. *Situation awareness analysis and measurement,* 227–246.

Wang J., et al. (2009). Security Metrics for Software Systems. *the 47th Annual Southeast Regional Conference.*

Watters J., et al. (2009). *The Risk-to-Mission Assessment Process (RiskMAP): A Sensitivity Analysis and an Extension to Treat Confidentiality Issues.*

Zhou S., et al. (2003). Colored petri net based attack modeling. *Rough Sets, Fuzzy Sets, Data Mining, and Granular Computing: the 9th International Conference* (pp. vol. 2639, pp. 715–718). Chongqing, China: Springer.

Mission Resilience

Gabriel Jakobson

1 Introduction

As we come to the end of the book, we look at the end-goals of achieving CSA. In this chapter we explain that the ultimate objective of CSA is to enable situation management, i.e., continuous adjustments of both the network and the mission that the network supports, in order to ensure that the mission continues to achieve its objectives. Indeed, several previous chapters stressed that CSA exists in the context of a particular mission, and serves the purposes of the mission. A mission that is able to absorb the attacks and keep returning to an acceptable level of execution is called a resilient mission. It can be said that the purpose of CSA is to maintain mission resiliency. This chapter explains that mission-centric resilient cyber defense should be based on collective and adaptive behavior of two interacting dynamic processes, cyber situation management in the cyber space, and mission situation management in the physical space. It discusses architecture and enabling technologies of such mutually adaptive processes that keep the mission persisting even if the network that supports the mission may be compromised by a cyber attack.

Human activities, organized as space and time bound processes, are usually referred to as business processes in civilian applications, and missions in military, security, and exploratory applications.[1] As business processes and missions proceed with their operational goals they rely on information technology (IT) assets as their operational recourse. Protection of IT assets from cyber attacks has been a constant goal of IT-centric cyber defense, which traditionally boils down to three operational goals: confidentiality, integrity and availability of IT assets (Aceituno 2005). Under

---

[1] Within the scope of issues discussed in this paper the notions business process and mission are handled as semantically equivalent concepts, and they will be collectively referred as missions, business or military ones.

G. Jakobson (✉)
Altusys Corporation, Princeton, NJ, USA
e-mail: jakobson@altusystems.com

© Springer International Publishing Switzerland 2014
A. Kott et al. (eds.), *Cyber Defense and Situational Awareness*,
Advances in Information Security 62, DOI 10.1007/978-3-319-11391-3_14

the umbrella of IT-centric cyber security, several different cyber defense paradigms were proposed, including perimeter bound cyber defense (Buecker et al. 2009), intrusion tolerant data (Fraga and Powell 1985), critical infrastructure protection (US GAO 2011), net-centric cyber security (US DoD 2012; Kerner and Shokri 2012), and resilient infrastructure systems (Mostashari 2010). Regardless of the different approaches to achieve cyber security, the IT-centric methods, in principal, looked on protection of IT assets as the primary goal of cyber defense. At the same time, everyday practice of cyber defense has revealed that often it is technically unconceivable or financially prohibitive to protect each and every IT component, especially while dealing with large IT infrastructures, or where the IT assets are used in dynamic and unpredictable operational environments. In order to address the above-mentioned issues, in recent years research has focussed on assessing the impact of cyber attacks directly on missions (Musman et al. 2010; Jakobson 2011b; Jajodia 2012). This move in cyber defense towards mission operational assuranse in compromised cyber environment lead to the notion of a cyber attack resilient mission (Goldman 2010; Peake and Williams 2014; Jakobson 2013).

Motivated by the resilient behavior in nature, the resilient systems are designed to resist the disruptive events happening in their operational environment, survive the impact of the disruptive events, and recover from those impacts. Our interest is on a specific class of resilient systems, namely resilient missions, where the success of cyber defense is measured by the trusted level of mission continuity achieved under cyber attacks. In this chapter, which is based on our work in resilient cyber defense (Jakobson 2013) and uses the framework of situation management (Jakobson et al. 2006), we describe a method how mission-centric resilient cyber defense can be achieved using the model of cyber-physical situation awareness. The focus of the chapter will be on architecture and enabling technologies of mission-centric resilient cyber defense, including:

(a) The use of models of cyber-physical situation awareness to sense, perceive, comprehend, project and reason about situations happening in the cyber-physical world.
(b) Collective and adaptive behavior of two interacting dynamic processes, cyber situation management in the cyber space, and mission situation management in the physical space; this collective and adaptive behavior assures mission continuation with an acceptable level of trust, even if the IT infrastructure that supports the missions may be compromised, while being under a cyber attack.
(c) The proposed framework is in principal cognitive, i.e. while modeling the entities, relations, situations, events and actions we are interested mostly in the meaning of those objects.

The chapter is organized in the following way. Section 2 discusses how the notion of resilience is understood in different disciplines, provides a definition of a mission-centric resilient cyber defense, and reviews related work. Section 3 describes the cyber-physical situation awareness based approach and the basic architectural framework of mission-centric resilient cyber defense. Section 4 reviews the models of the basic conceptual elements of the proposed approach, including missions, cyber terrain, and cyber attacks. Section 5 presents a method of real-time cyber situation awareness and how it is applied to resilient cyber defense. Section 6 describes resilient cyber defense that is achieved through assessment of plausible future cyber situations and their impact on future planned missions. Section 7 describes a method of achieving mission resilience through adaptation of mission behavior. Section 8 draws conclusions and refers to some future research directions.

2 Overview: Resilient Cyber Defense

2.1 On Resilient Behavior in Complex Systems

Resilience is a fundamental behavioral feature of complex dynamic systems, being natural or artificial ones. It has been studied extensively in several scientific and engineering disciplines. In psychology and behavioral neuroscience, resilience is an individual's ability to adapt successfully in the face of stress and adversity. This coping may result in the individual "bouncing back" to a previous state of normal functioning, or simply not showing negative effects (Wu et al. 2013). Similarly, in social science, resilience is understood as an ability of individuals and groups to overcome challenges, like trauma, tragedy, crises, and isolation, and to bounce back stronger, wiser, and more socially powerful (Cacioppo et al. 2011). Recent studies in molecular genetics have shown that the mechanisms of resilience in biological systems are mediated by adaptive changes in neural circuits (Feder et al. 2009). In engineering disciplines, especially those ones that are dealing with complex distributed systems, the system resilience is designed to anticipate and avoid disruptive incidents, survive, and recover from natural disruptions, system faults or adversary actions (Westrum 2006). In business enterprise management domain research on resilient behavior is conducted under the term of business continuity planning (Davenport 1993).

Despite the diversity in the physical nature of complex systems that exhibit resilient behavior, the defining feature of them is to resist the disruptive events happening in the environment, survive the impact of the disruptive events, and recover from those impacts. The resilient system has a strong "motivation" to survive, even if not all individual components of the system are functional or are surviving. In other words, the system resilience is achieved through emergent collective and adaptive behavior of all components of the system. Similar viewpoint, applied to cyber defense systems, was expressed recently in King (2011), where a research plan was proposed to achieve resilience in a complex system that contains brittle components by introducing the mechanisms of system adaptation and self-organization.

2.2   Understanding of Misson-Centric Resilient Cyber Defense

The defining features of resilient systems, mentioned in the previous section, are also true for mission-centric resilient cyber defense systems. We will further classify the different acts of resilient behavior by mapping them to a timeline, and examine how a system behaves before, during and after the disruptive event. We will refer to the corresponding list of time-dependent resilient behaviors as the Baseline Resilience Model (BRM):

- **Before the disruptive event**, which might or might not happen, the resilience relates to a vigilant behavior of detecting current or predicting future disruptive situations, detecting and minimizing existing system vulnerabilities, or undertaking deceptive or any other behaviors that disorient potential adversaries.
- **During the disruptive event**, the resilient behavior concerns how to reorganize and adapt to new operational situations in order to maintain the required system's functionalities within an acceptable level of trust, and how to assess the inflicted impact of the disruptive events.
- **After the disruptive event**, the resilient behavior focuses on restoration, reconfiguration and damage control, back-track reasoning and forensics, as well on planned organizational and technical advancements.

While talking about resilient missions and cyber defense we assume the existence of a combined cyber-physical operational space, which contains two interacting processes: the mission operations control and command process in the physical operational space, and the mission cyber defense management process in the cyber space. Mission-centric resilient cyber defense is a combined behavioral capability of these two processes that interacting together to assure effective mission continuation in reaching mission goals, even if mission operations may be embedded into a compromised cyber infrastructure environment.

2.3   Review of Related Work

A general problem statement and outline of the technical roadmap to cyber attack impact assessment on missions was given in Musman et al. (2010), which focuses on cyber mission impact assessment framework and maps the enterprise network and information technology assets to the enterprise businesses processes (missions). Paper Grimaila et al. (2009) discusses general design concepts of a system that provides the decision makers with notifications on cyber incidents and their potential impacts on missions. Assessment of cyber attack impact on missions requires modeling of the topology of the networks and cyber assets, as well as mapping from cyber assets to missions within vulnerability constrains specific to cyber assets. The notion of a virtual terrain was introduced in Argauer and Young (2008), which was used to model physical topology of a network, network services, and vulnerabilities of the network objects. The paper described a method on how to assess cyber attack impact on networks, services and users, based on an algorithm of overlaying correlated cyber attack tracks on virtual terrain. Several efforts have been made in research of attack graphs and in generation of cyber attack scenarios for automatic detection of cyber attacks (Cheung et al. 2003a; Noel et al. 2004; Qin and Lee 2004a).

A method for deploying mission tasks in a distributed computing environment that minimizes mission exposure to cyber asset vulnerabilities by taking into account dependencies between missions and cyber assets was presented in Albanese et al. (2013a). The proposed solution is based on the A* algorithm for optimal allocation of mission tasks into potentially vulnerable distributesd cyber infrastructures. In D'Amico et al. (2010) scenarios and ontology are described to express relationships between cyber assets, missions and users. A direct mapping from missions to cyber services was used in the Cauldron system (Albanese et al. 2013b).

One of the promising paradigms of resilient cyber defense is the act of cyber maneuver, also known as moving target defense (Moving Target Defense: An Asymmetric Approach to Cyber Security 2011). Similar to the concept of radio frequency hopping, the moving target cyber defense utilizes the randomization algorithms to diversify hardware platforms, operating systems, network segments, software applications, and services. The Net Maneuver Commander presented in Beraud et al. (2011) is a research prototype cyber command and control system, which constantly maneuvers across network and cyber assets to deceive potential cyber attackers.

In June 2011, The Defense Advanced Research Projects Agency (DARPA) announced a project called Mission Oriented Resilient Clouds, which aims to build resilience into existing cloud networks to preserve mission effectiveness during a cyber attack (Mission-Oriented Resilient Clouds 2011). The project defined an ensemble of interconnected hosts acting in concert. Loss of individual hosts and tasks within the ensemble is allowable as long as mission effectiveness is preserved. A model of increasing mission survivability based on reinforcement learning was proposed in Carvalho (2009). The paper defines the measure of mission survivability as a ratio between the successfully completed workflows of the mission to the total number of the workflows. The paper examines two core capabilities of increasing mission survivability: redistribution of the network resources to ensure mission continuity, and learning of the attack patterns to estimate the level of vulnerability of other nodes. Both of these capabilities dealt with the network resource management, while adaptation of the mission was not addressed. A model of adaptation of mission operations to achieve resilient behavior under a cyber attack was presented in Jakobson (2012).

3 Cyber Situation Awareness Based Approach to Resilient Cyber Defense

3.1 A General Situation Awareness and Decision Support Model

As mentioned in the Introduction, we are interested in two specific situation awareness processes, the mission situation awareness in the physical mission operational space, and the mission cyber situation awareness in the cyber space. We will show that interactions between these two situation awareness processes serve as a basis for mission assurance. In this section, we will describe a general model of situation management that will be used for describing the processes of mission and cyber situation awareness.

A widely used model of situation awareness (SA) was proposed by Endsley (1995). The model defines SA as "the perception of the elements in the environment within a volume of time and space, the comprehension of their meaning and the projection of their status in the near future. Endsley considered SA as the main precursor to decision-making, however, not always as a guarantee for effective decision-making. Advancement of the SA model towards capturing the specifics of cyber defense has been the focus of an increasing number of research activities (Tadda and Salerno 2010; Barford et al. 2010; Jakobson 2011a).

In our model of situation management (SM) (Jakobson et al. 2006), we follow the same point made by Endsley, and consider SA and Decision Support (DS) as two separate, but closely interacting processes. Schematically, a general SM process is depicted in Fig. 1. Time-wise, the overall SM process is mapped into three main sub-processes, the Situation Control process that is performed at the current time of attention, the Past Situation Awareness process, and the Future Situation Awareness process. The Situation Control process is essentially a real-time process that aims to bring the Reality World into a goal state, and is driven by the difference between the current and goal states of the Reality World. As shown in Fig. 1, the Situation Control process forms a loop through the current state of the Reality World and the corresponding state of the current Situation Model. Situation Model is a subjective reflection of the objective reality in the mind of an agent (or multiple agents) that is responsible for the overall situation management process. The Situation Control loop is further broken down into the current Situation Awareness and the Decision Support processes.

The current Situation Awareness process includes three consequent stages: situation sensing, perception and comprehension. Situation sensing is the stage of instrumentation of the entities in the Reality World in their spatial and temporal settings, and transformation of the obtained measures into a stream of data, possibly locally analyzed, unified and fused. The sequence of the processes of information sensing, perception and comprehension are characterized by an increasing level of abstraction of the processed information. It is also a process where the data of the objective reality is transformed step-by-step into a subjective reality depending on the interpretation power possessed by the agents involved in the sensing, perception and comprehension processes. During the Decision Support process that involves the steps of reasoning, plan generation and execution of the actions defined in the plan, we see the similar changes in the generality and objectivity of the processed information, but only moving from a declarative specification of the intended tasks to the executable procedures that affect the state of the Reality World. This completes the Situation Control loop, and a new sensing stage can start, upon which the control loop moves into a new cycle.

The Past Situation Awareness process deals with the analysis to determine the reasons and give explanations why the system is in the current state, while the

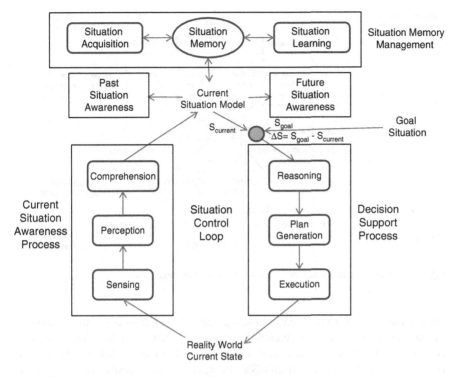

Fig. 1 Situation management process—a schematic view

Future Situation Awareness process deals with prediction of future plausible situations that the system may end up in. The Past, Current and Future Situation Awareness processes comprise the overall Situation Awareness process present in the SM model.

3.2 Integrated Cyber-Physical Situation Management Architecture

The overall system architecture of a synergistic mission operations and mission cyber defense situation management is given in Fig. 2. It is modeled using the general SM process described in the previous section and contains two main interacting closed-loop situation management processes: cyber situation management (CSM) process in a cyber operational space, and mission situation management (MSM) in a physical operational space. The CSM and MSM processes act collectively in one combined cyber-physical operational space. The processes interact through a common object of interest—the Mission Model. As mission progresses in time, CSM receives IT service requests from the mission and provides the requested services

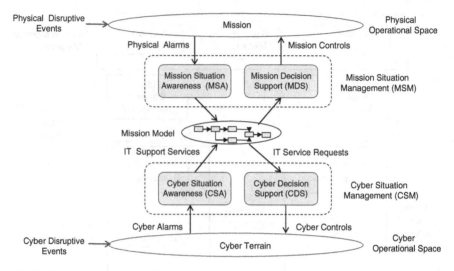

Fig. 2 Diagram of an integrated cyber-physical situation management

back to the mission. Concurrently to this process, MSM proceeds with the tasks of mission situation awareness, undertakes mission decision support functions, and transitions the mission into a new state. The new mission state might require renewed IT support services from CSM. In order to achieve resilience to withstand the impact of cyber attacks, the above-described interaction between CSM and MSM requires mutual adaptation of the cyber terrain and the mission, e.g. reconfiguration of dependencies among the cyber assets and services, replacing or upgrading certain assets, changing the logical or temporal order of mission tasks, or proceeding with a graceful degradation of the mission goals.

MSM acts according to the mission model, and mission control policies and rules. The MSM includes two sub-processes, the Mission Situation Awareness (MSA) and the Mission Decision Support (MDS) processes. MSA and MDS themselves are fairly complex operations: MSA performs the tasks of (a) sensing and pre-processing of real-time data coming from sensors and human reports; (b) perception of the collected data and construction of the tactical situation model; (c) current mission impact assessment caused by the actions and forces in the physical operational space; and (d) assessment of the future mission impacts caused by adversary actions, natural forces and external disruptions in the physical operational space. MDS performs the tasks of mission operations planning, mission adaptation and resource allocation, selection of mission execution agents, and mission execution and monitoring.

Like the MSM process, the closed-loop CSM process contains two major subprocesses, cyber situation awareness (CSA) and cyber decision support (CDS) processes. The CSA process includes the following sub-processes: (a) real-time cyber situation sensing, (b) cyber situation perception, (c) cyber situation comprehension, and (d) plausible future cyber situation assessment. The CDS process contains the following sub-processes: (a) CT vulnerability scanning and preventive maintenance, (b) CT adaptation as response to the cyber attacks and as reaction to IT service requests from the missions, and (c) CT recovery and restoration actions. For performing of the above-mentioned sub-processes, the CSA and CDS processes need a variety of data and knowledge sources, including the models of cyber terrain, the mission models and the cyber attack model that will be discussed in Sect. 4.

The diagram of mission operations and mission cyber defense situation management shown in Fig. 2, gives a fairly wide and multi-faceted picture of the processes happening in mission and mission cyber defense operations. Not all of those processes will be covered in equal detail here due to the specific focus of this chapter on mission-centric resilient cyber defense, and also due to space limitations. As a result, we will pay more attention to the issues of cyber situation awareness and mission adaptation process, which is a part of mission decision support process.

4 Modeling Missions, Cyber Infrastructure and Cyber Attacks

4.1 Mission Modeling

We will treat missions and business processes as conceptually equivalent terms, and informally define them as a goal-directed structured order of space and time-bound actions to resolve operational situations in favor of the agent that is conducting the mission or the business process. In order to proceed with its goal, a mission has to be supported (consumes) physical, human and/or IT (cyber) resources. Mission is a time-dependent dynamic process, it has its start-time and end-time, it is controlled by a mission agent, its goal is usually given by a higher-level controlling agent, and it takes place in some operational space. Mission possesses a certain amount of operational capacity, and its importance to a more high-level mission is measured by mission criticality. Mission operational capacity can be reduced by the impact of an attack. Structurally, a mission can be a fairly complex embedded flow containing mission steps, and other missions. The content of the actions executed at a mission step is defined by a mission task.

The missions are modeled as sequential or parallel flows of mission steps that are controlled by AND/OR logic and by temporal operators that are based on James F. Allen's interval algebra (Allen 1983). In addition to Allen's operators, a relation UNDEFINED is introduced that does not require any specific temporal order to be placed among the mission steps. The relation UNDEFINED is used in a flow "cloud", where all nodes are tied with AND-logic, however, the temporal order of execution of those nodes could be arbitrary.

Figure 3 illustrates a Mission A that has two main parallel flows that are forked by an AND-node. The first branch contains a sequential flow, while the second flow contains an OR-forked parallel flow, and a "cloud".

Grouping steps into flows or sub-missions, and defining logical and temporal relations between mission flows is a mission design task that is out of the scope of this chapter. There is difference in organizing steps into flows or missions: usually flows are smaller scale processes tied with the same operational environment, similar goals, and comparable time-frame. Contrarily, a sub-mission of a mission could take place in a different operational environment, has its own goals, and usually refers to larger-scale actions. For example, in Fig. 3, Mission B is designed as a submission of Mission A.

The existence of temporal order between missions and mission steps, and the options to change the order, e.g. advance or delay the order of execution of mission flows, opens an opportunity to adapt the mission in order to minimize the cyber attack impact on missions. Such methods of mission adaptation will be discussed in Sect. 6. As the embedded structure of missions unfolds during the mission execution process, all mission steps will be ultimately turned into executable mission tasks. Knowing the current and the unfolding future mission states, we can adjust the future mission steps so that only such branches are taken or modified that will reduce the impact of a cyber attack on the overall mission. A more detailed description of the mission model described above is given in Jakobson (2011a).

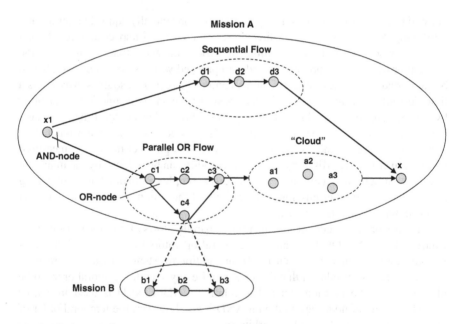

Fig. 3 Mission task flows

4.2   Cyber Terrain

Network topology was probably first looked at from the cyber security viewpoint in Argauer and Young (2008), where the notion of virtual terrain was introduced to model the physical topology of a network, network element configurations, and vulnerabilities of the network objects. The notion of cyber terrain was introduced in Jakobson (2011b) as a multi-level IT infrastructure that models cyber assets and services, their inter-dependencies, vulnerabilities and operational capacities. CT contains three sub-terrains: network infrastructure (NI), software (SW) assets, and IT services sub-terrains.

The NI sub-terrain is a collection of interconnected network hardware components like routers, servers, switches, firewalls, communication lines, terminal devices, sensors, cameras, printers, etc. All the dependencies between the components, like connectivity, containment, location, and other relations, represent the physical/logical topology of the NI sub-terrain. The SW sub-terrain describes different software components such as operating systems, middleware, applications, etc., and defines dependencies between the components, e.g., application software might contain several sub-components, or an operating system supports an application. The service sub-terrain presents all the services and their intra-dependencies. The most common dependencies among services include: enabling of one service by other, and containment of one or multiple services within a package of services. CT also defines dependencies between the sub-terrains: a NI sub-terrain component may "house" one or more SW sub-terrain components, and a SW sub-terrain component may enable some services in the services sub-terrain.

While supporting the missions, the CT possesses a certain "operational capacity", i.e. the ability to provide resources and services to the missions with a certain level of quantity, quality, effectiveness, and cost to the missions. The overall operational capacity of the CT is an aggregate of the operational capacities of each of its components. Operational capacity (OC) is considered as a relative measure of the current operational capacity against its maximum value, and is measured in an interval [0, 1], which indicates to what level the component of CT was compromised by a cyber attack. The value $OC = 0$ means that the component is totally compromised, and $OC = 1$ means that the component is fully operational.

In a general attack situation, a software asset can be either directly hit by a cyber attack causing permanent damage to it, or the asset may be indirectly impacted by a remote attack via inter-asset dependencies. The permanent damage caused to the asset is measured by the asset's permanent operational capacity (POC). POC is an internal feature of a software asset only. It stays unchanged until either its value is reduced by the next direct cyber attack, or it can be changed by a human, usually by resetting $POC = 1$.

A sequence of direct attacks might reduce the operational capacity of an asset, or totally destroy the asset bringing its operational capacity to 0. Contrary to the effect of the direct attack, an indirect cyber attack does not cause permanent damage to the cyber asset. There is nothing inherently wrong with the asset that is under an indirect attack. However, its operational capacity might be reduced because of its dependency on other assets that either suffer from direct attacks or are also indirectly impacted.

4.3 Impact-Oriented Cyber Attack Modeling

A cyber attack is a sequence of deliberate actions using malicious code carried out by individual or organized attackers to gain access to protected IT assets, alter/compromise computer code and data, and ultimately disrupt or destroy systems, business processes and missions whose operations are supported by attacked IT assets. Cyber attack modeling is a central task in many cyber security solutions. Depending on the goals set for these solutions, e.g., multi-step attack detection, insider attacks, attacker motivation, etc., different aspects of a cyber attack are captured by these models. In our work, we limit our interest to aspects that are related to the attack impact on cyber assets, services, and missions. Doing so, we are interested in two types of relations concerning the cyber attack: the logical relations that allow us to model the processes of detection and propagation of an attack impact, and computational relations that allow us to calculate the level of those impacts. The cyber attack model (see Fig. 4), which is an impact-oriented model, contains four concepts (rectangles): Attack, Hardware Platform, Asset, and Vulnerability, and 5 conceptual relations (ovals):

R1: Targets (Attack, Hardware-Platform)—attack targets a hardware platform, usually identified by an IP address
R2: Exploits (Attack, Vulnerability)—attack exploits a vulnerability
R3: Houses (Hardware-Platform, Asset)—hardware platform houses a software asset
R4: Has-Vulnerability (Asset, Vulnerability)—software asset possesses a vulnerability
R5: Impacts (Attack, Asset)—attact impacts asset

The model on Fig. 4 follows the notion of *conceptual graph* introduced by John Sowa (2000). However, in addition to the Sowa's model, the conceptual graph shown on Fig. 4 illustrates two extensions: first, the concepts can be parameterized, and second, it is allowed to use computational relations between the parameters. For example, the model has parameter Impact Factor (IF) for the concept Attack, and parameter Permanent Operational Capacity (POC) for the concept Asset. Second, computational relations can be defined among parameters, e.g., relation POC Calculator between the parameters IF and POC. In Sect. 5.2, we will will show how POC will be calculated. The computational relations are depicted in conceptual graphs as small circles.

In the proposed model, the impact factor (IF) of an attack is a measure defined on an interval [0, 1]. Impact factor indicates a level of how much the attack is capable of compromising the attacked asset. IF = 0 means that the attack has no

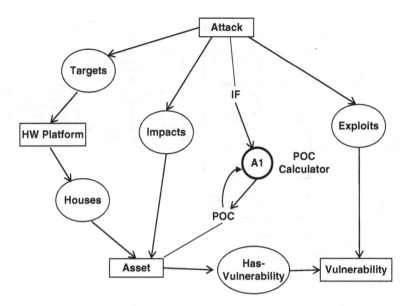

Fig. 4 Impact-oriented cyber attack model

impact on the asset, and IF = 1, means that the attack is totally destroying the asset by bringing its permanent operational capacity to 0. Assigning values for impact factor of cyber attacks is an important knowledge acquisition task, which requires analysis of historic attack data as well as consultation with cyber security experts. In this work, we use the asset vulnerability scores from the Open Source Vulnerability Database (OSVDB 2010) to calculate the attack impact factors as it is shown in Jakobson (2011b). If a vulnerability score is not available from this or any other similar software vulnerability database, an attack impact factor can be computed from the alert severity (priority) data, which is a common data field in all intrusion detection systems.

5   Cyber Situation Awareness and Resilient Cyber Defense

5.1   Cyber Situation Awareness Process

A general view of the cyber situation awareness (CSA) process was already presented in Sect. 3.2. Within the context of cyber defense, the sub-processes of CSA, Cyber Situation Sensing, Cyber Situation Perception, Cyber Situation Comprehension, and Plausible Future Cyber Situation Assessment sub-processes, have very specific content that reflects the nature of the domain of cyber defense, and will be correspondingly referred as Cyber Terrain Monitoring, Target SW

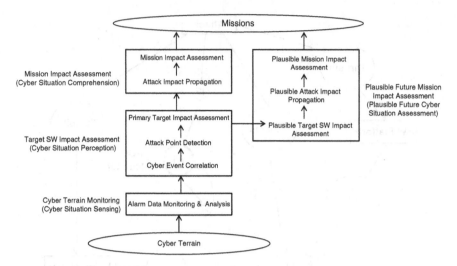

Fig. 5 Cyber situation awareness process

Impact Assessment, Mission Impact Assessment, and Plausible Future Mission Impact assessment (Fig. 5). Cyber Terrain Monitoring process includes the tasks of monitoring and analysis of cyber alert data that is coming from different hardware and software components of the cyber terrain. Target SW Impact Assessment process includes the tasks of (a) cyber event correlation that it is used for detecting cyber attack patterns in the stream of incoming cyber events, (b) the task of attack point detection that determines what primary SW asset was targeted and on what HW platform, and (c) the task of assessment of the impact on that primary software asset that was caused by the cyber attack. Mission Impact Assessment process contains tasks of attack impact propagation, and assessment of the impact of the cyber attacks on the currently ongoing mission steps. Finally, the Plausible Future Mission Impact Assessment process contains the tasks of plausible target SW asset impact assessment, propagation of the plausible attack impact through the cyber terrain, and assessment of the plausible impact on missions.

Several critical components of the described method of building mission-centric resilient cyber defense system, including cyber attack impact propagation, plausible future cyber attack impact assessment, situation-aware BDI multi-agent system architecture have been implemented and tested in SAIA (Situation Awareness and Impact Assessment)—an experimental prototype system developed at Altusys in 2008–2010 under a contract with AFRL, Rome.

5.2 Target Software Impact Assessment

Target SW Impact Assessment (Fig. 5) starts with the task of cyber event correlation, with the goal of recognition of cyber attacks. In this work, we are using our previous results on model-based temporal event correlation and intrusion detection

(Jakobson et al. 2000; Jakaobson 2003). An event correlation agent possesses beliefs (facts) about the structure of a particular application, i.e. all the entities and inter-entity relations in the cyber terrain, and beliefs about the signature and anomalies of cyber attack situations. Corresponding models are built and maintained in the agent's knowledge bases, such as Domain Ontology (classes of cyber terrain entities and relations), Situation Ontology (classes of cyber attack signatures and anomalies), and Domain Constraints (constraints representing the semantics of the entities, relations, and entity parameters). Situations occurring in the world are recognized by applying a situation recognition rule. During the event correlation process, several time-dependent functions are performed, including: (a) time-dependent counting of event occurrences; (b) monitoring the duration of the situations and lifespan of the entities; (c) monitoring the correlation time window; (d) scheduling the time dependent actions; and (e) managing temporal relations between events.

The next step in Target SW Impact Assessment is the task of cyber attack point detection, i.e. determining whether the targeted asset is vulnerable to the attack. Not every cyber attack succeeds in attacking a SW asset, e.g., there may be situations where the attack is targeting a SW asset does not have vulnerabilities, which can be exploited by the attack. An attack might succeed if the following logical constraints hold:

IF (Attack C targets hardware platform H)
AND (Hardware platform H houses software asset A)
AND (Asset A has vulnerability V)
AND (Attack C exploits vulnerability V)
THEN (Attack C succeeds in impacting the asset A)

There are several known algorithms of logical constraint resolution (Dechter 2003). A specific method based on fast database search and match was implemented in Jakobson (2011b).

The final step of Target SW Impact Assessment is assessment of the impact on the primary software target. The impact is measured by the OC of the asset that is the result of combination of two factors: the reduction of the permanent operational capacity of the asset due to the direct cyber attack and indirect impact due to the dependency of this asset from other assets. Lets suppose that an asset A that depends also on asset B was a direct target of a cyber attack X. The combined operational capacity of asset A can be calculated as follows:

$$OC_A(t) := Min\left(Max\left(POC_A(t) - IF_X(t), 0\right), OC_B(t)\right)$$

where

$POC_A(t)$ is the current permanent operational capacity of an asset A at time t
$IF_X(t')$ is the impact factor of an attack X at time $t' > t$
$OC_B(t')$ is the operational capacity of the asset B at t'
$OC_A(t')$ is the operational capacity of the asset A at t'.

In the case where asset A is a terminal node in the cyber terrain, i.e. it does not depend on any other software assets, the above-given expression can be simplified:

$$OC_A(t) := Max(POC_A(t) - IF_X(t), 0)$$

We should say that in the above-mentioned case, $POC_A(t') = OC_A(t')$, since the asset A is a terminal node.

Since only software assets can be targets of direct cyber attacks, they can only be characterized by POC: no service, mission step, or mission has POC. Usually, the initial value of POC for all software assets is set to 1, i.e. the asset is claimed to be in a full operational order at the beginning of the mission.

5.3 Mission Impact Assessment

Mission Impact Assessment includes two main tasks: the task of cyber attack impact propagation and the task of mission impact assessment. As a cyber attack hits a SW asset in the cyber terrain, the impact of that attack starts to propagate through the cyber terrain via the links between the SW assets and IT services, reaches the missions, and continues propagation through the links between mission steps and missions until the top-level missions are affected. The cyber attack impact propagation process is formally described by the impact dependency graph (Jakobson 2011b). The impact dependency graph (IDG) is a mathematical abstraction of assets, services, mission steps and missions and all of their inter-dependencies as they were initially described in the cyber terrain and in the mission model (see Fig. 6). In addition to the nodes of assets, services, mission steps and missions, IDG has two special nodes: logical AND and OR-nodes. The AND-node defines that the parent node depends on all of its children nodes, while the OR dependency defines the required presence of at least one child node. The OR dependency is introduced in order to capture possible options to reconfigure cyber terrain or missions.

During the attack propagation from the attacked nodes (e.g. the red-colored node in Fig. 6), the operational capacities of all dependent nodes will be calculated. The node that is in the linear path in the IDG gets the operational capacity from its child node, while the operational capacities of the AND and OR nodes are calculated as follows:

$$OC_{OR}(t) = AVE(OC_1(t), OC_2(t), ..., OC_n(t))$$

$$OC_{AND}(t) = MIN(OC_1(t), OC_2(t), ..., OC_n(t)),$$

where

$OC_{OR}(t)$ is the operational capacity for an OR-node
$OC_{AND}(t)$ is the operational capacity for an AND-node
$OC_1(t), OC_2(t), ..., OC_n(t)$ are the operational capacities of the child nodes for the
    OR and AND nodes.

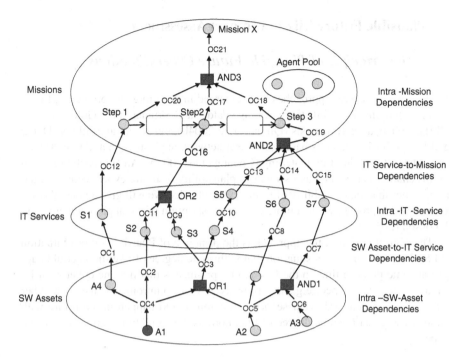

Fig. 6 Impact dependency graph

The mission part of the IDG is illustrated in Fig. 6 by Mission X, which has three sequential steps Step 1, Step 2 and Step 3 that are logically connected by the AND3 node. IDG explicitly represents the temporal relations between mission components as it was discussed in Sect. 4.1. For example, the Mission X has two AFTER relations between the shown mission steps.

While calculating the operational capacities for missions we need to take into account the particular operational state of a mission. During real-time mission monitoring, the impact of a cyber attack on a mission depends on two major factors: (1) what impact the attack has on steps of the mission, and (2) what operational state— planned, ongoing, or completed state, the mission steps are in. For example, lets suppose that a cyber attack happened when the Mission X was already executing Step 2. In this case, the impact of the cyber attack on those assets that support Step 1 could be considered irrelevant, since Step 1 was already completed. Contrarily, the ongoing Step 2 will be affected by the attack. The case for Step 3 that is planned for execution at the moment when the cyber attack is happening needs a special analysis. First, since Step 3 has not yet been undertaken, its operational situation will not be accounted for in the calculation of the operational situation of the overall mission. However, we are able to calculate a potential impact on Step 3, which could happen. One practical action would be to reconfigure the cyber terrain or the mission. Since mission is a process that unfolds step-by-step as time progresses, its operational capacity is getting its starting value $OC = 1$, and then it is steadily decreasing depending on the operational capacities of its executed steps.

6   Plausible Future Mission Impact Assessment

6.1   The Principle of Plausible Future Cyber Situations

In recent years several approaches have emerged in detecting and predicting future attacks, including probabilistic reasoning (Valdes and Skinner 2001; Goldman et al. 2001), statistical alert analysis (Qin and Lee 2004b), clustering algorithms (Debar and Wespi 2001), methods based on causal network analysis (Qin and Lee 2004c), and cyber attack condition matching (Cheung et al. 2003b). An approach presented in this chapter is based on assessment of plausibility of future cyber security situations rather than on probability of future cyber attacks. We will give a general overview of the approach, while a more detailed description of the approach is given in Jakobson (2011a).

The central notion of the approach is the principle of Plausible Future Situation (PFS). PFS is defined as a situation that with some degree of likelihood could happen at some point in time in the future. Our premise is that if some cyber security situation happened once, e.g., a certain asset was compromised due to a cyber attack then the detected cyber security situations could happen in the future with another asset that to some degree of likelihood is "similar" to the already attacked cyber asset.

6.1.1   The Principle of Plausible Future Cyber Situations

For any assets $a, b \in A$

$$\frac{\text{Compromised } (a(t), OC_a(t)) \ \& \ \text{Similar } ((a(t), b(t)), q(a, b))}{\text{Plausible (Compromised } (b(t'), OC_b(t') = OC_a(t)), p = q(a, b)), t' > t}$$

The PFS principle states that if at some time moment **t** an asset **a** is compromised to the level of $OC_a(t)$ and the strength of similarity between the assets **a** and **b** is equal to $q(a, b)$, then the plausibility that the asset **b** could be compromised at a future time $t' > t$ to the same level that the asset a was compromised at moment t, i.e. $OC_b(t') = OC_a(t)$, is equal to the level (to the strength) of similarity between the assets **a** and **b**.

Example: Let's assume that at some time **t** a database was hit by a cyber attack with an impact factor 0.3, which, by exploiting a vulnerability of the database reduced its operational capacity from the original value of 1.0 to 1.0 - 0.3 = 0.7. It is known that in the targeted network, in some other host, resides the same database, however, with a different release. Let's assume that due to the difference in releases, the similarity level of the databases is 0.85. Application of the PFS allows us to come up with a conclusion that some time in the future (not exactly when) it is plausible with certainty 0.85 that the other database could lose its operational capacity to the level of 0.7.

As was stated already, the crucial factor in calculating the plausible future cyber security situations is to identify the methods and algorithms for assessing the similarity between the assets. For this purpose, we are introducing several specific asset similarity relations:

1. Vulnerability-Similarity—similarity of assets is based on the set of their common vulnerabilities, like type, criticality, and the number of common vulnerabilities of the assets.
2. Configuration-Similarity—the similarity measure depends on the software product type, version, release, manufacturer, and other structural characteristics of the product.
3. Location-Similarity—the similarity measure depends on the location of the asset in the network, e.g. are the assets in the same subnet or LAN, geographic location of the servers, etc.
4. Functional-Similarity—the similarity measure depends on a set of common functions provided by the assets.
5. Temporal-Similarity—calculates the similarity measure depending on the closeness of the time-dependent correlation of the activities performed by the assets.
6. Mission-Similarity—calculates the similarity measure depending on the number of common missions supported by the assets.
7. Usage-Similarity—calculates the similarity measure depending on common traffic patterns, where the assets are involved.

Construction of the functions for calculating the different similarity measures requires focused knowledge acquisition efforts, including interviewing IT experts and mission management experts, analysis of historical statistical data, and using the automatic algorithms of data mining.

Example: For illustration purposes, let's discuss the asset similarity relation that is based on common vulnerabilities. We will use the asset vulnerabilities listed in the Open Source Vulnerability Database (OSVDB) (Feder et al. 2009). For a given vulnerability, the OSVDB records identify the versions of a vendor/product that share the same vulnerability. For example, vulnerability # 22919 "Oracle Database XML Database DBMS_XMLSCHEMA_INT Multiple Procedure Remote Overflow" affects the product/versions from the vendor "Oracle Corporation" as it is shown in Table 1.

Table 1 Common vulnerability table

Product	Product #	Release	Version
Database	10 g	2	10.2.0.1
Database	10 g	1	10.1.0.3
			10.1.0.4
			10.1.0.5
			10.1.0.4.2
Database	9i	2	9.2.0.6
			9.2.0.7
Database	8i	3	8.1.7.4
Database	9i	1	9.0.1.4
			9.0.1.5
			9.0.1.5
Database	8	8.0.6	8.0.6.3

Table 2 Asset similarity function

Similarity class	Product	Product #	Release	Version	q_{vs}
1	1	1	1	1	1.0
2	1	1	1	0	0.9
3	1	1	0	0	0.75
4	1	0	0	0	0.5
5	0	0	0	0	0.0

Table 2 contains practically feasible combinations of similarities (measured by binary 1) and dissimilarities (binary 0) between two software assets along Product, Product #, Release, and Version coordinates as shown below. In consultation with IT personnel, an asset vulnerability-based similarity function p_{vs} was constructed as shown in the last column in Table 2.

In general, two assets might be related with multiple similarity relations. In this case, an asset similarity index is introduced that calculates a combined effect of them.

6.2 Plausible Future Mission Impact Assessment Process

Plausible Future Mission Impact Assessment process (see Sect. 5.1) contains three tasks, the tasks of plausible target SW impact assessment, propagation of the plausible attack impact through the cyber terrain, and assessment of the plausible impact on missions. Below we will give a brief description of the process:

1. During the first task, those plausible target SW assets are determined that based on application of the Principle of Plausible Future Cyber Situations have a high level similarity to already compromised SW assets. Let's call those assets high plausibility target SW assets.
2. During the second step, the method of cyber attack impact propagation through the IDG (that was described in Sect. 5.3) will be applied to all assets in the set of high plausibility target SW assets.
3. During the third step, the plausible cyber attack impact propagation process will be carried over to the mission portion of the IDG, and plausible impacts to mission will be assessed.

7 Mission Resilience Through Adaptation

7.1 Adaptation in Federated Multi-Agent Systems

The resilient cyber defense system has to adapt to the changes in the operational environment, adversary activities, and available system resources. It is assumed that an adaptable system should exhibit autonomous run-time behavior without outside intervention, including the following types of adaptation:

- Structural adaptation—adaptation to the internal structural changes, e.g., loss of inter-node connectivity in the cyber terrain, or loss of agents capable of implementing mission tasks.
- Functional adaptation—adaptation to the changes in the functional role of system components, e. g. changes in the tasks performed by the mission nodes or cyber services.
- Resource adaptation—adaptation to the changes in the physical, cyber and human resources made available to the system, e.g. changes in the volume, quality and availability of cyber assets and services that support missions.

All three types of adaptations are useful in adaptation of the cyber terrain and missions to achieve mission resilience under a cyber attack. As we discussed in Sect. 4.1, missions are modeled as flows of mission steps, where a mission step could be another mission, another flow, or an executable mission task. From a mission execution viewpoint each mission task is implemented by an agent that is assigned to the task. Such an approach to modeling of mission tasks by an agent allows us to represent all mission tasks collectively as a multi-agent system (MAS). MAS is widely used for modeling complex distributed systems due to such features as a capability to act independently in a persistent manner, rational reasoning, interaction with the world, and mobility (Wooldridge 2002). One of the most popular formal models of MAS is the Belief-Desire-Intension (BDI) model. It was conceived as a relatively simple rational model of human cognition (Norling 2004). It operates with three main mental attitudes: beliefs, desires and intentions. Rao and Georgeff (1995) replaced the declarative notion of intentions with a procedural specification of instantiated and executable plans. Our approach of constructing the internal structure and behavior of a mission agent is based on the model of adaptable situation aware Belief Desire Intension (BDI) agent (Jakobson et al. 2008).

7.2 Mission Resiliency Preserving Adaptation Policies

Mission adaptation policies are rules that are used by an agent to modify the mission, its components and inter-dependencies between the mission components. As we talk about missions as objects of adaptation, two important aspects should be considered:

(a) *Single Entity Level Adaptation.* Each entity, e.g. a mission, a mission task, or an agent that implements the mission task, can be modified. For example, one can change the criticality index of a mission or a task, or operational capacity of a task or an agent. An important adaptation function is the selection of an agent from a pool of pre-defined agents to implement a particular mission task. For example, IDG on Fig. 6 shows that an agent pool containing three agents is assigned as potential alternative implementers to mission Step 3.

(b) *Inter-Entity Relations Level Adaptation.* The inter-entity relations adaptation covers the functions of changing or modifying the structural, temporal, logical, and domain-specific relations between the entities. For example, adding or deleting a mission task, changing the AND-nodes and OR-nodes in a mission flow, changing the temporal order of tasks in a mission flow, delaying or speeding up the start or end time of a mission or its components.

Below we will present a sample list of Mission Adaptation Policies that are divided into two sets, those that are designed for currently ongoing missions, and for those missions that are planned for future execution.

Adaptation policies for ongoing mission tasks that are under execution at the time of a cyber attack:

A1. For every currently active mission task, select an agent from a corresponding agent pool that has the highest operational capacity, which is equal to or greater than the required operational capacity specified in the mission task. If no agent is found, use Policy A2.

A2. Reduce, incrementally, the value of the task's required operational capacity from the current value to the lowest trusted level. For each incremental required operational capacity value perform the Policy A1. If no agent is found that matches Policy A1, use Policy A3.

A3. Modify the mission task flow so that the tasks with no matching agent are moved to a later time of execution. Issue a CT reconfiguration order to replace/ or repair the CT node with low operational capacity.

A4. Stop execution of those mission tasks, where (a) the stop task execution permission is granted, and (b) no agent could be found with operational capacity that is at least equal to the required operational capacity of the task.

A5. Select from the alternative mission flows (mission flows that are in OR condition among themselves) a flow where all tasks have the matching agents, whose operational capacities are greater than the required operational capacities in the corresponding tasks.

A6. First select those tasks from the "Cloud" in the mission flow that satisfy the required operational capacity condition. For the rest of the tasks issue CT reconfiguration orders.

Adaptation policies for future tasks that are planned for execution:

B1. Issue a request to Mission Command and Control to modify the future part of the ongoing mission to satisfy the required operational capacity conditions for all planned tasks.

B2. For all tasks, whose corresponding agents have operational capacities that are below the required ones, issue CT reconfiguration orders.

B3. Follow policies A1 and A5.

B4. Make all required calculations to implement policies A2, A3, A4, and A6.

8 Summary

Cyber Situational Awareness supports the situation management process that aims to achieve mission resiliency. The system resilience is designed to anticipate and avoid disruptive incidents, survive, and recover from natural disruptions, system faults or adversary actions—this is also true for mission-centric resilient cyber defense systems.

The quality of cyber defense should be measured by the level of success of missions that are achieving their operational goals, even if they are forced to operate in a compromised cyber environment. A solution to cyber defense is found in adopting a resilient mission-centric cyber defense architecture, where collective and adaptive operations of missions and cyber terrain resources allow mission continuation. A synergistic cyber-physical situation awareness system includes two interacting processes, the process of mission operation situation management and mission cyber defense situation management. The Situation Management Process involves a loop that includes the Current Situation Awareness process and Decision Support Process. Cyber terrain is a multi-level IT infrastructure that models cyber assets and services, their inter-dependencies, vulnerabilities and operational capacities. Cyber terrain contains three sub-terrains: network infrastructure, software assets, and IT services. Cyber attack is a sequence of deliberate actions of using malicious code carried out by individual or organized attackers to gain access to protected IT assets, alter/compromise computer code and data, and ultimately disrupt or destroy systems, business processes and missions whose operations are supported by attacked IT assets. The sub-processes of CSA include Cyber Terrain Monitoring, Target SW Impact Assessment, Mission Impact Assessment, and Plausible Future Mission Impact assessment. The Resilient cyber defense system has to adapt to the changes in the operational environment, adversary activities, and available system resources. An adaptable system should exhibit autonomous run-time behavior without outside intervention, including structural, functional and resource adaptation. Mission adaptation policies are rules that are used to modify the mission, its components and inter-dependencies between the mission components. Mission-centric resilient cyber defense is in an extensive stage of research and development. There are several major challenges ahead. The first challenge is related to the development of a common "lingua franca" for specifying and modeling basic elements of mission-centric cyber defense: we are eager to manipulate the terms like cyber attack, cyber defense, cyber attacker, system resilience, adaptation, events, situations, context, etc. but still do not have a consensus on their meaning, and very often lack adequate languages and models describing them. The second major challenge is related to the matrices of expected quality achieved for the proposed solution of cyber defense. The future road from resilient cyber defense to active cyber defense and then to offensive cyber actions still needs conceptual, technological and legal attention.

References

Aceituno, V. "On Information Security Paradigms," *ISSA Journal*, September, 2005.

Albanese, M., Jajodia, S., Jhawar, R., and Piuri, V. "Reliable Mission Deployment in Vulnerable Distributed Systems". In *Proceedings of the 1st Workshop on Reliability and Security Data Analysis (RSDA 2013)*, Budapest, Hungary, June 24, 2013a.

Albanese, M., Jajodia, S., Jhawar, R., Piuri, V. "Secure Mission-Centric Operations in Cloud Computing," ARO Workshop on Cloud Security George Mason University, USA, March 11–12, 2013b.

Allen, J. F. "Maintaining Knowledge About Temporal Intervals," *Communications of the ACM* 26 (11), pp. 832–843, 1983.

Argauer, B., and Young, S. *"VTAC: Virtual Terrain Assisted Impact Assessment for Cyber Attacks,"* Proceedings of SPIE Security and Defense Symposium, Data Mining, Intrusion Detection, Information Assurance, and Data Networks Security Conference, Orlando, CA, 2008.

Barford, P., Dacier, M., Dietterich, T. G., Fredrikson, M., Giffin, J., Jajodia, S., Jha, S., Li, J., Liu, P., Ning, P., Ou, X., Song, D., Strater, L., Swarup, V., Tadda, G., Wang, C., and Yen, J. "Cyber SA: Situational Awareness for Cyber Defense," in Issues and Research, Editors: S. Jajodia, P. Liu, V. Swarup, C. Wang, Advances in Information Security, Volume 46, 2010.

Beraud, P., Cruz, A., Hassell, S., and Meadows, S. "Using Cyber Maneuver to Improve Network Resilience," Military Communications Conference, MILCOM 2011.

Buecker, A., Andreas, P., Paisley, S. Understanding IT Perimeter Security. IBM Redpaper Report REDP-4397-00, 2009, http://www.redbooks.ibm.com/redpapers/pdfs/redp4397.pdf.

Cacioppo, J. T., Reis, H. T., Zautra, A. J. "Social Resilience: The Value of Social Fitness with an Application to Military," *American Psychologist*, Vol. 66, No. 1, pp. 43–51, 2011.

Carvalho, M. "A Distributed Reinforcement Learning Approach to Mission Survivability in Tactical MANETs," *ACM Conference CSIIRW 2009*, Oak Ridge, TN, 2009.

Cheung, S., Lindqvist, U., and Fong, M. W. "Modeling Multi-Step Cyber Attacks for Scenario Recognition," 3rd DARPA Information Survivability Conference and Exhibition, Washington D. C., 2003a.

Cheung, S., Lindqvist, U., and Fong, M. W. "Modeling Multi-Step Cyber Attacks for Scenario Recognition", In Proceedings of the 3rd DARPA Information Survivability Conference and Exhibition,Washington, D. C., 2003b.

D'Amico, A., Buchanan, L., Goodall, J., and Walczak, P. "Mission Impact of Cyber Events: Scenarios and Ontology to Express the Relationships Between Cyber Assets, Missions and Users." Proceedings of the 5th International Conference on Information Warfare and Security (ICIW), Thomson Reuters ISI, 2010, 388–397.

Davenport, T. *Process Innovation: Reengineering work through information technology*. Harvard Business School Press, Boston, 1993.

Debar, H., and Wespi, A. "The Intrusion Detection Console Correlation Mechanism", In 4th International Symposium on Recent Advances in Intrusion Detection (RAID), 2001.

Dechter, R. *Constraint Processing*, The Morgan Kaufmann Series in Artificial Intelligence, 2003.

Endsley, M. R. "Toward a Theory of Situation Awareness in Dynamic Systems," *Human Factors*, 37(1), pp. 32-64, 1995.

Feder, A., Nestler, E., and Charney, D. "Psychobiology and Molecular Genetics of Resilience," Nature Reviews Neuroscience 10, June 2009.

Fraga, J. S., Powell, D. "A Fault- and Intrusion-Tolerant File System," In *Proceedings of the 3rd International Conference on Computer Security*. 203–218, 1985.

Goldman, H. *"Building Secure, Resilient Architectures for Cyber Mission Assurance,"* Technical Papers, The MITRE Corporation, November 2010, http://www.mitre.org/sites/default/files/pdf/10_3301.pdf

Goldman, R. P., Heimerdinger, W., and Harp, S. A. "Information Modeling for Intrusion Report Aggregation", In DARPA Information Survivability Conference and Exhibition, 2001.

Grimaila, M. R., Fortson, L. W., and Sutton, J. L. *"Design Considerations for a Cyber Incident Mission Impact Assessment (CIMIA) Process,"* Proceedings of the 2009 International Conference on Security and Management (SAM09), Las Vegas, Nevada, July 13–16, 2009.

Jajodia, S. (ed.) *Moving Target Defense: An Asymmetric Approach to Cyber Security*, Springer, 2011.

Jajodia, S. A Mission-centric Framework for Cyber Situational Awareness, Keynote at ICETE 2012.

Jakobson, G. "Technology and Practice of Integrated Multi-Agent Event Correlation Systems," International Conference on Integration of Knowledge-Intensive Multi-Agent Systems, KIMAS'03, September/October 2003, Boston, MA.

Jakobson, G. "Extending Situation Modeling with Inference of Plausible Future Cyber Situations", 1st IEEE International Conference on Cognitive Situation Awareness and Decision Support 2011 (CogSIMA 2011), Miami, FL., 2011a.

Jakobson, G. "Mission Cyber Security Situation Assessment Using Impact Dependency Graphs," Proceedings of the 14th International Conference on Information Fusion, 5–8 July 2011, Chicago, IL., 2011b.

Jakobson, G. "Using Federated Adaptable Multi-Agent Systems in Achieving Cyber Attack Tolerant Missions," 2nd IEEE International Conference on Cognitive Situation Awareness and Decision Support 2012 (CogSIMA 2012), 6–8 March, 2012, New Orleans, LO.

Jakobson, G. "Mission-Centricity in Cyber Security: Architecting Cyber Attack Resilient Missions," 5th International Conference on Cyber Conflict (CyCon 2013), Tallinn, Estonia, 2013.

Jakobson, G., Weissman, M., Brenner, L., Lafond, C., Matheus, C. "GRACE: Building Next Generation Event Correlation Services," IEEE Network Operations and Management Symposium NOMS 2000, Honolulu, Hawaii, 2000.

Jakobson, G., Buford, J., Lewis, L. "A Framework of Cognitive Situation Modeling and Recognition," *The 2nd IEEE Workshop on Situation Management, in Proceedings of the Military Communications Conference (MILCOM 2006),* Washington, D. C., September, 2006.

Jakobson, G., Buford, J., and Lewis, L. "Models of Feedback and Adaptation in Multi-Agent Systems for Disaster Situation Management," SPIE 2008 Defense and Security Conference, Orlando, FL, March, 2008.

Kerner, J., Shokri, E. "Cybersecurity Challenges in a Net-Centric *World, "Aerospace Crosslink Magazine*, Spring 2012.

King, S. Cyber Science & Technology Steering Committee Council Research Roadmap, NDIA Disruptive Technologies Conference, November 2011.

Mission-Oriented Resilient Clouds. 2011, DARPA, Information Innovation Office, http://www.darpa.mil/Our_Work/I2O/Programs/Mission-oriented_Resilient_Clouds_(MRC).aspx.

Mostashari, A. Resilient Critical Infrastructure Systems and Enterprises, *Imperial College Press,* 2010.

Musman, S., Temin, A., Tanner, M., Fox, D., and Pridemore, B. *"Evaluating the Impact of Cyber Attacks on Missions,"* MITRE Technical Paper #09-4577, July 2010.

Noel, S., Robertson, E., Jajodia, S. *"Correlating Intrusion Events and Building Attack Scenarios through Attack Graph Distance,"* 20th Annual Computer Security Conference, Tucson, Arizona, December 2004.

Norling, E. "Folk Psychology for Human Modeling: Extending the BDI Paradigm," *In International Conference on Autonomous Agents and Multi-Agent Systems*, 2004.

OSVDB. The Open Source Vulnerability Database, 2010.

Peake, C., Williams, D. "An Integrative Framework for Secure and Resilient Mission Assurance," 4th Annual Secure and Resilient Cyber Architectures Workshop, May 28–29, 2014.

Qin, X., and Lee, W. "Attack Plan Recognition and prediction Using Causal Networks," in Proceedings of the 20th Annual Computer Security Applications Conference, pp. 370–379, 2004a.

Qin, X., and Lee, W. "Discovering Novel Attack Strategies from INFOSEC Alerts", In Proceedings of the 9th European Symposium on Research in Computer Security, Sophia Antipolis, France 2004b.

Qin, X., and Lee, W. "Discovering Novel Attack Strategies from INFOSEC Alerts", In Proceedings of the 9th European Symposium on Research in Computer Security, Sophia Antipolis, France 2004c.

Rao, A., and Georgeff, M. "BDI Agents: From Theory to Practice," In *Proceedings of the First International Conference on Multi-Agent Systems, 1995.*

Sowa, J. F. *Knowledge Representation: Logical, Philosophical, and Computational Foundation,* Brooks Cole Publishing Co., Pacific Grove, CA, 2000.

Tadda, G. P., Salerno, J. S. Overview of Cyber Situation Awareness Cyber Situational Awareness in Issues and Research, Editors: Sushil Jajodia, Peng Liu, Vipin Swarup, Cliff Wang, Advances in Information Security, Volume 46, 2010.

US DoD. 2012, "Department of Defense Net-Centric Data Strategy", http://dodcio.defense.gov/docs/net-centric-data-strategy-2003-05-092.pdf.
US GAO. Critical Infrastructure Protection. Cybersecurity Guidance Is Available, but More Can Be Done to Promote Its Use", *USA GAO Report to Conressional Requesters GAO-12-92*, 2011.
Valdes, A., and Skinner, K. "Probabilistic alert correlation". Proceedings of the Fourth International Symposium on Recent. Advances in Intrusion Detection (RAID 2001), 54–68.
Westrum, R. A Typology of Resilience Situations, in (Eds. E. Hollnagel, D. Woods, D. Lelvenson) *Resilience Engineering Concepts and Precepts. Aldershot, UK: Ashgate*, 2006.
Wooldridge, M. An Introduction to Multi-Agent Systems, John Wiley and Sons, 2002.
Wu, G., Feder, A., Cohen, H., Kim, J., Calderon, S., Charney, D., and Mathé, A. *"Understanding Resilience,"* Frontiers in Behavioral Neuroscience, Vol. 7, Article 10, 15 February, 2013.

Concluding Thoughts

Alexander Kott, Cliff Wang, and Robert F. Erbacher

1 Challenges

As we conclude this book, it is worth pointing out that although the research community has made quantum leaps in science and technology of information security, especially in the area of cyber situation awareness, we are far from perfect in defending our cyber systems. Challenges ahead of us are abundant.

Some of these challenges arise from the uncertainty about the exact nature of similarities and differences of SA in physical and cyber worlds, and from the unique characteristics of cyber operations. To what extent can we transfer our insights and theories of SA from largely physical or "kinetic" domains to the domains of cyber security? One may argue that important extensions, adaptations, and even major paradigm shifts could be required to accommodate the unique aspects of SA in cyber domains. Are the differences real, and how critical are the influences of these differences? In the following, let us consider briefly several such aspects:

A. Kott (✉)
RDRL-CIN, United States Army Research Laboratory,
2800 Powder Mill Rd., Adelphi, MD 20783, USA
e-mail: Alexander.Kott1.civ@mail.mil

C. Wang
RDRL-ROI-C, United States Army Research Office,
4300 S Miami Blvd, 27703 Durham, NC, USA
e-mail: Xiaogang.X.Wang.civ@mail.mil

R.F. Erbacher
RDRL-CIN-D, United States Army Research Laboratory,
2800 Powder Mill Rd., Adelphi, MD 20783, USA
e-mail: Robert.F.Erbacher.civ@mail.mil

© Springer International Publishing Switzerland 2014

A. Kott et al. (eds.), *Cyber Defense and Situational Awareness*,
Advances in Information Security 62, DOI 10.1007/978-3-319-11391-3_15

1.1 Human Actors in the Cyber Space

Cyber operations involve extensive participation of humans, as users, defenders and attackers. This is largely comparable to the domains of physical or "kinetic" SA in military or other settings where active adversaries are present. In the cyber world, however, one difference worth noting is the oversized role played by users. These legitimate and generally friendly citizens of the cyber space are responsible for an enormous volume of observable activities, many of which happen to be difficult to distinguish from malicious activities by adversaries. Thus, the adversary is afforded endless opportunities to hide within the mass of legitimate users' activities. Unlike "kinetic" SA in military settings, the boundary between attackers and defenders has never been well defined. Further, our attackers also enjoy asymmetric advantages over us (in terms of their operation modes and visibility of such operations), as will be discussed in the next section.

The resulting complexity might be compared to SA in counter-insurgency, anti-terrorism, and crime fighting domains where the adversaries hide among innocent civilians. Still, the cyber world presents an important distinction: users of computer systems can often—mainly due to naïve or erroneous use of the systems—produce a large volume of suspicious looking actions that have few similarities in a physical domain. To put it differently, an unwitting user of a computer network has far more opportunities to produce malicious-looking behaviors than an innocent shopper has chances to appear as a dangerous terrorist.

For these reasons, cyber defenders not only have to build an adequate SA of our cyber infrastructure, but they also have to understand well the behaviors of regular users and their associated tasks, objectives, misconceptions and errors. In addition, a challenging task of the defenders is to establish SA of the adversary in the confusing context of regular users' activities: their intention, capability, objective, and process. The challenges of SA that differentiates adversary from an unwitting user in cyber environments are further multiplied by the facts that cyber adversaries can operate with far greater stealth than is possible in a physical environment.

Perception and comprehension of the adversary has been and will continue to be hard challenges of cyber SA. A human adversary could be highly irrational while intelligent, and highly disciplined yet unpredictable. They could be sponsored by a nation state, with dynamic capabilities and more than sufficient resources. The adversaries could be great learners of our defensive capabilities and procedures as well. The dynamic, adaptive, and intelligent nature of today's adversaries pose a great challenge to the SA process since our understanding of adversarial behaviors could be short lived, and our projection based on their transient state could lead us into a wrong direction when they evolve their techniques quickly.

1.2   Highly Asymmetric Nature of Cyber Attacks

Cyber space attacks are exceptionally asymmetric in nature, arguably even more so than those in the domains of terrorism and insurgency that are well known to be asymmetric. Defenders are charged with the mission of fighting with almost entirely unknown attackers and protecting cyber assets from zero day attacks that are by definition unknown to the defenders. Any applicable knowledge may be extremely limited and short lived, making it hard to predict attackers' rapidly evolving behaviors, approaches, and strategies. Particularly for zero day attacks, the defenders must learn and understand the situation and its details swiftly. Perhaps the best strategy may rely on rapid learning (which, to be sure, brings its own great difficulties), and on fast reactions based on limited and partly uncertain comprehension.

On the other hand, the adversary has excellent opportunities for achieving accurate CSA, because today's cyber defense systems are mostly static, and our defense strategies are only marginally adaptive. Our adversary benefits from learning from us, a process which could be carried out in a well planned and well timed manner, given that our defensive approaches are relatively stable and change only slowly. The adversaries could benefit from knowing our extant processes for forming and utilizing our SA, in order to understand our cyber operations well and to craft new attacks that can exploit our related weaknesses effectively.

In essence, due to the static nature of our cyber systems and operating processes, and current passive defense strategy, the asymmetry of our current cyber defense tends to offer attackers great benefits. For this reason, it is critical for the researchers and practitioners of cyber defense to work towards ways to reverse the asymmetry to benefit the defense side. Among the promising approaches are new techniques such as moving target defense.

1.3   Complexity Mismatch Between Human Cognition and Cyber World

Following Moore's law, computational power grows exponentially, while human cognitive capability remains largely unchanged. In addition, advances in machine intelligence have made computing much more powerful, as measured by both the speed of number crunching as well as by the sophistication of computational methods and processes. As a result, cyber defenders are facing future attacks that are highly sophisticated and that can be launched on a much larger scale.

Our cyber infrastructure continually increases in its complexity and in the number of critical missions that it is expected to support. In the meantime cyber sensors grow ever more powerful and ubiquitous, bringing in much more data than we can process. For example, during a large-scale coordinated denial of service attack that combines several attacking schemes and uses effective camouflage to hide its true attack vector, a tremendous number of alerts could be generated in a very short period of time and overwhelm human analysts. On the other end of the spectrum, for a slow and stealthy type of attack, the true attack trace could be deeply and carefully embedded in the high volume of normal traffic, making it hard for an analyst to identify and observe.

In essence, cyber systems are getting bigger, tasks more complicated, and attacks more sophisticated—all of which lead to a tremendous growth in the amount of data for a human analyst to absorb—while our cognitive capabilities remain the same. In order for human defenders to be effective in identifying and defeating future cyber attacks, novel tools and models that can help fill the gap between cyber data and situation comprehension by cyber analysts are highly desired.

1.4　Disconnect Between Cyber Operations and Mission

The current practice of cyber defense is often fragmented and inadequately integrated with the broader goals of assuring effective mission execution. While one cyber analyst may focus on maintaining computer security, he or she may not interact with another analyst monitoring the network status. This fragmentation of cyber operations is partially due to the lack of an effective mission model that ties all parts of a cyber operation together. A mission model is important for SA in any domain, not only in cyber security. However, in more physical domains, a mission model tends to be driven by well understood, intuitive physical causal chains, easier to form, and often may remain implicit. Not so in the cyber domain where it is often difficult to understand the dependencies between the physical or cyber mission, and the cyber effects that may negatively impact the mission.

A cyber mission model and CSA are mutually dependent: CSA is difficult to achieve without a mission model while at the same time the mission model—often rapidly evolving during an operation—is impossible without CSA. Adversarial information, including the possible adversarial impacts on the mission, is also important in forming SA and making decisions for mission operations. Well established and insightful cyber mission models translate mission assurance requirements into well orchestrated cyber operations, and help turn cyber defense from being merely reactive to one that is proactive and focused on mission assurance.

2　Future Research

Although the interactions between cyber attackers and defenders can be highly dynamic, and the nature of the interactions may evolve rapidly, a theoretical model that captures key invariants related to cyber defense can be helpful in maintaining CSA and in devising, optimizing and executing defensive actions. Such a model would focus on capturing several unique aspects of cyber operations.

First, cyber situation continually evolves for both defenders and attackers. Our cyber assets change from time to time. Different missions start and end continuously. Our adversaries may pose different threat levels, and our monitoring and surveillance give us continually updated information on their techniques and capability. The key issue is how we can form the awareness of the dynamically changing situation in quantifiable ways that support rational decision-making.

Second, the defenders' SA and decision-making must be based on criteria that maximize the effectiveness of the defense. The set of criteria would capture important considerations such as satisfying minimum necessary requirements for mission assurance, or minimizing the adversary's ability to observe our cyber assets or to launch damaging attacks. To this end, it may be possible to leverage new concepts and advances in control theory and system modeling to guide CSA, and to enable better cyber defense and mission assurance, such that our dynamic strategy and proactive actions will increase the cost to the adversary for launching attacks while in the meantime not incurring a huge cost to the defense side.

Third, the cyber dynamics model would support multiple levels of abstraction, e.g., it would reflect operations—and the corresponding CSA—at both strategic and tactical levels. The dependencies between different levels are also important to capture in the model and need to be understood well. It could be quite possible, for example, that in order to achieve strategic mission assurance, certain sacrifices at tactical levels may be needed, such as reducing bandwidth allocation for certain non-essential traffic types, or isolating certain nodes for quarantine purposes.

Obviously, comprehensive modeling of cyber operations is a daunting task due in part to the highly complex nature of cyber systems and the dynamic missions they execute or support. Active human participation by both users and malicious attackers further complicate the picture. Nevertheless, promising research directions exist that may help meet these challenges. For example, game theoretic approaches offer opportunities for analyzing and modeling two party and multi-party interactions, and help decision making to maximize defender's returns. However, current approaches have limited successes in dealing with the exponential growth in complexity as the game must become ever more sophisticated in order to model rapidly evolving sophistication of cyber operations.

Recent research interests have focused on advancing game theory and its applications to cyber systems. Advancement in this line of research may bring insights and new techniques that would help cyber defenders at two distinct levels. In macro-level strategy, the research would yield a set of guiding principles for cyber operation that can satisfy mission assurance requirements under resource constraint, and under known and assumed threats and attacker capabilities. In micro-level decision support, the research results may point to specific actions to deal with real time or near real time threats, in order to defeat ongoing attacks or to prevent future ones. It should be possible to link the two levels (or multi-level) of strategy and decision making. For example, while the macro-level strategy provides security guarantees from a long-term, security assurance perspective, the micro-level actions support mission assurance for both the ongoing operations and the long term assurance objective. The multi-level perspective may shed new light on how to form and maintain SA that simultaneously supports strategic and tactical decisions.

It is also critical to turn around the asymmetry of our current cyber defense operations. For far too long, this asymmetry has provided cyber attackers with significant advantages. In particular, our current cyber systems, due to their static nature, allow the attackers to observe our defense for extensive periods of time, and to obtain highly accurate CSA before launching decisive attacks. One fundamental question is how to change the asymmetry around in a fundamental way.

Moving target defense is a new approach that suggests that defenders should continually and dynamically modify their systems. But how? New research is needed towards theoretical models that can guide the system updates in an optimal way. In particular, any such approach should make sure that frequent updates of the defenders' systems do not produce a negative impact on the defenders' CSA.

For example, it may be possible to leverage advances in control theory and to develop models of cyber operations where defenders and attackers have their own distinct sets of objectives, approaches and techniques. This would enable novel formulations that seek to minimize the observability and more generally the adversary's CSA of our cyber systems by proactive and adaptive system changes, while maintaining maximum control, accessibility and CSA for defenders. Such approaches may help future defense to be much more proactive, to offer asymmetric advantages to the defenders, and ultimately to offer a high level of mission assurance. It is anticipated that with research advancement and new capability creation, we will be more adaptive, more proactive, and ultimately more effective in future cyber defense.

Acknowledgements and Disclaimers

The authors of the Formation of Awareness chapter acknowledge that the work presented in the chapter has been supported by a Multidisciplinary University Research Initiative Award (MURI; # W911NF-09-1-0525) from the Army Research Office.

The authors of the Cognition and Technology chapter acknowledge that this research was supported by a Multidisciplinary University Research Initiative Award (MURI; # W911NF-09-1-0525) from the Army Research Office; by the Army Research Laboratory under Cooperative Agreement Number W911NF-13-2-0045 (ARL Cyber Security CRA); and by a Defense Threat Reduction Agency (DTRA) grant (HDTRA1-09-1-0053) to Cleotilde Gonzalez and Christian Lebiere. The views and conclusions contained in this document are those of the authors and should not be interpreted as representing the official policies, either expressed or implied, of the Army Research Laboratory or the U.S. Government. The U.S. Government is authorized to reproduce and distribute reprints for Government purposes notwithstanding any copyright notation here on. The authors would like to thank Hau-yu Wong, Dynamic Decision Making Laboratory, for help with editorial work in the paper.

The authors of the Inference and Ontology chapter acknowledge that this work was sponsored by the US Naval Research Laboratory under contract N00173-11-2007. Thanks, also, to Mike Dean, of BBN, who provided technical consulting during the project.

The authors of the Cognitive Process chapter acknowledge that this research was supported by a Multidisciplinary University Research Initiative Award (MURI; # W911NF-09-1-0525) from the Army Research Office and by a Summer Faculty Fellowship at Army Research Laboratory.

The authors of the Metrics of Security chapter make the following disclaimer: This paper is not subject to copyright in the USA. Commercial products are identified in order to adequately specify certain procedures. In no case does such identification imply recommendation or endorsement by the National Institute of Standards and Technology, nor does it imply that the identified products are necessarily the best available for the purpose.

© Springer International Publishing Switzerland 2014

329

A. Kott et al. (eds.), *Cyber Defense and Situational Awareness*,

Advances in Information Security 62, DOI 10.1007/978-3-319-11391-3

Printed in the United States
By Bookmasters